Date Due

DEC 6			
OCT 9			
NOV 6			
NOV 20			
OCT 4			
DEC 14			
MAR 7			
MAY 24			

THE BIBLE IN CURRENT CATHOLIC THOUGHT

THE BIBLE IN CURRENT CATHOLIC THOUGHT

Edited by

JOHN L. McKENZIE, S.J.

HERDER AND HERDER

1962
HERDER AND HERDER NEW YORK
232 Madison Avenue, New York 16, N.Y.

SAINT MARYS THEOLOGY STUDIES, 1

Imprimi Potest: John R. Connery, S.J., Provincial of the Chicago Province
November 19, 1962
Nihil Obstat: John B. Amberg, S.J., Censor deputatus; November 20, 1962
Imprimatur: Geo. J. Casey, Vicar General, Archdiocese of Chicago
November 21, 1962

Library of Congress Catalog Card Number: 62-21949

Made and printed in the United States of America

To the Memory of

the Reverend

MICHAEL J. GRUENTHANER

of the Society of Jesus

1887 - 1962

CONTENTS

EDITOR'S PREFACE

JOHN L. McKENZIE, S.J.

The pleasant European custom of presenting to senior scholars a testimonial volume has not yet become common in the United States, and our scholarship has been poorer because of this lack. Such volumes have often included some of the finest scholarship in the generation in which they were written. Whether this volume can be so described must be left to the judgment of its readers. We have attempted to assemble here the work of men who are recognized as competent by their colleagues in the field of biblical studies. The bond which unites them in this volume is not only their professional dedication to the field of their research and teaching; it is also the friendly esteem which they feel for the man to whom this volume is dedicated. Many of our contributors have known Father Gruenthaner as teacher, and for a number he is the man who introduced them to biblical studies; others have known him as a colleague and as a friend through many years. To each of the contributors and to the editor the volume is a confession of a debt which is too great to be repaid in any other way than the way in which Father Gruenthaner desired: by the continuation of the scholarly work to which his life has been devoted.

[*Seventeen days before the seventy-fifth birthday on which this tribute was to have been presented, its recipient ended a life of vigorous activity and, at the last, great suffering. Our offering is thus transformed into a Memorial Volume. The appreciation embodied in each of the essays remains unaltered.*]

Forty years have elapsed since Father Gruenthaner began his career as a biblical scholar. The life of a scholar seems to the outside world to be a life of tranquillity so undisturbed that it approaches dullness; his colleagues in biblical studies know that these forty years were an exciting period. Father Gruenthaner entered upon his work at the time when Palestinian archaeology began its tremendous activity after the first world war. The discoveries at Ugarit, which revolutionized the study of pre-Israelite and Israelite religion, occurred in 1929. The languages and history of Mesopotamia, in which Father Gruenthaner was long and deeply interested, saw a development which was scarcely less than explosive. In exegesis these were the years of the growth of Form Criticism, of the *traditionsgeschichtlich* analysis of Albrecht Alt and Martin Noth, of the studies of oral tradition carried on by the Scandinavian school, of the flowering of biblical theology initiated by Walther Eichrodt and continued by so many others. Father Gruenthaner was an active participant in a great intellectual movement.

Of more intense personal interest to Father Gruenthaner was the rapid growth of Catholic exegesis, particularly in the United States. For some years he enjoyed the peculiar distinction of holding the only doctorate in Sacred Scripture in the United States. No one rejoiced more than Father Gruenthaner himself when he lost this distinction. When he had begun the study and teaching of the Old Testament, Catholic exegesis was timid at best, and often insecure. The effect of biblical studies on theological studies was slight, and practically negligible in the Church at large. Our biblical scholarship was probably not much behind our scholarship in other areas; there is very little creative work of permanent value which has remained from this period. Father Gruenthaner must be numbered among those men who were dissatisfied with the inertia of Catholic scholarship, and whose patient and dedicated toil, often unappreciated or received with hostility, created the atmosphere which made possible the appearance of the encyclical *Divino Afflante Spiritu* in 1943. The younger generation of scholars who enjoy the benefits of this encyclical can never forget their debt to their seniors who prepared the ground for subsequent work, even when the seniors have sometimes been astonished at the fruit which grows on the trees they planted.

The story of Father Gruenthaner's life is the story of two places quite dissimilar and remote from each other; St. Mary's College in Kansas and the Catholic University in Washington, apart from a few brief excursions to other seminaries; in his early years the Jesuits of North America did not have enough qualified teachers of exegesis to staff their own seminaries. The number of men who came under his influence in his years of teaching is beyond calculation; so also beyond calculation is the conviction which he communicated that the Bible is holy, that its study can be interesting and profitable. Those who came under his personal direction for advanced studies went away with the awareness that there is no easy and simple way to biblical understanding, that understanding is the fruit of rigorous and disciplined method. Father Gruenthaner lived to see that fulfilment which is the unique joy of the teacher: the employment by his students of the methods and principles which they had learned from him to reach conclusions different from his own.

Father Gruenthaner's prodigious capacity for work has long been legendary at both the institutions where his life has been spent, and some amusing exaggerations of folklore have assembled about him; all the same, it is difficult to exaggerate his singleness of purpose and his ability to improve the time. It is a matter for regret that the commitments laid upon him did not allow him more time for scholarly literary production. When one considers his activities, it is remarkable that his production reached the volume it did. He was one of the founders of the Catholic Biblical Association of America and a collaborator in the revision and the translation of the Old Testament. He was the second editor of the *Catholic Biblical Quarterly*, a post which he held for eleven years. No one except Father Gruenthaner himself could tell, and he would not, the problems involved in assuring the simple survival of a journal which in the opinion of many was a project far too ambitious for the Catholic biblical scholars of the United States. His rugged faith in the capacity of his colleagues to reach the level necessary to sustain a journal has long since been justified.

Father Gruenthaner could attest that the apparent serenity of the scholar's life is often deceptive in appearance. When we compute the legacy he has left to his students, perhaps more precious than anything else is the example of the kind of courage which the scholar needs if he is to meet setbacks and discouragement and continue his work without losing heart. Such courage arises from the conviction that the work the Church gives us to do is highly important and worthy of the total dedication which it demands. This conviction was transparent in Father Gruenthaner; if it lives in the present generation of scholars, many of them learned it from him. We need the genuine professional attitude now as much as it was ever needed, and we are fortunate in having such splendid examples.

Father Gruenthaner's active career barely extended into the period in which the biblical movement began to reach the clergy and the laity in large numbers. Here he was a pioneer. For several years he was a pillar of the faculty of theology for the laity instituted at St. Mary's College, Notre Dame, Indiana. He was convinced, as all of us now are, that if biblical scholarship produces genuine results these results should be communicated to all the faithful, primarily through the Catholic educational system. It is astonishing to recall now that there were many who did not share this conviction. Doubts and fears about biblical studies led to the opinion that these matters had better be confined to the restricted public which reads the learned journals, and that for the clergy and the laity in general ignorance was a guarantee of security. It would be premature to say that this attitude is dead; but one must also note that the type of popular exposition in which Father Gruenthaner was a pioneer has now become commonplace.

In dedicating this volume to Father Gruenthaner we render a tribute which is late to one who has led the way in almost every area in which biblical scholars work. He met difficulties which we have not had to meet just because he and his contemporaries met and overcame them. With the development of biblical studies new problems have arisen; we shall solve them if we meet them as our senior scholars met their problems. A volume such as this, we hope, will be as much a warrant of the future of biblical scholarship as it is a tribute to one from whose leadership we have received so much. The editor of this volume wrote a review a few years ago of a collection of papers which were presented at a Catholic biblical congress held at Brussels in 1958. The words which I used to describe that collection are applicable to this one as well, and I take the liberty of repeating and expanding them.

One can see in this and similar collections that Catholic biblical scholarship has arrived at a consensus which deserves close study. It is not a consensus of opinion; Catholic scholarship encourages an atmosphere of free and friendly controversy. It is a consensus of principles and methods, and the principles and methods are those set forth in the encyclical *Divino Afflante Spiritu.* That these principles and methods are Catholic is evident from their acceptance by the Holy See; that they are scholarly is evident from their acceptance by scholars who are not Catholics, and who recognize that in the methods recommended by the Church there is nothing which offends the scholarly ideal of free investigation. This massive agreement is one of the assured fruits of the scholarly endeavor of the last forty years.

Catholic scholarship is critical in the best sense of the word. It is methodical. It examines its own conclusions thoroughly and proposes them with due reservations. It investigates and tests all the available evidence and argues carefully from one step to the next. It avoids the extremes of skepticism and credulity. It does not treat the Bible as a homogeneous mass of detached sayings, but as an articulate literature with form and structure. It attempts to find the meaning of the Bible, not to impose a meaning from outside the Bible.

Catholic scholarship is historical. It places the Bible in the time and place of its composition and attempts to recreate the experience of those who wrote or spoke its contents and of those who heard them. It studies language and culture as deeply as it can. The Bible is the story of the encounter of a people with God, and its development is not unlike the development of a living organism. To understand it one must retrace the steps in this development as they were lived. Catholic scholarship has that respect for the monuments of the past which forbids it to distort them for any purpose, however pious the purpose may seem.

Catholic scholarship is traditional. The Bible is the book of the Church and can never be treated as anything else. Catholic scholars respect tradition too much to permit themselves to be misled by spurious traditions. The meaning of the Bible for the Church cannot be ascertained without a deep knowledge of how the Church herself has used and presented the Bible. This tradition is not dead but living, and the use and presentation of the Bible in the Church, which has always grown with the Church herself, must live and grow in the present and in the future. To the Catholic scholar tradition is not a tomb in which the past is enshrined, but the living voice of the Church. Hence Catholic scholarship is also theological. It recognizes that the Bible is a theological source and seeks to do all it can to make that source more intelligible and available. We need not be defensive about the amount and the quality of the theological interpretation produced by modern Catholic scholarship. Catholic scholars do not believe that the theological interpretation of the Bible has been exhausted, nor do they think that they themselves will exhaust it. They know that the value of their work will lie in the possibilities it offers their successors to advance the theological understanding of the Bible beyond the point which this generation reaches.

Thus Catholic scholarship is apostolic. No Catholic interpreter forgets that he is an officer and a servant of the Church associated in a subordinate position with the hierarchy in its office of teaching. If his work does not serve the Church he regards it as wasted. What he can do may be little, but it will be done by no one if he fails to do it. He has a responsibility which the Church has committed to him, and which he can fulfil only within the framework of the Church. His identification with the Church is his ultimate assurance that his work will be worth while.

Finally, Catholic scholarship is creative—a bold claim which perhaps modesty should forbid. Nevertheless, the essays collected here show that Catholic scholarship has learned that strength and independence of judgment which enables the scholar to present new insights as the fruit of his personal study. Catholic scholars have outgrown the timidity and the imitative dependence which justly or unjustly were so often alleged against Catholic biblical scholarship in the past. In seeking this creative fecundity Catholic scholars are doing no more than what Pius XII pointed out is their duty. One avoids this duty for many motives, of which the fear of failure is perhaps the most powerful. The scholars whose work is assembled here are representative of the body of Catholic scholarship in their readiness to take the risks which creative writing imposes. Their work is also an illustration of the achievements which creative work can attain.

In speaking of the work of Catholic scholarship in such terms I express my own feelings. Catholic biblical scholarship includes a group of men with whom it is an honor to be associated, an honor which one feels is greater than one deserves. I speak also for Father Gruenthaner and the men of his generation, the teachers of the present generation of scholars. If Catholic biblical scholarship is what I have described—and I am personally convinced that it is—Father Gruenthaner's labors have produced a hundredfold; and we of the present generation can reflect that we have reaped where we have not sown. The scholar recognizes his debt to his colleagues; in the above lines I have attempted to express my own indebtedness to Father Gruenthaner as well as to my colleagues, those represented in this volume and the many who are not, who have contributed to the richness of modern biblical scholarship.

MICHAEL J. GRUENTHANER, S.J., M.S., S.T.D., S.S.D.

FRANCIS A. PETRU, S.J.

Father Michael J. Gruenthaner, S.J. was born in Buffalo, New York, on October 1, 1887. After completing his elementary schooling at St. Boniface School and his high school education at Canisius High School in Buffalo, he entered the Society of Jesus on August 31, 1905 in what was then the Buffalo Mission of the German Province. After two years of noviceship at St. Stanislaus Novitiate, Brooklyn, Cuyahoga Co., Ohio (Cleveland), he pronounced his first religious vows on September 8, 1907. Toward the end of his noviceship, when part of the Buffalo Mission was joined to the Missouri Province of the Society of Jesus, Fr. Gruenthaner became a member of that Province. He began his undergraduate studies in the humanities and sciences at St. Stanislaus Novitiate, but in 1908-1909 he continued his courses at St. Stanislaus Seminary, Florissant, Missouri.

During the next three years, 1909-1912, Fr. Gruenthaner pursued the study of Philosophy at St. Louis University, St. Louis, Missouri. This was followed by a year of graduate studies in Science and Mathematics, and upon its completion Fr. Gruenthaner earned the degree of M.S. from St. Louis University in 1913. From 1913 to 1916 he was instructor in Chemistry, Mathematics, and German at Marquette University, Milwaukee, Wisconsin. He held the same position in 1916-1917 at the University of Detroit, Detroit, Michigan.

Fr. Gruenthaner then made his theological studies at St. Louis University from 1917 to 1921, and was ordained to the Holy Priesthood on June 27, 1920. After the completion of his theological studies, he went to Rome for graduate studies in Sacred Scripture at the Pontificio Istituto Biblico, where he gained the degree of Licentiate in Sacred Scripture in 1924.

Upon returning to the States, Fr. Gruenthaner taught Sacred Scripture and Hebrew at the Theological Seminary of St. Mary of the Lake, Area, Illinois (Mundelein) in 1924-1925. In the following year he completed the final year of spiritual training (Tertianship) at St. Stanislaus Novitiate, Cleveland, Ohio.

In 1926 Fr. Gruenthaner returned to Rome for further graduate studies in Sacred Scripture. He successfully defended his doctoral dissertation before the Pontifical Biblical Commission in 1927 and received the degree of Doctor in Sacred Scripture in 1928. In 1929 was conferred on him the Gregorian University Doctorate of Sacred Theology.

From 1928 to 1931, Fr. Gruenthaner taught Scripture and Hebrew at Weston College, Weston, Massachusetts, and from 1931 to 1961 he held the same position at St. Mary's College, St. Marys, Kansas. This became in 1931 the School of Divinity of Saint Louis University.

It was during this period that Fr. Gruenthaner made his important contribution toward the advancement of American Catholic higher scholarship in Sacred Scripture. He was a charter member of the Catholic Biblical Association of America, which was organized in 1936. In 1939 he was appointed to translate the book of Ezechiel for the Biblical Association's revision of the Challoner-Douay Old Testament.

In 1941 he became editor-in-chief of the Catholic Biblical Quarterly and served in that capacity until 1951. During those ten years, his diligence and skill brought the Quarterly to a recognized and honored status among the pioneering periodicals of the Judeo-Christian exegetical world. The editor himself contributed interesting items of biblical news and several research articles especially on the prophecy of Daniel.

In addition to his duties at the Kansas seminary, Father Gruenthaner in 1941 accepted the position of teaching Sacred Scripture, Biblical Archaeology and Geography at the Catholic University of America, Washington, D. C. and lectured there during the second semester of each school year until 1951. During the years 1943-1956 he also served as Chancellor of the Graduate School of Sacred Theology for Laywomen at St. Mary's College, Notre Dame, Indiana. Here he lectured in Sacred Scripture and allied subjects each summer session during this period.

On August 31, 1955, Fr. Gruenthaner celebrated the Golden Jubilee of his entrance into the Society of Jesus. At the Twenty-first General Meeting of the Catholic Biblical Association of America, held on September 3-4, 1958, at Christ the King Seminary, Olean, New York, in conjunction with the centennial observance of St. Bonaventure University, Fr. Gruenthaner was awarded by St. Bonaventure University a citation in recognition of outstanding contributions to Catholic biblical scholarship. In 1959 illness forced him to retire from his teaching, and in 1961 he was declared Professor Emeritus at St. Mary's College, St. Marys, Kansas. After a lingering illness there, while appreciatively awaiting the appearance of this volume in his honor, he was hospitalized in Topeka and there called to the reward of his labors on September 14, 1962.

Fr. Gruenthaner had been a member of the American Association for the Advancement of Science and of the American Oriental Society.

DOCTORAL DISSERTATION: *The Authorship and Date of Daniel,* Rome, 1927

1. CONTRIBUTIONS TO COLLECTIVE WORKS:

"The World of the Old Testament and its Historicity," in *European Civilization, Its Origin and Development,* Edward Eyre, edit., Oxford, 1934, Vol. 1, 501-965

"Mary in the New Testament," in *Mariology I,* Milwaukee, 1955, 80-108

"Angel", *Encyclopaedia Britannica* [1947-1962], 1, 920-921.

2. ARTICLES IN JOURNALS:

"Chaldeans or Macedonians? A Recent Theory on the Prophecy of Habakkuk," *Bib* 8 (1927) 129-160; 257-289

"The Seventy Weeks," *CBQ* 1 (1939) 44-54

"Enuma Elis and the Hexaëmeron," *HPR* 39 (1939) 1052-1060

"Jews as a Race," *Thought* 14 (1939) 36-51

"The Future Life in the Psalms," *CBQ* 2 (1940) 57-63

"The Liturgical Piety of the Psalms," *HPR* 40 (1940) 817-824

"Antichrist in the Scriptures," *HPR* 42 (1941-42) 448-460

"The Messianic Concepts of Ezechiel," *TS* 2 (1941) 1-18

"The Old Testament and Retribution in This Life," *CBQ* 4 (1942) 101-110

"The Date of Abraham," *CBQ* 4 (1942) 360-363; 5 (1943) 85-87

"The *Providentissimus Deus,*" *CBQ* 5 (1943) 3-5

"Fiftieth Anniversary of the Encyclical *Providentissimus Deus,*" *CBQ* 5 (1943) 115-116

"*Divino Afflante Spiritu:* The New Encyclical on Biblical Studies," *AER* 110 (1944) 330-337; 111 (1944) 43-52; 114-123

"An Unfounded Charge of Heresy (Phil 2,6)," *AER* 110 (1944) 407-415

"The Name of Moses", *AER* 111 (1944) 72-73

"*Divino Afflante Spiritu,*" *CBQ* 6 (1944) 3-5

"The Demonology of the Old Testament," *CBQ* 6 (1944) 6-27

"Hebrew Tribal Intermarriage," *AER* 113 (1945) 149

"The Serpent of Gen 3:1-15," *AER* 113 (1945) 149-152

"The Confraternity Version of Phil 2:6,7a," *CBQ* 7 (1945) 231-235

"Recent Theories about Ezechiel," *CBQ* 7 (1945) 438-466

"The New Latin Psalter," *Review for Religious* 5 (1945) 365-372

"Century of Jewish Life," *Thought* 20 (1945) 17-20

"The Last Verse of Psalm 109," *AER* 115 (1946) 463-467

"The Four Empires of Daniel," *CBQ* 8 (1946) 78-82; 201-212

"The Book of Tobias and Contraception," *CBQ* 8 (1946) 98-100

"The Scriptural Doctrine on First Creation," *CBQ* 9 (1947) 47-58; 206-219; 307-320

"Monsignor Knox's Version of the Psalms," *CBQ* 10 (1948) 42-54

"Two Sun Miracles of the Old Testament," *CBQ* 10 (1948) 271-290

"Pope Pius XII and the Scriptures," *AER* 120 (1949) 233-238

"The Last King of Babylon," *CBQ* 11 (1949) 406-427

"Evolution and the Scriptures," *CBQ* 13 (1951) 21-27

English Translation of "An Instruction of the Pontifical Biblical Commission on the Proper Way to Teach Scripture in the Seminaries of Clerics and the Colleges of Religious", *CBQ* 13 (1951) 123-134

Biblical and Archaeological News, *CBQ* 10 (1948) 210-218 (with Joseph P. Lilly); 10 (1948) 334-340; 439-444; 11 (1949) 98-107; 220-226; 337-343; 459-463; 12 (1950) 91-98; 226-232; 340-345; 464-469; 13 (1951) 98-105; 213-222; 336-343; 447-452; 14 (1952) 71-73; 146-150; 255-261; 355-358; 15 (1953) 60-64; 208-212; 339-343.

3. BOOK REVIEWS

J. A. Montgomery, *A Critical and Exegetical Commentary on the Book of Daniel, Bib* 9 (1928) 101-104

E. Seraphim, J. Kelly, *Maps of the Land of Christ, CBQ* 1 (1939) 193-194

Rand McNally, *Historical Atlas of the Holy Land, CBQ* 1 (1939) 194

Samuel Belkin, *Philo and the Oral Law, CBQ* 2 (1940) 276-277

G. A. Cooke, *A Critical and Exegetical Commentary on the Book of Ezekiel, TS* 1 (1940) 84-85

H. Torczyner, L. Harding, A. Lewis, J. L. Starkey, *Lachish I: The Lachish Letters, TS* 1 (1949) 193-195

Cuthbert Lattey, *The First Book of Psalms* (*Pss. I—XLI*), *TS* 1 (1940) 327-328

Erwin R. Goodenough, *An Introduction to Philo Judaeus, CBQ* 3 (1941) 187-188

Harold W. Clark, *Genes and Genesis, TS* 2 (1941) 603

An Indexed Bibliography of the Writings of William Foxwell Albright, CBQ 4 (1942) 282-283

George L. Robinson, *The Bearing of Archaeology on the Old Testament, TS* 3 (1942) 464-465

David Jacobsen, *The Social Background of the Old Testament, CBQ* 5 (1943) 482-484

C. S. Lewis, *The Problem of Pain, AER* 111 (1944) 312-313

Joseph C. Plumpe, *Mater Ecclesia, An Inquiry into the Concept of the Church as Mother in Early Christianity, CBQ* 6 (1944) 371-372

Charles T. Fritsch, *The Anti-anthropomorphisms of the Greek Pentateuch, CBQ* 6 (1944) 378-379

Charles T. Callan, *The Psalms, Translated . . . with Introductions, Critical Notes and Spiritual Reflections, AER* 113 (1945) 72-75

Raphael M. Huber, *A Documented History of the Franciscan Order, CBQ* 7 (1945) 360-362

Abraham E. Millgram, *Sabbath, the Day of Delight, CBQ* 8(1946)365

James Keller, *The Priest and a World Vision, AER* 117 (1947) 156-157

James Brodrick, *The Progress of the Jesuits, AER* 117 (1947) 236-238

Père Lagrange and the Scriptures, (translated from the French by Richard T. Murphy), *AER* 117 (1947) 472-474

E. C. Messenger, *The Sunday Epistles Simply Explained, AER* 117 (1947) 476-477

Walter Duffey, *The Tribal-Historical Theory on the Origin of the Hebrew People, CBQ* 9 (1947) 125-126

Charles C. Torrey, *The Lives of the Prophets, CBQ* 9 (1947) 487-488

H. and H. A. Frankfort, John A. Wilson, Thorkild Jacobsen, William A. Irwin, *The Intellectual Adventure of Ancient Man, Modern Schoolman* 25 (1947-1948) 206-209

J. Coert Rylaarsdam, *Revelation in Jewish Wisdom Literature, TS* 8 (1947) 149-150

G. Sholem, *Major Trends in Jewish Mysticism, TS* 8 (1947) 510-512

Nahum N. Glatzer (edit.), *In Time and Eternity: A Jewish Reader, Thought* 22 (1947) 556-557

Humphrey J. T. Johnson, *The Bible and Early Man, AER* 119 (1948) 237-238

Joseph B. Frey, *My Daily Psalm Book, CBQ* 10 (1948) 223

Nils Messel, *Ezechielfragen, TS* 9 (1948) 472-473

R. P. J. Prado, *Praelectionum Biblicarum Compendium, II, Vetus Testamentum, Liber Primus: De Sacra Veteris Testamenti Historia,*[5] *AER* 120 (1949) 363-364

Q. Septimius Florens Tertullianus, De Oratione, Critische Uitgabe met Prolegomena, Vertaling en Philogisch-Exegetisch-Liturgische Commentar door G. F. Diercks, AER 120 (1949) 446-447

H. Pinard de la Boullaye, *S. Ignace de Loyola, AER* 120 (1949) 522-524

Sefer Tehilloth likebhod Ha-Qadosh Ignaṣiyos, Liber Precum in Honorem Sancti Ignatii, CBQ 11 (1949) 108

Albert Gelin, *Les Idées Maîtresses de l'Ancien Testament, CBQ* 11 (1949) 116-117

Joseph Ziegler, *Ezechiel*; Friedrich Nötscher, *Daniel* (Echter-Bibel), *TS* 10 (1949) 458

Eugenio Zolli, *The Nazarene, Studies in New Testament Exegesis* (translated by Cyril Vollert), *AER* 123 (1950) 236-237

Alfred O'Rahilly, *The Family at Bethany, AER* 123 (1950) 237-238

E. K. Lynch, *Whither Goest Thou? Conferences for Religious, AER* 123 (1950) 319

The Old Testament. Newly translated from the Latin Vulgate by Msgr. Ronald Knox, Vol. I: Genesis to Esther; and *The Holy Bible, Book of Genesis. Translated from the Original Languages with Critical Use of All the Ancient Sources by Members of the Catholic Biblical Association of America, AER* 123 (1950) 479-480

J. M. Paul Bauchet, *Sefer dibhre ha-yamim lenefesh Tirsah, haqetannah, CBQ* 12 (1950) 107

Saadia Gaon, *The Book of Beliefs and Opinions, CBQ* 12 (1950) 110

Paul Heinisch, *Probleme der biblischen Urgeschichte, TS* 11 (1950) 409-410

Paul Heinisch, *Geschichte des Alten Testaments,* Part I, *TS* 11 (1950) 604-605

Pedro Leturia, *Iñigo de Loyola* (translated by Aloysius Owen), *AER* 124 (1951) 76-77

Michael Schmaus, *Katholische Dogmatik: Erster Band, Erstes Heft, Einleitung; Zweites Heft, Gott der Dreieinige, AER* 124 (1951) 236-237

Giovanni Rinaldi, *Daniele*; D. Pietro de Ambroggi, *Le Epistole Cattoliche di Giacomo, Pietro, Giovanni, e Giuda, AER* 134 (1951) 399

Paul Heinisch, *Geschichte des Alten Testaments, Ergänzungsband II, AER* 125 (1951) 78-79

Franz M. Willam, *Der Lehrstück-Katechismus als ein Träger der katechetischen Erneuerung, AER* 125 (1951) 319-320

John B. Steinmueller and Mother Kathryn Sullivan, *Catholic Bible Encyclopedia, New Testament, CBQ* 13 (1951) 106-107

James B. Pritchard, edit., *Ancient Near Eastern Texts Relating to the Old Testament, CBQ* 13 (1951) 108-109

The Code of Maimonides, Book Thirteen, The Book of Civil Laws (translated by Jacob J. Rabinowitz); *Book Fourteen, The Book of Judges* (translated by Abraham M. Hershman), *CBQ* 13 (1951) 224

La Sacra Bibbia, Tradotta dai testi originali con note a cura del Pontifico Istituto Biblico di Roma, Vol. I; II Pentateuco; Vols. II, III; I Libri Storici; Vol. IV Libri Poetici, Giobbe, Salmi, CBQ 13 (1951) 225-226

Lionel Casson and Ernest Hettich, edits., *Excavations at Nessana, Vol. II: Literary Papyri, CBQ* 13 (1951) 346-347

Alexander Heidel, *The Babylonian Genesis, The Story of Creation,*[2] *AER* 127 (1952) 477-478

H. C. E. Zacharias, *Human Personality: Its Historical Emergence in India, China, and Israel, CBQ* 14 (1952) 205-206

Edward Robertson, *The Old Testament Problem, TS* 14 (1953) 93-95

Jean Steinmann, *Le prophète Jérémie: Sa vie, son oeuvre, et son temps, TS* 14 (1953) 298-299

Rudolph Schnackenburg, *Die Johannesbriefe, TS* 16 (1955) 283-284

Eric F. F. Bishop, *Jews of Palestine: The Local Background to the Gospel Documents, CBQ* 19 (1957) 154-155

M. E. Boismard, *Du Baptême à Cana* (*Jean* 1,19—2,11), *CBQ* 19 (1957) 288-289

Adrien M. Malo, *L'épopée inachevée de nos Lieux Saints, CBQ* 20 (1958) 586-587

"A KINGDOM OF PRIESTS"

WILLIAM L. MORAN, S.J.

The problem of *mamleket kôhᵉnîm* in Ex 19,6 hardly needs introduction; so often studied, it remains a *crux interpretum*. In the ancient translations alone, with their many divergences, one sees the ambiguity of the apparently simple Hebrew expression.[1] And among modern scholars discussion touches the central question: who are the priests? Most maintain that "kingdom of priests," like the parallel expression "holy nation," should be understood of all Israelites, though there are many differences of opinion on the function and theological implications of this, in some sense, common priesthood. Others argue that the priests are to be distinguished from the general body of the Israelites; they are priests in the narrower, technical sense, and therefore the *mamleket,* whether it mean realm or office, is theirs alone.

This much seems clear: *mamleket kôhᵉnîm* and *gôy qādôš* must be interpreted as parallel expressions. This follows not only from the structural relationship but from the evident connection of "priests" and "holy" and from the fact that *mamlākâ* and *gôy* are frequently found in parallelism (see below). "Priests" therefore is an attribute of "kingdom" just as "holy" is an attribute of "nation."[2]

On this basis we may not only rule out some of the ancient translations,[3] but we may also exclude what until recently at least was perhaps the most common interpretation: Ex 19,6 predicates priesthood of the individual Israelite as such.[4] For if holiness is predicated of the collectivity, the nation, then the priesthood is also collective, belonging properly to the kingdom. This too fits the general context, in which

---

1. See R. B. Y. Scott, *OTS* 8 (1950) 213-215, and add *mlkwt khnwt'*, "priestly kingdom," of the Aramaic fragment of the Testament of Levi [D. Barthélemy, O.P., and J. T. Milik, *Discoveries in the Judaean Desert*, (Oxford: 1955), 88]. For the Palestinian, Alexandrian, New Testament, and early Patristic interpretations, see Lucien Cerfaux, *RevScPhTh* 28 (1939) 5-39 = *Recueil Lucien Cerfaux* II (Gembloux: 1954), 287-302.
2. Scott, *OTS* 8 (1950), 216.
3. Peshitta: "kingdom *and* priests and a holy nation" (cf. Apc 1,6; 5, 10; Jubilees 16, 18); Targums: "kings (and) priests."
4. So for example, Georg Beer, *HAT* 3, (Tübingen: 1939), 97, who sees in Ex 19,6 a more elevated religion, which like the ideal of Jer 31,34 dispenses with the mediation of priests and thus reaches towards the New Testament; cf. also Num 16, 1ff.

there is question of the covenant with the people as a whole, the sons of Israel and the house of Jacob (v. 3).[5]

Another view is that Israel is here given a priestly rôle to be exercised on behalf of the other peoples from whom it has been chosen (cf. v. 5); Is 61,6 is cited to illustrate the same conception of Israel's vocation.[6] Scott's criticism, however, seems valid: " . . . there is no support whatever for it in the immediate context . . ., where what is emphasized is rather the separation of Israel from all other nations."[7]

J.-B. Bauer goes his own way.[8] He takes *mamleket* as *status absolutus* and as the abstract for the concrete. The Israelites are kings sharing in the kingship of Yahweh through the victories he gives them over their enemies. Syntactically, "priests" is in apposition with "kings," but with the force of an adjective. The Israelites are "priestly kings" because they alone worship the true God and therefore they alone have a true cult. It is however highly questionable whether military victories may be said to confer royalty and whether participation in the true cult of the true God may be said to confer priesthood.[9] Moreover, the alleged apposition is an extremely rare construction and not at all at home in prose.[10]

The views of Wildberger and Buber are alike in leaning heavily on 2 Sm 8,18 and 1 Kgs 4,5.[11] In the former passage David's sons are said to be priests, and in the latter Zabud, "friend" of the king,[12] is also called a priest. From these texts Wildberger, following Baudissin,[13]

---

5. The collectivity is stressed in the recent studies of J.-B. Bauer, *BZ* 2 (1958) 283-286; H. Junker, *TTZ* 56 (1947) 10-15; R. B. Y. Scott, *OTS* 8 (1950) 217; H. Wildberger, *Jahwes Eigentumsvolk, (AbTANT* 37; Zürich: 1960), 81.
6. Scott, *OTS* 8 (1950) cites Ehrlich and McNeile; Israel's mediatory rôle also appears in Junker, *art. cit.*; M. Noth, (*ATD* 5²; Göttingen: 1961), 126; Noth, *Amt und Berufung im A. T.*, (Bonner Akademische Reden 19; Bonn: 1958), 33, n. 47; H. Schneider, *Die Heilige Schrift, Exodus*, (Echter-Bibel; Würzburg: 1952), 42.
7. Scott, *OTS* 8 (1950) 217.
8. Bauer, *BZ* 2 (1958) 283-286.
9. Cf. the criticisms of Wildberger, *Jahwes Eigentumsvolk*, 81, n. 29.
10. Bauer refers to Joüon, *Grammaire de l'Hébreu biblique*, 131c, who finds most of the examples strange. They can now be explained for the most part in the light of enclitic *mem* in the construct-chain; cf. H. D. Hummel, *JBL* 76 (1957) 87-103 [the writer cannot on comparative grounds accept Svi Rin's explanation in *BZ* 5 (1961) 258, n. 19].
11. Wildberger, *Jahwes Eigentumsvolk*, 81-83; M. Buber, *Moses* (Zürich: 1948), 155-156; Buber, *Königtum Gottes*³, (Heidelberg: 1956), 103-104.
12. On this title see most recently H. Donner, *ZAW* 73 (1961) 269-277.
13. *Die Geschichte des alttestamentlichen Priestertums* (Leipzig: 1889) 191-192. Baudissin, however, makes no connection between this title and Ex 19,6. Buber also cites 2 Sm 20,26 in favor of a purely profane priesthood, but as Baudissin, 192, remarks, Ira, the priest of David, is mentioned immediately after Zadok and Abiathar, and therefore must be considered a priest of the cult.

concludes that "priest" was a title of honor conferred on the king's sons and on high court-officials, none of whom had any special relation to the cult. In this sense the Israelites are called "priests"; they are the intimates of the king Yahweh. Buber even maintains that these passages show that "priest" could be used without any sacral associations whatever, and David's sons and Zabud occupied a profane office at court called "priest." This office he finds defined in 1 Chr 18,17, the parallel to 2 Sm 8,18, as "the first at the hand of the king." Such are the Israelites in the kingdom of Yahweh.

These texts are a very slender basis for the interpretation of *mamleket kôhᵃnîm,* especially in view of its parallelism with "*holy* nation." In 1 Kgs 4,5 *hakkôhēn* is secondary,[14] and in 2 Sm 8,18 the priestly status of David's sons, if admittedly not completely understood, can be explained and is hardly proof of the existence of a simply honorific title.[15] Certainly it was understood by the Chronicler as implying priesthood in the strict sense; for this reason he changed the sons' titles in conformity with the later Aaronite monopoly of the cult.

For Scott "kingdom" is simply a synonym of "nation," and "of priests" he understands in the light of the ritual sanctification of priests, who are therefore "the sanctified" (cf. *nᵉgîdîm* in Prov 8,6 and *šᵉmānîm* in Is 28,1.4). Israel is "a kingdom set apart like a priesthood," and the phrase does no more than describe the Israelites as Yahweh's worshipers, "a positive counterpart of the idea of separation from the worship of other gods expressed in *gôy qādôš.*"[16]

The writer's principal objection against Scott's explanation does not really touch the main issue. It is that v. 6, like 5b, is a blessing, a reward for obedience to the covenant (v. 5a), and so must by implication at least promise more than that, if Israel remains faithful to Yahweh, it will be his worshipers.[17] This minimal sense, however, does not seem essential to Scott's explanation. The postulated use of a concrete noun with adjectival force is, and apart from genitives of material this construction is not normal. Recourse to Prov 8,6 and Is 28,1.4 indicates the difficulty of explaining the plural form if indeed its force is that of an adjective. In a prose passage like Ex 19,3-6, so traditional for the most part in its phraseology and so normal in its syntax, one does not expect such a combination of grammatical rarities in two words, and one understands Scott's caution in proposing his solution.

---

14. See Donner, *ZAW* 73 (1961) 270, n. 9.
15. R. de Vaux, O.P., suggests that David's sons substituted for him in the cult (*BJ ad loc.*).
16. Scott, *OTS* 8 (1950) 219.
17. On the literary form, see below, note 65. *A fortiori,* therefore, we do not believe Ex 19,6 announces a program of moral holiness in keeping with Israel's priestly dignity [A. Clamer, *La Sainte Bible, Exode* (Paris: 1956) 168-169; P. Heinisch, *HS* 1/2 (Bonn: 1934) 146]; the reward for the fulfilment of obligations should not be additional obligations. This is not to deny *noblesse oblige*—cf. the use of *'am qādôš* in Dt 7,6, etc.—but to restrict ourselves to the meaning of the terms in Ex 19,6.

In the principal alternative, namely, that the priests of Ex 19,6 are only a relatively few Israelites, no one denies its freedom from all difficulties of grammar and general prose usage, nor does it labor under the problem of explaining what is meant by priesthood. It is context which is urged as the most serious objection: reference to a small group is felt to be discordant when it occurs between two designations of the whole people, "personal possession" in v. 5 and "holy nation" in v. 6. Moreover, those who find evidence for an early date for the composition of Ex 19,3-6 argue that the implied political power of priests would be an anachronism in an early text and historically would make sense only in the post-exilic period.

Recently Cazelles, who admits the implications for the date, has attempted to decide the question simply on the basis of Old Testament usage.[18] He finds that *mamlākâ* is used 24x in the *status constructus*, and with one possible exception (1 Sm 24,21) the complement, noun or possessive suffix, refers not to the ruled but to the ruler. "Kingdom of priests" therefore is "un royaume (dirigé par) des prêtres."[19]

Important as these observations are, they leave some unsolved questions and areas of doubt. First, does *mamleket* mean "kingdom?"[20] Second, the exception cannot in our opinion be explained away.[21] Third, if in an expression like *mamleket yiśrā'ēl* Israel is a genitive of apposition (the kingdom of Israel), then it can no more become "its (Israel's) kingdom" than "River Euphrates" (*nᵉhar pᵉrāt*) can become "its (the Euphrates') river"; if Israel is an objective genitive (dominion over Israel), we can still see why common usage would avoid the ambiguity of *mamlaktô*. In other words, the relevant cases for the problem at hand seem to be only 11 (those with nominal complement), not 24 (by inclusion of the 13 with possessive suffixes). Finally, one may wonder if it is legitimate to ignore the usage of the plural construct *mamlᵉkôt* (25x), the nominal complement of which is never the ruler. At least it is hard to see the reason for the distinction in the use of the singular and plural, especially since the synonyms

---

18. *GLECS* 8, 57; see also *Introduction à la Bible*[1] ed. Robert-Feuillet (Tournai: 1957) 1, 376; *VT* 10 (1960) 93.
19. So in *Introduction à la Bible*.
20. Perhaps Cazelles himself now leans towards Caspari's view (see below). In his brief remarks in *VT* 10 (1960) 93 he writes: "Pour nous un royaume, c'est un pays qui a un roi. Dans l'antiquité le royaume, c'est plutôt le règne, une personne qui exerce un pouvoir."
21. Cazelles in *VT* 10 (1960) 93 would explain "kingdom of Israel" in 1 Sm 24,21 as referring, not to the people Israel, but to the eponym, Jacob-Israel. This does not seem probable because, aside from the fact that Jacob himself never possessed royal power and the origins of Israelite kingship are nowhere associated with his name, in v. 15 Saul is explicitly called "king of Israel" and nothing in the context invites us to see in "kingdom of Israel" anything but the dominion and its object which David is to have in Saul's place.

malkût and *mamlᵉkût* take nominal complements which do not refer to the ruler.[22]

Caspari's arguments were quite different, as to a certain extent was his conclusion.[23] He began with the use of *mmlkt* in Phoenician inscriptions, where it means "king." It refers however to the individual king only in so far as he embodies the institution of kingship; in his personal individuality he is called *mlk*.[24] As such *mmlkt* prescinds from the individual king; it is rather the royal office with its power as a constitutive part of the body politic, which is completed by the members (*'dm*) of the commonalty: *mmlkt* and *'dm* therefore form a totality. Since, however, *mamlākâ* is attested in the Old Testament with the meaning of "king" (1 Sm 10,18), and since numerous passages show king and people as the constitutive parts of Israel, Caspari concluded that *mamleket kôhᵃnîm* and *gôy qādôš* were best explained in this light—a regime of priests and a holy nation, the two parts of the totality, Israel.[25]

Against Caspari the principal objection has been that the comparison with Phoenician *mmlkt* is irrelevant, because in biblical Hebrew *mamlākâ* does not mean "king."[26] The only example he cited admits of another explanation; the masculine plural form of the participle (*hallôḥᵃṣîm*) modifying *hammamlākôt* can be explained if "kingdoms" be understood of the *peoples* oppressing the Israelites.[27]

However, Caspari's case is considerably stronger than he presented it, and cannot be so easily dismissed. Albright has proposed four examples[28]: 1 Kgs 10,20; Am 7,13 (*bêt mamlākâ* in parallelism with *miqdaš melek*); Ps 68,33 (*mamlᵉkôt hā'āreṣ*, sing to God!); Lam 2,2 (*mamlākâ* usually emended to *malkāh*, "her king," because of sense[29]). 1 Kgs 10,20 can hardly be doubted. Vv. 18-20a describe Solomon's throne, 20b says that *lo' na'ᵃśā kēn lᵉkol mamleket*. The last phrase is usually translated

---

22. Cf. Dn 9,1; 1 Sm 15,28; Os 1,4.
23. *ThBl* 8 (1929) 105-10. He is followed most recently by W. Beyerlin, *Herkunft und Geschichte der ältesten Sinaitraditionen* (Tübingen: 1961) 84-85. G. von Rad, *Gesammelte Studien* (Munich: 1958) 47-48, inclines in favor of Caspari's interpretation.
24. In the Karatepe inscriptions *hmmlkt* and *hmlk* occur together, so that the latter here cannot mean "king"; most probably it means "counselor, prince" [cf. Albright, *VT Suppl.* 3 (Leiden: 1955) 15, n. 2 and Hirschberg, *VT* 11 (1961) 378].
25. Caspari also argued negatively against taking all Israelites as in some sense priests, but the writer finds his arguments overly subtle and failing to take account of the use of parallelism in Ex 19,3-6.
26. So Buber and Wildberger. The meaning "king" is also not accepted by Köhler-Baumgartner, though Ex 19,6 seems to be set aside as a special case with references given to Caspari's and Scott's articles.
27. So Buber, *Königtum Gottes*³, 206, n. 68.
28. *JAOS* 60 (1940) 422; *HUCA* 23 (1950-51) 34. Siegfried-Stade, *Hebräisches Wörterbuch zum A.T.* (Leipzig: 1893) had already ascribed the meaning "king" to *mamlākâ* in Jos 10,2; 1 Sm 27,5; 2 Kgs 11,1; Am 7,13; Jer 27,1; Lam 2,2.
29. H.-J. Kraus, *BK* 20 (Neukirchen: 1956), would retain MT in the sense of "kingdom."

"in any kingdom."[30] This however would require *b*^{e}, and furthermore *na'*^{a}*śā l*^{e} is well attested in the meaning of "done to" or "done for" (Ex 2,4; 21,31; Is 3,11; Jer 5,13, etc.). In context "done to" is excluded, and unquestionably "done for" makes far better sense if we take *mamleket* in the meaning of "king," for one makes thrones for kings rather than for kingdoms. Also *mamleket* provides the right nuance, for the throne as the symbol of royal authority belongs rather to the office than to the individual.

In addition to the passages proposed by Albright, Zorell cites[31]: 2 Chr 12,8; Is 47,5; Jer 1,15; 25,26; Ps 79,6; 102,23; 135,11. Jer 1,15 is convincing. The *maml*^{e}*kôt* of the North are summoned to Jerusalem where each will set up a throne at the entrances to the city-gates.[32] The meaning "kings" is evident, not only from the fact that it is only kings who set up thrones, but from *'îš kis*^{e}*'ô*, "each *his* throne." In 2 Chr 12,8 Yahweh says that the Israelites will be Shishak's servants, and he contrasts the divine service with that of *maml*^{e}*kôt hā'*^{a}*rāṣôt*. Since the service of persons is contrasted—the text does not say that the Israelites will be Egypt's servants—"the kings of the lands" would preserve the lines of contrast much more sharply than "the kingdoms of the lands." Jer 25,26 is the conclusion of a long enumeration of the kings of the various nations who are to drink the cup of wrath; in this context therefore "all the kings on the face of the earth" fits better than "all the kingdoms . . ." In Ps 135,11 the mighty kings mentioned in v. 10 are specified: Sihon, king of the Amorites; Og, the king of Bashan; finally, "all the *maml*^{e}*kôt* of Canaan." Again context undoubtedly favors "kings" rather than "kingdoms."

Loretz has proposed 1 Kgs 5,1 where instead of ruling "kingdoms" he would have Solomon rule "kings," in favor of which he might have observed that in the parallel passage of 2 Chr 9,26 *m*^{e}*lākîm* replaces *mamlākôt*.[33] Similarly, in 2 Chr 17,10 Yeivin would have the fear of Yahweh fall upon "all the *kings* of the lands."[34]

We would add 2 Chr 9,21. A sin-offering is made for the *mamlākâ*, the sanctuary, and Judah. It is clear that *mamlākâ* does not mean "kingdom," for the only kingdom of which there could be question is later explicitly mentioned, namely, Judah. We find therefore *la monarchie* (*BJ*), *das Königshaus* (Rudolph, *HAT* 21; cf. also Curtis, *ICC*), as well as *the kingdom* (*RSV*). Comparison with Phoenician

---

30. So *BJ*, the Chicago University Translation, Rudolph in *HAT* 21, etc. The parallel passage in 2 Chr 9,19 reads *mamlākâ*, and the construction (*lô' . . . kol*) decidedly favors the singular; read consonantal MT as *mamleket*, *status absolutus* (cf. Mich 4,8).
31. *Lexicon hebraicum et aramaicum V. T.* (Rome: 1961) 445.
32. For the omission of *mišp*^{e}*ḥôt* see Rudolph, *HAT* 12² (Tübingen: 1958) 8. K. Budde, *JBL* 40 (1921) 32-33 argued for *malkê* on the basis of the LXX, Aquila and Theodotion.
33. *BZ* 2 (1958) 290.
34. *JQR* 50 (1959-60) 220, n. 129. Yeivin adds 1 Kgs 10,20; Is 13,4 (see below n. 37) etc.—I owe this reference to Father Mitchell Dahood.

mmlkt solves the problem: the sin-offering is for the king, but not for him personally so much as for the royal office and power he embodies and which through Ahaz's sins, explicitly mentioned in v. 19, has contracted guilt.

In some examples, therefore, the meaning "king" seems virtually certain; in others, if not necessary, it removes certain inconcinnities. In a given case one may hesitate. It should be noted that this development from abstract to concrete is already attested for *mulku*, "kingship," in the Amorite language of the 18th century,[35] and in the Taanach letters *šarrutu*, "royalty," seems to have the concrete sense of "king" with the connotation in context of "royal service."[36] There is therefore nothing improbable in the development postulated for Hebrew *mamlākâ*, as of course there is nothing surprising in the fact that we should find the same development of the same word in two so closely related dialects as Phoenician and biblical Hebrew.[37]

Even more important, however, for Ex 19,6 are a certain number of passages in which *mamlākâ* and *gôy* occur together and, we submit, the former means "king." We may first remark that it is precisely because Israel is in Ex 19,6 a *mamlākâ* that it is also a *gôy*, not an *'am*, *qādôš*. In Deuteronomy Israel is, as in Ex 19,5-6, *qādôš* and a *segullâ*, but in these passages always an *'am*.[38] However, in Deuteronomy Israel is never a *mamlākâ*, and the two differences cannot be separated. This is shown by the intimate connection between *mamlākâ* (*melek*) and *gôy* elsewhere in the Old Testament, and is illustrated by a similar variation in the Priestly tradition in Genesis.[39] Twice the patriarchs are promised that they will be made a *qehal 'ammîm* (28,3; 48,4), but when they are promised "*qehal gôyîm* will come from you," another promise immediately follows, "and *kings* will come forth from your loins" (35,11). Similarly in 17,6, "I will make you into *gôyîm*," is in parallelism with "and kings will come forth from you." In brief, where

---

35. Albright, *Archaeology and the Religion of Israel* (Baltimore: 1946) 162.
36. See A. Malamat, *Scripta Hierosolymitana* VIII (Jerusalem: 1961) 221, n. 10. This would be a Canaanitism and reflect *mamlaktu* or another abstract. Cf. *malkûtām* in Jer 10,7, which in context—parallelism with "the wise men of the nations," Yahweh as "king of the nations"—is better translated "in all their royalties" (so Chicago University Translation).
37. For this reason we do not understand Wildberger's assumption (*Jahwes Eigentumsvolk*, p. 80) that the meaning "king" would presuppose Phoenician influence on biblical Hebrew. It should be noted that not infrequently *mamlākâ* is translated by *basileus* in the LXX; some of the occurrences are to be explained by an inner Greek corruption of *basileia*, but not Is 13,4; 13,19 (*mamlekût*); 14,16; 23,11; 60,12; Jer 28 (51), 20; Lam 2,2; [cf. Joseph Ziegler, *Septuaginta V. T. Graecum auctoritate Societatis Litterarum Gottingensis editum*, XIII (1943), XIV (1939), XV (1958), Göttingen]. This may point to a knowledge of *mamlākâ* = "king" among some of the Alexandrians; cf. also the Targums' translation of *mamleket* by "kings" in Ex 19,6.
38. *'am qādôš* and *segullâ*: Dt 7,6; 14,2; 26,18-19; without *segullâ*: 14,21; 28,9.
39. The variation has been noted by J. Hoftijzer, *Die Verheissungen an die drei Erzväter* (Leiden: 1956) 9-11.

royal descendants are mentioned, the *'ammîm* become *gôyîm*.[40]

We would first examine the expression *gôy ûmamlākâ* (*haggôy wehammamlākâ*), and we begin with 1 Kgs 18,10. It is prose, and therefore we need not consider the possibility of synonyms simply for the sake of metre, etc. Obadias meets Elias and tells him that there is no *gôy ûmamlākâ* where Ahab has not sought him, and if they said he was not with them, Ahab would put under oath *'et hammamlākâ we'et haggôy* that it could not find the prophet.

What are "nation and kingdom?" The strong associations with a territory, which Rost has remarked in his study of *gôy*,[41] are here evident in the use of *šām* to refer back to "nation and kingdom." They are however people, for they speak and are put under oath. They are also in the same place (not "nation *or* kingdom"): (1) the oath ceremony seems to describe one action binding the "kingdom" and "the nation", and the LXX betrays this by translating *haggôy* as *tas chōras autēs*; (2) in Jer 18,7-8 and 27,7-8 *haggôy hahû'* refers back to *gôy ûmamlākâ*, so that in some sense *gôy - mamlākâ* constitute *one* nation; (3) *mutatis mutandis* the same is true of *gôy* and *mamlākâ* in Is 60,12 (see below); (4) there would be no point to the addition of *mamlākâ*, since every *gôy* already includes every *mamlākâ*[42]. But if they are in the same place, they are also distinct: (1) hendiadys (a kingly nation, a nation with a king) cannot explain the inversion of the order ("the kingdom and the nation"); (2) a stock expression in which no special meaning is any longer attached to the terms is also not inverted. Distinct but in one place, constituting one people—these can only be the king and the nation.

Montgomery-Gehman have already appealed to Phoenician *mmlkt* to explain *mamlākâ* in 1 Kgs 18,10.[43] We may briefly remark how well the passage fits in with other ancient Near Eastern documents. The distinction of king and people as two juridical persons is found in texts of both the second and first millennium.[44] To mention only one example not too far from the time of the events described in 1 Kgs 18, the Sefîrē treaty clearly distinguishes the oaths of the royal house from those of the people in general.[45] Since too we may suppose the author

---

40. In Gen 17,16 we have *gôyîm - malkê 'ammîm*.
41. *Festschrift Procksch* (Leipzig: 1934) 140-141.
42. *Ibid.*, 138-139; *id.*, *Die Vorstufen von Kirche und Synagoge im A. T.*, (*BWANT* 4/24; Stuttgart: 1938) 54 (*gôyîm* = "staatlich organisierte Völker"); see also E. A. Speiser, *JBL* 79 (1960) 159; N. A. Dahl, *NTS* 4 (1958) 325.
43. ICC (Edinburgh: 1951) 299 and 309.
44. For the second millennium, see Viktor Korošec, *Hethitische Staatsverträge* (Leipzig: 1931) 57-58; also 52 for the obligations put on a vassal king's subjects, and cf. Klaus Baltzer, *Das Bundesformular*, (*WMzANT* 4; Neukirchen: 1960) 85-87, and the writer's remarks in *Biblica* 43 (1962) 105-106, on the possibility of distinguishing the covenants with Moses and the people in Ex 34.
45. A. Dupont-Sommer, *Les inscriptions araméennes de Sfiré* (Paris: 1958) Stela I p. 17 and Stela II p. 61.

of 1 Kgs 18 was thinking of states bound to Ahab by some sort of alliance, as Ahab could otherwise have hardly sent envoys and put anyone under oath, it should be noted that the restoration of fugitives is one of the commonest obligations imposed by the treaty texts, and the clauses regarding their restoration are binding primarily on the king.[46] In a passage therefore concerning a fugitive we must in a sense almost expect some mention of a king. And two texts from Alalakh also illustrate this point.[47] The king to whose territory a fugitive has presumably fled, if he disclaims knowledge of where the fugitive is, must still provide the fugitive's owner an escort for a search in outlying villages (cf. *māṣā'* in v. 10!), and in these villages it is again the leading authorities, the "mayor" and his five elders or notables[48], who must take an oath that they too know not where the fugitive is. The "mayor" was probably subject to the approval of, if not directly appointed by, the crown, and therefore was in some sense the crown's representative.[49] In any event, both in the capital and in the villages, it is, as we would expect, the highest authorities who are involved most directly in the restoration of a fugitive.

Re-examined in the light of 1 Kgs 18,10 the remaining passages in which *gôy ûmamlākâ* (*haggôy wᵉhammamlākâ*) occurs, all in prose, acquire new meaning. In Is 60,11 the riches of nations are to be brought to Jerusalem and their kings (*malkêhem*) led (leading?) to the city. The following verse, a secondary prose addition, continues: For *haggôy wᵉhammamlākâ* who will not serve you will perish, the nations will be utterly wasted. Following immediately upon v. 11 (cf. also v. 3, *gôyîm-mᵉlākîm*, and v. 10, *bᵉnê nēkār-malkêhem*), v. 12a can only mean that the possibility is considered of a nation and its king who refuse service to Israel.

In 2 Chr 32,15, if we translate *gôy ûmamlākâ* by "nation and king," Sennacherib's speech becomes much more pointed. Vv. 10-12 warn the people under siege specifically against Hezekias and his promise that Yahweh would deliver them. Sennacherib appeals to history: no people has been saved so far, "the gods of the nations of the lands" and "the gods of the nations" have proved helpless before Assyrian power (vv. 13-14). V. 15 returns to the first point: Do not let Hezekias deceive you, "for no god of any *gôy ûmamlākâ* can save his people . . ."

---

46. For the second millennium, Korošec, *Hethitische Staatsverträge*, 80-81; for the first, Stela III from Sefîrē [cf. J. A. Fitzmyer, *CBQ* 20 (1958) 449, 451].
47. Donald J. Wiseman, *The Alalakh Tablets* (London: 1953) texts 2:27ff, 3:36ff.
48. On the notables (*damqūti*) see Tsevat, *HUCA* 29 (1958-59) 126.
49. This at least seems to be the system at Mari; cf. Jean Kupper, *Les nomades en Mésopotamie au temps des rois de Mari* (Paris: 1957) 17. At Alalakh the "mayor" is attested chiefly as a witness to documents, once as the leader of a revolt; on the latter, see D. J. Wiseman, *JCS* 12 (1958) 126:19-24; Anne Draffkorn, *JCS* 13 (1959) 94-97; W. G. Lambert, *JCS* 13 (1959) 132. A. Goetze, *Kleinasien*² (Munich: 1957) mentions regions in eastern and northeastern Anatolia ruled by nobles or elders, at whose head there was probably a "mayor."

Unquestionably, an implicit reference to Hezekias in *mamlākâ* fits the context perfectly; previously it was only question of the gods of the nations, but when Sennacherib drives home his point, "no god of any nation and *king*" must be declared unavailing.

Jer 27,7-8 says that all nations (*kol haggôyîm*) will serve the king of Babylon; "the nation and the kingdom" which do not serve him, Yahweh will punish that nation (*haggôy hahû'*). The progression of thought is the same as that of Is 60,11-12, and it is evident that "nation and kingdom" refers to the same people as *haggôy hahû'*. Unless, however, *mamlākâ* is to become virtually meaningless, it must be an explicit reference to the king of the rebellious nation, who is only implicit in "that nation." The same process of shifting between the explicit and implicit is found in Jer 27,7: all the nations will serve, then comes the reversal of fortune, and it is not only nations that will subject the king of Babylon, but also kings (*gôyîm rabbîm ûmelākîm gedōlîm*).[50] We thus have this scheme in vv. 7-8: *gôyîm*: *gôyîm-melākîm*: *gôy-mamlākâ*: *gôy*.[51]

Though the remaining passages in which *mamlākâ* and *gôy* are found together, often in parallelism, are relatively numerous, they are for the most part inconclusive.[52] In Ez 37,21-22 it is predicted that the Israelites will be made into one nation (*gôy 'eḥād*) and all of them will have one king (*melek 'eḥād*), no more will they be two nations (*šenê gôyîm*) and no more will they be divided *lištê mamlākôt*. Certainly it cannot be said that "into two kingdoms" in itself presents any special difficulties, but the parallelism of nation/nations and king/*mamlākôt* is in view of what we have already seen at least suggestive.[53] If we conceive of Israel as originally consisting of one *gôy* and one *mamlākâ*, then we can understand how the period of the divided monarchy could be conceived as a division into two *mamlākôt*—not two kings, but two royal offices.[54] In Agg 2,22 Yahweh promises to overthrow *kissē' mamlākôt* and destroy *ḥozeq haggôyîm*.[55] Since thrones properly belong to kings rather than kingdoms, the LXX's "thrones of kings" is probably correct, though it cannot be proved (cf. *kissē' hammelākîm*, 2 Kgs 11,19).

Ps 105,13 (1 Chr 16,20) is clearly an example in which *mamlākâ* and *gôy* are simply synonyms, and in Ex 29,13ff Egypt is a "kingdom"

---

50. On retaining MT in v. 7 see Rudolph, *HAT* 12², 161.
51. Jer 18,7-9 also contains the sequence of "nation and kingdom" followed by "that nation." Cf. Jer 25,11: "the king of Babylon and that nation."
52. Is 13,4 (LXX "kings"); Jer 1,10; 29,18; 51,20 (LXX "kings"); 51,27-28; Nah 3,5; Soph 3,8; Agg 2,22; Ps 46,7; 79,6 (Zorell "kings"); 2 Chr 20,6.
53. If the LXX is followed and *nāśî'* read instead of *melek*, the force of the parallelism is not really diminished, since it would still be question of rulers.
54. In Ez 35,10 we have two nations and two lands, but this does not necessarily imply that *mamlākôt* in 37,22 is a territorial term; in Ez 35,10 there is no reference to rulers.
55. MT *ḥozeq mamlekôt haggôyîm* is probably secondary (Horst, *HAT* 14, 202).

among the nations. In Jer 10,25 the *gôyîm/mamlākôt* parallelism of Ps 79,6 is replaced by *gôyîm/mišpāḥôt,* which suggests, if it does not prove, that in Ps 79 *mamlākôt* means "kingdoms" rather than "kings." The parallelism of poetry may conceal other exceptions to our hypothesis.[56] In prose passages, however, which are of greater relevance for the interpretation of Ex 19,6, *mamlākâ* and *gôy* seem to stand in the relation of ruler and ruled.

In favor, therefore, of Caspari's interpretation of *mamleket kôhᵃnîm* we can now point to a greater number of passages in which *mamlākâ* most probably means "king, royalty," and among them are some in which *mamlākâ* together with a *gôy* constitutes a state. If we take this evidence along with Cazelles' observation on the usage of *mamlākâ* and weigh it against the alternative that all Israel is called priestly, with all the difficulties this view has in explaining the nature and function of this priesthood, it seems to us that Caspari has still given the most probable exegesis of Ex 19,6.[57]

The objection from context has no validity against this interpretation. For *mamākâ* is not synonymous with *gôy,* and the latter does not refer to the whole people, but only to those who are not priests. It is the *mamleket kôhᵃnîm* plus the *gôy qādôš* which form the totality, the personal possession of Yahweh.

What then are the implications of this interpretation for the political power of priests? Are they such that *mamleket kôhᵃnîm* could be said only of the post-exilic priesthood?[58] We think not.

We may safely assume that an expression like "a royalty of priests," if it refers to anyone other than kings, would not have arisen during the period of the monarchy. Apart from a priestly polemic against the monarchy, of which we have no evidence, the royal presence on the throne would not favor an expression which conflicted too openly with the facts.[59] "A royalty of priests" reflects, therefore, either the

---

56. We do not consider the parallelism of *mamlākâ* and *'am,* since the latter is to be carefully distinguished for the most part from *gôy* as Rost, Dahl and Speiser have rightly insisted (see n. 42). Note Speiser's observation, *JBL* 79, 159, that the individual in the *gôy* is *'ādām,* in the *'am* however *'îš,* and cf. Phoenician *mmlkt* and *'dm* as the components of the totality.
57. It is to be hoped that further publication of the Mari texts may throw new light on the exact meaning of the still somewhat obscure *gāyum* and thus help us better understand the origins of the *gôy* and *mamlākâ* relationship; on Mari *gāyum* see most recently M. Noth, *Die Ursprünge des alten Israel im Lichte neuer Quellen* (Arbeitsgemeinschaft für Forschung des Landes Nordrhein-Westfalen, Heft 94; Cologne and Opladen: 1961) 15-16.
58. So Cazelles (n. 18), and cf. Winnett, *The Mosaic Tradition* (Toronto: 1949) 163.
59. We may thus explain why *māmleket kôhᵃnîm* disappears in the Deuteronomic tradition; the king of chapter 17 is not compatible with a royalty of priests.—K. Koch, *ZTK* 55 (1958) 40-41 detects an antimonarchical attitude in the Priestly tradition, but this cannot be transferred to the monarchical period.

post-exilic or the pre-monarchical period.

The latter possibility is seen first from the author's emphasis, which falls, not on "royalty" and "nation," but on "priests" and "holy." Israel is to have, and be maintained by God in a corporate national existence, and thus take its place among the nations of the world.[60] Its similarity to these nations is expressed by the fact that like them it is organized according to a distinction of *mamlākâ* and *gôy*. This similarity, however, only throws into bolder relief the uniqueness of Israel, which is in each of its parts consecrated to God, separated from the profane and drawn into the sphere of the sacred, and therefore peculiarly belonging to God and under his special protection.[61] Like *qādôš*, therefore, *kôhanîm* in its own way shows the distinctive nature and privileged status of this people which from all others has been chosen to be God's personal possession, a *segullâ*.[62]

Seen in this light, "a royalty of priests" is not the charter for an Israelite hierarchy. It allows for other figures who probably played a more important political rôle.[63] But the political power which, as Albright rightly insists,[64] the priests of the central sanctuary did enjoy would be sufficient basis for singling out the priests, in whose power the sacral character of Israel as a nation could be felt to find expression.

This onesidedness is also explained by the very close dependence of Ex 19,3-6 on the cult. The literary form of vv. 4-6a has been established by the studies of Muilenburg, Baltzer and Beyerlin.[65] It is a parenetic formulation of the basic form, the covenantal genre. In v. 4 we have the equivalent of the historical prologue, in v. 5a reference to the fundamental stipulation (*Grundsatzerklärung*), in vv. 5b-6 to the blessing.[66] Muilenburg does not hesitate to call the pericope *"in nuce* the *fons et origo* of the many covenantal pericopes which appear throughout the Old Testament."[67] It is the form which we find especial-

---

60. Implicit too is the promise of a territory, since *mamlākâ-gôy* are inconceivable without a territory; cf. n. 41.
61. See Wildberger, *Jahwes Eigentumsvolk,* 97-98; also Dt 28,9-10, interpreting Dt 26,19, explains "holy" as implying divine ownership with the consequent fear of the peoples of the earth.
62. On this term see most recently Moshe Held, *JCS* 15 (1961) 11-12.
63. We may think of the *nesî'îm* and the so-called Minor Judges; cf. M. Noth, *Geschichte Israels*² (Göttingen: 1954) 94-104.
64. *Archaeology and the Religion of Israel,* 108-109.
65. Muilenburg, *VT* 9 (1959) 351-357; Baltzer, *Bundesformular* (n. 44) 37-38; Beyerlin, *Herkunft* (n. 23) 78ff.
66. We cannot accept Baltzer's analysis of vv. 5-6a as "Grundsatzerklärung," 6b as a statement of Israel's status granted by God. Beyerlin too sees in v. 5a a statement of God's exclusive claims comparable to that of a suzerain upon his vassal. But the form is clearly that of a conditional blessing, of which we have numerous examples in Deuteronomy (11, 13ff; 11,22ff; 28,1ff, etc.). Besides, if *segullâ* may imply divine claims, it no less clearly implies privilege.
67. Muilenburg, *VT* 9 (1959) 352.

ly developed in Deuteronomy, and it unquestionably goes back originally to the cult.[68]

The remarkable style of the passage must also be considered.[69] In v. 3, the beginning of Yahweh's discourse, *libenê yiśrā'ēl* is balanced by the final words in v. 6, *'el benê yiśrā'ēl.* In the message itself to the people (vv. 4-6a) the first and last clauses are both introduced by the emphatic *'attem.* The prose is rhythmical,[70] clauses are carefully balanced (If you carefully heed my voice—and keep my covenant), there is even genuine *parallelismus membrorum* (Thus shall you speak to the house of Jacob and declare to the sons of Israel). These devices together with alliteration (*kî lî kol*: k-l-k--l) and repetition of references to persons (*'attem* twice, *'etkem* twice, *lî* three times, *my* voice, *my* covenant), which emphasize so forcibly the deep personal relationship involved in the covenant, make Ex 19,3-6 an example of Hebrew high prose at its best.

This is not the style of our Pentateuchal traditions, but it fits perfectly in a cultic setting. The reference to "the house of Jacob" points in the same direction. As a designation of the people it is without parallel in the entire Pentateuch.[71] It is however frequent in the prophets and occurs once in the Psalms.[72] Yet it is hardly a creation of the prophets. Micheas (3,9) addressing the leaders of Jerusalem uses it in parallelism with "the house of Israel." This can hardly be explained unless "the house of Jacob" was strongly rooted in tradition as a designation of the chosen people. In view of Micheas' dependence on the old amphictyonic traditions,[73] we may safely assume that "the house of Jacob" goes back to pre-monarchical days, from which time it could hardly have been kept alive except in the cult.[74]

If, however, Ex 19, 3-6 is an old independent tradition of the Israelite amphictyony,[75] then in its cultic setting the singling out of

---

68. G. von Rad, *Gesammelte Studien,* 33ff, and his *Deuteronomium-Studien* (*FRLANT* 58; Göttingen: 1948) also the studies of Baltzer and Beyerlin, and the survey of the question in H. Reventlow, *Das Heiligkeitsgesetz* (*WMzANT* 6; Neukirchen: 1961) 22ff.
69. Muilenburg, *VT* 9 (1959) 351-7, and cf. also M. Haelvoet, *ETL* 29 (1953) 375ff.
70. First remarked by Ehrlich.
71. Gn 46,27 refers to Jacob's family.
72. Am 3,13; 9,8; Mi 2,7; 3,9; Ob 17,18; Is 8,17; 10,20; 14,1; 29,22; 46,3; 48,1; 58,1; Jer 2,4; 5,20; Ps 114,1.
73. W. Beyerlin, *Die Kulttraditionen Israels in der Verkündigung des Propheten Micha* (*FRLANT* 72; Göttingen: 1959).
74. It is these features of style and vocabulary which in the writer's opinion argue strongly against ascribing Ex 19,3-6 to P. The cultic background also explains the so-called Deuteronomic language; cf. Beyerlin, *Herkunft und Geschichte der ältesten Sinaitraditionen,* 83, n. 1, and Wildberger, *Jahwes Eigentumsvolk,* 19ff.
75. Its independence of course is no argument against its being incorporated by E, to which we would ascribe Ex 19, 3-6 along with the *opinio communior.*

the priests as the possessors of the *mamleket* becomes even more intelligible. Gathered at the central sanctuary, not only is Israel visibly a holy nation, but in these circumstances the rôle of the priests is especially prominent.[76] In fact, it may be called royal, in so far as ancient Near Eastern royalty was sacral and had a cultic function. This kingship, however, which is not like that of "all the nations," witnesses to the fact that this royalty of priests, like the holy nation, belongs and is subordinate to Israel's invisible king.[77] "You will be *for me* a royalty of priests and a holy nation."

With a passage so difficult and so often studied one can only hope, not to have solved the problem, but to have perhaps made some remarks which may eventually lead to a solution. However, whatever the merits of our efforts may be, of this at least we are confident: the subject has been well chosen for a volume which honors a priest and Old Testament scholar for his services in the New *mamleket kôhanîm.*

---

76. Cf. M. Haran, *JBL* 80 (1961) 158: "From the sacral-cultic point of view, the preëxilic biblical sources, excluding P, admit the existence of two classes only: the priests and common people."
77. See Beyerlin, *Herkunft . . .*, 85ff., who rightly sees in the association of Yahweh with a *mamlākâ* and in the literary form, which is based on that of suzerain treaties, an implicit recognition of Yahweh's kingship. The argument from literary form was anticipated by Eugene H. Maly in his P.I.B. thesis, *The Anti-monarchical Attitude in Pre-exilic Israel* (1959) 287ff. W. Schmidt, *Königtum Gottes in Ugarit und Israel,* also sees a connection between Ex 19,6 and 1 Sm 8, 12 [on the theocratic ideal of 1 Sm 8, see Weiser, *ZTK* 57 (1960) 141-161].

RECENT MELKIZEDEK STUDY

IGNATIUS HUNT, O.S.B.

Of all the figures that make their appearance in the Bible "Melkizedek is assuredly the most enigmatic",[1] and we are under no illusions about completely extricating him from the shrouds of mystery that have surrounded him for so long a time. Nonetheless, many aspects of this elusive personage have been clarified in our times. This is largely due to a better understanding of the literary methods of the ancient orientals, to archaeological discoveries touching on Canaanite antiquities, and to a more mature text-study, guided and helped by all the information that has been pouring in from the ancient Near East.

Melkizedek makes but one fleeting *appearance* in the Bible: in Gn 14,18-20. In Ps 110,4 and Heb 5-7 he does not appear. He is merely called up from the past by way of illustration or figure. This means that the Gn passage has a special claim on our attention since it is basic to the others. We cannot, however, exclude the possibility of its having been retouched in the light of later conditions, such as those reflected in Ps 110, for the matter of inter-composition chronology is still the subject of scholarly debate.[2]

Gn 14, as is now well-established, belongs to none of the standard tradition-strands that make up the bulk of the Pentateuch. Whatever this chapter's provenance, it stands apart, "a world in itself."[3] This conclusion has been reached by an impressive number of scholars of the most varied background.[4] The chapter, once adjudged by critics

1. A. Gelin, "Sacerdos tuus Melchisedech," *AmiCl* 62 (1952) 33.
2. cf. R. Tournay, "Le Psaume CX," *RB* 67 (1960) 19ff; G. W. Ahlström, "Der Prophet Nathan und der Tempelbau," *VT* 11(1961) 114, with further references; H. H. Rowley, *The Old Testament and Modern Study* (Oxford: 1951) 55, with references to Pfeiffer and Eissfeldt.
3. cf. G. von Rad, *Das erste Buch Mose* (ATD; Göttingen: 1952) 147; *Genesis,* translated by John H. Marks (Philadelphia: Westminster, 1961) 170, citing Köhler.
4. cf. John Bright, *A History of Israel* (Philadelphia: 1959) 66; A. Bentzen, *Introduction to the Old Testament*[4] (Copenhagen: 1958), II, 59-60; R. de Vaux, "Les patriarches hébreux et les découvertes modernes," *RB* 55 (1948) 327ff.; H. Gunkel, *Die Urgeschichte und die Patriarchen: Das erste Buch Moses*[2] *(Die Schrift des ATs,* Göttingen: 1921) 189ff.; W. F. Albright, *Recent Discoveries in Bible Lands* (Pittsburgh: 1955) 75-6 (and in many other of his writings); H. Cazelles, "Patriarches," in VDBS 7, c. 122 merely dissociates Gn 14 from the J tradition; R. Tournay, *RB*

to be utterly devoid of historical foundation,[5] is now generally regarded as rooted in history,[6] though it would be a serious mistake to think of it as anything like historiography in the present-day sense of the term. The material is ancient, carrying us back, in Albright's opinion, to the 17th century B.C.[7] It presents Abraham in a military and "world-scene" setting, quite distinct from the rest of Gn.

For many years now scholars have exchanged views regarding the originality of verses 8-20 within the framework of Gn 14. The affirmative viewpoint finds its principal argument in the reference to "Yahweh 'El 'Elyôn" in 14,22, which, it is stated, "is unintelligible apart from vv. 18-20."[8] Aside from this doubtful argument, the verses may be omitted from the chapter without being missed; nor would the episode dealing with the king of Sodom be fractured or thrown into confusion as it is in the present condition of the text. It is quite plausible that the Melkizedek incident, regarded by Gunkel as a variant to the episode involving the king of Sodom,[9] was once a detached account and was later inserted both into the chapter and into the account regarding Abraham's encounter with the king of Sodom.[10] The fact that the name Yahweh has been prefixed to 'El 'Elyôn in 14,22 in the MT but fails to appear in the LXX or Peshitto, is already a sign of textual instability,[11] though the presence of " 'El 'Elyôn, creator of heaven and earth" in the same verse (14,22) is not so easy to explain.[12] At all events, whatever may have been the original con-

---

67 (1960) 20, states that "beaucoup d'exégètes admettent que dans sa rédaction actuelle, abstraction faite de ses sources, Gen., XIV s'apparente à la tradition sacerdotale. Les indices de cette origine sont en effet nombreux et significatifs." These indications have so far seemingly failed to impress Père Tournay's colleague at the École Biblique, Père R. de Vaux.

5. cf. views listed, but not followed, by E. Kutsch, in RGG[3] (Tübingen, 1960), 4, 843-4.
6. W. F. Albright, *Recent Discoveries,* 75-6; idem. *Archaeology of Palestine* (revised Penguin ed., Baltimore, 1960) 237; idem, "Abram the Hebrew: a New Archaeological Interpretation," *BASOR* 163 (1961) 36-54 passim; G. von Rad, *Das erste Buch Mose,* 147; R. de Vaux, *RB* 55 (1948) 327ff.
7. *Archaeology of Palestine,* 237.
8. J. Skinner, *A Critical and Exegetical Commentary on Genesis* (ICC; Edinburgh: 1910) 292; T. Hanlon, "The Most High God of Gen 14,18-20," *Scr* 11(1959) 115.
9. *Genesis Übersetzt und Erklärt*[3] (Göttingen Handkommentar zum AT, ed. Nowack: 1910), 284.
10. The term "insertion" refers to the chapter as we have it and may not be the most accurate as far as the entire text-history of Gn 14 is concerned, for extractions may also have taken place. Thus D. N. Freedman, "Notes on Genesis," *ZAW* 64 (1952) 193-4, referring to W. L. Moran, "The Putative Root 'tm in Is 9,19" *CBQ* 12 (1950) 154, remarks that "it is generally recognized that Gn 14 is based upon an old poem, excerpts of which are still partly embedded in the prose text."
11. In the light of this and other remarks to come, Tournay's rejection of the "insertion"-hypothesis [*RB* 67 (1960) 20] as a "pétition de principe" does not seem justified.
12. The phrase may possibly have occurred in both the Melkizedek and the King of Sodom fragments. It is more likely that it was added in at least one instance.

dition of 14,18-20, the verses are assuredly the highpoint of the chapter as it now stands and are filled with significance.

The passage as we have it in the MT may be translated as follows: "And Melkizedek, king of Salem,[13], brought out bread and wine; and, since he was a priest of 'El 'Elyôn, he blessed Abram and said: 'Blessed be Abram by 'El 'Elyôn, creator[14] of heaven and earth. And blessed be 'El 'Elyôn, who delivered your enemies into your hands.'[15] Thereupon Abram [16] gave him a tenth of everything." This translation agrees with LXX except that we have Melkizedek's deity in the Hebrew form.

Few biblical critics would assert today, as did Julius Wellhausen in 1899,[17] that Melkizedek is a purely fictional character created to fill a need. Hermann Gunkel pointed out only three years later that the

---

13. W. F. Albright, *BASOR* 163 (1961) 52, makes the following important remark which could change nearly every standard treatment of the Melkizedek question: "The name *Malkîṣedeq* has parallels for both elements in the 20-18th centuries B.C. The figure of Melchizedek seems to have been misunderstood. Nothing is said in Gen 14 about any relation to Jerusalem, which seems to be a much later notion. I should read the pertinent words in 14:18 as follows: u-Malkî-ṣédeq mélek šelom (-oh) hôṣî léḥem wa-yayin, "And Melchizedek, a king allied to him brought out bread and wine" (with the simplest possible haplography)." In a footnote attached to "a king allied to him", Dr. Albright states: "Parallels are numerous and good: e.g. 'iš-šelômî (Ps 41:10); 'anšê sêlômeka parallel to 'anšê beriteka (Obad 7); 'anšê šelômî (Jer 20:10); 'anše sêlômeka (Jer 38:22); be(îš) šêlômô (!) parallel to bĕrito (Psalm 55:21); berit šelômî (Is 54:10). Needless to say, šelômôh (with the most obvious haplography) is the normal preexilic spelling of standard sêlômô, 'his alliance, allied to him'." This remark may well carry the field as time goes on. If so, it will mean that reference to Jerusalem in the Ps and Heb passages rests on a misunderstanding, and is hence basically invalid. Apart from the haplography that must be postulated, it is noteworthy that the chapter is fond of attaching a city to each of the personages to which it refers. We cannot as yet look upon the unusual "šalem" as an impossible reference to Jerusalem, though all have noted the oddity of the term. Albright's concluding remarks are as provocative, original, and ingenious, as his suggestion already cited. He refers, among other things, to the transmission of the ancient Abraham sagas in poetic sung-form through the donkey or ass nomads ('Apiru) at their oases.
14. Evidence for this translation has been assembled by Paul Humbert, "Qânâ en Hébreu Biblique," *Festschrift für A. Bertholet* (Tübingen: 1950) 259-266, with reference to the Phoenicio-Canaanite origin of the term *qânâ;* Stanley Gevirtz, "West-Semitic Curses and the Problem of the Origins of Hebrew Law," *VT* 11 (1961) 143, with select bibliography; and H. Cazelles, *VDBS* 7, 146.
15. For a plausible reconstruction of the primitive form of this blessing, cf. D. N. Freedman, *ZAW* 64 (1952) 194.
16. The subject of the verb is not entirely clear, and in the episode involving the King of Sodom, broken by the Melkizedek incident, Abraham renounces all disposition of the spoils (Gn 14,23); cf. A. van den Born, "Melchisedek," *Bijbels Woordenboek* (Roermond en Maaseik: 1954-7), c. 1110.
17. *Composition des Hexateuchs und der historischen Bücher des ATs*[3] (Berlin: 1899) 311ff.

Hebrews, whose contempt for the Canaanites from Conquest-time on was proverbial, would not have "invented" a personage such as Melkizedek, and even less have allowed him to serve as a figure of the ideal king of Judah.[18] "If not an historical figure," said Skinner,[19] "Melkizedek was at least a traditional figure of great antiquity, on whom the monarchy and hierarchy of Jerusalem based their dynastic and priestly rights."

Though the Hebrew "Malkî-zedek" is edifyingly and popularly explained in Heb 7,2 as meaning "king of justice", the name may well mean "Zedek (a pagan deity) is my king." This is confirmed by Jos 10,1.3 where Adonizedek, another Jerusalem king, is presented. With our present knowledge of local Canaanite deities, plus other information on the god Zedek from Phoenician and Sabaean sources,[20] this conclusion seems unavoidable.

Melkizedek is listed as king of "Salem". We have already given our reasons for not accepting the recent interpretation of this name by Albright, as tempting as it may be.[21] In a chapter where kings are associated with places,[22] and where many places mentioned are not far from the area of Jerusalem, we adhere to the opinion, certainly that of the majority of scholars,[23] that Salem is Jerusalem, as it is in Ps 76,3, and as is supposed in Ps 110,4, where the Davidic king of Zion reigns in the same place as Melkizedek of old.[24]

There is a popular etymology stating that Jerusalem means "vision of peace"[25]—but this is probably incorrect. The name more likely

---

18. *Genesis* . . .², 525. As in n. 9 supra, we will refer generally to the 1910 edition, though there is a 1917 edition which is not available. As far as Gunkel's information on Melkizedek we noted practically no change in the third edition over the second.
19. *Genesis ICC*, 270.
20. J. Chaine, *Le Livre de la Genèse* (Paris: 1948) 204; M.-J. Lagrange, *Le Livre des Juges* (*Études Bibliques,* Paris: 1903) 3; A. Clamer, *La Genèse* (*La Sainte Bible*; Paris: 1953), 1/1, 256; P. Dhorme, "Abraham dans le cadre de l'histoire," *RB* 40 (1931) 514.
21. cf. supra, n. 13.
22. The chapter has nine such identifications, apart from the one in question.
23. For other views cf. e.g. E. Dhorme, *La Bible* (Pléiade; Paris: 1956), 1/1, 45, who states: "Il s'agit du bourg qui porte encore aujourd'hui le nom de *Salem,* à environ 5 km à l'est de l'antique Sichem. Nous retrouverons cette localité dans xxxiii.18." J. Milik, *Bib* 42 (1961) 84 expresses the same conviction as that of Dhorme, making 14,17 responsible for *šalim's* later identification with Jerusalem: J. Chaine, *Genèse,* 204-5, following Dussaud, believes that *šalim* is the name not of a place but rather of the Phoenician-Semitic god *šalim.* This view is only another way of stating the more standard opinion, for authors commonly explain the etymology of Jerusalem with reference to this god.
24. R. Tournay, *RB* 67 (1960) 23, points out that the *Genesis Apocryphon,* xxii,13, makes this identification, thus being the oldest document explicitly to make it.
25. cf. the Vesper hymn for the Dedication of a church: "beata [in Benedictine breviary is retained *dicta,* the more primitive form] pacis visio."

refers to the god Salem (or Salim) who was credited with having built the city. The most ancient name of the city, Urusalim, found in the 14th century Amarna Letters, would mean, according to L.-H. Vincent's explanation: "Salem built it".[26] Gn 14,18 is the only place in the book where Jerusalem is mentioned. The name Salem, closely resembling *šalôm* (=peace), may have been used here for purposes of avoiding the all-too-evident pagan faith-overtones that Jerusalem had when this account was drawn up,[27] and of employing a term, never used in common parlance,[28] that brought out positively the idealism of the city.

It is noteworthy that we have already encountered probable references to two pagan deities.

Well-attested in all three biblical passages is the fact that Melkizedek was both king and priest[29]—a combination of functions now known to have been very common in the ancient Near East.[30] What differentiated Melkizedek from many others like him was his contact with Abraham, father of the Chosen People, whom Melkizedek blessed (a priestly function), and for whom he provided a pact-repast (a kingly function), and from whom he received priestly tithes[31]—meant to serve here as a stimulus to the regular payment of tithes at Jerusalem (cf. Dt 12,11; 14,22ff). Of great significance is the fact that all this took place (under our assumption) at the future religious and political capital of Israel, where the Davidic line of kings was to rule.[32] Thus the founder of the Holy People came into contact for the first time with the Holy City in the presence of one who was to serve as an ideal to the Davidic monarchs. Abraham is presented as acknowledging Melkizedek's god, sanctuary, and priesthood.

Three times, in rapid succession, within the area of 14,18-20, and once again in v. 22, the name 'El 'Elyôn occurs. The name is certainly used by the final redactor as a title for the Unique God of the Israelites: in other words, Melkizedek is presented as a monotheist whose God is precisely the same as Abraham's. This has been the common Jewish and Christian understanding of the account.[33] The

---

26. L.-H. Vincent, "Abraham à Jérusalem," *RB* 58 (1951) 364.
27. G. von Rad, *Das erste Buch Mose,* 151,=Genesis, 174.
28. Bruce Vawter, *A Path Through Genesis* (New York: 1956) 132.
29. R. Tournay, *RB* 67 (1960), 20, prefers to play down the kingship, and emphasizes the priesthood. This fits his peculiar post-exilic situation for the episode's redaction and use, and is allied to his chronology for Ps 110.
30. cf. Clamer, *Genèse,* 257.
31. cf. A. van den Born, *Bijbels Woordenboek,* 1110 for the problem involved here and mentioned above in the text.
32. cf. von Rad, *Das erste Buch Mose,* 152,=*Genesis,* 175.
33. Defended along with nearly every other "traditional" view by G. T. Kennedy, *St. Paul's Conception of the Priesthood of Melchisedech: An Historico-Exegetical Investigation* (Washington: 1951), and note review by P. Benoit, *RB* 60 (1953) 613-4. For an approach similar to Kennedy's, cf. *A Catholic Commentary on Holy Scripture* (London: 1953) 194.

same title, 'El 'Elyôn, comes up again in Ps 78,35, perhaps under the influence of Gn 14,[34] while the two names occur in a balanced construction in Nm 24,16.[35]

On the other hand, there is strong archaeological evidence that the Canaan of Abraham's time was solidly polytheistic, local and regional gods being worshiped everywhere—often with lofty names.[36] Specific examples are not wanting to show that pagan deities were given the title 'El 'Elyôn, although the god given this name usually headed the pantheon.[37] In his *Praeparatio Evangelica*[38] (written between 312-322),[39] Eusebius reports indirectly on a Phoenician deity "Elioûn kaloúmenos Hypsistos". This Elioûn was father of 'El, but was soon supplanted by him.[40] In more recent times an Aramaic stele of the 8th century B.C., found at Sefire, contains a reference to 'El and 'Elyôn as two distinct deities.[41] Leaving aside less important discoveries,[42] we may at least allow the possibility that the name 'El 'Elyôn was applied to various deities of Phoenicia and of Canaan,[43] including Jerusalem.

---

34. T. Hanlon, *Scr* 11 (1959) 110.
35. In "Erwägungen zur Etymologie des Gottesnamen 'El šaddaj'," *ZDMG* 111 (1961) 61, M. Weippert suggests that in Gn 14,18-20.22 and in Ps 78,35 the name 'El 'Elyôn should be grammatically construed as "'El, nämlich der 'Aelyôn." Cf. also R. de Vaux, *Ancient Israel* (New York: 1961) 310 [=*Les Institutions de l'Ancien Testament* (Paris: 1960) 2,144] for the same view.
36. cf. E. Jacob, *Ras Shamra et l'Ancien Testament* (Neuchâtel: 1960) 90-92.
37. For a thorough treatment of the term 'Elyôn, as related to 'El, cf. R. Lack, "Les origines de 'ELYON, le Très-Haut, dans la tradition cultuelle d'Israel," *CBQ* 24 (1962) 44-64. One of the many conclusions reached in this study is that 'Elyôn did not enter Israel's theology exclusively through Jerusalem, but was rather "the epithet of the great god of the moment in a given place," 57. It would be impossible to give anything like a summary of this paper as it is very detailed and much longer than the present communication.
38. I,10. cf. *MG* 21/80.
39. B. Altaner, *Patrologie*[5] (Freiburg: 1958) 209. Philo of Byblos, whom Eusebius is quoting, died around 140 A.D. cf. R. Follet, "Sanchuniathon, personnage mythique ou personne historique?" *Bib* 34 (1953) 82: O. Eissfeldt, *RGG*,[3] 5,346.
40. cf. Chaine, *Genèse*, 206; T. Hanlon, *Scr* 11(1959) 112-3.
41. First published in *Mélanges de l'Université de S. Joseph*, 15 (1931) 237-260, and reproduced in ANET 503-5. Levi della Vida, "El 'Elyôn in Gn 14,18-20," *JBL* 63 (1944) 1-9, maintains that 'El and 'Elyôn are two distinct deities, the former corresponding to Ghê, the latter to Ouranos. Note that in Gen 14,18-20.22 'El 'Elyôn is creator of heaven and earth. M. Pope, '*El in the Ugaritic Texts* (Supplements to VT; Leiden: 1955) 52, regards it as certain that 'El and 'Elyôn were once distinct deities.
42. cf. R. de Vaux, *Institutions* 2, 144 = *Ancient Israel* 307.
43. cf. W. Eichrodt, *Theologie des Alten Testaments*[5] (Göttingen: 1957), 1, 113; G. von Rad, *Das erste Buch Mose*, 151; E. Jacob, *Theology of the Old Testament*, tr. A. W. Heathcote and P. J. Allcock (New York: 1958) 45 ff; R. Lack, *CBQ* 24 (1962) passim, whose study, however, is more concerned with the term 'Elyôn than with the combination 'El 'Elyôn; and R. de Vaux, as in footnote 42.

Even more fundamentally, it is now clear that nearly all the names used for God in Genesis[44] have pre-Israelite origins.[45] This is especially true of the generic and common name 'El, with all its forms and compounds, of which 'El 'Elyôn is but one. Consequently the odds against Melkizedek's monotheism are extremely heavy. It would have been extraordinary, almost miraculous, had he been a monotheist. We might note here that Samuel Driver[46] was not convinced that 'El 'Elyôn was really the name of Melkizedek's divinity, while Chaine[47] suggests that Salem once stood in the account in place of the present 'El 'Elyôn. Walther Eichrodt speaks of the designation 'Elyôn as having been used by way of a bridge between specifically Jewish conceptions and the loftier pagan notions of God—the name being eminently suitable by reason of its universality and indefiniteness: "Die dem Wort ursprünglich anhaftende polytheistische Färbung ist dabei ganz vergessen und nur noch die darin liegende Erhabenheit und Allmacht empfunden."[48]

While admitting the antiquity of the account, Gerhard von Rad[49] thinks that it was sponsored by the Davidic kings and priestly circles at Jerusalem: a) to offer some justification for making Jerusalem, so long a pagan shrine, the political and religious capital of Israel; b) to justify the break with the ancient patriarchal order through the institution of monarchy; and c) to encourage the payment of tithes. He points out that nowhere else in the patriarchal sagas does Abraham show such deference to anyone as he does to Melkizedek.

In an article dealing with Melkizedek's divinity, Thomas Hanlon remarks: "When Melkizedek blessed Abraham in the name of 'El 'Elyôn, his thoughts were obviously centered on the God of Abraham;"[50] "Abraham recognized Melkizedek as a friend of God!"[51] and "Melkizedek was monolatrous because he was a priest of 'El 'Elyôn."[52] None of these assertions approach the Genesis account from the standpoint of the final editor's mentality and purposes, but rather as if we had before us a photographically-accurate, completely objective, rigor-

---

44. The sacred name Yahweh is considered by most scholars as a special case. Compare, however O. Eissfeldt, "Jahwe" in *RGG*,[3] 3,515-6, who suggests that the name came to Moses through the Midianites. He states, nonetheless, that Yahweh was venerated only in Israel and in those regions that fell under Israelite influence; cf. E. Jacob, *Theology* . . . . 48ff.
45. J. Bright, *History* 90; H. Cazelles, *VDBS* 7, 127 (re 'El 'Olam) ; Th. C. Vriezen, *Hoofdlijnen der Theologie van het Oude Testament*[2] (Wageningen: 1954) , 208-9; M. Pope, *El in the Ugaritic Texts,* 14 and 55.
46. *The Book of Genesis*[9] (London: 1913) , 165.
47. *Genèse,* 207.
48. *Theologie,* I, 113.
49. *Das erste Buch Mose,* 152,=*Genesis,* 175.
50. *Scr* 11 (1959) 110.
51. *ibid.,* 110.
52. *ibid.,* 117.

ously historical reproduction—to such a degree that perceptive readers may even discern the precise religious outlook of Abraham and Melkizedek at the moment of their meeting! The same writer, while admitting that "from an historical point of view it is impossible to maintain that Melkizedek was a monotheist in the strict sense,"[53] attempts a compromise by postulating common Amorite background for both Abraham and Melkizedek, and therefore a common interest in, and loyalty to, 'El—of whom Abraham had a more lofty conception than did Melkizedek.[54] The latter's state of mind is compared to that of Abraham before his call. Such a construction fails to consider that the patriarchal accounts (including Gn 14,18-20) were redacted by men whose monotheism was well-developed; who had already heard the lofty doctrine of Second Isaiah;[55] and who tended to project, to some degree, their own monotheism back into the patriarchs. While conceding that the patriarchs were monotheists of a primitive sort, there is good reason to believe that they were far from being complete monotheists. The sacred writers succeeded in veiling over much of this weakness, as they felt justified to do, but they did not entirely finish their task. There are several vestiges in Gn of an imperfect monotheism, e.g. Jacob's provisional acceptance of Yahweh in 28, 20ff. and 35,2ff.

With Hans Urs von Baltasar,[56] Melkizedek is best classed among the "holy pagans" of old. It was an enthusiastic Hebrew writer who lifted up both Melkizedek and his deity to the rank of full monotheism. There is no reason for asserting that this was done with an intent to deceive, or because a later writer didn't know any better.[57] The matter has been well-stated by Bruce Vawter: "The Jews reasoned that Yahweh, not the pagan gods, had the real right to be called Most High and Everlasting. Far from cheapening their theology, this process testifies to their uncompromising monotheism."[58] We may refer to this process, without intending any disrespect, as "propaganda,"[59] of which this is no isolated instance in the OT (cf. the frequent acknowledgement by outsiders of Israel's God in Jer 25,9; Is 45,1; and especially Dn 2,47; 3,28; 6,26). In general, our overly tense Catholic preoccu-

---

53. *ibid.,* 117.
54. cf. A. Gelin, *AmiCl* 62 (1952) 33. A similar approach is taken up by V. Hamp, "Monotheismus im AT," *Sacra Pagina* (Paris: 1959) I, 518; cf. M. Pope, *El in the Ugaritic Texts,* 82ff, for what we regard as a more carefully stated view.
55. C. H. Dodd, *The Bible Today* (Cambridge: 1946) 48-9; L. H. Grollenberg, *Atlas of the Bible,* tr. Joyce M. H. Reid and H. H. Rowley (London: 1956) 100.
56. cf. *The Liturgy and the Word of God,* tr. by the monks of St. John's Abbey (Collegeville: 1959) 47.
57. H. Gunkel, *Genesis* . . . 285.
58. *Path Through Genesis,* 135.
59. W. Eichrodt, *Theologie* 1, 113; Gunkel, *Genesis* . . ., 285; E. Jacob, *Ras Shamra* . . . . 91.

pation with inerrancy has made us shy away from conclusions that were accepted by independent scholars of the highest repute decades ago.

Psalm 110

Ps 110 is genuinely messianic, for it is centered around the Davidic king, the Messiah.[60] The psalm in its primitive form was probably used for the enthronement of king David,[61] and may also have been recast as it was used over and over.[62] In v. 4 Melkizedek is summoned up from the past, perhaps by way of legitimizing the Davidic dynasty,[63] which was "regarded as in some sense heir to the royal priesthood of Melkizedek."[64] The fact that Melkizedek had reigned as king and priest in Jerusalem, that he had received tithes from Abraham even as they were received in Jerusalem by the priesthood,[65] that Melkizedek blessed Abraham, just as both king (cf. 2 Sm 6,18-20; 1 Kgs 8,14.55) and priest issued blessings in the times of the monarchy; that Melkizedek's dignity was thought to have been received from some higher source (this is perhaps hinted at in Ps 110,3)[66] just as the Davidic monarch was divinely authorized in his dignity—all this was reason for the famous words addressed to David's heir: "Yahweh has sworn and will not retract: 'You are a priest forever after the manner of Melkizedek.'" Heavy emphasis undoubtedly lies upon the word "forever"—termed the "central affirmation" by Tournay.[67]

It has been suggested that David's conception of his office was derived from the ancient Jerusalem-Jebusite priest-king ideal handed down in the form of a "hieròs lógos"[68] for generations, and ultimately represented by Zadok who would have been functioning in this way immediately prior to David's capture of Jerusalem around 1030 B.C. Zadok, in turn, would have been converted to Yahwism and retained by David as a priest, the ancient ideal being transferred to David in whole or in part.[69] G. von Rad shows marked reservations to this

---

60. For an accurate presentation of this psalm in simple language without footnotes, cf. P. Guichou, *Les Psaumes Commentés par la Bible,* vl. 3 (Paris: 1959) 44-48.
61. E. Podechard, cited by Gelin, *AmiCl* 62 (1952) 34.
62. R. de Vaux, *Ancient Israel* 110[= *Institutions* 1, 168].
63. Gunkel, *Genesis* . . . 286.
64. J. Bourke, "The Ideal King of Judah," *Scr* 11 (1959) 102; E. Jacob, *Theology* . . . , 331-2; H. Ringgren, *The Messiah in the Old Testament* (London: 1956) 15; E. Podechard, *Études de critique d'histoire religieuse* (Lyons: 1948) 15.
65. R. Tournay, *RB* 67 (1960) 47.
66. E. Jacob, *Theology* . . . , 332; R. Tournay, *RB* 67 (1960) 18.
67. *RB* 67 (1960) 18.
68. cf. remarks by A. van den Born, *Bijbels Woordenboek* 1110; G. W. Ahlström, *VT* 11 (1961) 113-5 explains this approach with a heavy stress on syncretism.
69. J. Bourke, *Scr* 11 (1959) 102; H. H. Rowley, "Melchizedek and Zadok," *Festschrift für A. Bertholet,* 461ff; E. Jacob, *Theology* . . . 331ff makes a highly sensible defense of this view.

hypothesis,[70] though he admits as certain, as do most other scholars, that Zadok was not an Aaronid and that his descendancy from Aaron in 1 Chr 6,1-8 (cp. with 1 Sm 22,20) is no more than a fiction, at best based on adoption.[71]

Independently of this, it is evident that the Hebrew monarchs at times performed certain priestly functions. An impressive list was assembled by R. de Vaux in his recension of de Fraine's dissertation on Israelite Royalty,[72] as well as his *Institutions de l'Ancien Testament*.[73] In the early years of the monarchy even more of these functions may have been handled by the kings;[74] but later writers, at a time when these functions had become increasingly confined to the official priesthood, would tend to present their materials accordingly, "suppressing the sacral character of the king."[75] Without accepting all the conclusions of the Scandinavian sacral-kingship school, there is sufficient reason today for applying Ps 110,4 to the Davidic monarch without having recourse to a so-called "directly messianic prediction."[76]

HEBREWS 5-7

The author of the Epistle to the Hebrews was interested in establishing "the infinite superiority of the new order of salvation"[77] over the old, placing emphasis on the pre-eminence of Christ's priesthood over the Aaronic priesthood. To this end he took up once more[78] the Melkizedek theme, exploiting it much more exhaustively than had the Psalmist.[79] In arriving at his conclusions he dealt not so much with Melkizedek himself as with Melkizedek as he is concretely presented in

---

70. G. von Rad, *Theologie des Alten Testaments*³ (Munich: 1961) I, 247, cf. also R. de Vaux, *Ancient Israel* 114; 311; 374 [*Institutions* 1, 176; 2,145.235], who regards the hypothesis as "insuffisamment fondée".
71. J. Bourke, *Scr* 11 (1959) 102; cf. also R. de Vaux, *Les Livres de Samuel*² (*BJ*; Paris 1962) 177.
72. cf. *RB* 61 (1954) 586 where Père de Vaux reviews Jean de Fraine's work: *L'aspect religieux de la royauté israélite* . . . (Rome: 1954).
73. I, 174-5=*Ancient Israel* 113.
74. G. von Rad, *Theologie*. . . . I, 50 and 321 shows marked reservation to this idea.
75. J. L. McKenzie, "Royal Messianism," *CBQ* 19 (1957) 36; R. de Vaux, *RB* 61 (1954) 586.
76. Cf. G. Glanzman's review of Pius Drijvers' commentary on the Psalms; *TS* 20 (1959) 112; J. L. McKenzie, *CBQ* 19 (1957) 35; R. de Vaux's view on this point was altered from *RB* 61 (1954) 586-7 to *Institutions,* I, 175-6 (four years later). In the later work he is not unwilling to allow the kings to be called in some way priests—a thing which he excluded in his 1954 review. Note R. Tournay, *RB* 67 (1960) 27, who applies this psalm to the priesthood from the time of Ezra on—not to David nor to the monarchs of Judah.
77. J. van der Ploeg, "L'exégèse de l'AT dans l'Epître aux Hébreux," *RB* 54 (1947) 187.
78. Pre-Christian tradition had shown considerable interest in Melkizedek cf. K. H. Rengstorf, *RGG*,³ 4,844. A good summary of Melkizedek speculation prior to, and during, the early Christian era may be found in O. Cullmann, *Christologie du NT* (Neuchâtel: 1958) 74ff.
79. A lengthy treatment of Melkizedek in Heb may be found in C. Spicq, *Épître aux Hébreux* (Paris: 1953) II, 111ff., and 181ff.

the sacred history of the Bible.[80] Furthermore, the author made use either of the rabbinical principle: "What is not in the Torah is not in the world," or of the Alexandrian principle: "Even the silence of Scripture is significant" (or of both).[81] This permitted him to press into Christological service additional aspects of the ancient Canaanite priest-king: no father, no mother, no genealogy, no earthly source of office, etc. But the feature he most insists upon is not the dual office of Melkizedek, but his *everlasting* priesthood.[82] After all, Scripture doesn't say that Melkizedek died, and the Psalm verse had said: "You are a priest forever . . ." It is worthy of note that this author, so quick to capitalize on every possible feature of Melkizedek, did not even hint at a bread-wine typology or at sacrifice.

Chaine,[83] following Bardy,[84] remarks that few biblical personages have had the good fortune in the history of exegesis that Melkizedek has enjoyed. As time went on, some of the loftiest, as well as some of the most fantastic and ridiculous, honors were conferred upon him. He became Shem, son of Noah;[85] anticipation of the Incarnation;[86] the Logos;[87] the Holy Spirit;[88] an angel;[89] a virgin,[90] etc. In two nearly contemporary Church Fathers, viz. Clement of Alexandria[91] (died 211-5) and Cyprian of Carthage[92] (died 258), Melkizedek's bread and wine suddenly emerge, first as a type of the Eucharist, and then also as a true sacrifice. This became a prevalent notion and remains such in the average Catholic mind today—in fact it is the most popular notion connected with Melkizedek. It is found in vol. 3 of our Confraternity OT.[93] None of the biblical passages, however, hints at an offering of bread and wine in sacrifice. Melkizedek merely *brought out* these elements—a refreshment more generous than the customary bread and

---

80. cf. van der Ploeg, *RB* 54 (1947) 216, who refers to Westcott.
81. *ibid.*, 215-6; cf. also C. Spicq, *L'Épître aux Hébreux* (Paris: 1952) I, 59-62.
82. cf. van der Ploeg, *RB* 54 (1947) 213-4; F. X. Durrwell, *The Resurrection: A Biblical Study,* tr. Rosemary Sheed (New York: 1960) 139.
83. *Genèse,* 208.
84. G. Bardy, "Melkisédek dans la Tradition patristique," *RB* 35 (1926) 496-509; 36 (1927) 24-45.
85. cf. Epiphanius, *Haereses,* 55,6,1, *MG* 41/982 (opinion of "Samaritans") and Jerome, Ep. 73, *CSEL* 55/22.
86. cf. Epiphanius, ibid., 55,5, 1-3 and 7,3 *MG* 41/986; Ambrose *De Mysteriis* VIII, 46, *ML* 16/404 and 607.
87. Philo of Alexandria, *Leg. Alleg.* III, 25-26; 79-82, cited by Bardy *RB* 35 (1926) 496-7.
88. For a list of Egyptian writers who taught this doctrine, cf. Bardy, *RB* 36 (1927) 25ff; also Epiphanius, *MG* 41/980.
89. Jerome, Ep. 73, *CSEL* 55/14 and 22, asserts that Origen taught this. It is not however found in the extant writings of Origen. The doctrine is referred to by Cyril of Alexandria, *Glaphyra* in Gn 2,3, *MG* 69/84.
90. cf. Ignatius to the Philadelphians, IV, *MG* 5/824.
91. *Stromata* IV, 25, in *MG* 8/1369.
92. Ep. 63,4 *CSEL* 3-2/704.
93. *The Holy Bible, The Sapiential Books* (Paterson: 1955) 287.

water mentioned in Dt 23,4. In Gn, the priestly function of Melkizedek is the blessing he bestows; the bread and wine were a kingly gift,[94] very likely used in a repast that was connected with a friendly pact.[95] Though the bread-wine Eucharistic typology has become popular, it lacks solid foundation, unless we "validate" it through the notion of "covenant" or pact.[96]

The Roman Liturgy

And what about the Roman Rite liturgy? The Canon of the Mass, for example, implies both the monotheism and bread-wine sacrifice of Melkizedek: ". . . et quod tibi obtulit summus sacerdos tuus Melchisedech, sanctum sacrificium, immaculatam hostiam." Does not the venerable adage "legem credendi lex statuat supplicandi"[97] apply here? There is good reason to doubt that it does. In both *Divino Afflante Spiritu*[98] and *Mediator Dei,*[99] Pius XII spoke of qualifications in the use of the adage, which had originally been applied to a particular doctrine and was only later turned into general use.[100] Several qualifications regarding its use were recently made in a study by Hermann Schmidt,[101] viz. that the doctrine in question must be otherwise generally taught; that its mode of being taught in the liturgy makes a great difference as regards its force; that the liturgy has a strong poetical and accommodational side, relying often on interpretations of Church Fathers; and that the liturgy, especially in its ancient form, is seldom interested in the scientific or academic statement of truth. When sound evidence opposes the two ideas contained in the Canon's use of Melkizedek (not to mention other liturgical applications, e.g. the Feast of Corpus Christi), we need have no qualms about abandoning the liturgical application—which is only brought up in passing.[102]

Conclusion

Melkizedek, then, is at least a traditional, if not an historical character; a person of perfectly respectable qualities for his time and position; a priest-king in ancient Jerusalem, already a shrine in his

---

94. Cf. H. Gunkel, *Genesis* . . . 286.
95. So H. Junker, *Genesis* (AT, Echter, 1949) 51; A. Gelin, *AmiCl* 62 (1952) 33; G. von Rad, *Das erste Buch Mose,* 152, cf. Jos 9,14 and Gn 31,46.
96, A. Gelin, *AmiCl* 62 (1962) 33.
97. Denzinger . . . . *Enchiridion Symbolorum*[30] (Freiburg: 1955), 66, #139.
98. cf. *AAS* 35 (1943) 311.
99. *AAS* 39 (1947) 540-1.
100. Hermanus A. P. Schmidt, *Introductio in Liturgiam Occidentalem* (Rome: 1960) 131.
101. *ibid.,* 132-4.
102. cf. A. Baumstark, *Liturgie Comparée, Conférences faites au Prieuré d'Amay* (Chevetogne: 1940) 64, for the resolution of one feature of the Latin Rite Canon, viz. the word "summus," which, in the translation made from the Greek original, was misconstrued as belonging to Melkizedek. The word originally went with "of you", referring to God as "summus". This point was brought to my attention by Vladimir Vancik of Chicago.

time and the Holy City of the future; whose deity 'El 'Elyôn, too, could be subsumed by the monotheistic redactor Gn 14 under the authentic Most High God, and thus forward the Hebrew faith. This was sufficient reason for the fame of Melkizedek. If there is any lesson in all of this for us, it is that we must expand our often narrow outlook on the OT, on the Hebrew mentality and its literary methodology, which were more supple than we at times allow.

The footnote to Gn 14,18 in the BJ by R. de Vaux is a model of synthesis and diplomacy, summing up rather well the entire Melkizedek question.[103] We should also point out that Hermann Gunkel in the 1902 edition of his Genesis Commentary in the *Göttingen Handkommentar zum AT,* had already assessed the Melkizedek question with an amazing accuracy and breadth. It has taken us a long time to catch up to him.

---

103. "Après le Ps 76,2, toute la tradition juive et beaucoup de Pères ont identifié Shalem avec Jérusalem. Son roi-prêtre, Melchisédech, porte un nom cananéen (cf. Adonisédech, roi de Jérusalem, d'après Jos 10,1). Il adore le Dieu Très Haut, El 'Eliôn, nom composé dont chaque élément est attesté comme une divinité du panthéon phénicien. 'Eliôn, généralement seul, est employé dans la Bible comme un titre divin, surtout dans les Psaumes. Ici, au v. 22, El 'Eliôn est identifié au vrai Dieu d'Abraham. Ce Melchisédech, qui fait dans le récit sacré une brève et mystérieuse apparition, comme roi de Jérusalem où Yahvé choisira d'habiter, comme prêtre du Très Haut dès avant l'institution du sacerdoce lévitique, et auquel le Père de tout le peuple élu paie la dîme, est présenté par le Ps 110,4 comme une figure du Messie, roi et prêtre. L'application au sacerdoce du Christ est magnifiquement développée dans l'Épître aux Hébreux, chap. 7. Toute la tradition patristique a exploité cette exégèse allégorique. Elle y a ajouté: Clément d'Alexandrie avait vu dans le pain et le vin apportés à Abraham une figure de l'Eucharistie, saint Cyprien le premier y reconnut un véritable sacrifice, figure du sacrifice eucharistique, et cette interprétation a été reçue dans le Canon de la Messe. Plusieurs Pères, dont saint Ambroise, ont même admis qu'en Melchisédech était apparu le Fils de Dieu en personne; quelques auteurs secondaires l'ont assimilé au Saint-Esprit et certains hérétiques ont fait de lui une puissance céleste supérieure au Christ."

GERHARD VON RAD'S *GENESIS*

FREDERICK L. MORIARTY, S.J.

Biblical scholars can only be grateful to the SCM Press for including in its "Old Testament Library"[1] a translation of *Genesis* by a scholar of international renown, Professor Gerhard von Rad of Heidelberg.[2] The translation, by John H. Marks, is made from the fourth edition of *Das Erste Buch Mose, Genesis,* published in 1956 as part of the series *Das Alte Testament Deutsch.* The translation is, apart from a very few lapses, clear, faithful, and readable. In fact, it is far better than the translator's prefatory remarks might have led us to expect. Though one's reaction to the book may be mixed, as is true in the writer's case, it would be unfair to leave the impression that this work is anything but an important contribution to biblical scholarship, which must be taken with the utmost seriousness.

It should be said at once that, although this work on Gn ranks as a full-scale commentary, it is conceived and executed according to the clearly stated purpose of the series and the dominant interests of von Rad himself. *ATD* was designed as a series of theological expositions of individual books for the benefit of both clergy and laity. For this reason we should not expect to see in von Rad's work that detailed treatment of philological, linguistic, or archaeological problems which we look for in commentaries aimed at the professional scholar.[3] On the other hand, von Rad shuns no basic hermeneutical

1. This is a publishing project deserving of attention and support since it promises to include authoritative works, some accessible up to now only in foreign languages, on important aspects of Old Testament science. In the U. S. the *Library* is published by the Westminster Press.
2. Gerhard von Rad, *Genesis* (London: SCM Press, 1961) pp. 434.
3. Von Rad notes in a Foreword that, since limits were set to the discussion of philological and archaeological problems, his book does not dispense the student from consulting the more exhaustive commentaries. Typical of the latter would be *Genesis, übersetzt und erklärt,* by Hermann Gunkel, (5th ed. 1922) ; *Genesis,* by John Skinner, International Critical Commentary (New York: Scribners, 1910) , and Paul Heinisch *Das Buch Genesis* (Bonn: Hanstein, 1930) . It should be added, however, that all these works need extensive revision in the light of new material now available in biblical philology and archaeology. It cannot be said too often that older commentaries on the historical books of the bible, especially the Pentateuch, are quite thoroughly outdated by the rapid advances made in this area.

questions and he does not hesitate to make demands of readers who seek to understand the profound meaning of the Gn traditions. The distinction, less familiar to English-speaking people, between *Historie* and *Geschichte* is essential to his exposition and, along the same line, his classification of the traditions as saga forces us to approach the material in a spirit thoroughly alien to the historical materialism of the last century.

Von Rad works, of course, with the traditional sources which have been isolated by critical study of the Pentateuch. Taking only those sources which would come into play in Gn (therefore omitting Dt) he would date the Yahwist around 950 B.C. during the reign of Solomon, and the Elohist probably one or two centuries later. Latest of all is the Priestly tradition whose actual composition falls in the postexilic period, between about 538 and 450 B.C. Von Rad wisely warns the reader, however, not to attach undue importance to the dates of these sources because the dates refer only to the completed literary composition. The age of the traditions embodied in the source is quite another matter. For example, the Priestly tradition, latest of all as far as literary fixation goes, contains the reflective theological doctrine of a long sacerdotal tradition along with much that is very ancient and often in a practically unaltered and very archaic form. His awareness of the complexity and continuities of the material in the Hexateuch is very clear from his concluding remarks about the three narrative sources:

> Many ages, many men, many traditions and theologies have constructed this massive work. Only the one who does not look superficially at the Hexateuch but reads it with a knowledge of its deep dimension will arrive at true understanding. Such a one will know that revelations and religious experience of many ages are speaking from it. *For no stage in this work's long period of growth is really obsolete; something of each phase has been conserved and passed on as enduring until the Hexateuch attained its final form.*[4]

You may call this element of his methodology the Graf-Wellhausen hypothesis, if you wish. But the reader cannot fail to see how von Rad has avoided any rigidity in its application, and is well aware of its limitations.

Besides the documentary hypothesis, two other elements enter into von Rad's method of understanding the historical narratives. There is the problem of literary analysis. He frankly acknowledges his great debt to Hermann Gunkel who, in his well-known commentary on Gn, isolated the original preliterary units which were later embodied in the narratives, and then analyzed them with what von Rad felicitously calls a "distinctive aesthetic charisma". Von Rad does not neglect these smaller units in his commentary but he is more interested in the larger contexts within which the smaller, once isolated, units must now be interpreted. He insists time and again on the new perspectives given

---

4. Von Rad, *Genesis*, 27.

the material by its progressive re-interpretation over the centuries.[5] In the Gn which we now have theological reflection has reached a term. The modern exegete, von Rad believes, has perhaps spent an excessive amount of time and energy on separate incidents embodied in the Gn narrative without giving sufficient attention to the hermeneutical task of understanding the unified composition. The combination of these separate traditions was not the helter-skelter work of an "obtuse archivist"—to use von Rad's own expression—but the construction of an organic theological end-product. It is this work which places great demand on the exegete who must, in the long run, interpret Gn *as it now stands.* To assist us in grasping the theological message of the book he has added to his exegetical treatment a series of "epilogues" which expound the deeper meaning of the various sections. These are particularly helpful for the reader who might otherwise feel swamped by exegetical detail.

The third element in von Rad's method concerns his understanding of Israel's history, and here he obviously depends to a considerable extent on the school of Albrecht Alt and Martin Noth. That this school has its defects as well as its virtues has been pointed out recently in a book review article by W. F. Albright:

> And yet he (E. Voegelin) is definitely wrong in following the Alt-Noth-von Rad School so closely. He cannot be blamed, since Albrecht Alt was a great scholar, and his pupils Martin Noth and Gerhard von Rad are first-class men, whose work made very important historical contributions, and von Rad is surpassed by no one in his insight into certain problems of Old Testament religion. But after the middle thirties Alt himself was cut off almost completely from direct contact with Palestine as well as from non-German research. His pupils were in much the same situation, and the attempt to replace the influx of empirical data from Palestine and the ancient Near East by systematic research along a priori lines led to increasing loss of touch with archaeological and philological fact. Today there is a very sharp cleavage between the dominant German school and the archaeological school, best represented in America and Israel.[6]

To this it might be added that the school described above shows a certain lack of openness, even today, to the important contributions made to our understanding of Israel's history by British, French, American, and Israeli scholars. The omission of up-to-date archaeological information shows up in section after section of von Rad's *Genesis.* From this viewpoint the treatment is antiquated, and herein lies von Rad's weakness. His strength lies in his unusual power of pene-

---

5. See von Rad, *Genesis,* 314ff, for his analysis of Jacob's struggle at Penuel, in Gn 32,22-32.
6. *Theological Studies* 22 (1961) 275. The excerpt is taken from W. F. Albright's review of Eric Voegelin's *Israel and Revelation,* the first volume of his massive work, entitled *Order and History* (Baton Rouge: Louisiana State University Press, 1956) cf.p. 533.

tration into the theological message of a given section and into the work as a total composition.

And yet one cannot help but feel a certain uneasiness over von Rad's form-critical approach to the Israelite historical tradition. I suspect that, in place of speaking about an "historical tradition", he would prefer to substitute "cultic tradition". But, we should ask, what is recoverable from this cultic tradition, these various cult legends now assembled around a canonical framework which itself is based on cultic worship? Is it possible to recover authentic traditions about Abraham and Moses from the material as it has come down to us? These are serious questions for the biblical scholar and they cannot be evaded. As far as I can see, von Rad does not forbid the quest for the historical Abraham; he is simply lukewarm to it.[7] He appears to say that kerygma or confession, created by the cult, has come between us and historical events so that instead of bothering about verification of the underlying historical tradition we should concentrate on the new meaning created by the kerygma which, in turn, is the product of the cult.

In answering the question about the historicity of these narratives, however, von Rad is not espousing the cause of a liberal theology which took them as so many fictional representations of universal religious truths. Quite the contrary! He maintains that this kind of explanation "cannot be fought emphatically enough". His own view of the relationship between narrative and event sees in the former an enlarging of "the inner events from a unique to a kind of typical occurrence". But then what has become of the relationship between the theological expressions of Israel's faith and the facts of her history? Is there not a danger that, in von Rad's understanding of the problem, the facts have not only been transmuted but arbitrarily manipulated so that they may stand for Israel's self-understanding and her experience of faith? It would seem that the inner coherence of faith and historical fact has been weakened, if not dissolved. Historical memory, in other words, has been made subordinate to *creative cultic liturgies*.[8]

A very different school of biblical interpretation while respecting the theological character of our historical material, has used all available tools, but especially archaeology in the wide sense, to demonstrate the basic authenticity of the patriarchal and Mosaic traditions. Its emphasis lies in setting the early traditions of Israel in the framework of the Middle and Late Bronze periods respectively. Albright, de Vaux, G. E. Wright, Glueck and many others are representative of this viewpoint. It seems to me that they are fully justified in the claim that a fundamentally reliable historical tradition comes before all else in

---

7. See his article, "History and the Patriarchs", *Expository Times* 72 (April, 1961) especially p. 214.
8. On this question see the remarks of G. E. Wright in "Cult and History", *Interpretation* 16 (Jan., 1962) 13-14.

Israel's narratives about her past. Tradition precedes and governs the cult, even when we grant that the latter has had a subsequent influence in shaping the tradition for liturgical purposes.[9] It is not out of place here to recall the remark made many years ago by W. F. Albright when he issued a warning against the historical nihilism always possible when one tries to make the analysis of oral and written compositions *(Gattungsgeschichte)* carry more historical weight than it should:

> Since all ancient literary composition had to conform to fixed patterns of oral delivery and formal styles of writing—a fact which cannot be doubted by anyone who is familiar with the literature of Egypt and Mesopotamia—the ultimate historicity of a given datum is never conclusively established nor disproved by the literary framework in which it is imbedded: there must always be external evidence.[10]

Form criticism, in its widest sense, can neither prove nor disprove the historicity of the units it isolates. It may tell us approximately when an oral tradition was first committed to writing and how this written document compares with others. But as long as form criticism remains faithful to its own principles and methods it is powerless to evaluate the historical value of the material transmitted by the documents. The form critic must use other measuring-rods, distinct from his own critical tools, before he can safely construct an historical situation—or demolish it. One such measuring-rod is archaeology.[11]

To understand von Rad's approach to Gn it is important to note the first sentence of his Introduction, where he says that "Gn is not an independent book that can be interpreted by itself. On the contrary, the books Gn to Jos (Hexateuch) in their present form constitute an immense connected narrative". There are two statements here, the first more certain than the second. Consistent with his earlier and more elaborate study on the formation of the early books of the Bible,[12] von Rad, as already noted, sees the first six books, from Gn to Jos, as one unified narrative which takes us from Creation to the entrance of the Israelite tribes into the Promised Land. The dominant, creative figure in welding together this material was the Yahwist, with whom the rest of the paper will be mostly concerned. Should one object that a disproportionate time is spent on this particular tradition we can only answer that von Rad's own viewpoint has made this necessary. The Elo-

---

9. For the new respect accorded these historical sources, see G. E. Mendenhall in "Biblical History in Transition", a chapter in *The Bible and the Ancient Near East,* ed. G. E. Wright (Garden City, N. Y.: Doubleday, 1961) 32-49.
10. *BASOR* 74 (1939) 12.
11. See the remarks of Mendenhall in *The Bible and the Ancient Near East,* 34.
12. *Das Formgeschichtliche Problem des Hexateuchs,* 1938; reprinted as the first essay in *Gesammelte Studien zum Alten Testament* (Munich: Chr. Kaiser, 1958) 312.

hist and Priestly traditions, in his opinion, bring little or nothing essentially new to the Yahwist tradition.

Not to overlook entirely another tradition however, let us look briefly at von Rad's handling of the Elohist narrative in Gn 22, one of the high points in the patriarchal saga. He claims that originally the pericope was a cult legend, aetiological in character, attached to a sanctuary. In its primitive form the story was concerned with the abolition of child sacrifice and the legitimation of a cult center.[13] The original narrative closed, in von Rad's opinion, with v.14 and the following verses radically changed the old significance of the story and tied it up with the theme of promise to the patriarchs, a theme which unites all the Gn narratives. But what is the meaning which Gn 22 has now, as it stands?

Von Rad answers his own question by saying that in the narrative we have, above all, the idea of a radical test of obedience. Abraham undergoes a testing greater than any he had ever experienced, for God now seemed ready to destroy the very possibility of salvation which began with the promise to Abraham.[14] God appears here as the enemy of His own work; He is really confronting Abraham with the question of whether or not he is able to renounce God's gift of promise. Far out on the road of Godforsakenness Abraham is brought face to face with the utter gratuity of the promise which escapes all human demand. Von Rad concludes his study of this theological revision of what was originally but an isolated cult legend by extending its meaning to Israel's own history:

> Finally, when Israel read and related this story in later times it could only see itself represented by Isaac, i.e., laid on Yahweh's altar, given back to Him, then given life again by Him alone. That is to say, it could base its existence in history not on its own legal titles as other nations did, but only on the will of Him who in the freedom of grace permitted Isaac to live. Is it too much to expect that the one who could tell such a story did not also make rather lofty demands on the thought of his hearers?[15]

With the reservations already made about the nature of the original narrative, it is impossible not to recognize von Rad's profound grasp of the theological values inherent in this episode.

Now let us turn to the Yahwist. He was the Israelite genius of the tenth century B.C. who, in von Rad's opinion, brought together in its final literary form this mass of traditions; at the same time his work represented the final stage of theological reflection on what, at an earlier period, were cult traditions tied to various centers of Israelite

---

13. In commenting on Gunkel's somewhat similar proposal, G. E. Wright has remarked, "This is a historical judgment of capital importance, for which, however, there is unfortunately no proof whatever": *Expository Times,* 71 (July, 1960) 294.
14. For a further development of this theme by von Rad, see his article "History and the Patriarchs", *Expository Times* 72 (April, 1961) 215.
15. *Expository Times* (April, 1961) 239-40.

liturgy. Von Rad, if I understand him correctly, believes that after the Conquest of the Land (in the time of the Judges), Israel's early traditions coalesced into two distinct and separate groups, the Sinai tradition and the Conquest tradition. The latter is the one which will claim our attention for the moment. It is well known that von Rad sees in the credos of Dt 26,5-9; Dt 6,20-24; Jos 24,2-13 the essential theme of the Hexateuch as well as the earliest recoverable form of the Conquest tradition. These credos become the point of departure for his form-critical studies of Israelite tradition. The short recitals follow an observable pattern or canonical scheme within which the different items of the Conquest tradition would be grouped. The short credo, or "festival legend", thus becomes the nucleus of the Conquest tradition. Von Rad holds that the festival in question was the Feast of Weeks, celebrated annually at Gilgal.[16] When the Twelve Tribe League, therefore, met at the cult center in Gilgal, their various traditions were harmonized into some kind of unity within the framework of the credo as we have it in Dt 26,5-9.[17] This is but another way of saying that Israel's traditions, as a unified national epic, grew out of the cult rather than that these traditions served as the basis of the liturgy celebrated at the cult centers. While there is no difficulty in granting that liturgical celebration can modify and, in some way, reshape the historical traditions it is surely going much too far to say that the cult *created* the traditions. Those familiar with liturgical services will reject at once the notion that the events celebrated are the product of the liturgy rather than its basis and whole *raison d'être*.

But in considering the Gn traditions as they existed at the time of tribal unity under the Judges we are still a long way off from their final stage as a literary work. Almost two centuries would pass before these traditions, circulating orally and closely bound to the cult, would find their literary and theological genius who would forge them into a new and meaningful unity without sacrificing the canonical order of the earliest credos. The genius was, in von Rad's view, the Yahwist and his accomplishment is described as one of the great creative achievements of all time. To consider the extent of his creativity one must consider the three steps he took with the old cultic material at his disposal.

The Yahwist was the first to incorporate the Sinai tradition into the Conquest tradition, thus uniting what had been two separate traditions with their own cultic centers. Von Rad claims that in this unification the Yahwist has given us the two basic elements of all biblical

---

16. For a sharp criticism of this hypothesis, see A. Weiser, *The Old Testament: Its Formation and Development* (New York: Association Press, 1961) 83-5.
17. H.-J. Kraus has attempted to reconstruct this ceremony in considerable detail in his study, "Gilgal, ein Beitrag zur Kultusgeschichte Israels", *Vetus Testamentum* 1 (1951) pp. 181-99. He considers it very likely, however, that the feast in question was not the early summer Feast of Weeks (Pentecost) but the spring Feast of Passover.

proclamation: law and gospel (kerygma). That this viewpoint has not been generally accepted is well known. A. Weiser, for example, has rejected as unfounded this alleged fusion of the Sinai and Conquest traditions.[18] An even stronger stand against this supposedly late joining of the two independent traditions, comprising law and kerygma, has been taken by G. E. Mendenhall in his study of the legal form of the Mosaic covenant.[19] This study has made it clearer than ever that we must look to the Mosaic period, and not later, for the basic structure of Israelite belief and proclamation. It is the covenant, inextricably associated with the Sinai event, which has provided the nucleus around which the early traditions and confessions of Israel coalesced. "And perhaps even more important", Mendenhall adds, "is the fact that what we now call 'history' and 'law' [von Rad's 'gospel' and 'law'] were bound up into an organic unit from the very beginnings of Israel itself".[20]

G. E. Wright, in a recent survey, has also appealed to Mendenhall's thesis as a decisive argument against late joining of the Sinai and Conquest traditions. He writes:

> If there is any merit at all to this [Mendenhall's] discovery, it means that credo and Mosaic covenant go together, that there can be no covenant without the historical confession. Indeed, it is the very genius of the covenant form in question that it permitted expression of the central tenet of Israelite theology: namely, that the bond between God and people was established through the gracious action (*ḥesed*) of God, and that legal duty on Israel's part should be a gracious response (*ḥesed*) to God's unmerited action.[21]

In view of these arguments von Rad's position that the Yahwist was the first to unite the Sinai and Conquest traditions may be judged extremely questionable.

---

18. *The Old Testament,* 83-90. To this we might add the critique of J. Bright in his book *Early Israel in Recent Historical Writing* (London: SCM, 1956) 105-6, where he is dealing explicitly with Noth's same position on the Sinai theme.
19. This is a very important monograph which first appeared in two articles of *The Biblical Archaeologist,* 17 (May and Sept. 1954) reprinted as *Law and Covenant in Israel and in the Ancient Near East* (Pittsburgh: The Biblical Colloquium, 1955). It is interesting to observe that a similar study, drawing on the Hittite suzerainty treaties for formal parallels but giving more attention to form critical factors, has been made by Klaus Baltzer as his 1957 Heidelberg dissertation, *Das Bundesformular* (Neukirchen: Neukirchener Verlag, 1960). See the notice in *Theologische Literaturzeitung,* 83 (Aug., 1958) 585-6; also the review by W. L. Moran in *Biblica* 43 (1962) 100-106.
20. *Law and Covenant,* 70.
21. "Old Testament Scholarship in Prospect", *Journal of Bible and Religion,* 28 (1960) 189. For a study of *ḥesed* and related concepts, see A. R. Johnson, *"Ḥesed and Ḥasid", Interpretationes ad VT pertinentes S. Mowinckel septuagenario missae* (Oslo: Land og Kirke, 1955) 110-112. See also D. N. Freedman, "God Compassionate and Gracious", *Western Watch* 6 (1955) 13.

The second creative work of the Yahwist was to extend the patriarchal tradition by uniting, in a work dominated by the theology of the Yahwist, the individual traditions and collections of traditions into an organic whole. The primitive credo, von Rad claims, had been extremely spare in its information about this period: "A wandering Aramaean was my father". From this simple statement the Yahwist, by creatively combining individual traditions which he transfigured as he united, put together a unified narrative governed by the one theme: the promise of the land. Although this was a very ancient promise, and can even be traced back to the cult of the "God of the Fathers" in pre-Mosaic times, it is under the hand of the Yahwist that this theme unites a mass of disparate material belonging to different tribes. The theme of the promise to the Fathers, running like a thread through the patriarchal narrative (Gn 12,7; 13,14f; 15,18; 24,7; 26,2f; 28,13; 50,24) has now been brought into relation with all Israel, while the Conquest itself is now understood as the fulfillment of that promise.

We can only delay a moment on the historical situation which von Rad believes underlies this step from oral, cult traditions to finished literary composition. He notes that Gn (and the rest of the Hexateuch) reached its final form at the very time when Israel faced a crisis in her national life. This consisted in the decline of Israel's old tribal unity and its replacement by a highly centralized state under David and Solomon. In this crisis there occurred a breakdown in the old sacral institutions, and the traditions became emancipated from their cult context. The old traditions, loosed from what held them together and guaranteed their transmission within the community, would now either be dissolved or assimilated into a new unity. That unity, we are told, was provided by the Yahwist who not only gave literary fixation to the traditions, but their new theological orientation as well. We have passed, therefore, from the stage of *Sitz im Leben* to that of *Sitz im Buch.*

The third and final creative step taken by the Yahwist was to prefix the primeval history of Gn 2—11 to the entire Hexateuchal narrative.[22] Von Rad admits that we cannot prove conclusively that nobody else anticipated the Yahwist in this theological fusion of primeval and sacred history. But he sees no evidence that the Yahwist was here guided by an established tradition.[23] What is the message or

22. See the remarks of J. Barr, reviewing von Rad's *Theologie des Alten Testaments,* in *Expository Times* 73 (Feb., 1962) 145. For von Rad, as for a number of other German exegetes of the present time, the Creation story belongs to a secondary place in the theology of the Hexateuch. But is there good reason in the texts for us to believe that this *must* be correct? Must we not consider the possibility that the domination of the subject by *Heilsgeschichte* simply forces a distortion of facts which will not fit in?

23. I now learn from B. D. Napier's article, "On Creation-Faith in the Old Testament", *Interpretation* 16 (Jan., 1962) 21, note, that von Rad no longer holds [as he did in the Gn commentary] that the theological

kerygma which these united traditions of the first eleven chapters proclaim? One would have to read the commentary on these sections for an adequate answer, but von Rad has summed it up in both his Introduction (pp. 22-23) and his Epilogue to the Yahwistic Primeval History (pp. 148-50). Let the author himself explain:

> What is described, therefore, is a story of God with man, the story of continuously new punishment, and at the same time gracious preservation, the story, to be sure, of a way that is distinguished by progressive divine judgment, but that, nevertheless, man could never have traveled without continued divine preservation. This consoling preservation, that revelation of God's hidden gracious will, is missing, however, at one place, namely, at the end of the primeval history. The story about the Tower of Babel concludes with God's judgment on mankind; there is no word of grace. The whole primeval history, therefore, seems to break off in shrill dissonance, and the question we formulated above now arises even more urgently: Is God's relationship to the nations now finally broken; is God's gracious forbearance now exhausted; has God rejected the nations in wrath forever? That is the burdensome question which no thoughtful reader of ch. 11 can avoid; indeed, one can say that our narrator intended by means of the whole plan of his primeval history to raise precisely this question and to pose it in all its severity. Only then is the reader properly prepared to take up the strangely new thing that now follows the comfortless story about the building of the tower: the election and blessing of Abraham. We stand here, therefore, at the point where primeval history and sacred history dovetail, and thus at one of the most important places in the entire Old Testament. Primeval history had shown an increasing disturbance in the relationship between humanity and God and had culminated in God's judgment on the nations. The question about God's salvation for all nations remains open and unanswerable in *primeval* history. But our narrator *does* give an answer, namely, at the point where sacred history begins.[24]

Throughout the commentary von Rad shows how the individuality of the Yahwist comes through as he transforms the rough material of the individual cycles of Gn traditions. Through his genius the early materials are assimilated into the history of *all* Israel as they are fitted into the perspective of promise and fulfillment in the light of the Conquest of the Promised Land. The Elohist, of course, worked along similar lines but the brilliance and vitality of the Yahwist are missing and his history is much closer to the original credo. The sacerdotal tradition differs considerably from the two preceding ones; it is not primarily a narrative but a didactic work, the end-product of a prolonged

---

sequence of the Yahwistic primeval history is due to the personal inspiration of the Yahwist [recent letter from von Rad to Napier]. Von Rad now refers to an article by Hartmut Gese, "Geschichtliches Denken im Alten Orient and im Alten Testament", *Zeitschrift für Theologie und Kirche* 55 (1958) 127f and esp. 142ff., which demonstrates the Yahwist's dependence on a much older Sumerian model.

24. Von Rad, *Genesis*, 149.

theological reflection, with the accent not on man but on what comes from God, His judgments, commands, and regulations which guarantee the salvation of God's people.

By way of conclusion, let us turn once more to the Yahwist and see how he has handled the Joseph story which von Rad has here, as elsewhere[25], conceived as belonging to the category of wisdom literature. The story, which has all the earmarks of the wisdom movement, so enthusiastically promoted in the Solomonic era, is far from homogeneous. Von Rad also doubts that the form in which we now have the story in the Yahwistic and Elohistic traditions is the original version. Again, he notes the creative skill of the Yahwist who has incorporated the story into the body of patriarchal traditions, giving it an organic unity from beginning to end. Such an artist was no mechanical collector of traditions. In keeping with his genius and purpose, it is the theology of the story which commands the Yahwist's attention. What is the story saying? Von Rad answers this question with his customary theological penetration. He believes that the key to the entire exposition is found in Joseph's words: "As for you, you meant evil against me; but God meant it for good, to bring it about that many people should be kept alive, as they are today" (Gn 50,20). In the whole morass of human sin God's hand is able to direct everything to His purpose, which is salvation. This divine plan for the salvation of all men, and not Israel alone, permeates all human life and not simply the sacred history of Israel. Man's evil cannot frustrate this secret design for God can even make our own sinful acts serve His purposes. The vision of the ancient author is as wide as the world, and the human heart itself becomes the theatre of God's mysterious and providential activity.

It is in the Joseph story that we find a good instance of von Rad's typological interpretation of the Old Testament.[26] While von Rad's application of this method to the Old Testament is not altogether free from the subjective and the arbitrary, the insight into the relation between the two Testaments and the analogy upon which it rests are valid. And this analogy comes down to the truth that the God who revealed Himself perfectly in the Word has begun this process of self-disclosure in the Old Testament, that both Testaments deal with *one* divine discourse. In von Rad's words: "One must therefore—at last to use the controversial word—really speak of a witness of the Old Testa-

---

25. "Josephsgeschichte und ältere Chokma", *Supplements to Vetus Testamentum* I (Congress Vol., Copenhagen, 1953) 120-7.
26. For a preliminary treatment of this hermeneutical question, see von Rad, "Typological Interpretation of the Old Testament", *Interpretation* 15 (April, 1961) 174-92. This is a translation of an article which appeared in 1952. He has returned to the question in *Theologie des AT*, Band II, 1960, pp. 329-424. It is a lengthier exposition and it has been severely criticized by F. Baumgärtel in his review of this second volume, in *Theologische Literaturzeitung* 86 (Dec., 1961) 895-907.

ment to Christ, for our knowledge of Christ is incomplete without the witness of the Old Testament".[27]

This inadequate summary of von Rad's *Genesis* has no more than begun to indicate the many profound insights, observations, and great erudition which mark this book. No review can do justice to a work of great learning and competence, and von Rad's book certainly belongs in this class. Despite the strictures made on matters which appear to be of capital importance since they concern our understanding of Israel's history and institutions, there can be no doubt that this book, in its English dress, will stimulate further reflection on the burning questions of sacred history and Old Testament theology.

---

27. Von Rad, *Interpretation* 15(1961) 192.

THE CONCEPT OF WISDOM LITERATURE

ROLAND E. MURPHY, O. CARM.

The purpose of this paper is to raise the question of the notion of wisdom literature in the ancient Near East and then to examine the concept of wisdom literature as exemplified in the Old Testament.

The vagueness of the term, "wisdom literature," is suggested by Professor W. G. Lambert's judgment in his recent work, *Babylonian Wisdom Literature*: "'Wisdom' is strictly a misnomer as applied to Babylonian literature. As used for a literary genre the term belongs to Hebraic studies and is applied to Job, Proverbs, and Ecclesiastes."[1] He goes on to remark that piety, or fear of the Lord, characteristic of Hebrew wisdom, is relatively absent from the Babylonian where wisdom usually refers to "skill in cult and magic lore." Thus, in the famous *Ludlul Bel Nemeqi,* Marduk is the "lord of wisdom," i.e., he is praised for his skill in the rites of exorcism.

This is not the first time that scholars have felt the ambiguity of the concept of "wisdom literature." Rudolf Anthes points out that the proper designation of Egyptian wisdom literature is "teaching" rather than wisdom.[2] In his recent work on Sumerian wisdom, J. J. van Dijk is forced to present a descriptive definition of wisdom as his *point de départ.*[3] Perhaps the broadest definition is given by Edmund Gordon:

> The generic term "wisdom literature" may be said to comprehend all literary writings current in ancient Mesopotamia (as well as in the neighboring lands of the Near East, including Egypt) whose content is concerned in one way or another with life and nature,

---

1. *Babylonian Wisdom Literature* (Oxford: 1960) 1.
2. *Lebensregeln und Lebensweisheit der alten Ägypter* in *Der Alte Orient* 32 (1933) 8.
3. *La Sagesse Suméro-accadienne* (Leiden: Brill, 1953) 3f. He contrasts wisdom with science, which is the knowledge acquired by induction and deduction; wisdom is also science, a knowledge from an esthetic point of view—the perception of something in an object that corresponds to our innate sense of the good and the beautiful: "Le problème du mal, considéré sous l'aspect de sa disharmonie avec notre sens du bon, c'est de la sagesse; quand on en analyse les causes, c'est de la science." The author's attempts were criticized by T. Fish in a review in *JSS* 1 (1956) 286-7.

> and man's evaluation of them based either upon his direct observation or insight. . . . In their mode of expression, the wisdom texts of Mesopotamia run the gamut from profound seriousness (in the "righteous sufferer" poems) to light ironic humour and biting satire (in the proverbs and miniature assays [*sic*]).[4]

One can fairly conclude from this representative sampling that there is considerable variability in defining wisdom and wisdom literature of the ancient Near East. There is no denying that the literatures of these areas have something basically in common that we can vaguely call "wisdom," but beyond that many distinctions would have to be made.

Is there any way of obtaining fairly definite and narrow limits for wisdom literature? I think it is best found in the *Sitz im Leben* provided by the Egyptian sources.[5] Here are clear examples of royal teachings over a long period of time: the instructions of Hor-dedef, Kagemni, Ptah-hotep, Merikare, Amenemhet, Kheti ("the instruction of Duauf"), Ani, Amenope, and the Insinger papyrus of the Ptolemaic period.[6] These works have definite characteristics:

1. They are instructions (*Sebayit*—"teaching") on a *modus vivendi,* transmitted from teacher to student (often in the form of father to son, such as Merikare). These are authoritative decisions about the good life, formed ultimately by observation and experience. Henri Frankfort has strongly insisted that they are not merely a pragmatic attunement to life's realities.[7] *Maat,* the divine order established since creation, is the key concept of this literature; by his activities man is to integrate himself into the existing order of things in an harmonious manner; the opposite is chaos, which cannot be tolerated.

---

4. "A New Look at the Wisdom of Sumer and Akkad," *BO* 17 (1960) 122-152; see 123. Gordon goes on to list, on the basis of form and content, the literary genres of both Sumerian and Akkadian wisdom literature: Proverbs, Fables and Parables, Folk-tales, Miniature "Essays", Riddles, "Edubba" Compositions, Wisdom Disputations or "Tensons", Satirical Dialogues, Practical Instructions, Precepts, "Righteous Sufferer" poems. These eleven categories correspond essentially to the genres mentioned by van Dijk (*Sagesse,* 4ff), with a "few exceptions"; "Riddles and Satirical Dialogues" take the place of "Letters to Gods and to Men" and "Maxims." See the classification(s) proposed for Sumerian literature by M. Lambert, "La littérature sumérienne à propos d'ouvrages récents," *Revue d'assyriologie et d'archéologie orientale* 55 (1961) 177-196; the continuation of this article will treat of the wisdom texts.
5. Besides Anthes mentioned above, see also P. Humbert, *Recherches sur les sources égyptiennes de la littérature sapientiale d'Israël* (Neuchâtel: 1929); H. Brunner, "Die Weisheitsliteratur," in B. Spuler, *Handbuch der Orientalistik* 1, 2, *Ägyptologie* (Leiden: Brill, 1952) 90-110.
6. Most of these texts are available in translation in *ANET*; for Kagemni see Gardiner in *JEA* 32 (1946) 71-74; for the Insinger Papyrus, cf. A. Volten, *Das demotische Weisheitsbuch* (Copenhagen: 1941).
7. H. Frankfort, *Ancient Egyptian Religion* (New York: Harper Torchbook, 1961) 54-87. Hartmut Gese transposes this idea to the OT wisdom literature; cf. *Lehre und Wirklichkeit in der Alten Weisheit* (Tübingen: 1958).

2. The persons concerned, as well as some of the topics treated, indicate that the instruction is designed to make the student a worthy figure in the royal court. Even if the teaching becomes more universal in application, the courtly origins are indicated by the characters concerned. Even should this framework be fictive, as some hold for the instruction of Amenemhet—that it was written after his death to support the royal claims of his son, Sesostris I—the courtly *Sitz im Leben* remains.

Such a life-setting and a corresponding literature have been only partially established for Mesopotamia,[8] and they are *assumed* for Israel. This assumption seems reasonable:

1. The Old Testament itself recognizes that wisdom is the property of Israel's neighbors, and in fact measures Solomon's wisdom by the wisdom of Egypt and Arabia (3 Kgs 5, 9-14 [4, 29-34]).[9] Such a comparison with foreign models is never made for any other aspect of Israel's thought.

2. We can point concretely to extant Egyptian works as parallels to biblical wisdom, e.g., Amenemope and Prv 22,17—24,22. We need not examine here the broad similarity in content between the Israelite wisdom books and the Egyptian instructions.[10] The international stamp of wisdom literature is further confirmed by references to Lamuel and Agur in Prv and by the striking paucity of references in the wisdom books to cult, covenant or sacred history.

3. In Israel the transmission of the advice for courtiers may not have assumed precisely the same form as the "Instructions" that have come down to us in Egypt. At least, we have no evidence. But we do have several royal proverbs in Prv 16 and 25, which betray the court atmosphere and the delicacy required in dealing with the anointed of Yahweh. This is no small gain, in view of the paucity of detail about the practical functioning of the Jerusalem court. The proverbs in these chapters provide a broad characterization of a careerist and what is expected of him: industry, a sense of responsibility, justice,

8. The only certain literary examples are the *Counsels of Wisdom* (in Lambert, *op. cit.*, 96-107; *ANET*, 426f) and the *Wisdom of Ahiqar* (*ANET*, 427-430, and see translation by Grelot in *RB* 68 [1961] 178-194). Ahiqar the vizier of Sennacherib/Esarhaddon, delivers at least two discourses advising his apparently incorrigible nephew. The book of Tobias, with the advice of Tobit (4,3-21) and of the angel (12,6-11) forms a sort of parallel. For Canaanite wisdom, see W. F. Albright, "Some Canaanite-Phoenician Sources of Hebrew Wisdom," *VTSup* III (1955) 1-15.

9. We know next to nothing about what is attributed to Solomon concerning "trees"—from the Lebanon cedar to the hyssop—or concerning "beasts, birds, and reptiles." Should this animal literature be considered part of the wisdom sayings, or better a kind of wisdom literature? See A. Alt, "Die Weisheit Salomos," *TLZ* 76 (1951) 139-144 (=*Kleine Schriften* II, 90-99). Albright has pointed to an ant proverb in the Amarna letters as a rough parallel to Prv 6,6; 30,25; see *BASOR* 89 (1943) 29-32.

10. See P. Humbert, *Recherches sur les sources égyptiennes . . .*

integrity, caution as regards strange women, etc. There is also the fact of royal associations of wisdom throughout the Old Testament literature: the ascription of Ecclesiastes and the Book of Wisdom to Solomon; the frequent coupling of royalty and wisdom, as in Prv 8,15; Eces 1,12f; Sir 9,17-10,5; Wis 6,9.20.

While therefore we recognize a certain limited dependence of Israel upon Egypt during the early years of the wisdom movement, this fact merely explains the existence and general direction of the movement. It does not mean that during the monarchy the Israelite sages contributed nothing of their own to the content of these teachings. It is almost impossible to characterize adequately the tenor of their sayings; there is some truth in all the emphases which various scholars have underlined. Zimmerli has stressed the absence of an appeal to authority (it is to experience itself), the orientation of the sayings to man's profit and interests.[11] Gerhard von Rad calls this literature *Erfahrungsweisheit*.[12] It is based on human experience and directed towards whatever pertains to human interest (*allgemein Menschliches*); thus it attempts to master reality, to catch the laws operating in nature and human society and man himself. He also allows a certain "theological" tendency—although it goes no further than recognize the limitation that God has put on human activity—in three types of sayings: 1) God is tester of hearts (Prv 16,2; 17,3; 21,2; 24,12; cf.15,3.11). 2) God finds certain actions abominable, while others please him (Prv 11,1.20; 15,8.9.26; 16,5.7; 17,15; 20,10.23; 21,3; 22,11; cf. also 14,25; 19,5; 18,5; 22,28, which approach the laws in the Pentateuch). 3) There is a certain mysterious area of activity that belongs to Yahweh alone (16,9; 19,21; 21,2; 20,24; 21,30f). Such sayings as these caused the late Abbé Robert to speak of the "Yahwism" of Prv 10-29.[13] Working from the standpoint of *style anthologique*, he pointed to some typical Yahwistic attitudes in some of the proverbs (e.g., 15,24; 22,10). But his argument hardly touches the core of the material in these chapters.[14]

Let us conclude this consideration of the wisdom literature in the ancient Near East by stating that it is essentially the literature concerned with the courtly education of young men. This is its proper origin and purpose, by which it differs from popular sayings or moral

---

11. Walther Zimmerli, "Zur Struktur der alttestamentlichen Weisheit," *ZAW* 51 (1933) 177-204. His position has been challenged by H. Gese, *Lehre und Wirklichkeit*, 33-41.
12. *Theologie des Alten Testaments* (Munich: 1957) 415-439.
13. "Le Yahwisme de Prov 10,1—22,16; 25-29," *Mémorial Lagrange* (Paris: 1940) 163-182.
14. P. W. Skehan ["A Single Editor for the Whole Book of Proverbs," *CBQ* 10 (1948) 115-130] has made a strong case that the proverbs in 14,26-16,15 are due to the arrangement of the postexilic editor (who is also the author of cc. 1-9). In these middle chapters there are some nineteen sayings about Yahweh (more than one-third of the fifty-three Yahweh sayings in 10,1-22,16); this shows the religious preoccupations of the editor, even if the Yahweh sayings are pre-exilic.

treatises or fables, or any other kind of literature to which it might bear some similarity.

* * *

What importance do the courtly origins and international stamp of this literature have for our *understanding* of the Old Testament wisdom books? Relatively little. They are very important for understanding the growth and direction of this literature, but not for the religious message. For one thing, the sayings themselves are not limited to courtly occupations. All of these books in their present form date from the post-exilic period when there was no longer king or court, when the concept of *ḥokmah* was completely religious.

This is true even for Prv, which is clearly a collection, and which contains pre-exilic elements that were directed towards courtly training, as we have seen. But even in this case, have the pre-exilic sayings preserved completely their original character?[15] Are we to think that the editor retained them as antiquarian notices? Rather, a significant change has taken place: the atmosphere of the court career has been replaced by something distinctly Yahwistic. The context of these early sayings is more than ever now the principles of Yahwist faith: "the fear of the Lord is the beginning of knowledge" (Prv 1,7; cf 9,10; 15,33). The French term, *relecture,* which properly refers to a later, interpretative, reworking of a text, is perhaps not too strong here: the old text has not been touched, but the old standards of conduct have been assimilated into a more religious framework.[16] Indeed, one may ask if this assimilation is any the less remarkable than the other more widely recognized instances of Israel's power of assimilation, whether in cult, or in terminology applicable to Divinity. There is no way of ascertaining the whole range of the original corpus of Israelite wisdom literature. Presumably, it could have dwelt on many varied topics (the trees and animals of 3 Kgs 5,10ff?), but only those with more directly religious application were preserved.

For this reorientation one need merely recall Prv 1-9, in which the urgent, didactic tone, so reminiscent of Dt, comes alive in the appeal of the wisdom teacher to his student.[17] Wisdom is held out as divine and utterly desirable. If the youth observes the wisdom counsels, he will have life (Prv 8,35; Sir 4,12), just as the Deuteronomic

---

15. There is no intention of denying that most of the sayings in Prv 10-29 were originally destined for the *gens du roi* as H. Duesberg calls them [*Les Scribes Inspirés* (Paris: 1939) I, 447-453], and as recent authors have emphasized. But the point is that the scope of these inherited sayings has been now broadened by the Yahwistic interpretation of *ḥokmah* as primarily religious literature. Dom Duesberg seems to admit this on pp. 572ff.
16. See also G. Fohrer, "Tradition und Interpretation im Alten Testament," *ZAW* 73 (1961) 1-30 especially 19-24.
17. See the fundamental studies on Prv 1-9 by Abbé Robert in *RB* for 1934 and 1935; there is also the influence of Jeremia and Isaia in the *style anthologique* that characterizes these chapters.

preachers set before their audience the choice of life and prosperity or death and doom (30,15-20), assuring them that if they followed exactly the way prescribed in "the commandments, the statutes and the decrees" they would "live and prosper" and have long life in the land (5,33).[18] In one important respect the wisdom viewpoint differs from that of Dt. The latter had a definite legal corpus to propagate and it worked within the framework of covenant renewal. The Sage, however, propagates a way of life, not the Torâ (except for Sirach); it is the way of life that combines loyalty to the covenant God—or rather assumes this loyalty—with a backlog of practical observations about life and man that are in harmony with devotion to the God of the covenant and observance of His law.

The editor and collector of the book of Prv wants his readers to interpret his work in the light of his introductory chapters. The word of the prophets and the torâ of the priests had aimed at the more obvious areas of Yahwist belief, morality and ritual. But what about the large grey area—the concrete details of daily life—that area which was less immediately connected with clear-cut moral decisions? Here was the place for a practical morality, or propaedeutic to morality, to develop, that would equip man for the smaller experiences which at the same time mold his moral character: how should one react to bad companions (13,20)? What are the effects of jealousy (14,30)? What are the consequences of pride (29,33)? One might say that what had been deduced by experience and observation was seen to be a confirmation of what had been believed in: a kindly man benefits himself; but a merciless man harms himself (11,17); the start of strife is like the opening of a dam; therefore, check a quarrel before it begins (17,12); the soul of the sluggard craves in vain, but the diligent soul is amply satisfied (13,4). If a proverb such as 17,12 were ever originally derivative from the context of the Egyptian ideal of the silent man with *maîtrise de soi,* it simply has a new quality and direction as it now stands. While 13,4 offers prosperity as a reward for industry and diligence, the reward is not just the

---

18. It is because he fails to appreciate the Deuteronomic preaching of the Law that Bauckmann claims that the Law was sacrificed to Wisdom. See E. G. Bauckmann, "Die Proverbien und die Sprüche des Jesus Sirach," *ZAW* 72 (1960) 33-63. According to this writer the apodictic character of amphictyonic law has yielded to a "profit" motive, in man's interest as conceived by the sages. But the wisdom writers no more falsified obedience to Yahweh than did the Deuteronomic writers, or Amos (5,14; cf. also Ex 23,24-26) by the emphasis on life and prosperity as a reward. It is true that the reward is conceived in more individualistic terms than in Dt. The nationalization of wisdom described by J. Fichtner *(Die altorientalische Weisheit in ihrer israelitisch-jüdischen Ausprägung* [*BZAW* 62; Giessen: 1933]) is merely a *closer* tie-in between the morality of Law/Prophets and the inheritance of the wisdom writers. This union had already begun in pre-exilic times, and it culminated in the identity of Wisdom and Law proposed by Sirach.

conclusion of the worldly-wise; it fits into the retribution schema accepted by the Deuteronomic thinker and the religious sage.

How was the gap between courtly training and religious wisdom bridged? What factor enabled the postexilic sage to incorporate the less obviously religious proverbs into his message?[19] For one thing we have seen that such sayings could be considered a propaedeutic to morality, because of their pertinence to every-day life. Secondly, the reward promised by these proverbs (success, prosperity) was seen as identifiable with the life promised by the religious-minded sage. The rewards held out by Dt for observance of the law are in every way comparable to the success envisioned by the early wise men. The blessings of the "produce of your soil, and the offspring of your livestock" (Dt 28,4) were seen to have some relation to the diligence, independence and other traits fostered by the sages. The good life, then, is the common denominator between observance of the law as conceived by Deuteronomy and the pursuit of wisdom preached by the wisdom writers. Ultimately this common denominator is a basis for the identification between Law and wisdom—stated unequivocally by Sirach and found already in Dt 4,6, "Observe [the statutes and decrees] carefully for thus will you give evidence of your wisdom and intelligence to the nations, who will hear of all these statutes and say, 'This great nation is truly a wise and intelligent people.' "

Finally, the religious orientation of this literature is not lessened by the absence of explicit treatment of cult, covenant and salvation history (but for the latter, see Sirach's "Praise of the Fathers," cc. 44ff., and also Wis 11 ff). It is true that the humanistic approach born of the original *Sitz im Leben* of court training gave a certain impetus to the study of human experience and conduct in and for itself. To this extent, the influence of its origins was still at work.

Can we go further and specify the *Sitz im Leben* of the postexilic wisdom literature? The only concrete evidence is to be found in the description of Coheleth as one who "taught the people knowledge, and weighed and scrutinized and arranged many proverbs" (Eces 12,9), and in the allusion which Sirach makes to his school and to his lessons (51,23.29). The sages must have been concerned with the

---

19. Abbé Cazelles finds the explanation in the development of personal religion in Dt and especially Jeremia (the new covenant). In this manner, the doctrine of the sages who were attacked by the prophets (Is 29,14; Jer 8,9; 9,11; 18,18, etc.) came to be canonized in the postexilic period. See "A propos d'une phrase de H. H. Rowley," *Wisdom in Israel & in the Ancient Near East* (Rowley *Festschrift; VTSup* III; Leiden: 1955) 26-32. However, one may question the precise point of the attack. It would seem that the sages were attacked by Is and Jer for their political advice (reliance upon politics for salvation) and not for their professional schooling of courtiers; the class, rather than their wisdom literature was at fault.

education of youth, which was predominantly moral formation.[20] The remarkable thing is that the old wisdom tradition continued to influence these sages to such an extent that they left almost no directions about cult or sacred history. It is quite clear from the picture of the sage drawn by Sirach that the training was not the same as might have been given a priest. By this time, it is true, the study of the Law is part of the schooling; but Sirach himself is clearly a collector and assayer of sayings of the past:

How different the man who devotes himself
 to the study of the Law of the Most High!
He explores the wisdom of the men of old
 and occupies himself with the prophecies;
He treasures the discourses of famous men,
 and goes to the heart of involved sayings;
He studies obscure parables
 and is busied with the hidden meanings of the sages.
He is in attendance on the great,
 and has entrance to the ruler.
He travels among the peoples of foreign lands
 to learn what is good and evil among men. (39,1-5)

Coheleth is perhaps the most genuine representative of the postexilic tradition in so far as he insisted on human experience and the testing of values urged by the sages. It is this aspect of his thought that has made him vulnerable to charges of scepticism. But he does not reject "fear of the Lord" or subjection to the divine will; he sees many questions left unanswered in the accepted wisdom teachings of his day. His predilection for these difficult problems once again bears witness to the fact that the humanistic, experiential bent initiated by the court teachers never came to an end.

The author of the book of Job belongs also to this tradition. He is occupied with a problem that became acute in the wisdom teaching —retribution, the promise of life that wisdom is expected to insure. The collector of Prv touched lightly on this problem: "For whom the Lord loves he reproves, and he chastises the son he favors" (3,12). One psalmist was an incurable optimist (Ps 37). In the book of Job the problem is aired on the level of wisdom. Here the sages—Arabs, at that—discuss the problem within the framework of wisdom and fear of the Lord (c.28).

One final remark on the activity of the wisdom teachers is suggested by Père Audet. He is inclined to regard them as responsible

---

20. See Lorenz Dürr, *Das Erziehungswesen im Alten Testament und im Antiken Orient,* (*MVAG,* 36/2; Leipzig: 1932) 106ff, 116ff; H. Ludin Jansen, *Die spätjüdische Psalmendichtung. Ihr Entstehungskreis und ihr "Sitz im Leben"* (Oslo: 1937).

for the preservation and orientation of the Canticle of Canticles in the wisdom orbit.[21]

We may conclude with this summary[22] of the concept of Israelite wisdom literature:

1. It was originally a courtly training for young men, along the lines of Egyptian models; several examples of this education are preserved in the older portions of the book of Prv, where they have been reinterpreted in the framework of wisdom and fear of the Lord.

2. For the most part, it is essentially a postexilic, religious, interpretation of human conduct, carried on in the light of the traditional Israelite moral ideals and motivation of Dt, but also continuing the experimental, humanistic tradition inherited from courtly origins.

---

21. "Le Sens du Cantique des Cantiques," *RB* 62 (1955) 197-221, esp. 216. One might compare here the final verse in Os 14,10, where the sage's gloss has the air of an official interpreter. For examples of wisdom in the prophetic corpus, see J. Lindblom, "Wisdom in the Old Testament Prophets," in *Wisdom in Israel and in the Ancient Near East* (Rowley *Festschrift; VTSup* III; Leiden: 1955) 192-204.

22. This description by no means exhausts the nature of Old Testament wisdom; it leaves untouched the divine, inaccessible character of wisdom, as well as its identification with the Law. See now the thought-provoking review article by Guy Couturier, "Sagesse babylonienne et Sagesse israélite," *Sciences Ecclésiastiques* 14 (1962) 293-309, who would push the *Sitz im Leben* of wisdom literature beyond the sphere of the court into that of the family.

NORTHWEST SEMITIC PHILOLOGY AND JOB

MITCHELL J. DAHOOD, S.J.

One reviewer has taxed N. H. Tur-Sinai in his Commentary on Job with trying to solve all the obscure passages in the most difficult book of the Hebrew Bible when we simply do not begin to have the necessary tools of research.[1] Job will surely yield some valuable theological insights when new literary discoveries make it possible to determine the meaning of its numerous obscure words and phrases. It is evident, for example, that 19,25-27 are verses of capital theological content, but it is equally plain that modern biblical philology is not in a position to establish their precise sense and interpretation. In the meantime, we must possess our souls in patience.

The following textual notes seek to apply to a number of verses some of the gains that have been registered in Northwest Semitic research. For example, Ugaritic occasionally uses a common Semitic word with a specific nuance that is reflected in Job. Phoenician attests the qal passive of *śm,* "to place," which serves to clear up a morphological difficulty in 20,4. Perhaps only one emendation—in 4,20—proposed some 60 years ago, finds support in subsequent discoveries. Even here, it turns out that no emendation was needed after all; a redivision of consonants and their revocalization provide the sense desired.

4,20 *mibbōqer lāʿereb yukkātû*
mibbelî-m šēm (MT *mibbelî mēśîm*) *lāneṣaḥ yōʾbēdû*
Between morning and evening they are crushed,
Without a name, they perish forever.

The emendation of *mēśîm* to *šēm* proposed by N. Herz[2], adjudged *sehr beachtenswert* by T. Noeldeke[3] but discountenanced by É. Dhorme[4], should be reconsidered, now that it is possible to explain as enclitic the *mem,* deleted by Herz.[5] An equivalent phrase, without the enclitic,

1. W. F. Albright in *BASOR* 144 (1956) 39.
2. In *ZAW* 8 (1900) 160.
3. *Beiträge zur semitischen Sprachwissenschaft* (Strassburg: 1904) 37, n.3.
4. *Le Livre de Job* (Paris: 1926) 50.
5. H. Hummel, "Enclitic *MEM* in Early Northwest Semitic, especially Hebrew," in *JBL* 76 (1957) 85-107, esp. 105.

occurs in 20,8, *b^e^nê b^e^lî šēm,* "sons without a name."

5,26a *tābō' b^e^kelaḥ 'ĕlê qāber*
You will come to the grave in manly vigor.

30,2 *gam kōaḥ y^e^dêhem lāmmâ llî*
'ālêmô 'ābad kālaḥ
Indeed, what need have I of the strength of their hands?
Manly vigor has fled from them.

Though "firm strength, manly vigor" is the sense indicated by both contexts, the etymology of *kelaḥ* has remained obscure.[6] Ugaritic, with its several examples of composite words,[7] opens up new possibilities for Hebrew lexicography. Thus *kelaḥ* may have originated in congeneric assimilation of the two words *kōaḥ,* "strength" and *lēaḥ,* "freshness." A similar formation is perhaps found in Ugaritic *ḥrb mlḥt,* "a succulent knife." Though usually identified with Arabic *malîḥ,* "good,"[8] *mlḥt* may be combined from the two roots *mḥḥ,* "to be fat, full of marrow," and *lḥḥ,* "to be moist, fresh." By metonymy, the adjective *mlḥt,* primarily predicated of animals, is transferred to the knife which cuts the fatling. Cf. Is 34,6, *ḥereb . . . huddašnâ mēḥēleb,* "a sword made fat with fatness." In an economic text from Ras Shamra, this adjective is predicated of fattened geese: *uz mrat mlḥt,* "fattened, succulent geese" (*PRU* II, 128.20, p.162f.). It is, however, possible to explain *mlḥt* as a passive participle from *lḥḥ.*

Another possible instance of a composite noun is Ugaritic *šlyṭ,* which Albright has analyzed as a combination of two words like Heb. *šallîṭ* and *šayiṭ* (?), an obscure destructive agency of some kind (Is 28,15).

Other Hebrew instances include Is 51,9, *mḥṣbt,* composed of *mḥṣ,* "to smite" and *ḥṣb,* "to slay," which are found four times in parallelism in Ugaritic; e.g., 'nt:II:23f., *mid tmḫṣ wt'n tḫtṣb wtḥdy 'nt.*[10] Contamination may account for the apparently anomalous verb in Ps 88,17, *ṣmttny.* Congeneric assimilation of the verbs *ṣāmat,* "to annihilate" and *môtēt,* "to slay" would parallel the sense and the formation of *mḥṣb.*[11]

The translation of *'ālêmô 'ābad kelaḥ* reveals *'alê* in the sense of "from," as not infrequently with verbs of "fleeing."[12] In other words,

---

6. See S. R. Driver-G. B. Gray, *The Book of Job* (*ICC*), (Edinburgh: 1921) 2,33f.
7. C. H. Gordon, *Ugaritic Manual* (hereafter *UM*; Rome: 1955) § 8.64; Ch. Virolleaud, *Palais Royal d'Ugarit II* (henceforth *PRU II*; Paris: 1957) 100.3, p. 127.
8. *UM*, no. 1117, p. 288; G. R. Driver, *Canaanite Myths and Legends* (*CML;* Edinburgh: 1956) 162a, relates *mlḥ* to Arabic *lāmiḥu,* "shining."
9. In *BASOR* 83 (1941) 40, n. 6.
10. See I. L. Seeligmann in *Supplements to Vetus Testamentum I,* (Leiden: 1953) 169, n. 4.
11. For the Punic composite verb *'bbn,* "to adopt," see M. Cohen in *GLECS* 6 (1952) 12.
12. M. Dahood in *TS* 14 (1953) 85.

the force of *ʾābad* here is virtually that of Arabic *ʾabada*, Accadian *abātu*, "to flee." Similar sentiments are expressed in Dt 32,36, *kî ʾāzᵉlat yād*, "For strength had departed"; 34,7, *wᵉlōʾ nās lēḥōh*, "nor his virility abated," and Jer 49,4, *zāb ʿimqēk*, "your strength has drained."[13] See below for *ʿălê*, "from" in 29,7.

6,4c *bîʿûtê ʾĕlōah yᵉʿārᵉkûnî* (MT *yaʿarᵉkûnî*)
The terrors of God disarray me.

To arrive at the sense desiderated by the context, commentators suppose the ellipse of *milḥāmâ*, "they draw up in battle array," but Driver-Gray[14] are quite correct in terming such an ellipse "certainly harsh." The use of the *piel privativum* was evidently more extensive than the standard Hebrew grammars allow.[15] To the examples generally listed one might add Ps 52,7, *yᵉḥattēk* (!), "He will unfather you,"[16] Ezek 21,20, *ḥereb . . . mᵉʿuṭṭâ lᵉṭābaḥ*, "the sword unsheathed for slaughter" (cf. 21,33, *ḥereb pᵉtûḥâ lᵉṭebaḥ*, "the sword drawn for slaughter"), and Job 36,30, *hēn pāraś ʿālāyw ʾôrô wᵉšoršê hayyām kissâ*, "If He spreads His light over it, He exposes the roots of the sea." Perhaps in this fashion is to be explained Is 44,25b, *mēšîb ḥăkāmîm ʾāḥôr wᵉdaʿtām yᵉśakkēl*, "Who turns wise men backward, and renders senseless their knowledge."

11,7 *haḥēqer ʾĕlōah timṣāʾ*
ʾim ʿad taklît šadday timṣāʾ
Can you find out the designs of God?
Or can you reach the perfection of the Almighty?

The verb *timṣāʾ* of the second colon is often emended; *tiggaʿ* or *tābōʾ* are among the more widely accepted conjectures. N. Peters[17] considered the possibility of relating *timṣāʾ* to Ethiopic *maṣeʾa*, "to come, arrive," but finally discounted it. Ugaritic usage shows this equation to have been correct. Very frequent is the root *mǵy* "to reach, arrive," related to *mṣa* "to find, reach," occurring also in the variant form *mẓa*.[18] Particularly relevant for the context of Job which uses *timṣāʾ* twice but in different senses is 75:I:36f., *ymǵy aklm wymẓa ʿqqm*, "he reaches the eaters and finds the devourers (?)."

11,8 *gobhê šāmayim mah tipʿāl*
ʿimqē (h) -m šᵉʾôl (MT *ʿămuqqâ miššᵉʾôl*) *mah tēdāʿ*
The heights of heaven! what can you do?
The depths of Sheol! what do you know?

Some commentators, to gain a balance of construction, emend *gobhê šāmayim* to *gᵉbōhâ miššāmayim*,[19] but Prov 9,18, *ʿimqê šᵉʾôl*,

---

13. M. Dahood in *Bib* 40 (1959) 166f.
14. *The Book of Job*, 2,36.
15. Gesenius-Kautzsch-Cowley, *Hebrew Grammar*, 28th ed., p. 142; P. Joüon, *Grammaire*, §52d.
16. For full discussion, see A. F. Scharf in *VD* 38 (1960) 213-222, esp. 218.
17. *Das Buch Job* (Münster in Westf.: 1928) 118.
18. *UM*, p. 290, nos. 1142 and 1145 where the relationship of *mǵy* to *mṣa* is treated.
19. É. Dhorme, *Le Livre de Job*, 145; G. Hölscher, *Das Buch Hiob*² (Tübingen: 1952) 32.

"the depths of Sheol," suggests that the balancing is to be achieved by attaching the *mem* of *miššeʾôl,* in the second colon, to consonantal *ʿmq,* and explaining it as an enclitic *mem* in a construct chain.[20]

12,7-8 *weʾûlām šeʾal nāʾ behēmôt wetōrekkā*
weʿôp haššāmayim weyagged lāk
ʾô śîaḥ lāʾāreṣ wetōrekkā
wîsapperû lekā degê hayyām
But now ask the beasts, and they will teach you;
And the birds of the heavens, and they will tell you;
Or speak to the nether world, and it will teach you;
And the fishes of the sea will inform you.

If *ʾereṣ* is here understood as "nether world" (as in 10,21.22; 15,29), a quadripartite division of the universe comes to the fore. The beasts represent the earth, the birds the heavens, the fish the sea, and the lower world, itself. The theme of conversing with the nether world seems to have literary antecedents in ʿnt:III:19-21, *rgm ʿṣ wlḫšt abn tant šmm ʿm arṣ thmt ʿmn kbkbm,* "Speech of wood, whisper of stone, converse of heavens with the nether world, the deeps with the stars."

On the analogy of *śyḥ,* "to complain, converse," U. Cassuto[21] has derived *tant* from *ʾānâ,* "to mourn," and *ʾōneh,* "a lament." He translates *tant* by Heb. *śîḥâ,* "conversation"; the balance with *rgm* and *lḫšt* supports such a version and our Job passage would seem to confirm it.[22] Though Ugaritic specialists invariably take *arṣ* as "earth," the chiastic arrangement would favor the meaning "nether world": *tant šmm ʿm arṣ thmt ʿmn kbkbm.*

As a corollary, the view of Dhorme[23] that *bekol ʾēlleh* in v. 9 should be rendered *dans l'univers* is strengthened by our version of *ʾereṣ,* since in an enumeration of the different regions of the universe the nether world should be included.

12,25 *yemāšešû ḥōšek welōʾ ʾôr*
wayyittāʿû-m (MT *wayyatʿēm*) *kaššikkôr*
They grope in darkness with no light,
They wander about like a drunken man.

On the basis of the LXX reading and the needs of parallelism, many commentators (e.g., Dhorme, Peters, Driver-Gray) read *yittāʿû,* deleting the *mem* as vertical dittography. It may now be retained and explained as enclitic.

13,14 *ʿōlāmāh* (MT *ʿal-māh*) *ʾeśśāʾ beśārî beśinnāy*
wenapšî ʾāśîm bekappî
Forever will I take my flesh in my teeth,
And put my life in my hand.

---

20. For other examples, see H. Hummel in *JBL* 76 (1957) 97-99.
21. *Hāʾēlāh ʿAnath* (Jerusalem: 1951) 81.
22. For another proposal regarding the meaning of *tant,* cf. W. F. Albright in *BASOR* 150 (1958) 38, n. 13.
23. *Le Livre de Job,* 157.

Often deleted as dittography of the immediately preceding *ʿālay mah,*[24] consonantal *ʿlmh* may be vocalized *ʿōlāmāh* and parsed as the substantive *ʿōlām* with the terminative suffix *-h,* used temporally. The same construction occurs in 1 Aqht: 154=161, *pʿlmh,* "and to eternity."[25] The author of Job also employs the *-h directionis temporalis* in 24,5, *meśaḥerê laṭṭārep ʿarbāh* (MT *ʿărābâ*), "seeking for prey till evening" (cf. Ps 104,23).[26]

The phrase "I will take my flesh in my teeth," as idiomatic for "I will expose my life to mortal danger," does not occur elsewhere in the Bible, but does seem to find an echo in the ninth-century Kilamuwa Inscription A,6-7, *wkl šlḥ yd ll[ḥ]m wkt byd mlkm kmʾš ʾklt zqn w[km]ʾš ʾklt yd,* "And each one stretched forth his hand to consume me. And I was in the power of the kings as though I were eating my beard, and (as though) I were eating my hand." Because of the powerful surrounding kings, Kilamuwa was in constant danger of having his kingdom annexed.[27]

13,26 *kî tiktōb ʿālay merōrôt*
wetôrîšēnî ʿăwōnôt neʿûrāy
For You write against my account acts of violence,
And make me inherit the sins of my youth.

An exegetical problem in this verse is to determine the nature of the metaphor. Driver-Gray argue that in view of the second colon, a judicial is more probable than a medical figure in the first part of the verse. The sense is not, therefore, that You prescribe for me bitter medicines. There is now a third alternative. Economic texts from Ras Shamra frequently use the preposition *ʿl* in the sense of "against the credit of," or, as Virolleaud translates it, *à la charge de.*[28] Accordingly, *tiktōb ʿālay* may be taken as a commercial term denoting, "You write against my account" (cf. Lk 16,8). The basis for defining *merōrôt* as "acts of violence" lies in Hab 1,6, *haggôy hammar,* "the violent nation," Jgs 18,25, *ʾănāšîm mārê nepeš,* "men of violent temper," and Ugaritic-Arabic *mrr* "to be bitter," but also "to be

---

24. Peters, *Das Buch Job,* 140, calls it *lediglich Dittographie.* The most recent commentary on Job, F. Horst, *Hiob* (*BKAT*; Neukirchen: 1962) 177; 188, also deletes *ʿal mah.*
25. *UM,* §11.1; M. Dahood in *Greg* 43 (1962) 68; L. Krinetzki in *BZ* 4 (1960) 73, on the basis of Ugaritic *ʿlmt,* has vocalized Ps 48,15, MT *ʿal mût* as *ʿōlāmôt,* "to eternity," an accusative of time.
26. It will now be seen that Dhorme's emendation of Job 24,5, *ʿrbh* to *ʿad ʿereb* is unnecessary. The morphological relation of *ʿarbāh* in 24,5 to *ʿădê ʿāreb* in Ps 104,23 is the same as that of *amth* to *ʿd tkm* in Krt:157f, *yrḥṣ ydh amth uṣbʿth ʿd ṯkm,* "He washes his hands to his elbow, his fingers to his shoulder."
27. For text and commentary, see M. Lidzbarski, *Ephemeris für semitische Epigraphik* (Giessen: 1915) 3,218-238. F. Rosenthal in *ANET,* 2d. ed., (Princeton: 1955) 500, gives a different version of these lines which to the present writer seems unacceptable. The biblical parallels favor the commonly-held translation; see *CBQ* 22 (1960) 40f.
28. *PRU II,* p. 212.

strong."[29] The Peshitta reads *mardûtê*, "rebellious acts," which also makes a fine parallel to "sins of my youth." There is no need, however, to adopt this emendation.

The commercial sense of *ʿal* also appears in 2 Kgs 15,20 where the inability to explicate the syntax has often resulted in the emendation of *wayyōṣēʾ* to *wayeṣāw*.[30] The text reads: *wayyōṣēʾ menaḥēm ʾet hakkesep ʿal yiśrāʾēl ʿal kol gibbôrê haḥayil lātēt lemelek ʾaššûr ḥămiššîm šeqālîm leʾîš ʾeḥād wayyāšob melek ʾaššûr welōʾ ʿāmad šām bāʾāreṣ*, "And Menahem brought forth the money, against the account of Israel, against the account of all the wealthy magnates, to give it to the king of Assyria—fifty shekels of silver per person—and the king of Assyria returned and did not stay in the land." Menahem handed over to Tiglath-pileser III a lump sum which he planned to get back later from the Israelites—more specifically, the affluent Israelites, who were to be taxed fifty shekels apiece. The phrase *hakkesep ʿal yiśrāʾēl* will be seen to be syntactically identical with *PRU* II, 144.4 [*ḫm*] *šm ksp ʿl gd*[ ], "fifty shekels of silver against the account of Gad—."

14,2 *keṣîṣ yāṣāʾ wayyimmāl*
wayyibraḥ kaṣṣēl welōʾ yaʿămôd
He shines like a blossom and fades,
And flees like a shadow, and does not endure.

There is some dispute about the reading *yāṣāʾ*, but perhaps a measure of certainty can be added by noting here the Arabic-Ugaritic sense of *yṣʾ*, "to be clean, to shine." This creates a word-play with *ṣîṣ*, "blossom," which is related to the root *ṣwṣ* "to shine," and sets up a contrast with the darkness of a shadow in the second colon.[31] A similar pun is found in Jer 48,9, *tenû ṣîṣ lemōʾāb kî nāṣōʾ tēṣēʾ*, "Put salt on Moab, for shining she will surrender."[32] Covered with glistening salt crystals, the Moabites will go forth to surrender.

15,29-30a *lōʾ yeʿšar welōʾ yāqûm ḥêlô*
welōʾ yiṭṭeh lāʾāreṣ menōlem (MT *minlām*)
lōʾ yāsûr minnî ḥōšek.
He will not be rich, and his substance will not last;
And his possessions will not go down to the nether world;
He will not escape the darkness.

Though Koehler labels MT *minlām* "unerklärt," the Arabic etymology given in Zorell and other lexica appears satisfactory. Zorell

---

29. *UM*, p. 292. no. 1170; M. Dahood in *Bib* 39 (1958) 208f.
30. J. A. Montgomery-H. S. Gehman, *The Book of Kings* (*ICC*; Edinburgh: 1951) 450.
31. The evidence for this meaning will be examined below in connection with 28,1.
32. W. L. Moran in *Bib* 39 (1958) 71 offers a slightly different version. The frequent Ugaritic use of *l*, "upon," with verbs of placing, such as *ʿdb, ṯpd, št*, and the occasional biblical use of *la* in this sense (Ps 9,5; 29,10) authorize the translation of *tenû ṣîṣ lemōʾāb*, "Put salt on Moab."

(after Saadya) compares it with Arabic *manāl,* "res acquisita," from *nâla* (û), "to give, donate," but in the sixth form, "to receive, acquire." The root very probably appears in Is 33,1.[33] This definition nicely balances with *yeʿšar* and *ḥêlô*. Once the sense of *mnlm* is clarified, it becomes tolerably clear that *lōʾ yiṭṭeh lāʾāreṣ* denotes, "It will not descend to the nether world," and rings the same theme as Ps 49,18, "For he will take nothing with him when he dies; his wealth will not descend with him." Since, moreover, *ḥōšek* is a poetic name for Sheol (Job 10,21; 17,13), the contextual relevancy of 30a, described by the relatively conservative commentary of Driver-Gray as "an isolated stichos—looks like a variant of 22a,"[34] becomes obvious. That *ʾereṣ* often denotes "nether world" is well established and needs no demonstration here (cf. Job 10,20-21; Is 29,4; Jer 15,7; 17,13; Pss 141,7; 147,6; Prov 11,31).[35]

The apparent suffix in *mnlm* is really the enclitic *mem* used to balance the suffix of *ḥêlô;* this practice may be documented in Is 33,2; Mi 7,19; Pss 10,17; 12,8; 65,10; 109,13; Job 36,15.[36]

Our vocalization *menōlem* inserts an epenthetic vowel between the substantive and the enclitic *mem.*

16,18 *ʾereṣ ʾal tekassî dāmî*
weʾal yehî māqôm lezaʿăqātî
O earth, cover not my blood,
And let its cry have no burial-place.

In their commentary to this verse, Driver-Gray saw that the sense desiderated by *māqôm* was "grave," though in their translation it is rendered "(resting) place." They comment: "let his blood lie uncovered that its voice may not be gagged with the dust of the grave."[37] It is possible to provide a philological basis for simply translating *māqôm,* "burial-place." The Hadad Inscription from Zincirli reads in line 14: *w[h]qmt nṣb hdd zn wmqm pnmw br qrl,* "And I erected this statue of Hadad and the burial-place of Panamuwa, son of QRL."[38] Cooke[39] briefly comments on this passage that *mqm,* "place" was possibly like *topos,* "a burial-place" in Greek inscriptions. He translates it, however, "place." A similar nuance may be noticed in Eshmunazar, lines 3-4, *wškb ʾnk bḥlt z wbqbr z bmqm ʾš bnt,* "And I am lying in this casket and in this grave, in a tomb which I built." Though no scholar seems to have recognized this nuance of *mqm*

---

33. And probably in the Phoenician Inscription of Tabnit, line 7, *ʾl ynl zrʿ bḥym,* "May he beget no seed among the living." See S. Gevirtz in *VT* 11 (1961) 149, n. 4, who also compares *PRU III,* 15.89, *LUna-ya-li.*
34. *Book of Job,* 1, 139.
35. Full treatment may be found in *Bib* 40 (1959) 164ff.
36. H. Hummel in *JBL* 76 (1957) 95; M. Dahood in *CBQ* 20 (1958) 45f.
37. *Book of Job,* 1, 148.
38. G. A. Cooke, *A Text-Book of North-Semitic Inscriptions* (Oxford: 1903) 159ff.
39. *Ibid.,* 167.

here, it seems imposed by its balance with *ḥlt* and *qbr* and by its being the nearest object to *bnt*, which, to judge from the direct objects of this verb in Hebrew, desiderates an object less amorphous than generic "place." This conclusion is strongly seconded by Ezek 39,11, *ʾettēn legôg māqôm* (MT *meqôm*) *šām qeber beyiśrāʾēl*, "I shall give to Gog a burial-place there, a grave in Israel." Though the precise sense of Qoh 8,10 remains elusive, the proximity of *qebûrîm* shows that *māqôm qādôš* resembles the sense of Greek *hagios topos*, frequently used of a grave of a martyr or of a monastery associated with it.[40] Greek *topos* alone signifies "grave" and is found in this sense in Mk 16,6. In view of Old Testament and Semitic usage, it is difficult to understand why Liddell-Scott should propose an emendation of *topos* to *taphos* in this text. Latin *locus*, "burial-place" is very frequent in epitaphs.[41]

There is no need for the emendation to *zaʿăqātô* since Hebrew, like Phoenician, possessed a third sing. masc. suff. *-y*, in addition to *w-h*. Other examples in Job 19,28; 23,2; Jer 17, 13; Pss 16,8; 24,4; 36,2; 113,8; Qoh 2,25 etc.[42]

17,15-16 *weʾayyēh ʾēpô tiqwātî*
wetiqwātî mî yešûrennâ
baddê šeʾōl terēdannâ (MT *tēradnâ*)
ʾim yaḥad ʿal ʿāpār nēḥat (MT *nāḥat*)
Where then is my hope?
And my hope, who will see it?
It will descend into the hands of Sheol,
When we descend together upon the dust.

The key to the understanding of these verses lies in *baddê* which is contracted from *ba-yadê*, just as Ugaritic-Phoenician *byd* becomes *bd*, and Amarna *badiú* stands for an original *ba-yadihû*.[43] Among other texts that mention the hand of Sheol are Ps 49,16, *miyyad šeʾôl kî yiqqāḥēnî*, "From the hand of Sheol He will surely take me," Ps 89,49, and Hos 13,14. This contracted form also occurs in Is 16,6 = Jer 48, 30, *lōʾ kēn baddāyw*, "There is no justice in his hands," as first noticed by C. Rabin.[44] Cf. also Hab 2,13 = Jer 51,58. None of the Ugaritic texts speak of the hands of Mot, but there is mention of his throat in 67:1:6-7, *lyrt bnpš mt*, "I have indeed gone down into the throat of Mot," and of his mouth in 67:II:4.

---

40. Liddell-Scott-Jones, *A Greek-English Lexicon* (1940) 1806b, n. 5.
41. On the analogy of Latin *loculus*, "a coffin, a coffer for precious objects," one may attempt a definition of enigmatic *mqm* in Krt:126f, *qḥ ksp wyrq ḫrṣ yd mqmh*, "Take silver and yellow-glittering gold, along with its coffer."
42. On the origin of the Phoenician suffix of the third pers. masc. *-y*, see F. M. Cross, Jr.-D. N. Freedman in *JNES* 10 (1951) 228-230.
43. *UM*, p. 245, no. 310; p. 253, no. 450. See Jean-J. Hoftijzer, *Dictionnaire des inscriptions sémitiques de l'ouest*, I-II (Leiden: 1960) 104, lines 13-16.
44. In *JJS* 6 (1955) 112.

The form *t^erēdannâ* is third fem. sing. of the *modus energicus,* like Jgs 5,26, *tišlāḥannâ,*[45] Prov 1,20; 8,3, *tāronnâ* and Lam 1,13, *y^erēdannâ.*

In the sense of "when," *'im* is attested in 7,4, *'im šākabtî,* "when I lie down," and frequently elsewhere.[46] Job 21,13, *ûb^erega' še'ôl yēḥātû* (MT *yēḥāttû*), "And tranquilly they go down to Sheol," offers a good parallel to our derivation of *nēḥat* from *nāḥat,* "to descend."

18,20 *'al yômô nāšammû 'aḥărōnîm*
w^eqadmōnîm 'ūḥăzû (MT *'āḥăzû*) *śā'ar*
On his day they of the west are appalled,
And they of the east are seized by horror.

Since Schultens, the majority of commentators takes *'aḥărōnîm* as "they of the west," and *qadmōnîm,* "they of the east." The basis for this opinion is the expression *hayyam hā'āḥărôn* for the Mediterranean and *hayyam haqqadmônî* for the Dead Sea. Three modern versions, *RSV, Bible de Jérusalem,* and *La Bible de la Pléiade,* incorporate this reasoning into their texts. This view is buttressed by a similar merism in the description of Anath's wholesale slaughter in 'nt:II:7-8, *tmḫṣ lim ḫp y [m] tṣmt adm ṣat špš,* "She smites the people of the west, smashes the men of the east."[47]

The qal passive vocalization *'ūḥăzû* is dictated by several considerations. The usual analysis, "men take hold of fear," has an unnatural ring, while the texts cited to support it, Job 21,6 and Is 13,8, are patient of other explications. Thus Job 21,6 *w^e'āḥaz b^eśārî pallāṣût* may grammatically signify, "And horror seizes my flesh," since concord in gender is strictly not required when a word intervenes between predicate and subject.[48] Is 13,8, *ṣîrîm waḥăbālîm yō'ḥēzûn* is most naturally understood as, "Pangs and throes will take hold of them," and numerous translators accept this rendition. On the other hand, Ugaritic, with its frequent qal passives, confirms Böttcher's explanation of many biblical forms as qal passives (see discussion of 20,4).[49]

20,3b *w^erûaḥ mabnîtî* (MT *mibbînātî*) *ya'ănēnî*
And the spirit in my frame answers me.

The pointing *mabnîtî* is prompted by I Q Hodayot, 7,4, *wyrw'w kwl 'wšy mbnyty w'ṣmy yprdw,* "Then all the foundations of my frame were shattered, and my bones were thrown out of joint."[50] In

45. See D. N. Freedman in *ZAW* 72 (1960) 102.
46. F. Zorell, *Lexicon Hebraicum,* 61a; Brown-Driver-Briggs, 50a.
47. Cf. C. H. Gordon *apud* S. N. Kramer, ed., *Mythologies of the Ancient World* (New York: 1961) 197.
48. Other illustrations of this principle may be found in G. R. Driver in *JRAS* (1948) 166ff.
49. *Ausführliches Lehrbuch der Hebräischen Sprache,* II, §§ 903-907; *UM,* § 9.27.
50. Y. Yadin in *JBL* 74 (1955) 40-43; J. Maier, *Die Texte vom Toten Meer,* I (Munich: 1961) 91. For other occurrences of *mbnyt* in Qumran, see K. G. Kuhn, *Konkordanz zu den Qumrantexten* (Göttingen: 1960) 114. Accadian *nabnitu,* "frame, figure," should be compared.

other words, *rûaḥ mabnîtî* is the equivalent of 32,18, *rûaḥ biṭnî.*

20,4 *hăzōʾt yādaʿtā minnî ʿad*
minnî śîm ʾādām ʿălê ʾāreṣ
Do you know this as from of old,
Since man was placed upon the earth?

Advances in Northwest Semitic philology indicate that P. Joüon may have been correct when he described *śîm* here and in 2 Sm 14,7 as an infinitive construct of the qal passive conjugation.[51] The standard explanation takes *śîm* as an active infinitive construct with an indefinite subject; Joüon makes *ʾādām* the subject of passive *śîm.* Since the Ugaritic testimony for this qal passive conjugation is quite extensive, philologians are now in a position to offer a more satisfactory grammatical accounting of Eshmunazar, line 5, *ʾl ybqš bn mnm k ʾy śm bn mnm,* "May he not search in it for anything, for nothing whatever has been placed into it."[52] Scholars, save F. Rosenthal, have hitherto vocalized *śm* as *śāmû,* making the subject an indefinite "they."[53] A much smoother translation results from making *mnm* the subject of passive qal. In this light, it becomes clear that *śîm* in Obad 4, usually emended to *tāśîm,* is a preterite qal passive with *qinnekā* the subject: *weʾim bên kôkābîm śîm qinnekā miššām ʾôrîdekā,* "And if your nest has been placed among the stars, from there I will bring you down." As is well known, the qal passive of Arabic *qâla,* for example, is *qîla,* "it was said."

21,5 *penû ʾēlay wehāšammû*
weśîmû yād ʿal peh
Look at me and be astonished,
And lay your hand upon your mouth.

Though most commentators see in laying the hand upon the mouth a natural gesture merely for assuring silence (so Dhorme), some have recognized from the balance with *hāšammû* "be astonished," the added element of awe and amazement (also in Mi 7,16). Thus Driver-Gray call it a gesture of "awe-struck silence."[54] Here we would merely call attention to an Accadian seal of the late third millennium which represents Etana trying to rise skywards on eagle's wings, while both men and beasts look on in amazement. All fix their gaze on the ascending figure and one of the men holds his hand to his gaping mouth in a gesture of amazement.[55]

---

51. In *Bib* 1 (1920) 360, and *Grammaire,* § 58c.
52. Cooke, *Text-Book,* 30ff.
53. Z. S. Harris, *Grammar of the Phoenician Language,* p. 148; J. Friedrich, *Phönizisch-Punische Grammatik,* § 166; N. Slouschz, *Thesaurus of Phoenician Inscriptions* (in Hebrew), 21; Cooke, *Text-Book,* 31.
54. *Book of Job,* I, 183; in his study, "Mettre sa main sur sa bouche," in *RB* 67 (1960) 197-209, B. Couroyer does not consider this aspect of the problem.
55. A. Moortgat, *Vorderasiatische Rollsiegel,* (Berlin: 1940) no. 234, p. 104; pl. 32; reproduced in J. B. Pritchard, *ANEP,* no. 695, p. 333.

21,11-12 *yešallᵉḥû kaṣṣō'n 'ăwîlêhem*
wᵉyaldêhem yᵉraqqᵉdûn
yiśśᵉ'û kātīp (MT *kᵉtōp*) *wᵉkinnôr*
wᵉyiśmᵉḥû lᵉqôl 'ûgāb
They send forth their young like sheep,
And their children dance.
They take up the sword and harp,
And make merry to the sound of the flute.

The frequent phrase *tôp wᵉkinnôr* has rendered inevitable the emendation of consonantal *ktp* to *bᵉtōp*. However, Ugaritic-Egyptian *ktp*, "weapon, sword," makes it possible to retain the consonantal text and to propose, with due reserve, that we have here an allusion to the sword-dance about which much has been written in connection with Cant 7,1, *mᵉḥōlat hammaḥănáyim*, "the dance of the two camps."[56] This reading has two advantages: it obviates the need for the frequent alteration of *yiśśᵉ'û* to *yāśîśû*, or if *yiśśᵉ'û* is retained, of explaining it as elliptical for *yiśśᵉ'û qôl*[57], and renders causeless the change of *ktp* to *btp*. On the other hand, our interpretation merely requires the vocalic change to *kātīp* (based on Arabic *katīfun*, "sword"), while *yiśśᵉ'û kātīp* is the syntactic and semantic equal of Is 2,4 *yiśśā' . . . ḥereb*.

21,15 *mah ššadday kî na'ăbᵉdennû*
ûmah nô'îl kî nipga' bô
What need has the Almighty that we should serve Him?
And what does it profit us that we pray to Him?

A much sharper translation—God has no need, we gain no benefit—results from parsing *mah ššadday* as a piece of Canaanite syntax. Where Krt:38 reads *mat*, "What ails you" or "What do you need," Hebrew would say, *mah lāk*, and where Krt:137f. asks, *lm ank ksp wyrq ḫrṣ*, "What need have I of silver and yellow-glittering gold?", Hebrew would have to insert the preposition, *lamma lî* etc.[58] Hence the lack of a preposition in *mah ššadday* may be explained as a Canaanism. For the classical Hebrew construction, see 30,2; Jgs 18,23; 1 Sm 11,5; Is 22,1; Ps 114,5.

22,15 *ha'ōraḥ 'lm* (MT *'ôlām*) *tišmôr*
'ăšer dārᵉkû mᵉtê 'āwen
Will you keep to the way of ignorance,
Which wicked men have trodden?

Though *'ôlām* is attested by the ancient versions, it does not seem particularly relevant to the context and commentators have been sorely exercised to set forth the real import of the word here. In fact,

---

56. Consult the commentaries and C. M. Doughty, *Arabia Deserta*, II, 118; R. T. O'Callaghan, "The Word *ktp* in Ugaritic and Egypto-Canaanite Mythology," in *Or* 21 (1952) 37-46.
57. Driver-Gray, II, 146; N. Peters, *Job*, 230.
58. H. L. Ginsberg, *The Legend of King Keret* (New Haven: 1946) 35f.

Theodotion, who alone preserves the Greek, altered both parts of the verse: "You will not keep the ancient way, which just men trod."[59] For him, as well as for Hebrew tradition (e.g. Mal 3,4), the "ancient way" is the way of justice and innocence, not the path of wicked men. Nor will it do to try to explain his *ʾandres dikaioi* as an inner Greek corruption of *ʾadikoi.*[60] One is forced to conclude that *ʿlm* (vocalization uncertain) is the same word that occurs in Qoh 3,11, *gam ʾet hāʿlm nātan bᵉlibbām,* "Moreover, He placed ignorance in their heart."[61] The root is Ugaritic *ġlm,* Hebrew *ʿlm,* "to grow dark"[62] and is used with reference to knowledge in 42,3, *maʿlîm ʿēṣâ,* "who obscures counsel," which expresses the same idea as 38,2, *maḥšîk ʿēṣâ,* "who darkens counsel." A good parallel to our verse is found in Prov 2,13, *haʿōzᵉbîm ʾorḥôt yōšer lāleket bᵉdarkê ḥōšek,* "Those who leave the paths of uprightness to walk in the ways of darkness."

22,23 *ʾim tāšûb ʿad šadday tibbāneh*
tarḥîq ʿawlâ mēʾohŏlekā
If you return to the Almighty, you will be healed;
If you put iniquity far from your tent.

A new nuance of the root *bny* is brought out by Ugaritic usage in 1 Aqht:119, *bʿl ybn diy hmt,* "May Baal heal their wings." Such a meaning admirably fits our context since it would hark back to 2,7, "And (Satan) smote Job with malignant ulcers from the sole of his foot to the crown of his head." The specific force "to heal" seems preferable to more generic "to restore." The tentative nature of this proposal must not, however, be glossed over.[63]

23,4 *ʾeʿerᵉkā lᵉpānāyw mišpāṭ*
ûpî ʾămallēʾ tôkāḥôt
I would set my case in order before Him,
And I would fill my mouth with arguments.

The frequent emendation of *mišpāṭ* to *mišpāṭî* is required neither by grammar nor by meter; the practice of having one pronominal suffix do duty for two words in parallelism was widespread, especially among the biblical poets.[64] Another instance appears in 33,26, *yeʿtar ʾel ʾelôah wayyirṣēhû wayyarʾ pānāyw bitᵉrûʿâ,* "He prays to God and He accepts him, and He makes him see His face with joy." The suffix with *wayyirṣēhû* renders unnecessary another with *wayyarʾ*.

---

59. F. Field, *Origenis Hexapla Quae Supersunt,* II, 42.
60. So Dhorme, *Job,* 302.
61. M. Dahood in *Bib* 33 (1952) 206. This etymology is accepted by E. Jones in his recent work, *Proverbs and Ecclesiastes* (*Torch Bible Commentaries*; London: 1961) 296.
62. Ginsberg, *Keret,* 34, 45.
63. I am supposing that the reading is original and in its right place. The LXX reads *tēʿāneh,* and most modern commentators do not accept MT since *tibbāneh* unduly anticipates v. 25.
64. The writer has collected some 30 examples of this practice, in addition to those cited by G. R. Driver in *JRAS* (1948) 164f.

23,10 *kî yāda' derek 'immādî*
beḥānanî kazzāhāb 'ēṣē'
For He knows my way;
If He should test me, I would shine like gold.

28,1 *kî yēš lakkesep môṣā'*
ûmāqôm lazzāhāb yāzoqqû
For there is a smelter for silver,
And a place where they purify gold.

Prov 25,4 *hāgô sîgîm mikkāsep*
weyēṣē' (MT *wayyēṣē'*) *laṣṣōrēp kelî*
Remove the dross from silver,
And the vase will shine for the smith.

It has long been recognized that in certain contexts *yāṣā'* carries the meaning of Arabic *waḍu'a,* "to be clean, fair," and *ḍa'a,* "to shine."[65] H. L. Ginsberg's discovery of this signification in Ugaritic *yṣa* corroborates the view of earlier scholars on this point and authorizes us to find it in the three texts cited above.

The lack of the conditional particle before *beḥānanî* in 23,10, thoroughly discussed by commentators, is now matched by PRU II, 19.12-14, *ttn wtn wlttn wal ttn,* "If you give, then give; if you do not give, then don't give."[66]

Prov 17,3 (=27,21), *marṣēp lakkesep wekûr lazzāhāb ûbōḥēn libbôt yhwh,* "The smelter for silver, and the furnace for gold, but the tester of hearts is the Lord," offers a good parallel to Job 28,1, and indicates that *môṣā'*, elsewhere "source, origin," is a synonym of "a place where they purify gold" in the second part of the verse.[67]

23,13 *wehû' be'eḥād ûmî yešîbennû*
wenapšô 'iwwetâ wayyā'aś
For He alone is ruler, and who can gainsay Him?
And what He Himself desires, that He does.

The precise content of *be'eḥād* has remained something of a puzzle. Ugaritic usage, however, suggests that Abbé Le Hir may have been right when he rendered, *Mais il est seul maître, et qui peut l'arrêter?*[68] When Mot proceeds to challenge the sovereignty of Baal, he issued his claim partly in these terms: *aḥdy dymlk 'l ilm,* "I alone will rule over the gods." (51:VII:49f.) Scholars have compared *aḥdy,* an adverbial accusative, with Accadian *edišśiya,* "I alone," which on occasion occurs with verbs of "might, power"; e.g., *edišśā ṣirat,* "She

65. R. Kittel, *Die Psalmen,* 1st-2nd ed. (Leipzig: 1914) 266 (on Ps 73,7); S. Esh in *VT* 4 (1954) 350ff. (Jgs 5,31; Is 62,1; Os 6,5; Ps 36,6); M. Dahood in *Sacra Pagina,* ed J. Coppens *et al.* (Paris/Gembloux: 1959) 274, n. 3 (Jer 48,9).
66. Failure to grasp the conditional nature of the sentence put the correct translation out of the reach of Virolleaud.
67. P. Joüon in *Bib* 11 (1930) 323 proposed the alteration of *môṣā'* to *mimṣā'*, but this proposal does not commend itself.
68. Cited from Dhorme, *Job,* 318.

alone is mighty."[69] In other words, *be'eḥād* could be the semantic equivalent of *aḥdy*, but with the idea of ruling to be supplied.

24,11 *bên šûrōtēm* (MT *šûrōtām*) *yaṣhîrû*
yeqābîm dārekû wayyiṣmā'û
Between two rows they pass the noonday,
They tread the wine presses, yet suffer thirst.

There are several lexicographical problems in this verse, but here we limit our consideration to consonantal *šwrtm*, which is either emended to dual *šûrōtáyim*, or to plural *šûrōt*, with the final *mem* deleted. The consonants *šwrtm* may now be explained as Canaanite or Northern Israelite spelling of the dual feminine. Thus in Ugaritic one finds *bn qrytm*, "between the two cities," *mitm*, "200," and *thmtm*, "the two deeps."[70]

29,7 *beṣē'tî ša'ar 'ălê qāret*
bārehôb 'ākîn môšābî
When I went out the gate from the city,
Prepared my seat in the broad place.

Inscriptional discoveries revealing a number of new nuances possessed by *'ălê* shed valuable light on two problems in this verse. In the Mesha and Ahiram Inscriptions, *'l* denotes "from," and possibly also in Ugaritic.[71] G. R. Driver was accordingly justified in translating Ps 81,6, *beṣē'tô 'al 'ereṣ miṣráyim*, "when he went out of the land of Egypt" (cf. Ps 114,1; Is 11,16).[72] This version of *'ălê qāret*, "from the city," shows that Job was a city-dweller, and the theory, designed to meet the present text in the traditional translation, that Job was a resident of a country estate who used to go up toward the city, loses its basis. It also indicates that F. Hitzig was correct when he argued, by comparing 2 Sm 21,21 with 1 Sm 31,12 and citing Neh 8,1.3, that *reḥôb*, "broad open place" in this instance also stood outside the city gate.[73] Which is to say that *reḥôb* may also be a synonym of *gōren*, "threshing-floor," an open place outside the city-gate where royal court was held according to 1 Kgs 22,10 = 2 Chr 18,9; the Ugaritic texts offer a similar description of the *grn*.[74] Another example of *'ălê*, "from," is found in 30,2, discussed above in connection with 5,26.

29,8 *rā'ûnî ne'ārîm wenehbā'û*
wîšîšîm qāmû 'āmedû
The young men saw me and withdrew,
While the elders began to stand up.

---

69. W. F. Albright in *JPOS* 14 (1934) 130, n. 155; *CAD*, vol. 4, E, p. 38f.
70. *UM*, § 8.5.
71. Driver, *CML*, 141b for Ugar. *'l*, "from"; S. Segert in *Ar Or* 29 (1961) 228, discusses Moabite *'l*, while S. Gevirtz in *VT* 11 (1961) 147, briefly considers Phoenician *'l*.
72. *Die Welt des Orients*, 1950, 413.
73. *Das Buch Hiob*, (Leipzig: 1874) 212; Brown-Driver-Briggs, 932a, suggest that *reḥôb* in Nah 2,5 apparently stood outside the city-gate.
74. *UM*, p. 252, no. 441.

There can be no question but that the asyndetic construction *qāmû ʿāmedû* yields excellent sense, but a more dynamic version results when *qāmû* is taken as an auxiliary verb denoting inchoate action. In Arabic, *ʾaḫada, jaʿala, qâma* etc. in the perfect, and followed by the imperfect indicative, express the beginning of an action. Ugaritic attests to three verbs being used in this function: *qm, aḫd,* and *ndd;* thus *qm ytʿr,* "he began to serve."[75] Like Arabic, the *qtl* of the verb of beginning is followed by *yqtl,* except in one instance where an infinitive (or possibly *qtl*) succeeds: *yuḫdm šbʿr,* "He began to shine." Ugaritic evidently had more freedom in this respect than Arabic. This latitude of usage permits us to propose, with considerable caution, that in Hebrew the preterite verb of beginning could be followed by another preterite. The mordancy of 37,14 is considerably heightened when this theory is applied: *haʾăzînâ zzōʾt ʾiyôb ʿămōd hitbônēn* (MT *wehitbônēn*) *niplāʾôt ʾēl,* "Listen to this, Job; begin to understand the wonders of God." Since *ʿāmad* is often a synonym of *qām,*[76] it follows that it too might be employed as an auxiliary verb to signify incipient action. Job is thus reminded that he does not even begin to comprehend the power of God. The current attempts to explain *ʿămōd* as "stand still," or "stand erect," must be considered feeble.[77]

29,13 *birkat ʾōbēd ʿālay tābōʾ*
weléb ʾalmānâ ʾarnīn
The blessing of him about to perish entered my presence,
And I made the widow's heart sing for joy.

33,27a *yāšīr* (MT *yāšōr*) *ʿal ʾănāšîm wayyōʾmer*
He sings before men and says . . .

34,28 *lehābîʾ ʿālāyw ṣaʿăqat dāl*
weṣaʿăqat ʿănîyîm yišmāʿ
So that they cause the cry of the poor to come before Him,
And He hears the cry of the afflicted.

In his commentary on 29,13 Dhorme notes that, *L'emploi de ʿal après le verbe bwʾ nuance le sens de 'venir' en celui de 'monter' (venir de bas en haut)*. This insight is confirmed by Ugaritic *ʿl* (also inscriptional Aramaic), which with certain verbs denotes "in the presence of."[78] Thus 127:39f., *ʿl abh yʿrb,* "He enters his father's presence." The idiom *bwʾ ʿl* means substantially the same thing.

A. Dillmann saw that this was the sense of *ʿal* in 34,28, which he rendered, *um vor ihn zu bringen das Geschrei des Geringers.*[79] As proof, he cited 2 Sam 15,4, *mî yeśīmēnî šōpēṭ bāʾāreṣ weʿālay yābôʾ kol ʾîš ʾăšer yihyeh llô rîb ûmišpāṭ,* "Oh that I were made a judge in the

---

75. *UM,* § 13.24,47. For Arabic usage, W. Wright, *A Grammar of the Arabic Language*³ (Cambridge: 1933) II, § 42d.
76. Brown-Driver-Briggs, 764a (bottom of page).
77. A. Dillmann, *Hiob*⁴ (Leipzig: 1891) 317.
78. *UM,* § 10.13, and reference given there. Ps 104,34, *yeʿĕrab ʿālāyw śîḥî* is best translated, "Let my prayer enter His presence."
79. *Hiob,* 296.

land, that every man who has a suit or a cause might come before me," and 2 Kgs 25,20, *wayyōlek ʾōtām ʿal melek bābel riblātâ*, "And he brought them before the king of Babylonia in Riblath." To these texts might be added Gen 19,31; Lv 21,11; 26,1; Nm 6,6; Dt 25,5; 1 Sm 1,10, and perhaps all the cases of *ʿal* and *niṣṣab ʿal* which Brown-Driver-Briggs describe as "idiomatic."[80]

It was Abbé Le Hir who grasped the force of the idiom in 33,27 which he translated, *alors il chante devant les hommes.*[81] This expression also occurs in Prov 25,20, *wešār bašširîm ʿal lēb rāʿ*, "So is he who sings songs in the presence of a sad heart." Ugaritic specialists do not seem to have recognized this idiom in ʿnt:I:20f. (also 2 Aqht:VI;31), *yšr ǵzr ṭb ql ʿl bʿl bṣrrt ṣpn*, "The sweet-voiced lad sings in the presence of Baal in the recesses of Saphon." One finds *yšr ʿl* rendered "doth sing of Baal" (Ginsberg), "he sings in honor of Baal" (Driver), "sing over Baal" (Gaster), "sings of Baal" (Gray), "song about Baal" (Gordon).

31,16a *ʾim ʾemnaʿ-m* (MT *ʾemnaʿ mēḥēpes*) *ḥēpeṣ dallîm*
If I refused the desire of the poor.

Though *mānaʿ* is found with the accusative of the person and *min* of the thing refused in Num 24,11 and Qoh 2,10, the word order in our text appears too unnatural to suppose this construction here. One would have to render literally the colon, "If I withheld from (their) desire the poor."[82] This consideration permits one to propose that the *mem* of *mēḥēpeṣ* be attached as enclitic to the verb, with *ḥēpeṣ dallîm* forming a construct chain.[83]

32,14 *ûleʾaʿărōk* (MT *welōʾ ʿārak*) *ʾēlay millîn*
ûbeʾimrêkem lōʾ ʾăšîbennû
I will indeed prepare my own discourse;
And not with your arguments will I answer him.

Once the emphatic *lamedh* is recognized, a pellucid theme emerges which is reprised in vv. 17-18, "I also will answer my share, I too will declare my knowledge. For I am full of words; the spirit within me constrains me.[84]

34,3 *ki ʾōzen millin tibḥān*
weḥēk yiṭʿam leʾĕkōl
For the ear tests words,
And the palate tastes by eating.

The syntax of *yiṭʿam leʾĕkōl,* hitherto somewhat puzzling,[85] is notably clarified when it is recognized that *l* in Hebrew often has the

80. P. 756a.
81. Cited from Dhorme, *Job,* 460.
82. Brown-Driver-Briggs, 343a.
83. In *JJS* 6 (1955) 107ff., N. Sarna examines some possible cases of enclitic mem in Job; his most convincing example seems to be 15,18.
84. M. Dahood in *Greg* 43 (1962) 64f.
85. Driver-Gray, 2,253, discuss the syntactic possibilities.

force of *min,* in the present instance, of causal *min.* This usage reflects Ugaritic-Phoenician syntax, since in these dialects *min* is very rare (attested but once in Ugaritic). The function of *min* was fulfilled by *l.* Thus Karatepe A, III, 2-4 reads, *wbrk bʿl kr*[*n*]*trys ʾyt ʾztwd ḥym wšlm wʿz ʿl kl mlk ltty* etc., "And Baal KRNTRYS blessed Azitawadd with life and peace and mighty strength above every king by giving to him etc." It will be seen that the syntax of *ltty,* "by giving to him," is the same as that of *leʾekōl,* "by eating," save for the datival suffix in the former.

34,26 *taḥat rešāʿîm sepāqām*
bimeqôm rōʾîm
Among the wicked He slaps them,
In the place of onlookers.

In the light of 2 Aqht:V:6f., *yṯb bap ṯǵr tḥt adrm dbgrn,* "He sits at the edge of the gate, among the mighty men who are on the threshing floor," J. Greenfield[86] has proposed that *taḥat,* parallel to *b* in Isa 57,5b, denotes "among" and is correctly reproduced by LXX *ʾana meson,* "among." The recognition of this signification of *taḥat,* also parallel to *b,* but in reverse order, leads to a clearer, though not entirely satisfactory, understanding of the verse.

36,15 *yeḥallēṣ ʿānî beʿonyô*
weyigel ballaḥaṣ ʾoznem (MT *ʾoznām*)
He rescues the oppressed from his oppression,
And opens his ear in distress.

Friedrich Delitzsch,[87] working from the analogy of Accadian *ina,* "in, on,from,through", observed that with verbs of uprooting, rescuing, the prep. *b* denotes "from" (so in 20,20; 27,15;31,12). His version of the first colon: *Er errettet den Bedrückten aus seiner Bedrückung.* His argument may be corroborated by citing Vulg., *eripiet de angustia sua pauperem,* by noting the frequent Ugaritic-Phoenician use of *b,* "from," and by adding to his list of examples Job 5,19, *bešēš* (often emended to *miššēš*—so *BH*[3]) *ṣārôt yaṣṣîlekā ûbešebaʿ lōʾ yiggaʿ bekā rāʿ,* "From six dangers He will rescue you, and in seven, evil will not touch you." It will be noticed that in both 5,19 and 36,15, *b* denotes "from" in the first part of the verse and "in" in the second.

The third masc. suffix, in *ʿonyô* is balanced by an enclitic *mem* in *ʾoznem* (?), as in 15,29 and the texts cited in the discussion of that verse.

36,31 *kî bām yādîn ʿammîm*
yittēn ʾōkel lemakbîr
For with these He feeds the peoples,
He gives food in abundance.

G. R. Driver[88] has related *yādîn* to Arabic *dâna* V, "enjoyed absolute

86. In *ZAW* 73 (1961) 226-228.
87. *Das Buch Hiob* (Leipzig: 1902) 145.
88. *VTSup* 3 (1955) 89ff.

abundance," but in his discussion he makes no mention of Heb. *māzôn,* "food, sustenance," and the hophal participle in the phrase *sûsîm mûzānîm,* "well-fed horses." Since Houbigant, *yādîn* has very often been emended to *yāzûn,* "He feeds," but the impressive list of dialectal pairs involving the *d-z* sounds permits one to surmise that *yādîn is* dialectal for *yāzîn* (hiphil). Such pairs include: *ḥdy-ḥzy,* "to see,"[89] *ydʿ -yzʿ* "to sweat,"[90] *dky-zky,* "to be pure,"[91] *ndr-nzr,* "to vow,"[92] *pdr-pzr,* "to scatter." Especially relevant to the present discussion is the pair *dʿk-zʿk,* "to go out, be extinguished"; *dʿk* occurs four times in Job, but in 17,1, the hapax legomenon *nizʿākû* is attested. It is a mistake to emend it. One must agree with E. Ullendorff[93] that "some serious work ought to be undertaken, in the light of modern linguistic notions, on the question of dialects and colloquialisms in the Old Testament."

37,2a *šim*^{e}*ʿû maʿ* (MT *šāmôaʿ*) *b*^{e}*rōgez qôlô*
Listen closely to the roar of His voice.

In 13,17 and 21,2 is found the phrase *šim*^{e}*ʿû šāmôaʿ*, but here it produces the unusual rhythm 4:3; as a result, *šāmôaʿ* is often deleted. Part of the consonantal text can be salvaged and the discordant meter avoided by comparing it with the frequently recurring Ugaritic phrase, *šmʿ mʿ*, "hear, I pray."[94]

37,13 *ʾim l*^{e}*šebeṭ ʾim l*^{e}*ʾarṣô*
ʾim l^{e}*ḥesed yamṣiʾēhû*
Whether it be for correction, or for his own good pleasure,
Or from mercy, that He makes it arrive.

The context plainly requires that *ʾrṣw* be taken as a substantive from the root *rṣy*, "to be pleased with," with an *aleph* performative. The hapax legomenon *ʾaḥăwātî* in 13,17 reveals a similar formation with preformative *aleph* and elsewhere the present writer has analyzed *ʾîšôn* in Prov 7,9; 20,20, and Ps 13,4, as derived from *yšn* "to sleep".[95] It might be here remarked that the Palmyrene deity *ʾrṣw* appears in ancient North Arabic texts as *rḍw* and *rḍy.*[96]

38,7 *b*^{e}*ron yaḥad kôk*^{e}*bê bōqer*
wayyārîʿû kol b^{e}*nê ʾĕlōhîm*
When the morning stars sang together,
And all the heavenly beings shouted for joy.

The first colon, depicting the unity and harmony of the stars, in balance with *b*^{e}*nê ʾĕlōhîm* of the second member of the verse, may serve to confirm Driver's[97] restoration of *pḫr* in the badly damaged text

---

89. M. Dahood in *Bib* 36 (1955) 229; 40 (1959) 166.
90. T. Noeldeke, *Neue Beiträge,* 194f; cf. Prv 10,9,32; 14,33; Isa 53,11.
91. G. R. Driver, *JRAS* (1948) 168, n. 3.
92. Brockelmann, *Grundriss,* 1, 237.
93. In *Bulletin of John Rylands Library* 44 (1962) 464.
94. *UM,* § 9.18 cites five occurrences.
95. In a forthcoming monograph on Proverbs.
96. Lidzbarski, *Ephemeris,* 3,90ff.
97. *CML,* 116a.

76:I:3-4, *dl ydʿ bn il [dl ybn p] ḫr kkbm,* "That the sons of El may know, that the assembly of the stars may understand."

38,18 *hitbōnantā ʿad raḥăbê ʾāreṣ*
haggēd ʾim yādaʿtā kullāh
Have you surveyed the breadths of the earth?
Tell if you know it all.

Some critics have emended *kullāh* because the suffix *-ah* has no apparent antecedent. So N. Peters[98] who writes, *Für kulla(h) fehlt das Beziehungswort. Ich ziehe der neutrischen Fassung (es alles) nach Gr pose kamma vor.* This view becomes difficult to defend in view of 49:I:37, *wymlk barṣ il klh,* "And he rules over the wide earth, all of it."

39,3 *tikraʿnâ yaldêhen tᵉpallaḥnâ*
ḥeblêhem tᵉšallaḥnâ
They crouch, they drop their young ones,
They send forth their flocks.

A Ugaritic nuance may help clarify the precise import of much-canvassed *ḥeblêhem.*[99] Hebrew attests the use of *ḥebel,* "cord, territory, band" in connection with a group of prophets in 1 Sm 10,5.10, but Ugaritic also uses it of a flock of eagles, *ḥbl nšrm.* This usage allows one to infer that *ḥebel* could also be predicated of goats and hinds in our passage, and further suggests that *ḥeblêhem tᵉšallaḥnâ* is the semantic equivalent of 21,11, *yᵉšallᵉḥû kaṣṣōʾn ʿăwîlêhem,* "They send forth their young like sheep."

39,10 *hătiqšor rêm bᵉtelem ʿăbōt* (MT *ʿăbōtô*)
wᵉʾim (MT *ʾim*) *yᵉšaddēd ʿămāqîm ʾaḥărekā*
Do you bind the wild ox in the fertile furrow,
Or does he harrow the valleys after you?

In the first colon, MT literally reads, "the wild ox in the furrow of his cord," which is correctly rejected by N. Peters and other commentators. New light is shed on the problem by the collocation in 51:VIII:4, *ʿm tlm ǵṣr arṣ,* "toward the furrows of the fertile earth." The disputed root *ǵṣr* is most likely to be equated with Arabic *ǵaḍira,* "to be fertile, ample," as maintained by Gordon and Ginsberg, and not with Hebrew *ʿāṣar,* "to restrain, confine," as held by Gaster and Driver. The root is found in Jgs 18,7 *bāʾāreṣ yôreš ʿeṣer,* "in a land possessing abundance/fertility,"[100] and Prov 30,16, *šᵉʾôl wᵉʿōṣer rāḥam,* "Sheol, which is broad of bosom."[101] Since *ʿābâ* denotes "to be fat, thick," and

---

98. *Job,* 440.
99. G. R. Driver in *VTSup* 3 (1955) 93, equates it with Arabic *ḥabalu (n)*, "embryo of a camel."
100. So E. König, *Hebräisches und Aramäisches Wörterbuch,* 4th-5th ed. (Leipzig: 1931) 344.
101. On the appositional use of *waw* in the divine name *kṯr wḫss,* see W. F. Albright in *BASOR* 164 (1961) 36; another instance of this appositional or explicative *waw* may be seen in Sefire I, Face A, 9, *šmš wnr* "Shamash, who is the Lamp."

I Kgs 7,46, *maʿăbēh hāʾădāmâ* signifies "fertile ground," it follows that *telem ʿābôt* could be the semantic equivalent of *tlm ġṣr arṣ*.

It should be here noted that the root *ʿby* or *ʿwb* may underlie the divine name *yʿbdr* in the appellation *arṣy bt yʿbdr*.

In the second colon, *yeśaddēd ʿămāqîm*, "he harrows the valleys," should be compared with 62:5, *kʿmq tṯlṯ bmt*, "she plows her back like a valley."

39,16 *hiqšîaḥ bānehā lelōʾ lāh*
lerîq yegîāh belî pāḥad
She treats her young ones harshly, as though not hers;
In vain is her toil—without a flock.

Since vv. 13-18 describe the habits of the ostrich, *paḥad* must be identified with Ugaritic *pḫd*, "flock," as in *imr bpḫd*, "a lamb from the flock" (2 Aqht:V:17).[102]

39,23a *ʿālāyw tāronnâ* (MT *tirneh*) *ʾašpâ*
Around him rattles the quiver.

Hebrew lexicographers derive the hapax legomenon *tirneh* from *rnh*, a by-form of *rnn*. The frequency of the *modus energicus* in Ugaritic, the increasing number of Hebrew verbs that are now seen to belong to this mode, and the fact that *rnn* is attested in the energic form in Prov 1,20 and 8,3, *tāronnâ*, make it difficult to escape the conclusion that *tāronnâ* is the correct pointing in our text.[103] The energic form in 17,16 has been examined above.

102. On *paḥad* in Gen 31,42, see W. F. Albright, *From the Stone Age to Christianity* (Baltimore: 1940) 188f., 327.

103. Franz Delitzsch, *Hiob*, 479, considered this possibility, but discounted it on the ground that one should not remove from the lexica an authenticated root. He refers the reader to the *Thesaurus* which cites Arabic *ranaʾu*, "sound," from a postulated *rny*, but the *Thesaurus* specifically states that it is *rnn* I and IV that is used of the twang of a bow.

THE GREAT TREE AND NABUCHODONOSOR'S MADNESS

LOUIS F. HARTMAN, C. SS. R.

In the *Catholic Biblical Quarterly*, to which Father Gruenthaner, as editor, gave many years of yeoman service, three important articles were published by him on questions connected with the Book of Daniel.[1] We are led therefore to offer in homage to him here an investigation of one of the literary units which make up this fascinating book, which was one of his favorite fields of research.

We will limit this study to one of the haggadic stories that form the first half of Dn, that is, to the story of Nabuchodonosor's vision of the great tree and his subsequent madness (Dn 3,98 [31] -4,34). To discover some of the literary and traditional sources that its author used will be our principal endeavor, in the hope that this may cast light, not merely on his method of composition, but also on the meaning of the rather cryptic words that he frequently employs to convey his inspired message.

After the publication, in 1943, of the papal encyclical, *Divino afflante Spiritu*, which urged Catholic biblical scholars to study the various literary genres that were used by the inspired authors of the Sacred Scriptures, no doubt most of these scholars would now acknowledge that Dn belongs partly to the haggadic and partly to the apocalyptic literary genres. Inasmuch as neither of these genres is concerned with history, it is no longer the task of Catholic exegetes to try to solve the seeming inerrancies in historical matters where an inspired writer, such as the author of Dn, did not intend to write history.[2]

1. "The Seventy Weeks," *CBQ* 1 (1939) 44-54. "The Four Empires of Daniel," *CBQ* 8 (1946) 72-82; 201-212. "The Last King of Babylon" *CBQ* 11 (1949) 406-427.
2. While such a hagiographer employed the common ideas of his time about historical events (e.g., the idea that there was a period of a Median empire between the periods of the Neo-Babylonian and Persian empires) merely as tools to forge his own special religious message, without intending to pass any judgment whatever on the correctness of these ideas, many of his references to historical events or customs may, of course, be quite accurate. It is entirely to the credit of Father Gruenthaner that in his learned article on "The Last King of Babylon" [*CBQ* 11 (1949) 406] he could offer strong arguments to show that Dn is not wrong in calling Nabuchodonosor the "father" of king Belsassar (Dn

Moreover, the apocalyptic genre, which makes free use of the literary device of *prophetia post eventum*, is commonly conceded to be one of the ancient modes of writing which "in no wise contradicts the holiness and truth of God."[3] Therefore, it is taken for granted here, without repeating proofs which can easily be found elsewhere, that the detailed "prophecies" of Dn had already been fulfilled when this book was written ca. 166 B.C., but when the genuine prophecy in it, that the Lord would overthrow the pagan kingdoms of this world and establish the kingdom of God on earth, was still to be fulfilled.[4]

The part of Dn with which we are here concerned, the story of Nabuchodonosor's vision of the great tree and his subsequent madness, has for its purpose the illustration of this general thesis of the book, that we must "glorify the King of heaven, because all his works are right and his ways just; and those who walk in pride he is able to humble" (4,34). While this story is thus an integral part of the whole book and has numerous literary connections with other parts of the work, it forms, nevertheless, a distinct, self-contained unit, quite complete in itself. It may once have circulated separately in an earlier form, but in its present state it is surely from the same pen that wrote the rest of the book.

One unique feature is the general form in which it is cast. It is presented in the form of a letter, beginning in true epistolary style with the name of the sender (Nabuchodonosor), the name of the addressees (all the nations), and a greeting (abundant peace!): 3,98. This epistolary style was employed in Akkadian letters of the Neo-Babylonian period, in Aramaic letters of the Persian period, and in Greek letters of the Hellenistic period (cf the N.T. Epistles). But the combination of terms used to designate the addressees, "all the nations, peoples, and tongues" (*kol-'am^emayyā' 'ummayyā w^eliššanayyā'*), which also occurs in 3,4.7; 5,19; 6,26; 7,14, is particularly reminiscent of the many different peoples of the Persian Empire, to whom proclamations

---

5,2), if "father" is understood here in the sense of maternal "grandfather." But from the viewpoint of the biblical inerrancy of the book this is quite irrelevant.

3. *"Ut adhibitum dicendi genus Dei sanctitati et veritati haud quaquam repugnent," Divino afflante Spiritu, [2]Enchiridion Biblicum* 559. The decree of the Pont. Bibl. Comm. of 28 June 1908 ([2]Enchir. Bibl. 291), rejecting the possibility of *Prophetia post eventum* in Sacred Scripture, can reasonably be reinterpreted in the light of the subsequent papal teaching on the duty of Catholic exegetes to make a prudent use of the study of ancient literary genres. It may be noted that this decree is primarily concerned with the problem of the authorship of Deutero-Isaia, which is now commonly treated by Catholic biblical scholars in a manner somewhat contrary to this decree, yet apparently with the tacit consent of the present Pontifical Biblical Commission.
4. This is the date accepted, e.g., by P. J. DeMenasce, *Daniel* (La sainte Bible . . . de Jérusalem, Paris 1954, [2]1958) 15; Jean Steinmann, *Daniel* (Connaître la Bible, Paris/Bruges 1961) 19; CCD Version of *The Holy Bible, The Prophetic Books* (Paterson 1961) 501.

in their own languages were sent by the Persian kings;[5] cf Est 1,22; 3,12; 8,9. Because of its epistolary form this story is told by Nabuchodonosor in the first person, except for a short section (4,25-30) near the end, where the king is spoken of in the third person. Perhaps the shift in person is intentional here; the author may have felt that, because the king was not rational during his affliction, he should not be presented even later on as giving a rational account of it. Even apart from the epistolary introduction, this story may have been cast in the first person in imitation of the style of the royal inscriptions of the ancient Near East, which used this form of narrative. In any case, the boasting of the king in 4,27 about his building activity in Babylon is in the style of the dedicatory inscriptions on the new palaces built by the Assyrian and Babylonian kings, particularly by the historical Nabuchodonosor himself.

As in 2,1ff, so here also (4,2), Nabuchodonosor receives a vision in the form of a dream. The dream in which a god makes known his will to man, especially to a king, was a common motif in the ancient Near East, going back at least as far as Gudea of Lagash (end of the 3rd millennium B.C.), whose inscription, recounting the revelation he had received in a dream from the God, Ningirsu, is one of the longest texts in classical Sumerian prose that have come down to us. It is interesting to note that the last Babylonian king, Nabuna'id, who is apparently fused (if not confused) with the historical Nabuchodonosor in the Nabuchodonosor of Dn, records on his basalt stele, which is now in Istanbul,[6] that he had a dream in which his predecessor, Nabuchodonosor, appeared to him and explained to him the meaning of the astrological omen that he had just beheld in the same dream.

The account in Dn 4,2-6 about the failure of the Babylonian soothsayers to explain Nabuchodonosor's dream and about Daniel's successful interpretation of it is quite similar to the account in 2,1-27 in connection with the king's vision of the gigantic statue of various metals. But in Dn 4 the account is much shorter, and the king is easier on his soothsayers; at least he tells them here what he saw in his dream and he does not threaten dire punishments if they fail to divine its meaning. The satire on the stupidity of the pagan soothsayers in both of these stories in Dn owes something to the story of Joseph in Egypt, in which the Egyptian magicians are presented as unable to interpret Pharaoh's dream. The borrowing in Dn is evident from the fact that, with all the other words used here for various kinds of soothsayers, Dn (1,20; 2,2.10.27; 4,4.6) also uses the same word for "magicians" (Heb. *ḥarṭummîm*) that occurs in Gn 41,8.24 (cf also

---

5. On the writing of proclamations of the Achaemenid kings in the various languages of their empire, see J. Lewy, "The Problems Inherent in Section 70 of the Bisutun Inscription," *HUCA* 25 (1954) 169-208.
6. For an English translation of this inscription, by A. L. Oppenheim, see *ANET* 308b-311b; the part about Nabuna'id's dream is given here in col. 310a.

Ex 7,11.22; 8,3.14f; 9,11), although this is a loanword from Egyptian and should, strictly speaking, be used only in regard to Egyptian magicians (who would hardly be at the Babylonian court of Nabuchodonosor!).

The account of the vision of the great tree which Nabuchodonosor saw in his dream is woven together from several different strands. Its author is primarily indebted to the magnificent "Allegory of the Cypress" and its application in Ez 31, where the king of Egypt is likened to one of the great trees of Lebanon that is cut down, with its branches scattered. Not only for the general idea, but also in several of the details there is evidence here of borrowing. Compare, for instance, the picture in Dn 4,9.11.18 of the beasts resting under the shade of the tree and the birds nesting in its branches[7] with the same picture in Ez 31,6.13. In both cases the punishment is for the same sin, pride. In Dn the king of Babylon is "content and prosperous" (literally, "verdant": *ra'nan*) in his palace (4,1) and, like a tree of great height, "with its top touching the heavens" (4,8.17), his "majesty has become so great as to touch the heavens" (4,19); therefore he is "cut down" (4,11.20), that he may learn that "those who walk in pride God is able to humble" (4,34). In Ez the great tree of Lebanon, which is the king of Egypt (31,2f), is likewise "cut down" (31,12), "because it became lofty in stature, raising its crest among the clouds, and because it became proud in heart at its height" (31,10).

The concept of something "touching the heavens," that is, reaching to the heavens, is a symbol of insolent pride, of *hybris* against the divine, rising up against heaven, that is much older than either Dn or Ez. It goes back to the story of the Tower of Babel, whose builders made bold to raise "a tower with its top in the heavens" (Gn 11,4). The Sumerians, as well as the later Babylonians, intended such a *ziggurat* or temple tower to be a d u r - a n - k i, a "bond between heaven and earth"; but Israel regarded such a "skyscraper" as blasphemous arrogance. Compare also the proud boasting of the king of Babylon in Is 14,13f: "I will scale the heavens; above the stars of God I will set up my throne . . . I will ascend above the top of the clouds; I will be like the Most High."

In the allegory of Ez the great tree of Lebanon is "the envy of all Eden's trees in the garden of God" (31,9), for "the cedars in the garden of God were not its equal" (31,8); and its companions, "the

7. The same image is later used by Jesus in the parable of the mustard seed that grows up into a tree, in which the birds of the air "dwell" (*kataskēnoun*: Mt 13,32; Mk 4,32; *kateskēnōsen*: Lk 13,19; cf. the *yiškenû* in Ez 31.13 and the *yiškenān* in Dn 4,18). But W. Baumgartner (in Koehler's *Lexicon* 1079) is mistaken in thinking that, because the Christian-Palestinian lectionary renders this verb in Lk 13,19 by the *'af'el* of *ṭll*, in Dn 4,9 *taṭlēl* should mean "to make a nest"; in the latter passage the subject of the verb is *ḥêwat bārā'*, "wild beasts," who ordinarily do not "nest," but rather "find shade" under a tree.

trees of Eden," from which it had been stealing the life-giving water, are consoled at its downfall (31,16ff). Therefore, because of this "paradise" theme in Ez 31, we are justified in regarding the feature of the tree in Dn, that "its fruit was abundant and it provided food for all" (4,9.18), as an allusion to the tree of life in paradise; in his pride Nabuchodonosor pretends to take the place of God, who alone can sustain man's life.

Another feature in common between Ez 31 and Dn 4 is the abrupt shift that is made between the symbol and the thing symbolized, between the tree and the king. In Hebrew or Aramaic this is not quite as violent as it is in English since in these Semitic languages the word for "tree" is masculine. Thus, in Ez, when the tree is cut down, it descends (like a man) to the nether world (31,15-18). So also in Dn, the tree which is cut down suddenly has "its (his) mind changed from the human and given the sense of a beast" (4,11f). This characteristic, which continues in all later apocalyptic writings, may strike us moderns as too fantastic, but the people of the ancient Near East evidently thought it quite colorful.

Dn 4 is also indebted to the Messianic allegory in Ez 17,22ff, where a shoot from the cedar, that represents the royal house of David, grows into a majestic tree, so that "birds of every kind dwell beneath it, every winged thing in the shade of its boughs." The moral here, that "all the trees of the field shall know that I, the *LORD*, bring low the high tree, lift high the lowly tree, wither up the green tree, and make the withered tree bloom," is re-echoed, though rather freely in Dn 4,14: "That all who live may know that the Most High rules over the kingdom of men: he can give it to whom he will, or set over it the lowliest of men."

Somewhat more distant is the relationship between the stump and roots that are left in the ground in Dn 4,12 and the stump and roots of Jesse in Is 11,1, or "the oak whose trunk remains when its leaves have fallen" in Is 6,13.

Daniel thus explains the punishment to be inflicted on Nabuchodonosor for his pride: "You shall be cast out from among men and dwell with wild beasts; you shall be given grass to eat like an ox and be bathed with the dew of heaven; seven years[8] shall pass over you, until you know that the Most High rules over the kingdom of men and gives it to whom he will" (Dn 4,22). And a year later this dire fate overtakes him: "Nabuchodonosor was cast out from among men, he ate grass like an ox, and his body was bathed with the dew of heaven, until his hair grew like the feathers of an eagle, and his nails like the claws of a bird" (4,30).

There is no need here to inquire about the ideas that the ancients had of the form of insanity in which its victim acts like a sort of

---

8. The word, *'iddānîn,* really means merely "periods" of indefinite length, but the LXX is no doubt correct in translating it here as "years."

werewolf, nor to trace back the picture of a man, with "hair like the feathers of an eagle, and nails like the claws of a bird," to the composite images of ancient Mesopotamian art. What is more important is to know why this affliction is here attributed to Nabuchodonosor. It would be a hopeless quest to try to find any historical basis for it in the life of this great king of Babylon.

Ever since the publication of the so-called Nabonidus Chronicle in 1882[9] it has been suspected that the king with whom this folk tale was originally concerned was not Nabuchodonosor (605-562 B.C.), but Nabuna'id (555-539 B.C.). From this document we know that Nabuna'id spent a good part of his seventeen-year reign at the north-Arabian oasis of Tema. Although he no doubt had good reasons—military, commercial, and perhaps politico-religious—for his long stay there, the rumor could have arisen among the people that he remained away from Babylon for these long periods because he was out of his mind.

The publication of the "Verse Account of Nabuna'id" in 1924[10] confirmed this theory. This document, which is a biased account written by the Babylonian priests to justify the action of the gods in handing over Nabuna'id's realm to Cyrus, also makes him look as if he were not completely sane. The fourth column of this text is almost all lost, but one of its fragmentary lines begins, according to the translation of A. L. Oppenheim:[11] "The king is mad." One might conclude that this is an explicit statement that Nabuna'id was crazy.[12] Actually, since the Akkadian expression here is *a-gu-ug šarru*, Oppenheim, of course meant "mad" in the sense of "enraged, angry," and not in the sense of "insane, crazy."

It is now even more certain that the story about God afflicting a Babylonian king, as recounted in Dn 4, was originally concerned with Nabuna'id. The proof of this is the text from Cave 4 at *Qumrân* that was published in 1956 by J. T. Milik.[13] Although the very fragmentary Aramaic document itself which contains this text is ascribed by Milik to the second half of the first century B.C., it represents an older form of this folk tale. Because of its importance in connection with Dn 4, and since it is not readily available elsewhere, we give it here in transcription and translation, both based on Milik's work.

---

9. First published by T. G. Pinches, *Transactions of the Society of Biblical Archaeology* 7, (1882), 139ff; again published by Sidney Smith, *Babylonian Historical Texts Relating to the Downfall of Babylon* (London 1924) Pls. XI-XIV, pp. 110ff.
10. Published by Sidney Smith, *op. cit.* Pls. V-X, pp. 83ff.
11. *ANET* 314a.
12. Even J. T. Milik was misled by this English expression, which he translates as "Le roi est fou": *RB* 63 (1956) 410, note 5.
13. "' Prière de Nabonide' et autres écrits d'un cycle de Daniel", *RB* 63, (1956), 405-411: 415. Cf D. N. Freedman, "The Prayer of Nabonidus" *BASOR* 145, (1957), 31f.

Transcription: doubtful letters underlined; supplied letters in brackets

1 myl ṣlt' dy ṣly nbny mlk '[twr wb]bl mlk' [rb' kdy hwy ktyš]
2 bšḥn' b'yš' bptgm '[lh' 'ly]' btymn [mdynt' bšḥn b'yš]
3 ktyš hwyt šnyn šb' wmn ['nšy'] šwy '[nh wkdy hwdyt 'wyty]
4 wḥṭ'y šbq lh gzr whw' [gbr] yhwdy m[n bny glwt' bbbl whw']
5 hḥwy wktb lm'bd yqr w[rbwt hd]r lšm '[lh' 'ly' wkn ktb kdy]
6 ktyš hwyt bšḥn' b['yš'] btymn [mdynt' bptgm 'lh' 'ly']
7 šnyn šb' mṣl' hwy[t 'nth l'lhy] ksp' wdhb' nhš' przl']
8 "' 'bn' ḥsp' mn dy [ ]r dy 'lhyn h[mwn]

Translation: doubtful words in italics; supplied words in brackets

[1]The words of the prayer which Nabuna'i (d), the king of A[ssyria and Ba]bylon, the [great] king, prayed, [when he was smitten] [2]with a bad inflammation *by* the decree of the [*Most High God*] in [the *city* of] Tema. ["With a bad inflammation] [3]I was smitten (for) seven years and *from* [*men*] *I was put* (*away*). [But when I *confessed my sins* [4]and my faults, He (God) allowed *me* [ly!] (to have) a soothsayer. This was a Jewish [man *of the exiles in Babylon. He*] [5]*explained* (*it*) and wrote (me) to render honor and *g*[*reat glor*]*y* to the name of the [Most High God. Thus he wrote: 'When] [6]you were smitten with a b[ad] inflammation [in the city] of Tema [by the decree of the Most High God] [7](for) seven years, [you we]re praying to gods of silver and gold, [of bronze,] iron, [8]wood, stone, (and) clay . . . that *th*[*ese*] gods . . .' "

There are a few remarkable similarities between this text and Dn 4, but even more numerous and more striking differences between the two. The main similarities are these: in both accounts a certain Neo-Babylonian king is afflicted by God for seven years, during which time he is apart from ordinary social intercourse; a certain Jewish exile explains the meaning of his affliction to him and urges him to repent; thereupon he is cured and renders thanks to God. The principal differences are these: the names of the two kings, though both begin with "Nabu-," are not the same; one is afflicted with a sort of lycanthropic insanity, while the other is smitten with *šeḥîn* (literally, a "burning" or "inflammation"), a disease which causes the skin to break out in festering boils (Ex 9,9ff; Dt 28,27.35), resembling leprosy (Lv 13,18ff.23), which God sends to try men (Is 38,12; Jb 2,7); one king is at Babylon, the other at Tema (Is 21,14; Jer 25,23; Jb 6,19), when smitten. There is no sign of literary dependence of one story on the other; the relatively few words and expressions which they have in common are standard terms that could occur anywhere.[14] The name of the Jewish soothsayer (*gāzir*) of the *Qumrân* text (cf the same term in Dn 2,27; 4,4; 5,7.11) is not given in the present fragments. It may have been mentioned as "Daniel" elsewhere in the complete text.

The conclusion would seem to be that in the last pre-Christian centuries there was in circulation among the Jews a sort of "Daniel cycle" of stories, in which tales were recounted about a very wise Jewish exile in Babylonia who acted as a sort of counsellor to the Neo-Babylonian and Persian kings. The author of our canonical Dn, who wrote at the time of Antiochus IV Epiphanes (175-164 B.C.), as the second half of his book clearly shows, utilized some of these stories in the first half of his work. Although he brought them partly "up to date," as the story of Nabuchodonosor's dream of the gigantic statue in Dn 2 shows, he left a good deal of their older Neo-Babylonian and Persian coloring in them, and, if he intended his Babylonian kings as symbols of the wicked Epiphanes, he hardly stressed this point in any noticeable way.

That the Qumrân text represents an older variety of the story that is told in Dn 4 seems fairly certain from its closer relationship to the historical fact of Nabuna'id's long residence at Tema, as well as from the fact that it is more plausible than Dn in making the king of his story Nabuna'id rather than Nabuchodonosor. Even the use of the first person singular in telling the story is more easily explained on the supposition that in its earlier form it was cast as a prayer rather than as a letter or proclamation.

This analysis of the sources which the author of Dn used should not make him appear as a mere imitator or compiler. He is quite definitely a very original writer. Even in the use of technical terms he is the first, as far as we know, to designate an angel as an *'îr* (literally, "wakeful"), a "watcher" or "watchman" (4,10.14.20), a term for "angel" which later became common in the apocrypha. The concept itself probably goes back to "the angels who patrol the earth" and who are "the eyes of the *LORD* that range over the whole earth" in Zech 1,10f; 4,10, or even to the chariot-throne of the cherubim in Ez 1,18, of which the rims of the wheels are "full of eyes all around." Theologically, Dn 4 has an important "first," with Tb 12,9; 14,11, in its teaching that sins can be atoned for by good works (*ṣidqāh,* Heb. *ṣᵉdāqāh,* literally, "justice"; cf the *dikaiosynē* in Mt 6,1) and almsgiving to the poor (Dn 4,24). But Dn's greatest claim to originality lies in the fact that the author of this book took the eschatological images of the earlier prophets and developed this material into a new, apocalyptic style, that was to be of immense importance during the next few centuries.

---

14. The only noteworthy phrase, "gods of gold and silver, bronze and iron, wood and stone" (in the same order of the materials, but without the "clay" in Dn), does not occur in Dn 4, despite Milik's statement, but in the Belsassar story (Dn 5,23).

LEVITICAL MESSIANISM AND THE NEW TESTAMENT

BRUCE VAWTER, C.M.

It is frequently asserted that in the late biblical Judaism, especially under the early Hasmonean influence on Jewish thinking, a Levitical messianism tended for a time to displace the Davidic. In some instances, it is alleged, this Levitical messianism was the only one conceivable to men who had given up all hope of a Davidic restoration; in others, tradition reasserted itself, either to crowd out the Levitical idea altogether or to combine with it in a dual messianic expectation, the priestly together with the royal.[1] The so-called Zadokite document of the Damascus covenanters and, more recently, the Qumrân literature, have strengthened this position by their apparent references to an expectation of two Messiahs, the one "of Israel" and the other "of Aaron." It is the purpose of this paper to examine the sources in which this priestly messianism has been found, and to see how, if at all, such a conception has influenced the NT.

Jeremiah 33,14-26

Jer 33,14-26 is the longest continuous passage of Jer completely missing in the Greek. This is only one of the reasons that compel virtually all modern scholars to regard it as a post-Jeremian addition. It bears, in fact, various of the traits we have learnt to associate with such additions in the prophetic collections. The style is anthological of other passages of Jer: vv. 14-16 are a pastiche of 29,10 and 23,5f.; v. 17 comes from 35,19; 31,35-37 have served as the model of v. 19ff. and v. 25f.; and there are other reminiscences. Furthermore, Jeremiah's words have been used partly in a sense different from that of the authentic passages: the *Yhwh ṣidqēnû* and *ṣemaḥ ṣaddîq* of 23,5f. turn up in v. 14f. (MT has *ṣemaḥ ṣᵉdāqâ* in v. 15, but 4 MSS have *ṣaddîq*, and this was read by Theodotion), but the former now means Jerusalem rather than the messianic king, and the latter in turn refers to the kingship itself rather than to a scion of David.

The language of the passage appears to be late and retrograde.[2]

1. Cf. Sigmund Mowinckel, *He That Cometh*, tr. by G. W. Anderson (New York: Abingdon 1956) 286-290.
2. Cf. F. Giesebrecht, *Das Buch Jeremia* (HKzAT; Göttingen: Vandenhoeck & Ruprecht, 1907) 186 on v. 20.

An exception that impressed some earlier commentators is the Deuteronomic expression "Levitical priests," a term that is properly pre- rather than postexilic, in respect to the canonization of the Priestly legislation. But, as is the case with the Chronicler's similar usage, this now appears to be a deliberate archaism.[3]

We do not, it is true, have to agree with Rudolph's contention that such a prophecy would have been impossible for Jeremiah. Like Ezekiel, Jeremiah would have thought most naturally of a restored covenant in terms of the sacrifice and priesthood without which the worship of God was impossible.[4] But the author is not thinking simply of a continued priesthood in a renewed covenant. He is, rather, insisting that a covenant of perpetuity has been made with the tribe of Levi in its priestly function just as a covenant had been made with Judah in the royal function. The passage dates from a time when the priesthood had assumed an importance for the life of the nation equal to or even surpassing that of the kingship. This situation was not verified before the exile, but it was afterwards, particularly after hopes for a Davidic restoration were dashed with the passing of Zerubbabel and there was a consequent shift of political emphasis to the high priesthood.[5] We can probably be more precise than this: as Nötscher observes, it appears from the author's tone that he is encouraging those that had already been disillusioned with the priesthood.[6] Though Nötscher himself was disposed to date the passage as shortly after the exile, we may perhaps see in it a culmination of the disillusionment with the Zadokites that is reflected in the postexilic prophets and the work of the Chronicler, possibly of the time of Ezra and Nehemiah or even later.[7] Perhaps like the Chronicler the author awaited from the faithful Levites a priesthood of renewed fervor to replace the Zadokites, and perhaps, therefore, like the Chronicler again, his reference to "the Levitical priests" was not merely a piece of archaism.

At all events, it seems clear enough that Jer 33,14-26 belongs temporally as well as conceptually in the category of the texts which follow.[8]

---

3. Giesebrecht 183; Wilhelm Rudolph, *Der Prophet Jeremia* (HZAT; Göttingen: Vandenhoeck & Ruprecht, ²1958) 201.
4. C. von Orelli, *Der Prophet Jeremia* (KKzHS; Munich: Oskar Beck, 1905) 142f.; Albert Condamin, S.J., *Le Livre de Jérémie* (EB; Paris: Gabalda, 1920) 250.
5. Cf. William F. Albright, *The Biblical Period* (Privately printed: Pittsburgh, 1950) 49f.; reprinted from *The Jews: Their History, Culture and Religion*, ed. by Louis Finkelstein, 1949.
6. Friedrich Nötscher, *Das Buch Jeremias* (HSAT; Bonn: Peter Hanstein, 1934) 248-250.
7. Cf. Roland de Vaux, O.P., *Ancient Israel* (New York: McGraw-Hill, 1961) 390-394 [=*Les Institutions de l'Ancien Testament II* (Paris: Éditions du Cerf, 1960) 263-266]; Henri Cazelles, P.S.S., *Les livres des Chroniques* (B.J.; Paris: Éditions du Cerf, ²1961) 12. Rudolph believes the passage should be referred to this "literarisch dunkle Zeit."
8. T. Chary, *Les prophètes et le culte à partir de l'exil* (Tournai: Desclée, 1955) 166-171, finds the beginning of a covenant with Levi in Mal 3 and makes Jer 33,14-26 depend on this text.

MALACHI 1,6 - 2,9; 3,1-5

As it now seems to be generally agreed that Mal must be dated to shortly before the reforms of Ezra and Nehemiah—without entering into the fretted question of the relative chronology of these postexilic leaders—and obviously after the prophets Haggai and Zechariah,[9] these texts must belong roughly to the same era as the preceding; they perhaps even predate it. Much more explicitly than the preceding do they reflect a dissatisfaction with the Jerusalem priesthood. In 2,4.8 mention is made of the covenant with Levi, and in 3,3 a purification of the priesthood is promised.

The covenant with Levi is that found in Dt 33,9.[10] This covenant is invoked to give sanction against the unworthy priestly performance condemned in 1,6-14 and contrasted with the pure sacrifice ascribed to the Gentiles in vv. 11 and 14. Martin Rehm, in a recent article on the celebrated Mal 1,11, has rightly stressed the necessity of relating this prophecy to the messianic future.[11] In doing so, however, he seems to leave out of perspective the prophecy of 3,1-5 on the Levitical priesthood. According to Rehm, Mal 1,11 looks forward to a messianic age in which the prescriptions of the law of the single sanctuary and the Levitical priesthood will be impossible, when the plan of salvation must revert to former institutions, as when sacrifice was the prerogative of every family head.[12] As a kindred text he cites the postexilic Is 19,19 concerning the altar-to-be in Egypt. But Is 19,18-23 precisely regards an extension of *Israelite* covenant and law to Egypt. Furthermore, the entire passage has now taken as its model the description of the conquest in the Deuteronomic book of Joshua.[13] The altar of Is 19,19f which is *l*ᵉ*'ôt ûl*ᵉ*'ēd lYhwh* is patterned after the altar *'ēd hû'* of Jos 22,27ff.—a passage that expressly upholds the Deuteronomic law of the single sanctuary!

When we take into account the obvious devotion of the author of Mal to the Israelite cult and priestly purity, it is hardly realistic to interpret his messianic teaching apart from these. Whatever they might be in a Christian view, for him they were certainly no interim econo-

---

9. Cf. Otto Eissfeldt, *Einleitung in das Alte Testament* (Tübingen: J.C.B. Mohr, ²1956) 545f.; R. Pautrel, "Malachie," *VDBS* 5, 739-746.
10. Cf. Ernst Sellin, *Das Zwölfprophetenbuch* (KZAT; Leipzig: A. Deichert, 1922) 548; S. R. Driver, *A Critical and Exegetical Commentary on Deuteronomy* (ICC; New York; Scribners, 1895) 400f. A non-messianic expression of the covenant is the *b*ᵉ*rît hakk*ᵉ*hunnâ w*ᵉ*hal*ᵉ*wîyim* of Neh 13,29.
11. "Das Opfer der Völker nach Mal 1,11," *Lex Tua Veritas: Festschrift für Hubert Junker* (Trier: Paulinus-Verlag, 1961) 193-208.
12. So also Pautrel, *VDBS* 5, 744: the cult presupposed by Mal 1,11 "ne deviendra possible que par la substitution d'une loi nouvelle à l'ancienne, disons au temps de l'ère messianique." Cf. also A. van Hoonacker, *Les douze petits prophètes* (EB; Paris: Gabalda, 1908) 713, who asserts the same, though on p. 731 (on 3,3) he says the very opposite, insisting that there is no contradiction.
13. Cf. Edward J. Kissane, *The Book of Isaiah* (Dublin: Browne & Nolan, 1941) I, 218-220.

my.[14] If 1,11f is to be taken (rightly, I think) as a reference to the messianic age, it must be reconciled with 3,1-5; but just as certainly the solution is not to be had in denying the manifestly messianic character of 3,1-5.[15] It is not our task to make this conciliation here, but we might suggest that it would have lain in the line of thought of Is 66,21, and not in the abolition of a law which our author had constantly before him (3,22) as the ordinance of an unchanging God (3,6) of an eternal covenant.

ZECHARIAH 12,12f. (3,1-10; 4,11-14; 6,9-15)

The so-called Trito-Zech (12-14) seems to be in reality the second of three anonymous prophetic collections, the other two being Zech 9-11 and Mal 1-3, all of which originally stood at the end of the Book of the Twelve, each bearing the title *maśśā' d^{e}bar Yhwh*. In the present editing of the Bible, the first two have been gathered into Zech, whereas the third has been ascribed to the *mal^e'ākî* of Mal 3,1, taken now as a proper name.[16] There would seem to be no doubt that the two supplements to Zech are by separate authors and that both are subsequent to Mal.[17]

In "Trito-Zechariah" there is no covenant with Levi properly so

---

14. Cf. Rehm, *Junker-Festschrift,* 207, ftn. 67: "Die Fortdauer des levitischen Priestertums in der messianischen Zeit wird vom AT nicht gelehrt. Jer 33,18 handelt nicht vom Messias, sondern bezieht sich auf die Wiederherstellung nach dem Exil. Mal 3,3f erwartet die Beseitigung der augenblicklichen Missstände und die Besserung der Leviten in naher Zukunft." This judgment seems to disregard the context of Jer 33,18 entirely (an everlasting covenant paralleled with the everlasting Davidic covenant), to say nothing of what it implies Jewish messianism to have been.
15. Cf. M.-J. Lagrange, O.P., "Notes sur les prophéties messianiques des derniers prophètes," *RB* 15 (1906) 81: "Il [the author of Mal 1,11] songe encore aux Lévites, mais aux Lévites purifiés (III,3), à un sacrifice offert au nom de Iahvé connu comme tel." Whatever is to be said of Lagrange's insistence that *minḥâ* here is an unbloody sacrifice, finding an echo in the aspirations of some portions of Judaism, I think his judgment on the meaning of 1,11 is the only one consistent with the prophecy as a whole. Chary, *Prophètes,* 178-189 also recognizes the need to conciliate the two passages and to leave Malachi a Jew; he also admits a universalist influence (Iranian), however, in the construction of 1,11.
16. Cf. W. Nowack, *Kleine Propheten* (HKzAT; Göttingen: Vandenhoeck & Ruprecht, ^{2}1903) 422; Pautrel, *VDBS* 5, 739; Eissfeldt, *Einleitung*^{2}, 542f.
17. Von Orelli's attempt, among others, to establish a pre-exilic (late Hoseanic) date for Zech 9-11 is conceded to have failed, cf. *Die zwölf kleinen Propheten* (Munich: Oskar Beck, ^{3}1908) 178f. So also van Hoonacker's attempt, argued at length, *op. cit.* 650ff.; to ascribe the entire canonical book to Zechariah: cf. Sellin *Zwölfprophetenbuch,* 488ff.; Eissfeldt, *Einleitung,*^{2} 535-543. Both sections seem to presuppose the beginning of the Hellenistic period. Paul Lamarche, S.J., *Zacharie IX-XIV* (EB; Paris: Gabalda, 1961) 22f., 105-115, 148-157 defends an hypothesis of a single author for Zech 9-14, who was dependent on Deutero-Isaiah and whom he is inclined to date, contrary to the prevailing trend, in the period 500-480 after the (putative) death of Zerubbabel. However, he also concedes the possibility of an Hellenistic dating.

called. Neither is there properly a Davidic messianic expectation. In 12,12f., however, in describing the Jerusalem of the messianic age, the apocalyptist-prophet divides the people into "the families of the house of David," "the families of the house of Nathan," "the families of the house of Levi," and "the families of the Shimeiites" as those of note; "the remaining families" account for the rest of the eschatological Israel. The Davidic and Levitical elements of the people thus retain their preeminence, though no specific messianic functions are ascribed to them, and they are evidently put on a par.[18]

Despite all attempts to find other candidates, it would seem clear that the Nathan of v. 12 is the son of David by Bathsheba mentioned in 2 Sm 5,14; I Chr 3,5; 14,4 (the Targum identified him with Nathan the prophet, whom it calls "son of David"), and the Shimei of v. 13 is the Gershomite Levite of Ex 6,17; Nm 3,21, etc. (in the LXX Symeōn appears, while the Targum identified "the Shimeiite" with the Mordecai ben Jair ben Shimei of the book of Esther). Van Hoonacker's "conjecture assez hardie" to get rid of these names of no apparent importance[19] may, as a matter of fact, have been motivated by what precisely was their significance to the prophet. We are in the period long after the passing of Zerubbabel, when there was no longer any hope of a Davidic restoration from the normal line that had descended through Solomon. In "the house of Nathan" paired off with "the house of David" we may have the author's suggestion that the Davidic oracle will yet be fulfilled through another line of descent. Similarly, the pairing of "the Shimeiites" with "the house of Levi" can be another expression of dissatisfaction with the Zadokite priesthood, ideally descended from Aaron,[20] and the suggestion that another Levitical line will be substituted. This, in fact, is precisely the kind of apocalyptic

---

18. Cf. Chary, *Prophètes* 226f.
19. *Les douze,* 685.
20. On the Zadokite priesthood, cf. E. Auerbach in *ZAW* 49 (1931) 327f. It is generally thought that this was the priesthood of Gibeon (cf. 1 Chr 16,39), which remained a chief sanctuary during the time of David and Solomon (1 Chr 21,29; 2 Chr 1,3; 1 Kgs 3,4) after a long Canaanite history (2 Sm 21,9), cf. Henri Cazelles, "David's Monarchy and the Gibeonite Claim," *PEQ* 87 (1955) 165-175; J. Dus, "Gibeon—eine Kultstätte des Šmš und die Stadt des benjaminitischen Schicksals," *VT* 10 (1960) 353-374. Brought to Jerusalem by David with the Ark, it was later given the artificial genealogy of the Chronicler (1 Chr 5,29-41) associating it with the Aaronite and Eliite priesthood. Auerbach thinks these facts exclude the reliability of the data of Sm, according to which (2 Sm 8,17) Zadok was the son of Ahitub, one of the Eliite priests (1 Sm 14,3), apparently a younger son in view of Ahimelech's preeminence (1 Sm 21f). But whatever is to be said of the relation of the Eliites to Aaron, it is not impossible that in Israelite times the relations between Shiloh and Gibeon were as pictured in the Bible. After the loss of Shiloh, presumably in the Philistine wars, part of the Eliite priesthood may as readily have been transferred to Gibeon with the tabernacle as to Nob. No further light is shed by Sm on the origin of the Eliites save in the later 1 Sm 2,27. Cf. also de Vaux, *Ancient Israel,* 390-394.

fulfilment we might expect of this author.

We may now note several passages in Zech proper which have a bearing on the text we have just examined. In the vision of 3,1-10 the highpriest Jeshua is pictured as purified of the former sins of priesthood and people and elevated to a dignity beyond that ever enjoyed by the pre-exilic priesthood. He is endowed with many of the prerogatives possessed by the kings before the exile, though exclusively in the sacred domain. He is given (v. 7) "access" (probably read *mahᵉlākîm*) to the divine along with those who stand by, i.e., the angels. Sellin saw in this an absolute equation of Jeshua with the Davidic Messiah, and for him this was another reason to transfer 3,8-10 to a different context, after 4,10.[21] However, it does not appear that Zechariah has made such an advance over Haggai. The priesthood has, it is true, been given some of the royal prerogatives and there is a "separation of church and state"; but it is still the Messiah who will inaugurate God's kingdom.[22] All of this corresponds to the new responsibilities of the postexilic priesthood independent of royal interference in obedience to the prophecy of Ezekiel. Zechariah, however, professes a personal Davidic messianism, and the entire grandiose vision has as its climax the introduction of the theme of the *ṣemaḥ*. The highpriestly office is glorified, but not to the detriment of the hoped-for kingship, to which pre-eminence is still ascribed. The priesthood of the messianic age will be able to realize its potentialities only through the coming of the Davidic scion.

In 4,11-14, the explanation of the imagery in 4,1-3, it is evident that the two olive trees are Zerubbabel and Jeshua. They are called *bᵉnê-hayyiṣᵉhār* doubtless in reference to their separate anointings, Jeshua's in fact and Zerubbabel's in expectancy. The spirit is that of Jer 33,17f. The two serve their separate functions, however, each as the anointed of Yahweh, with neither equality nor subordination being implied. The olive trees do not represent equal suppliers of oil for the lampstand (v. 12 is a gloss), since the lampstand is (probably) designated in v. 10b as the eyes of Yahweh.[23]

It is hardly open to question that 6,9-15 originally referred to a symbolic crowning of Zerubbabel as king. According to v. 13, a priest

---

21. *Zwölfprophetenbuch*, 448: "In Unterschiede von Haggai, der ausschliesslich den Serubbabel in ein solches unmittelbares Verhältnis zu Jahwe rückt, hat er gerade hier zunächst nachdrücklich dem Josua ein analoges Recht zuerkannt, and von da an immer zu vermitteln gesucht, jedem der beiden Ämter, dem weltlichen wie dem geistlichen das Seine gebend und beide als gleich berechtigt und notwendig im Gottesreiche der Zukunft hinstellend vgl. 4,14; 6,13."

22. Chary, *Prophètes*, 148-152 more aptly observes that this marks the emancipation of the priesthood and the beginning of its glorification. It would be difficult to understand an alteration of the received text in the manner that Sellin imagined, in view of the opposite course that was followed in c. 6.

23. Cf. van Hoonacker, *Les douze*, 619f.; Albert Gelin, P.S.S. *Aggée—Zacharie—Malachie* (BJ; Paris: Éditions du Cerf, ²1951) 33.

(LXX: the priest) would stand by his throne (probably read *mîmînô* with LXX for the second *'al-kis*ᵉ*'ô*), and between the two there was to be peace. Again, it is Zerubbabel, the *ṣemaḥ,* who would build the temple of Yahweh and make possible the functioning of the priesthood.

This restoration of the original text from tendentious alteration is so axiomatic in view of the rest of Zech, there is no need to argue in its justification.[24] This alteration need not have been made only in Hasmonean times, of course; it could belong to any period after Zerubbabel, when the highpriest had by default become the sole depository of power in the postexilic community. It has resulted in what is verbally the only clear-cut example of Levitical messianism that lies in the texts before us. I need hardly add, however, that as this is the result of a purely mechanical substitution of a name without even an attempt to harmonize it with its conflicting context, it would be rash in the extreme to appeal to it as pointing to any elaborate theological development.

Ben Sira 45,15.23-26

Ben Sira mentions the covenant with Aaron in v. 15, and in the praise of Phinehas in vv. 23-26 he compares with the covenant made with David the everlasting covenant made with Aaron. The comparison is not to suggest their equality: he minimizes the Davidic covenant by contrasting it with the Levitical.[25] This is clear even if the Hebrew text of v. 25 is read as it stands:

*w*ᵉ*gam b*ᵉ*rîtô 'im dāwīd*
*ben yišay l*ᵉ*maṭṭēh y*ᵉ*hûdâ*
*naḥălat 'îš lip*ᵉ*nê k*ᵉ*bôdô*
*naḥălat 'ahărôn l*ᵉ*kōl zar*ᵉ*'ô*

The covenant with Aaron, says Ben Sira, is a covenant with all his descendants, whereas the covenant with David was with one man only. LXX and Syr further indicate that *lip*ᵉ*nê k*ᵉ*bôdô* should be read *lib*ᵉ*nô l*ᵉ*baddô,* in which case the sense is that the Davidic covenant was made in view of Solomon only, even as the Deuteronomic interpolator of 2 Sm 7,13 interpreted it. In either case, it is plain that the Davidic covenant has ceased to have any messianic significance for Ben Sira, and that in its place is the covenant with the priesthood.

This does not mean, however, that Ben Sira professed a Levitical messianism. Rather, he saw in the existing highpriestly office that was

---

24. Among those who have tried to preserve the received text, von Orelli, *Propheten* 196-198, made some sort of case for vv. 11-12, but foundered completely in trying to explain away v. 13, attested by LXX, which clearly demands two parties, of which the priest is a second. LXX has preserved enough of the original to make its restoration more than probable. Lagrange, "Notes" 71f. also tried to defend the received text of Zech 6,9-15 as original.
25. Norbert Peters, *Das Buch Jesus Sirach oder Ecclesiasticus* (EHzAT; Münster: Aschendorff, 1913) 391-393, following the uncorrected Hebrew text, makes it a simple comparison.

so soon to be degraded by the rivalries prior to the Maccabean age, something that had taken the place of messianism. Ben Sira's messianism, if it can be called that, is a realized messianism. By the same token, his covenant with Aaron is something quite different from the Levitical covenant we have seen in the preceding examples.[26]

Testaments of the Twelve Patriarchs

As is well known, in the Testaments of the Twelve Patriarchs Levi is given a pre-eminence over all the other tribes. This is generally explained as due to the Maccabean fervor of the time of the composition of this work.[27]

The pre-eminence of Levi, however, would appear to be one of the few things certain about this conjecture-ridden and puzzling book. It was in view of it that Charles concluded to the idea of a Levitical Messiah who had replaced the Davidic Messiah under Maccabean influence; with the break of Hyrcanus with the Pharisees, however, this aberration was abandoned, and first-century additions to the book have restored the traditional Messiah from Judah.[28] In the light of the Qumrân evidence, Karl Georg Kuhn has corrected this position: the two Messiahs from Judah and Levi co-exist in the Testaments, making them agree with the messianic expectation of the Qumrân sectaries. The Testaments, like the Damascus document and the Qumrân literature, are all Essenian, the only form of Judaism that held to this dual messianic idea.[29]

It is true that an imposing list of qualities is ascribed to Levi in the Testaments. To begin with what is certain, Test. Reub. 6,7 ascribes supremacy to Levi, and it is easy to agree that the rest of the words in this verse (ascribing the same supremacy to Judah, Reuben, Dan, and Joseph) are what Charles called them, "a foolish interpolation." The rest of the passage down to v. 10 inclusive extols Levi as the anointed highpriest (or, in the unamended text, "highpriest of the anointed one") who shall fulfil his priestly office *until* (*méchri*) the consummation: his function, in fact, as in v. 11f., is to bless the messianic line of Judah. The *en autô* of v. 11 chosen to be king over all

---

26. It is possible that Sir 48,10f. is a reference to the *Elias redivivus* of Mal 3,23f., as CCD takes it to be. LXX differs widely from the Hebrew, and the crucial words *lipen*[*ê* (*bô*) *yôm Yhwh*] have to be supplied in v. 10, which in turn must be depended on for the tense to be assigned *rō'ĕkā wāmēt* in v. 11. In any case, if Sir follows Mal here, it is in the original sense of Elijah as a forerunner of the Day of the Lord, not of the Messiah, and still less does it identify Elijah with the eschatological highpriest.
27. Cf. Hermann Strathmann, *"Leu (e) i," ThWNT* 4,242f.
28. R. H. Charles, *The Apocrypha and Pseudepigrapha of the Old Testament* (Oxford: Clarendon Press, 1913) II, 294.
29. "The Two Messiahs of Aaron and Israel," *The Scrolls and the New Testament*, ed. by Krister Stendahl (New York: Harper Brothers, 1957) 54-64. Lagrange appears to have been the first to identify the Testaments as Essenian.

the nation, however, is probably the Judah just mentioned, not Levi. Even if "anointed highpriest" is the title given to Levi, this does not mean Messiah in the technical Jewish sense: the title is that of Lv 4,3, etc., *hakkōhēn hammāšîaḥ*. In this passage there is not, therefore, at least necessarily, any eschatological Levitical highpriest.[30] It is true that v. 12 can as easily apply to Levi as to Judah, but here the Armenian text indicates that Levi (?) will be "eternal kings," not an eternal king, i.e., that he will continually fulfil the functions of warlike leadership ascribed to Levi (the Maccabeans) in Test. Sim. 5,5f.; Test. Dan 5,10-13 (corrected).

In Test. Lev. 8 Levi is given a crown as well as the diadem of priesthood and the ephod of prophecy (Moses). Probably the crown refers to the third stage in Levi's priestly career, which is also called a new priesthood, namely the Maccabean succession that replaced the Zadokites. Probably, too, this entails an assimilation to Levi of the role of Melchizedek, the association of temporal and priestly rule, as in Jub. 32,1 (in praise) and Ass. Mos. 6,1 (in reprobation).[31] But once again there is no eschatological priest or priestly Messiah. As Lagrange long ago pointed out, the reference to a king who will rise *from* Judah (so all the Greek MSS) in v. 14 must be a Christian interpolation in this much interpolated book; it is, at all events, at war with its context.[32]

The parade examples from the Testaments to prove a Levitical messianism are Test. Lev. 18 and Test. Jud. 24: in the former, a routine celebration of the new (Maccabean) priesthood becomes, in v. 6 and onwards, the prediction of an eschatological figure who will be a universal savior; in the latter, to a Judahite Messiah figured in vv. 4-6 another messianic figure is joined in vv. 1-3 who can only be (so goes the argument) the Levitical Messiah. But once again, when the

---

30. G. R. Beasley-Murray, "The Two Messiahs in the Testaments of the Twelve Patriarchs," *JTS* 48 (1947) 1-12 thinks that only in this passage is there an unambiguous portrayal of a Levitical Messiah. He also finds this idea in Test. Lev. 18, but dismisses the other texts alleged by Charles.

31. For a quite different interpretation, cf. T. W. Manson, "Miscellanea Apocalyptica III," *JTS* 48 (1947) 59-61. Manson takes the three stages to be Moses—Aaron—*benê ṣaddôq*: the king in v. 14 would be Solomon. If the figure of Melchizedek is invoked here to justify a change of priesthood, it is interesting to compare the view of H. H. Rowley, "Melchizedek and Zadok (Gen 14 and Ps 110)," *Festschrift für Alfred Bertholet* (Tübingen: J.C.B. Mohr, 1950) 461-472. According to Rowley the Zadokite priesthood, which he conceives to have been the Jebusite priesthood of Jerusalem accepted by David, itself was first legitimated by an appeal to the ancient story of Gn 14, and it is this legitimation that is reflected in Ps 110.

32. Cf. M.-J. Lagrange, O.P., *Le messianisme chez les Juifs* (EB; Paris: Gabalda, 1909) 72f. Similarly, v. 11f. of Test. Dan 5,10-13 appear to be Christian. When they are removed, together with the Judah of v. 10 which is doubtless due to the same interpolator (rather than to the "first-century Jewish" influence seen by Charles), the passage becomes merely a reference to the Maccabean wars and not messianic. Test. Lev. 17,2f. has undergone an interpolation of the same kind.

crucial verses are recognized as fairly obvious Christian interpolations (Test. Lev. 18, 6-12; Test. Jud. 24,1-3), the Levitical Messiah disappears.[33]

What remains in the Testaments, certainly, is the supremacy of Levi, but a purely priestly supremacy (Test. Lev. 4,1-6; 13). The kingship, it is made plain, resides with Judah (Test. Jud. 12,4). The author also takes pains to explain how it is that Judah has, for a time, forfeited his kingship (Test. Jud. 15,2f; 17,3), but he also insists that it is to be restored (Test. Jud. 17,5f.). Part of Levi's supremacy is that the priesthood should outrank the kingship; nevertheless, the kingship is Judah's eternally, and from it, not from Levi, will come the Messiah (cf. Test. Jud. 21f.; 25,1f.; Test. Iss. 5,7; Test. Naph. 5,3-5). In Test. Jos. 19,11 it is said that *a* savior (Armenian: "salvation") is to come from Levi and Judah, as a dual principle, and Levi and Judah together (Levi habitually mentioned first) are frequently coupled as this twofold source of salvation (Test. Sim. 7,2; Test. Lev. 2,11; Test. Gad 8,1; Test. Dan 5,4.7; Test. Naph. 6,6; 8,2). However, it appears to be clear enough what role each is to play in bringing about this salvation, and the role of the personal eschatological savior is assigned to Judah, not to Levi.

The tendency already discerned in Ben Sira has come to full term in the Testaments, to glorify the Levitical succession at the expense of the Davidic, for the reasons that have been seen. However, whereas messianism was of little or no concern to Ben Sira, it meant much to the apocalyptists. They, too, recognized that God had blessed Levi and diminished Judah. But when they look forward to the Messiah, the eschatological savior, they continue to look for him from Judah, whatever role they may assign to the priesthood in leading to him. This teaching of the Testaments, recognized for what it is, is not isolated. Precisely the same doctrine is taught in Jubilees, cc. 30-32, where Levi is given supremacy over Judah as the reward (contrary to Gn 49,5-7) of the slaughter of the Shechemites—but a savior is still awaited from Judah.

In the foregoing I have followed the hypothesis that I believe still has the greater probability, namely, that the Testaments of the Twelve Patriarchs is a Jewish work that has undergone considerable Christian interpolation.[34] We must also reckon with the possibility, however, that it was a Christian work in its inception. This position, not a new one,

---

33. Cf. Lagrange, *Messianisme,* 74-77. The verses can hardly be other than Christian: Test. Lev. 18,6 has a parallel only in the Gospel accounts of Christ's baptism; v. 11 recalls Ap 22,2, and v. 12 recalls Ap 20,2f. and Lk 10,19; v. 8 is the doctrine of Heb 7,23f.; the text further speaks of the conversion of the Gentiles and the probation of the Jews, etc. Test. Jud. 24,1-3 depends on the Gospel descriptions of our Lord's baptism and the Pauline doctrine of adopted sonship.
34. Cf. M. de Jonge, "Christian Influence in the Testaments of the Twelve Patriarchs," *NT* 3 (1960) 182-235. The author has returned to this position after previously defending the thesis of Christian authorship.

has recently been supported by new evidence from Qumrân.[35] Among the extensive apocrypha and pseudepigrapha possessed by the sectaries of Qumrân, no fragment of the Testaments of the Twelve Patriarchs has yet been identified. However, fragments of a Testament of Levi in Aramaic were found in Cave I, and still more extensive fragments in Cave IV; also in Cave IV were found fragments of a Testament of Naphtali in Hebrew. In both cases, the material of the fragmentary testaments is more extensive than the corresponding testaments in the Testaments of the Twelve Patriarchs. Thus it may be supposed that the fragments belong to some of the source material of the Testaments of the Twelve Patriarchs. The identical material—Testament of Levi in Aramaic and of Naphtali in Hebrew—was also recovered from the Cairo Genizah that yielded the Damascus document.[36] Presumably it, too, comes ultimately from Qumrân, from one of the earlier discoveries, probably that of c. 785 A.D., as related by Mar Timotheos I. Thus Qumrân may provide evidence of a pre-compilation state of at least part of the Testaments of the Twelve Patriarchs. Correspondingly, the compilation date of the finished work would have to be lowered considerably from the Maccabean or Hasmonean age that is usually considered.[37]

If the Testaments is a Christian work in the ultimate analysis, then of course the "interpolations" must be seen as the author's original intention in composing the work. This intention would then obviously be to show that Jesus Christ is the fulfilment of both a royal (Davidic) and a priestly (Levitical) messianism. In part, this would correspond to other early Christian attempts to find a Levitical as well as a Davidic ancestry for Jesus.[38] Such attempts need not have a more complex explanation than the fact that Luke could be interpreted as ascribing Levitical ancestry to Mary, the *syngenis* (1,36) of Elizabeth, who was *ek tôn thygatérōn Aarōn* (1,5). In the same line is the messianic conception of the third-century Hippolytus of Rome.[39] It seems to me more reasonable to suppose the Christian theorizing to be the result of this interpretation of Luke than to imagine Luke and

---

35. Cf. Eissfeldt, *Einleitung*², 784f.; J. T. Milik, *Ten Years of Discovery in the Wilderness of Judaea,* tr. by J. Strugnell (Naperville, Illinois: Allenson, 1959) 34f.
36. Monsignor Patrick W. Skehan has kindly called my attention to the significance of this fact.
37. An alternative hypothesis has been sustained by Marc Philonenko, *Les interpolations chrétiennes des Testaments des Douze Patriarches et les manuscrits de Qumrân* (Cahiers de *RHPhilRel*; Paris: Presses Universitaires, 1960): that the Testaments are integrally a Jewish work, the product of a Qumrân type of Judaism. The soteriological figure is not Jesus Christ but the Teacher of Justice. Besides the other obvious objections to this early-Dupont-Sommer kind of hypothesis, the absence of the Testaments at Qumrân is a decisive argument.
38. Cf. Strathmann, *ThWNT* 4, 244f.
39. Cf. L. Mariès, S.J., "Le Messie issu de Lévi chez Hippolyte de Rome," *Mélanges Jules Lebreton I* = *RechSR* 39 (1951) 381-396.

the theorizing together to be dependent on some Jewish tradition of a Levitical Messiah. For if Luke did intend to make such an insinuation, it is strange that it was never followed up. The idea is foreign to the rest of the NT, and it is deliberately excluded by the teaching of Hebrews.

Qumran

It has by now become virtually *sententia communis scholarum* that the Qumrân sectaries professed a Levitical, more properly an Aaronic, messianism which they had incorporated into the "normative" messianic expectation.[40] As the evidence, however, is somewhat ambiguous, we are not surprised to find a wide variety of opinion in the interpretation of this messianism.

Certainly, the existence of a priestly Messiah cannot be deduced simply from the famous passage IQS 9,11, which speaks of *nābî' ûmešîḥê 'ahărôn weyiśrā'ēl,* since *māšîaḥ* is patient of a double meaning in such a connection: it can mean the Messiah of Israel in the technical sense on the one hand, and it can also be the conventional highpriestly designation.[41] Rather, we must look to the qualities that are ascribed to the supposed priestly eschatological figure in the Qumrân expectation. 1QS 9,11 doubtless refers to the (literally: "a") prophet who was needed to settle so many religious questions in the contemporary Jewish world now bereft of the prophetic word (cf. I Mc 4,46; 14,41). One of the prophet's functions, for the sectaries, would be to restore the Zadokite priesthood, "the anointed of Aaron." Possibly, but not certainly, therefore, the prophet and the priest of this passage are eschatological figures. We have no assurance that the reference is not to a restored priestly line rather than to an individual eschatological priest.

Is the priest of 1QSa, who appears to be called *rô'š kôl 'ădat yiśrā'ēl* (2, 12), an eschatological figure? This might appear to be the case in view of the *be'aḥărît hayyāmîm* of 1,1.[42] However, this conclusion is

---

40. Cf. J. T. Milik, *Discoveries in the Judaean Desert I. Qumrân Cave I* (New York: Oxford University Press, 1955) 121f.; Raymond E. Brown, S.S., "The Messianism of Qumrân," *CBQ* 19 (1957) 53-82; F. M. Cross, Jr., *The Ancient Library of Qumrân and Modern Biblical Studies* (Garden City, New York: Doubleday, 1958) 165-173; A. M. Habermann, *Megilloth Midbar Yehuda* (Tel Aviv: Maḥberoth Lesifrut, 1959) 188.
41. Millar Burrows, *More Light on the Dead Sea Scrolls* (New York: Viking, 1958) 297-311 apparently believes such a distinction to be captious, reminding us that the sectaries had no way of making a written distinction between Messiah and messiah. While this is quite true, it should be no less evident that *māšîaḥ* was nevertheless capable of being employed in ways other than as the technical term for the object of messianic expectation. The *hakkōhēn hammāšîaḥ* of Lv, at Qumrân or elsewhere, is neither *a* nor *the* Messiah. In a comparable situation, Burrows himself is quick to point out that the *benê-hayyiṣehār* of Zech 4,14 are " 'sons of oil,' not 'Messiahs.' "
42. Theodor H. Gaster, *The Dead Sea Scriptures in English Translation* (Garden City, New York: Doubleday, 1957) 307-310 takes *both* the anointed king and the priest to be simply representatives of the two orders who will be present in the indefinite future. This seems improb-

not peremptory. As Cross has pointed out, the apocalyptic community of Qumrân is at one and the same time the future congregation of the elect and the present sect whose communal life foreshadows the new age.[43] The "messianic banquet" of 1QSa is simply the common meal of the sectaries, at which the Messiah, however, will be present (it is to be noted that "Messiah" and "Messiah of Israel" in this text are synonyms). The priest, therefore, may be simply the priest who *de facto* will be the head of Israel at the time of the Messiah's coming, who is represented here and now in the head of the Qumrân community. In a sense he could be called an eschatological figure, but he is hardly messianic. The role of the (presumed) highpriest in the formula of blessings (1QSb) is even more ambiguous, though it does seem likely that the *neśî' hā'ēdâ* of the blessings is the Messiah, or Messiah of Israel, elsewhere mentioned. Surely no one would attempt to establish the messianic character of the highpriest on the basis of 1QSb alone; those who find it there do so because of other considerations in other texts.

It might be thought significant that nowhere in the Qumrân literature do we find the expression "Messiah of Aaron" standing alone; the expression itself, as a matter of fact, occurs only the one time, if it occurs at all, as part of the designation of the Messiah of Israel in 1QS 9,11.[44] It is true, in the Damascus document the expression "Messiah of Aaron and Israel" occurs four times (12,23-13,1; 14,18;19,10f. [Charles 9b,10]; 20,1 [Charles 9b,29]: "Messiah from Aaron and from Israel"). The expectation that the fragments of this same work found in 4Q would show the singular Messiah of the Damascus document to be a medieval orthodox correction of a primitive plural Messiahs has not been realized: the singular occurs in the oldest exemplar of the document, which Milik dates 75-50 B.C.[45] This also rules out the suggestion that the repeated preposition of 20,1 indicated two Messiahs; the Damascus document clearly knows but one. That one, according to Milik, is the priestly Messiah who has taken over the title of the royal Messiah. The evidence does not seem to justify this assertion. "Aaron and Israel" appears to have meant simply "all Israel," that is, as embracing both the priestly and the lay elements (cf. 1,4-7, where *mîyiśrā'ēl ûmē'ahăron šôreš=še'êrît leyiśrā'ēl*; cf. also 10,5f.; in 1QM 3,12f. *yiśrā'ēl we'ahărôn='am 'ēl;* cf. also 5,1); therefore, "the Messiah of Aaron and Israel" corresponds to "the Messiah of all Israel."

---

able; *be'aḥărit hayyāmim,* which Gaster translates "in the future," doubtless means "at the end of time," given the eschatological preoccupations of the sectaries.

43. *Ancient Library,* 64, ftn. 63. Cf. also Edmund F. Sutcliffe, S.J., *The Monks of Qumran* (Westminster, Maryland: Newman, 1960) 111.

44. And for this reason it can scarcely be said that "the coming of two anointed chiefs" is "the main doctrine of the sect" on which supposition the whole of its messianism is to be restored. So Yigael Yadin, "A Crucial Passage in the Dead Sea Scrolls, 1QSa ii.11-17," *JBL* 78 (1959) 238-241.

45. Cf. Milik, *Ten Years* 125f.

He may, indeed, have been conceived as a priestly Messiah, but there is no proof of this. In view of the extraordinary denigration of David in 5,2-6 it may very well be, as Charles suggested,[46] that a non-Davidic Messiah was expected. The Damascus document, in other words, could be projecting the thought of Ben Sira into the eschatological future. It is perhaps worthy of note that the *n^e^śî' kol hā'ēdâ* of 7,20 (cf. the *n^e^śî' hā'ēdâ* of 1QSb), presumably the Messiah of Aaron and Israel, had an echo in the *n^e^śî' yiśrā'ēl* title of Bar Kochba, the non-Davidic Messiah proclaimed by Rabbi Akiba. All in all, though their affinities are plain, the Damascus document and the Qumrân literature contain too many obscurities to permit us as yet to explain the messianism of the one by the other.[47]

The rest of the original Qumrân material sheds no further light on an Aaronic Messiah. The War scroll makes frequent enough reference to the *kôhēn hārō'š,* but the highpriest of this document is no more eschatological than are the Levites, the other priests, and all the others who take part in the battle array. Strangely, the Messiah of Israel is not mentioned in connection with this eschatological battle; it is not immediately evident that the *n^e^śî' kôl hā'ēdâ* of 5,1 is the Messiah. Once again, as with the "messianic banquet," we seem to have merely a projection of existing Qumrân institutions (or would-be institutions) into the eschatological future.

Neither has the later Qumrân material provided as yet any solution to our problem. Documents published by John M. Allegro have satisfactorily defined the character of the Messiah of Israel, but say nothing of a Messiah of Aaron.[48] 4QpGen 49 (provisionally termed 4Q Patriarchal Blessings by Allegro), a *pēšer* on Gn 49,10, makes it quite clear that the Qumrân Messiah was the standard Davidic one of the tribe of Judah—something that, surprisingly enough, is not clear from the material that we have surveyed above. A second document, entitled by Allegro 4Q Florilegium, couples a *dôrēš hattôrâ* with the Davidic Messiah (*ṣemaḥ dāwîd*). Allegro identified this expounder of the Law with "the Messiah of Aaron." However, *dôrēš hattôrâ* is a fairly common figure in the Qumrân literature and the Damascus document, a figure who is not necessarily eschatological or even individualized. There seems to be no reason whatever to make him an Aaronic Messiah.[49] 4QpIs^a appears to speak of the Messiah (again explicitly identified as Davidic) as receiving priestly instruction (Fragment D, line 7f.), but priests are in question (*kôhănê haššēm*), not a priestly Messiah. 4Q Testimonia, doubtless the most important docu-

---

46. *Apocrypha and Pseudepigrapha,* 2, 795f.
47. Cf. Morton Smith, "What is Implied by the Variety of Messianic Figures?" *JBL* 78 (1959) 66-72. The writer, however, would not accept Smith's conclusion that no systematization was attempted by the sectaries or should be attempted by us.
48. "Further Messianic References in Qumran Literature," *JBL* 75 (1956) 174-187.
49. Cf. Brown, *CBQ* 19 (1957) 80f.

ment of the lot published by Allegro, is a catena of texts (from Ex, Nm, Dt, and an apocryphal 4Q Psalms of Joshua) which combine the prophetic, priestly, and royal aspects of messianism without distinguishing Messiahs; in view of the last text, which is not messianic, Allegro himself concludes that the common denominator of the texts is not messianism but eschatological doom.[50]

That the priesthood should figure largely in the eschatology of these true sons of Zadok is hardly to be wondered. However, to reconstruct from this the doctrine of a priestly *Messiah,* in all the technicality that we have the right to associate with this term, is, in the writer's opinion, an adventuresome step that has been too hastily taken.

The same judgment may be offered in respect to this entire investigation of the Judaism of the late biblical and intertestamental periods. Throughout the postexilic age the priesthood preoccupied the life and thought of Judaism, and this preoccupation inevitably affected Jewish eschatology in various ways. There is, however, no invariable pattern to this preoccupation, which was capable of quite disparate affirmations. It does not appear that in these affirmations there was sufficient consistency to allow us to speak of a Levitical messianism that either supplanted or shared the Davidic messianic expectation. We can speak of a priestly Messiah only by making the word "Messiah" mean something quite different from the meaning it has traditionally had both in Jewish and in Christian thinking.

The New Testament

If the line of reasoning we have followed above is correct, we should expect to find it confirmed by what we discover in the NT. There was, as we saw, a strand of Jewish thinking that brought a priestly figure into conjunction with the Davidic Messiah. We find that strand in the Gospels in the figure of John the Baptist, who is represented as Elijah the "restorer" of Mal 3,23f. (cf. Mt 17,12 *apokatastései,* Mk 9,12 *apokathistánei,* Mal 3,24 [LXX 4,6] *apokatastései*; also *apokathistáneis* in the question addressed by the as yet uncomprehending disciples to our Lord in Acts 1,6). It is true, the main emphasis of the Gospels is on John's and Elijah's prophetical status, not the priestly. Luke, however, is insistent on the Baptist's priestly origins: not only is he the son of a priest, but also of a mother who was a daughter of Aaron. John, therefore, was of priestly birth in the fullest sense.[51] That the Elijah-to-come would also be the eschatological Levitical highpriest who would anoint the Messiah was one form of the Jewish Elijah-expectation.[52]

---

50. Cf. also Patrick W. Skehan, "The Period of the Biblical Texts from Khirbet Qumrân," *CBQ* 19 (1957) 435-437.
51. Cf. Alfred Plummer, *A Critical and Exegetical Commentary on the Gospel According to St. Luke* (ICC; New York: Scribners, 1920) 9.
52. Cf. Joachim Jeremias, "*'Ēl (e) ias,*" *ThWNT* 2, 934f.; Strack-Billerbeck, *Kommentar zum Neuen Testament aus Talmud und Midrasch* (Munich: C. H. Beck, 1928) IV, 789-798; Joseph Klausner, *The Messianic Idea in*

This identification of the Baptist with Elijah the highpriest is certainly not one of the major emphases of the NT. What is equally clear is that when the NT attributes a priestly character to our Lord it is in no way dependent on the Levitical speculation of which we have been speaking above. Quite to the contrary, this attribution is premised on precisely the denial of what this speculation presupposed. The speculation, in whatever form it took, presupposed a covenant with Levi that would endure; the priesthood of Christ supposes that the Levitical priesthood has been definitely superseded. The Levitical speculation understood a renewed covenant with an entirely new priesthood.

According to Hebrews, Christ's priesthood is that of Melchizedek. Despite the claim that the author of Heb was dependent on the Alexandrian school of Philo for his Melchizedekian doctrine,[53] it should be quite evident that the resemblances are purely verbal.[54] It is hard to see how Cullmann—who, for that matter, completely confuses the Levitical and Melchizedekian highpriestly concepts in his search for a background for the NT doctrine—can instance Philo among those who treated of Melchizedek "eschatologically."[55] Philo's Melchizedekian "doctrine" (in *Leg. All.* III, 79-82 [*lógos*];*De Cong.* 99 [*automathê kai autodidakton*]; *De Abrahamo* 235, etc.) is the purest allegorism, totally unrelated to any history or eschaton. The treatment in Heb, on the contrary, exploits an historical typology, whose controlling term is throughout the antitype, and whose purpose is to explain the disappearance of Levitical cult and covenant. There is in Heb no Melchizedekian speculation for its own sake. It is to be noted, too, that Philo's celebrated dictum, *"légomen gàr tòn archieréa ouk ánthrōpon allà lógon theîon eînai pántōn ouch 'ekousiōn mónon allà kaì akousiōn adikēmátōn amétochon,"* was written as an allegorization of Nm 35,29 (in reference to the Levitical highpriest), the literal sense of which Philo considered an absurdity (*De Fug.* 108).

The doctrine of Heb is not the end result of a Jewish speculation, but a new revelation. Ps 110 and its Melchizedekian figure, when taken

---

Israel, tr. by W. F. Stinespring (New York: Macmillan, 1955) 456. This identification was based, in part, on the association of Mal 3,1-3 with 3,23f.

53. Cf. H. von Soden, *Hebräerbrief* (HCzNT; Tübingen: J.C.B. Mohr, ³1899) 6, 60f. This hasty conclusion of the older commentators has been almost completely abandoned today, cf. C. Spicq, O.P., *L'épître aux Hébreux* (EB; Paris: Gabalda, 1953) I, 39ff.; Otto Michel, *Der Brief an die Hebräer* (KEKNT; Göttingen: Vandenhoeck & Ruprecht, ¹¹ 1960) 16-27, 159f., 372f. However, Jean Héring, *Le royaume de Dieu et sa venue* (Neuchâtel: Delachaux & Niestlé, ²1959) 74 still makes Ps 110, Philo, and Heb together depend on a "mythe melchisédechien."
54. Cf. H. Windisch, *Hebräerbrief* (HzNT; Tübingen: J.C.B. Mohr, 1913) 58f.; Otto Michel, *"Melchisedék," ThWNT* 4, 574f.; Gottlob Schrenck, *"archiereús," ThWNT* 3, 275f.
55. Oscar Cullmann, *The Christology of the New Testament,* tr. by Shirley Guthrie and Charles Hall (London: SMC Press, 1959) 85.

messianically, could only be an embarrassment to Judaism.[56] What made it an embarrassment and what made it impossible to integrate Melchizedek into the Jewish messianic expectation, are capitalized on by the author of Hebrews. Faced with a new fact, that the awaited Savior had combined in himself both the Davidic hope and a priestly character, this author did what Judaism could not. He dispensed with the Levitical priesthood and consequently with the Mosaic Law, and appealed for his justification in prophecy to the typology of Melchizedek.

The other parts of the NT that identify Jesus as priest must also be independent of and in conflict with any conception of the continuation of a Levitical priesthood, for the reason made explicit in Heb 7,13f.[57] Jesus' depreciation of the temple in favor of his own mission (Mt 12,6), his substitution of himself for the temple (Jn 2,19; Lk-Acts), his repeated application to himself of Ps 110 (Mk 12,35ff. par. 14,62 par.), and the highpriestly prayer of John's Gospel, all presuppose a new priesthood that was not that of Levi and Aaron.

One may say, with Condamin, that Jesus Christ has fulfilled the spirit rather than the letter of OT prophecy and has realized its priestly ideal.[58] This is very true. But it seems more important to insist that the Christ-event, in its unicity, so far transcends the OT expectation as to have made all its expressions an inadequate anticipation. If this truth can be seen with more clarity here than in the apparently more literal fulfilment of the Davidic hope which was exploited so enthusiastically by the NT, still, in the one as in the other, fulfilment brought with it quite as much of the unexpected as it did of the expected.

---

56. Cf. Strack-Billerbeck, *Kommentar*, 4, 460-462.
57. Cf. Cullmann, *Christology*, 87-89, 104-107.
58. Condamin, *Jérémie*, 248: "On peut dire aussi que le prophète était éclairé par une lumière divine sur les traits essentiels du salut messianique, et non point sur le temps, les circonstances, les détails; pour ceci, il était laissé à ses conjectures probables, comme S. Pierre le note expressément I Pt 1,10-11."

THE QUMRAN RESERVOIRS

ROBERT NORTH, S.J.

The facts concerning the Dead Sea community have long riveted public attention. Their elaborate water-storage system is the most striking feature of the building they inhabited. And their writings suggest that these water-reserves served at least in part for a purification ritual.

Experts have already in passing broached all plausible variations explanatory of these two basic facts. Yet it would seem that no exhaustive analysis of them has been undertaken for its own sake, and that this would be a useful tribute to our honored teacher.

Literary Evidences

We will begin with a simple enumeration of the literary elements of our problem.[1]

SEREK HA-YAḤAD (COMMUNITY RULE)

1,16 - 2,18 The elaborate initiation ceremony for postulants (as also its referral in 5, 8) contains no utterance which could possibly be conceived as relating to a water-purification rite.

3,4-9 A proscription of the impenitent who are to be excluded from the community. This comes, not in connection with the reception rite, but after a passage prescribing annual reappraisal of even the most venerable members.

4 "Such a man **cannot be cleared by mere ceremonies of atonement** (*lô yukkeh b^{e}-kippurim*), **nor cleansed** (*yiṭhar*) **by any waters of ablution** (*niddâ*), **nor sanctified by [immersion in] lakes** (*b^{e}yammim*)
5 **or rivers, nor purified** (*yiṭhar*) **by any bath** (*mê raḥaṣ*). Unclean, unclean he remains so long as he rejects the government of God and
6 refuses the discipline [of communion with him] (*beyaḥad 'eṣatô*: in the community of his Essa[2]). For it is only through the [spiritual

1. Not only for convenience, but in view of its wide accessibility, we follow the edition of Theodor H. Gaster, *The Dead Sea Scriptures in English Translation* (New York: Doubleday Anchor, 1956), with our own occasional divergent renditions as [H:]. We have collated the Hebrew text from the realistic scroll-form facsimile of P. Boccaccio and P. Berardi (Fano: Seminary, 1953) based with permission upon the editions of M. Burrows (New Haven: American Schools, 1951) and Y. Yadin-Sukenik (Jerusalem: Bialik, 1954).
2. *'Êṣâ*, the Hebrew "council", would quite normally be transcribed in Greek as Essa, and thereby provide for Essene a derivation as plausible

apprehension] (*ru^{a}ḥ 'eṣat* = spirit of the Essa) of God's truth that man's ways can be [properly directed. Only thus can all his iniquities
7 be shriven] (*y^{e}kupp^{e}rû kol 'awônôtaw* = [his ways be] cleansed of all their iniquities) so that he can gaze upon the true light of life. Only through the Holy Spirit can he [achieve] union with (*leyaḥad* = unto the community of) God's truth [and] be purged of all his
8 iniquities.[3] Only by a spirit of uprightness and humility can his sin be atoned. Only by a submission of his soul to all the ordinances
9 of God can his flesh be made clean (*yiṭhar*). **Only thus can it really be sprinkled with waters of ablution. Only thus can it really be sanctified by waters of purification."**[4]

3,19 "The origin of truth lies in the fountain of light, and that of perversity in the Wellspring of Darkness."[5]

---

as any of the numerous others which have been suggested [A. Dupont-Sommer, *The Jewish Sect of Qumran and the Essenes* (New York, 1956 =*Nouveaux aperçus*; Paris: 1953) p. 92, and now *The Essene Writings from Qumran* (Oxford: Blackwell, 1961) 21n.3; 43]: despite the recent categorical rejection of Henri Serouya, *Les Esséniens* (Paris: Calmann-Lévy, 1959) 69n.—Jean-Paul Audet, "Qumran et la notice de Pline sur les Esséniens", *Revue Biblique* 68/3 (July 1961) 346-387 links *Ess-* of Essene rather with Ḥaṣaṣon[-Tamar] of 2 Chr 20,2 (p. 378); "this takes nothing from Qumran . . . except the right to be confused with Essenism". Despite the words "enter" and "admitted" in Gaster (*Serek* 2,25 has only *bō'* in 2,25 and a lacuna in 2,26) and the more cogent mention of "material resources" (*hôn, Serek* 3,2) not to be accepted into the *'Eṣâ* of the *Yaḥad*, it would seem that these strictures apply to the *dismissal* of members at any time as well as the refusal of admission.

3. The eloquent demand of interior dispositions is altogether conformed to the highest Jewish and Christian ideal; and as in Jer 7,4.22; Os 8, 13; Am 5,25; Heb 10,4, it does not disapprove but rather presupposes the use of that purification-rite which it calls inadequate. This problem is examined by Edmund F. Sutcliffe, "Baptism and Baptismal Rites at Qumran?", *Heythrop Journal* 1/3 (July 1960) 177-188.
4. Gaster p. 42-43.—For this obligatory water-purification rite, four separate techniques are expressly presupposed: sprinkling, [immersion in] a lake, [immersion in] a river, or washing in a bath. (The Hebrew root *ṭbl* which generally corresponds to the Greek *baptism* does not occur here.) The "river" would be presumably the Jordan, accessible at some five miles northeast of Qumran. "Lake" could be applied to the Dead Sea one mile east, or possibly to Fashkha-springs pool two miles south.—This passage *Serek* 3,4-9 is claimed by Otto Betz, "Die Proselytentaufe der Qumransekte und die Taufe im Neuen Testament", *Revue de Qumran* 1/2 (Oct. 1958) 213-234: p. 216, as the proof that *initiation* ceremonies included baptism. W. H. Brownlee, "John the Baptist in the New Light of Ancient Scrolls", *Interpretation* 9 (1955) 71-90, reprinted in K. Stendahl, *Scrolls and the New Testament* (New York: Harpers, 1957) 33-53, on p. 40, disallows this on the ground that the rite here is clearly to be repeated, and he claims that *Serek* 5,12 implies the *initiation* rite.
5. Gaster p. 43; more literally "In the springs (*mā'ôn*) of light are the generations of truth, and from the source (*māqôr*) of darkness the generations of perversity." Compare *Serek* 10,12, detached in Gaster p. 117 "Fountain of all knowledge, spring of holiness", and 11,6-7 p. 120 "Fount of righteousness, reservoir (*miqweh*) of strength, wellspring of all glory."

The word for water-source used here could perhaps be considered to refer literally to the water-rite from which spiritual truth comes; but then what of the "water" from which obfuscation comes? More plausibly the words are merely metaphorical, but the choice of metaphor may be a clue to the Sect's concrete preoccupations with water-rites.

4,20 [At the 'End'] "God will purge all the acts of man in [the
crucible of] his truth . . . cleansing (*li-ṭ^{e}hôr-ô*) him by the holy
spirit from all the effects of wickedness. **'Like waters of purification**
21 **he will sprinkle upon him the spirit of truth, to cleanse him of**
all the abominations' [H: and he will sprinkle upon him the spirit
22 of truth like purification (*niddâ*) from all abominations] **of**
falsehood and of all 'pollution through' [H: 'wallowing in'] the
spirit of filth."[6]

5,13 "No one is to go into water in order to attain the purity of
14 holy men. For men cannot be purified except they 'repent' ['turn
from'] their evil."[7]

The apparent sense here that all water-rites are forbidden is not nearly as strong as the implications of preceding passages that water-rites were in fact being used. However, we have here a point-blank direct statement whereas all other *Serek* references are mere implications.—More literally this passage might be taken to exclude total immersion as distinct from sprinkling or even bathing. But this is not borne out by the subjoined motive.—The prohibition does not seem to form part of the rite of postulant-reception which is repeated (from 1,16) in 5,7; since 5,10 has mean-

---

6. Gaster p. 45.—Here it would seem that the giving of "Truth" bears only a transferred or metaphorical relation to the water-rite, which here appears to consist in *sprinkling*.
7. Gaster p. 48. On p. 97 is the note "This is not a protest against baptism, as has been supposed [source not indicated], but rather against the idea that the act of immersion can *by itself* absolve sins."

   This is one of the passages cited by Oscar Cullmann, "Die neuentdeckten Qumrantexte und das Judenchristentum der Pseudoklementinen", in R. Bultmann Festschrift *Neutestamentliche Studien* BZNW 21 (1954) 35-51; 44, as part of his thesis that the Ebyonites were Qumranites who came over into Christianity; further "The Significance of the Qumran Texts for Research into the Beginnings of Christianity", *Journal of Biblical Literature* 74 (1955) 220. In a quite sweeping refutation of this thesis in dependence upon W. F. Albright, this passage is noted by Joseph A. Fitzmyer, "The Qumrân Scrolls, the Ebionites and their Literature", *Theological Studies* 16/3 (July 1955) 335-372 [reprinted in Krister Stendahl, *The Scrolls and the New Testament* (New York: Harpers, 1957) 208-23; see footnotes 40 and 77 below]. In note 74 of p. 363 is the rhetorical question "Are we sure that [IQS] 6:13ff refer to baths?" It would seem that 5,13 is meant; and the next page states "the passage in 5,13 may well allude to some bathing practice", and indeed more so than S 3, 3-6, which could just as well be "a rhetorical way of stressing the uncleanness and guilt of the man who rejects God's laws". Fitzmyer's note adds, "M. H. Gottstein, 'Anti-Essene Traits in the DSS', *Vetus Testamentum* 4(1954) 141-7, has gone to an opposite extreme in maintaining that the Qumrân sect was not a baptist sect, whereas the Essenes are known to have been definitely such." So also Millar Burrows, *Dead Sea Scrolls* (New York: Viking, 1955) 286: "There is no real reason to suppose that the attitude of the Essenes was essentially different from that expressed in the Manual of Discipline."

while treated the conduct of the initiate after his reception. There might well be question, however, of excluding the novice from customary water-rites for the year following his reception, in the light of the next citation.

6,16 " 'No candidate is to be admitted to the formal state of purity enjoyed by the general membership of the community' ['When (admitted by vote) one enters into the *'Eṣa* of the *Yaḥad,* he shall not
17 touch the Purity of the Many'] until, at the completion of a full year, his spiritual attitude and performance have been duly reviewed."[8]

Serek-b: It is noteworthy that neither in this important description of the controvertedly "sacred" Repast, nor in any above reference to water-rites, is there hinted a connection between the two: as is the case in Josephus' description of the Essenes.[9]

HODAYOT

Column 8: The only references to water (apart from *mire* or two metaphors of the hostile sea) are here in several allusions to waters "of holiness" in Eden or "of fertility" on earth, not implying purification rites.[10]

12,5 "Spring of knowledge, fountain of strength, waters unstinted, flood of ḥesed" metaphors as Serek 4,1 above.[11]

PESHARIM (HAB MICH NAH PS) AND BLESSINGS

No relevant allusions.

WAR

7,6 No one not cleansed of a bodily discharge is to go into battle.[12]

14,3 On return from battle, wash selves and garments clean of the blood of guilty corpses.[13]

FRAGMENTS

300 fragments from Cave 4 have been assembled in seven panels whose obverse gives "directives and prayer for a purification rite".[14]

CAIRO ṢADOQITE 'DAMASCUS' DOCUMENT

3,14 "He opened for them a well with water abounding, which they might dig. But them that spurned those waters he did not permit to live."[15]

6,1 "And these men 'dug the well', that well of which it is written

---

8. Gaster p. 51; p. 98 compares Josephus *War* 2 (137), 8,7: an Essene postulant was not admitted to "the holier water of purification" until after a year's probation.—Even apart from the significant Josephus-Essene parallel, the authorization of *Serek* 6,17 to "*touch* the Purity" only one year after the reception-ceremony, may well seem to imply purification by water-rite.
9. Gaster p. 309: *Serek-b* [D. Barthélemy-J. Milik, *Qumran Cave I* (Oxford: 1955) Plate 24] lines 3-20.
10. Gaster p. 166. Also *Ho*[*dayot*] 10,20, p. 175.
11. Gaster p. 183; cf. *Ho* 18,15, p. 200.
12. Gaster p. 290.
13. Gaster p. 299.
14. Claus-Hunno Hunzinger, "Le travail d'édition", *Revue Biblique* 61/1 (Jan. 1956) p. 67.
15. Gaster, *Dead Sea Scriptures,* p. 65.

'Princes dug it, nobles of the people delved it, with the aid of a *meḥôqeq*'. The 'well' in question is the Law."[16]

8,5 "All who turned away from the well of living waters shall not be reckoned with the community.'[17]

8,12 The only references to initiation-ceremony are oblique and do not mention water-rites.[18]

10,10 "Now concerning purification by water. No one is to bathe in
11 water that is dirty or too shallow. No one is to purify himself with water in a vessel or in a rock-pool that is too shallow. If an
12 unclean person come in contact with such water, he merely
13 renders it unclean; and the same is true of water drawn in a vessel."[19]

The last passage may be regarded as prescribing rather than merely prohibiting certain ritual-washings. All in all, though, it is surprising how silent or metaphorical or negative on this subject is this "code", as are all the Qumran finds except its "code".

Essene Portrayals

We repeat here our declaration "Specifically *we do not reject,* but rather acknowledge as commonly accepted, the identification with the Essenes, though there is still room for discussion and dissent on this hypothesis", and room especially for solving the problem of *why* the Qumran documents refer to their members as Sadducees (=*benê Ṣadoq*) whence the title of that article,[20] which has surprisingly been taken as disclaiming these obvious Essene links: an example perhaps of what scholarly conventions call "reading a paper by title".

Yet we still maintain with a significant group of commentators that the

---

16. Gaster, *Dead Sea Scriptures,* p. 68.
17. Gaster p. 72.
18. Gaster p. 72.
19. Gaster p. 77 notes that this portion of the manuscript applies to "*City*-communities". In the later regulations which he considers specific for *camp*-communities, no similar rite is described. It may be noted that in our opinion, admitted by several authorities, the territory called here "land of Damascus" is not the *city* of Damascus at all, and may well be the Qumran desert-camp itself. R. North, "The Damascus of Qumran Geography", *Palestine Exploration Quarterly* 87/1 (January 1955) 34-48; Millar Burrows, *More Light on the Dead Sea Scrolls* (New York: Viking, 1958) 219; Duncan Howlett, *The Essenes and Christianity* (New York: Harper, 1957) 115.—Jean Daniélou, *The Dead Sea Scrolls and Primitive Christianity* (Baltimore: Helicon, 1958) 97, expresses favor for the view of B. Z. Lurie, "History of the Jewish Community of Damascus", *Eretz-Israel Annual* [in Hebrew, Jerusalem, 1956; see our review in *Verbum Domini* 35/1 (Feb. 1957) 48] 4,111-18, making the town "Kokba" near Damascus a home of both Dositheus and the Zadokites.
20. R. North, "The Qumran 'Sadducees'" *Catholic Biblical Quarterly* 17/2 (O'Hara Festschrift, May 1955) 164. For pre-twentieth-century evaluation of the Essenes see now Siegfried Wagner, *Die Essener in der wissenschaftlichen Diskussion bis zum Beginn des 20. Jahrhunderts* (BZAW 79; Berlin: Töpelmann, 1960); alleged influence on John Baptist is noted p. 177; on Ebyonites p. 185; on Jewish baptism p. 233.

numerous striking identities between portrayals of the Essene and Qumran communities are not yet sufficient to warrant simply interchanging the terms in accurate scientific discussion. Nor do we see ultimate compelling force in the fact that no *other* historically-recorded group better fits the Qumran data than do the Essenes; it would be just as logical to conclude that the Essenes are identical with New Testament Christians, who never call themselves "Essenes" but never disclaim connection, and in an intriguingly close time-space context exhibit (along with noteworthy differences) closer kinship to the Essenes than to Pharisees, Sadducees, or Zealots.

It remains perfectly true and significant that the three ancient portrayals of the Essenes supply numerous details obviously similar and relevant to Qumran practice, which it would be unwarranted to overlook.

JOSEPHUS

W 2(123),8,3, "They think that oil is a defilement and wipe it off; they think sweat is a good thing."

W 2(129),8,5 "They labor diligently until 11 a.m. Then they **assemble in one place, put on white loin-cloths, and bathe their bodies in cold water.** After this they meet together in a building of their own, into which it is not permitted to any of another sect to enter. They go, **after a pure manner, into the dining-room as into a holy temple,**[130] and quietly sit down. [Then they go back to work][132] and afterwards return to supper, after the same manner."

W 2(137),8,7 "If anyone would come over to their sect, he is not immediately admitted, but he is prescribed the same method of living which they use, for a year, while he continues excluded. They give him a small hatchet, and the loin-cloth, and a white garment.[138] But when he has given evidence that he can observe their continence, he approaches nearer to their way of living, and is made a **partaker of the waters of purification;** yet even after this . . . he is tried for two more years [then must take certain oaths but no special ritual bath][139] before he is allowed to touch the common food."

W 2(147),8,9 "On the sabbath they do not go to stool;[148] on other days they dig a pit with the hatchet and cover it over afterwards, and wash themselves after, as if it were a defilement to them, though it is natural."

W 2(150),8,10 "If the seniors are touched by the juniors, they must wash afterward as if they had mixed with outsiders."[21]

W 2(161),8,13 [In the "marrying branch"] "the women go into the baths with some of their garments on, as the men go with a loin-cloth."

Ant 18(19),1,5 "When they send what they have dedicated to God into the temple, **they do not offer sacrifices, 'because they have more pure lustrations of their own'** [so Whiston: in Greek merely *diaphorótēti hagneiôn*]: on which account they are excluded from the common

21. Special importance is attached to this prescription by Joachim Gnilka, "Die essenischen Tauchbäder und die Johannestaufe", *Revue de Qumran* 3/10 (May 1961) 185-207; p. 187; and Joseph M. Baumgarten, "Sacrifice and Worship among the Jewish Sectarians of the Dead Sea (Qumrân) Scrolls", *Harvard Theological Review* 46/4 (Oct. 1953) 156.

court of the temple, but offer their sacrifices themselves."

No reference to water-ritual occurs in the minor allusions of Josephus: Ant 13 (172) ,5,9: Essenes hold fate governs all; 15 (371) ,10,4: live like Pythagoreans.

PHILO, PLINY

No mention of Essene water-purification.

The Reservoirs as Seen at Present

We have now completed all literary attestations directly relevant to use of water by the Qumran and/or Essene sects. We defer to later consideration all alleged or indirect relevance of John the Baptist or such sects as the Ebyonites and Mandeans. Our next factual material is drawn from the geographical setting and excavated remains of the Qumran community.

The Qumran building is at a distance of one mile southeast of Caves 1 and 2, where the eleven principal Scrolls were found. It is on the same plateau on a spur of which was found the Cave 4 richest in fragments. We have already noted the distances from this building to the Dead Sea a mile east, Fashkha spring two miles south, and the Jordan River five miles northeast. There are also copious springs at Jericho some twelve miles northwest, but virtually none in the whole "Desert of Juda" from Jericho-*Qilṭ* to Jerusalem-*Hôd*.

At present there are apparent to one visiting the site of Qumran, some thirteen reservoirs (chart Fig. 1, indicating photographs Plates I-VIII) . The name reservoir has been chosen with considerable deliberation to describe noncommittally various installations, each open at the surface and extending to various depths below, and large enough for a man to enter. This description fits cistern, pool, bath and *bassin* in the French sense as "St. Lawrence basin". It also fits, by dictionary definition, a place or large receptacle where even dry commodities can be stored, though special suitableness to fluid contents is always connoted. The situation and construction-era of the reservoirs is indicated on the accompanying Fig. 2.[22]

One of the reservoirs was eventually divided into two quite distinct parts, 56 and 58 (Plate IVc) . Another received from the excavators two locus-numbers, 48 and 49, for reasons not discernible, and north of it is a third Locus, 50, which is a separate "cistern, pool, or *bassin*" (all three terms are applied to it) . Locus 85 does not seem to be regarded in the excavation-report as a separate reservoir, perhaps because it merely furnishes the Steps of approach to 91. There is also an extensive area (137-132) now entirely on the surface, but equated by the excavators with other *bassins*, as is the Locus 119 *bis* "under the floor". Thus a total of twenty separately-numbered reservoirs is involved.

---

22. Based on *Catholic Biblical Quarterly* 19/2 (April 1957) 236, my adaptation of Père de Vaux's plan in *RB* 63 (1956) 576, with modifications now suggested by his 1961 Schweich volume. Père de Vaux kindly checked the correctness of locus-numeration of my photos.

The reservoirs generally contain steps, proportioned to the storage-space but really a lion's share in every case. The idealized diagram of Reservoir 48 in Fig. 5 shows how some 39% of the storage-space is lost on account of the stairs. A half-step or even smaller tread is noted at the bottom of the reservoirs 56, 71, and 117. But as a rule the steps run across the whole width of the reservoir.

In several, such as 48 and 71, stair-width is divided into "corridors" by low partitions clearly visible in photograph. (Plates Iab, Va). These partitions vary in height. In cistern 48 some survive to a height surpassing the next higher step. In 117 (Plate Va) they are more solid and stumpy. In 85 (Plate IVb) they have wholly disappeared and are represented merely by attachments left in the plaster of the risers. Our photos of 56 (Plate IVc) and 71 do not show the partitions but we have verified their trace. The most plausible, if not the most obvious, purpose of these partitions would be to enable two rows of persons to descend and return in a continuous line in a liturgical procession, without bumping into each other by reason of preoccupation with their devotions. The explanation of Dupont-Sommer is rather that "Essene baptisteries had different stairs of access in order not to mingle those who had need of a different degree of purification".[23] Another usefulness that has been suggested for the partitions is that of allowing the water to trickle down only that surface of the stair which its volume requires, thus diminishing evaporation.[24]

Naturally the smallest reservoirs do not have stairs across their whole width, but only a little "stepping-point" in the corner, as 83 (Plate IIIb). The round cistern 110 is the only one which exhibits maximum efficiency. As at present visible, it has a winding stair strikingly resembling that of the famed cistern recently discovered at Jîb-Gibeon[25] (Plate VIa). But since the excavation-report declares our reservoir was stairless, presumably the steps were left in place by the excavators to facilitate earthmoving operations. It is a frequent discouraging experience of excavators to see visitors exhibit special interest in such stairs as a uniquely-preserved "antique". The small pools 67, 68, 69, 75 and bath 68 seem to have had no step at all, nor did reservoir 91 (Plate IVa), though 56 seems to have provided originally the staircase for 58 (Plate IVc).

In several cases the reservoir has a built-in shelf or bench, best visible in the photo of 138 (Plate IIIa), along both the long sides.

---

23. Discussion following André Parrot's report, *Revue d'Histoire et de Philosophie Religieuses* 35 (1955) 65.
24. R. de Vaux, *Revue Biblique* 63 (1956) 540 "the partitions directed the flow of water and kept part of the stair dry" [omitted apparently in the parallel 1961 Schweich description]; on the claim of p. 539, "similar cisterns with broad stairs and sometimes partitions on the steps are found at the same period", see text accompanying footnotes 39-48 below.
25. James B. Pritchard, *The Water System of Gibeon* (Philadelphia: Pennsylvania U., 1962).

Fig. 1—Statistical Chart of Data Concerning the Reservoirs

Locus	Called	Length	Width	Estimated Depth[a]	Estimated Gross Volume[a]	Steps	Partition	Ledge	Estimated Net Volume[c]	Facing[c]	Roof	Photo
138	bath	1.7 m	1 m	1.3 m	2.21 m³	6	0	2	1.32 m³	NW	0	Plate IIIa
132-7	bassin	20 m	6 m	0.2 m	24	0	0	0	24	SE	0	
110	round cistern	—	d 5 m	4 m	54.5	b	0	0	54.5	S	0	II b, c
118	cistern	6.2 m	2.5 m	2.5 m	38.75	12	0	2	23.25	NNE	0	
117	cistern	7.4 m	2.5 m	2.5 m	46.25	13	2	2	27.75	SSW	0	V a
119B	covered bassin	2 m	0.7 m	0.2 m	0.28	0	0	0	1.35	E	1	
83	pool	2.2 m	1.6 m	1 m	3.52	3	0	0	2.11	SSW	0	III b
85	steps	3.8 m	2 m	1.5 m	8.4	5	1	0	5.04	SSW	0	IV b
91	cistern	12 m	4.5 m	3 m	162	0	0	0	162	SSW	0	IV a
56	steps	8.8 m	4.5 m	2.5 m	99	14	2	0	59.4	ESE	0	IV c
58	cistern	8 m	4.5 m	2.5 m	90	0	0	0	90	ESE	0	IV c
34	four tiny bassins	1.5 m	1.5 m	0.6 m	1.35	2	0	0	0.25	NNW	1?	
67	pool	1.5 m	1.2 m	1 m	1.8	0	0	0	1.8	ESE	0	
68	bath	2.2 m	2 m	0.6 m	2.64	5	0	1	1.58	WNW	0	
70	pottery pool	2 m	1 m	0.8 m	1.6	0	0	0	1.6	ESE	0	VIII b
69	pottery pool	2 m	1.5 m	0.8 m	2.4	2	0	0	1.4	WNW	0	VIII b
75	pool?	3 m	3 m	0.2 m	1.8	0	0	0	1.8	S	0	VI d
48-49	earthquake cistern	6 m	2.3 m	2.8 m	38.64	14	3	1	23.18	NNE	1?	I a-b
50	bassin	2 m	1.8 m	1.5 m	5.4	1	0	0	3.24	NNE	0	
71	cistern	17.4 m	4.5 m	3 m	225	16	3	0	135	SSW	0	V b
					TOTAL 809.54 m³				TOTAL 620.57 m³			

a. No published figures are available on the depth or volume of the reservoirs. Those given here are merely an educated guess with a view to representing the situation more concretely. b. Actual steps not original. c. On the basis of Fig. 5, the net volume of stepped

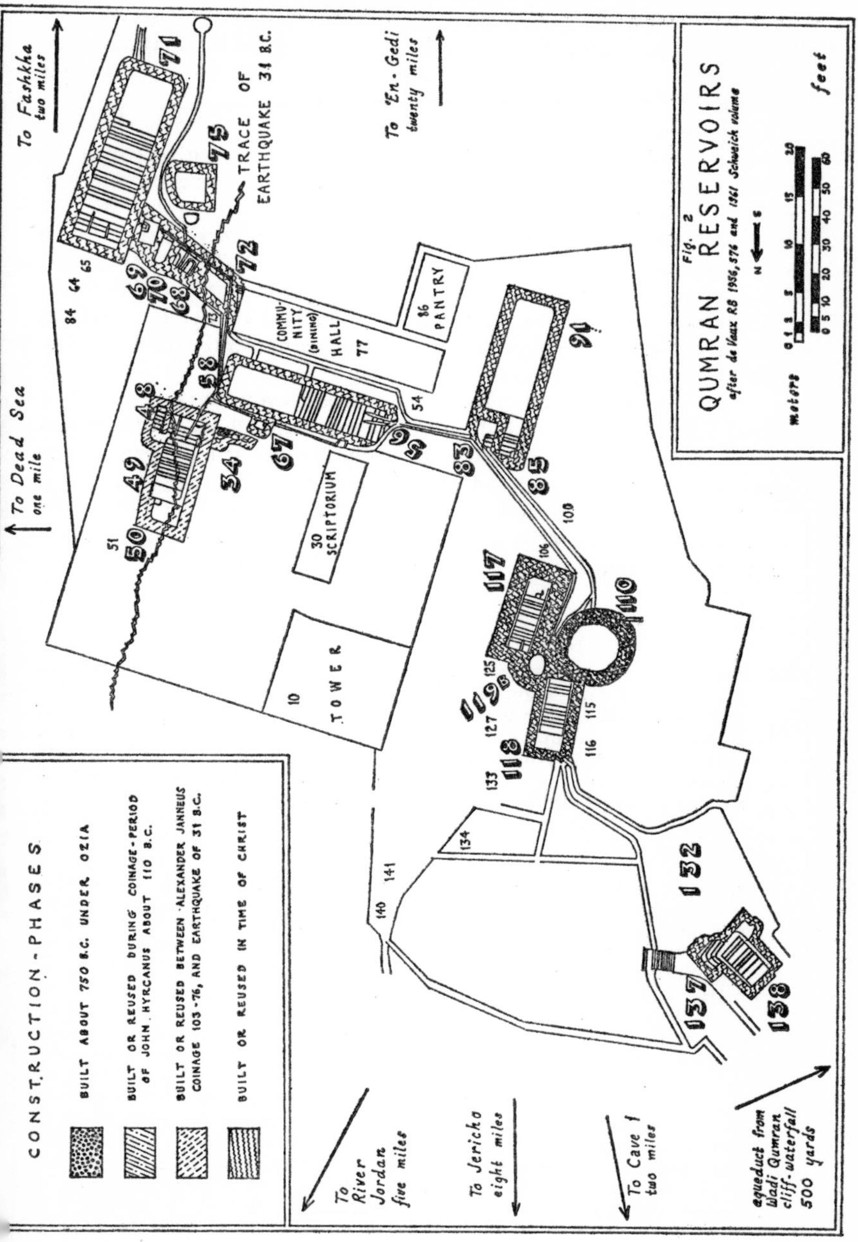
To Dead Sea
one mile
To Fashkha
two miles
TRACE OF EARTHQUAKE 31 B.C.
To 'En-Gedi
twenty miles
COMMUNITY (DINING) HALL 77
86 PANTRY
30 SCRIPTORIUM
10 TOWER
Fig. 2
QUMRAN RESERVOIRS
after de Vaux RB 1956, 576 and 1961 Schweich volume
metres
feet
CONSTRUCTION - PHASES
BUILT ABOUT 750 B.C. UNDER OZIA
BUILT OR REUSED DURING COINAGE-PERIOD OF JOHN HYRCANUS ABOUT 110 B.C.
BUILT OR REUSED BETWEEN ALEXANDER JANNEUS COINAGE 103-76, AND EARTHQUAKE OF 31 B.C.
BUILT OR REUSED IN TIME OF CHRIST
To River Jordan five miles
To Jericho eight miles
To Cave 1 two miles
aqueduct from Wadi Qumran cliff-waterfall 500 yards

The irreverent thought occurs that these would have been suited for sun-bathing; but this is a pursuit quite repugnant in hot climates. We should perhaps reckon with the possibility that the reservoir was used for some industry like tanning or dyeing which may have required that the surface of the water be level with the operator yet protected from spilling over onto the main floor.

The reservoirs are all connected with a single extremely elaborate system of conduits (close-up photo Plate IIa). The spout by which the conduit poured into the reservoir has been interestingly preserved, especially in 83. The conduit-system strongly suggests that *all* the reservoirs were for storing the same substance, namely water, which was brought from the cliff-face of Wadi Qumran (Plate VIIIa, rear left) by an ingenious tunnel and a long aqueduct still visible along the plateau (Plate VIIIa, midground center and right). However, in at least one case the reservoir was shut off permanently from the conduit by subsequent masonry.

ORGANIC DEVELOPMENT OF THE RESERVOIR-SYSTEM

Our Fig. 2 attempts to indicate the construction-dates of the respective reservoirs. The masonry was dated by Père de Vaux chiefly on the basis of coins found scattered about.[26] Five periods interest us:

(a) At an epoch shown by the *pottery* to be long before the earliest Scrolls-community, was built the deepest and only round cistern as part of a primitive but fairly extensive desert-lodge.

---

26. On certain academic issues raised by this dating, our reserves expressed in *Orientalia* 25/1 (Jan. 1956) 91, and *Catholic Biblical Quarterly* 16/3 (July 1954) 434-5, have been largely met by the accurate formulations of de Vaux's "Les manuscrits de Qumrân et l'archéologie", *Revue Biblique* 66/1 (Jan. 1959) 87-110, answering objections of Zeitlin, Dussaud, Teicher, Kahle, Lacheman, and especially H. del Médico, "Sept questions relatives aux ruines de Qumran", *Sanctuaires et pèlerinages* 9 (1957) 1-12, and *L'énigme des manuscrits* (Paris 1957). A comparison of pages 92 and 99 of this article of de Vaux will show how fully he admits that the ultimate criterion [contrary to usages normally insisted upon: W. F. Albright in Wright-Filson *Westminster Atlas* (Philadelphia: 1945) 10] is *numismatic,* not ceramic. See now my observations on P. Lapp's *Palestinian Ceramic Chronology* 200 B.C.-A.D. 70 (New Haven 1961) in *CBQ* 24/3 (July 1962) 309-313.—In his 1959 Schweich Lectures, *L'Archéologie et les manuscrits de la mer Morte* (London: Oxford, 1961) 17, amid numismatic data considerably augmented since the 1956 *Revue Biblique* report, de Vaux warns that "the data of stratigraphy, pottery, and coins are distorted" by the 1954 École Biblique fellow and excavation-collaborator E. M. Laperrousaz, "Le probème de l'origine des manuscrits découverts près de la mer Morte, à propos d'un livre récent [Dupont-Sommer, *Écrits esséniens* 1959]", *Numen* 7/1 (Jan. 1960) 26-76, especially p. 71 pushing back the abandonment of the monastery from 33 to 67 B.C.; and "Remarques sur les circonstances qui ont entouré la destruction des bâtiments de Qumrân à la fin de la période *Ib* de leur occupation", *Vetus Testamentum* 7 (1957) 337-49; 8 (1958) 92-4. —Fresh appraisal of largely Qumranic material is now available in Robert H. Smith, "The 'Herodian' Lamp of Palestine: Types and Dates", *Berytus* 14/1 (1961) 53-65.

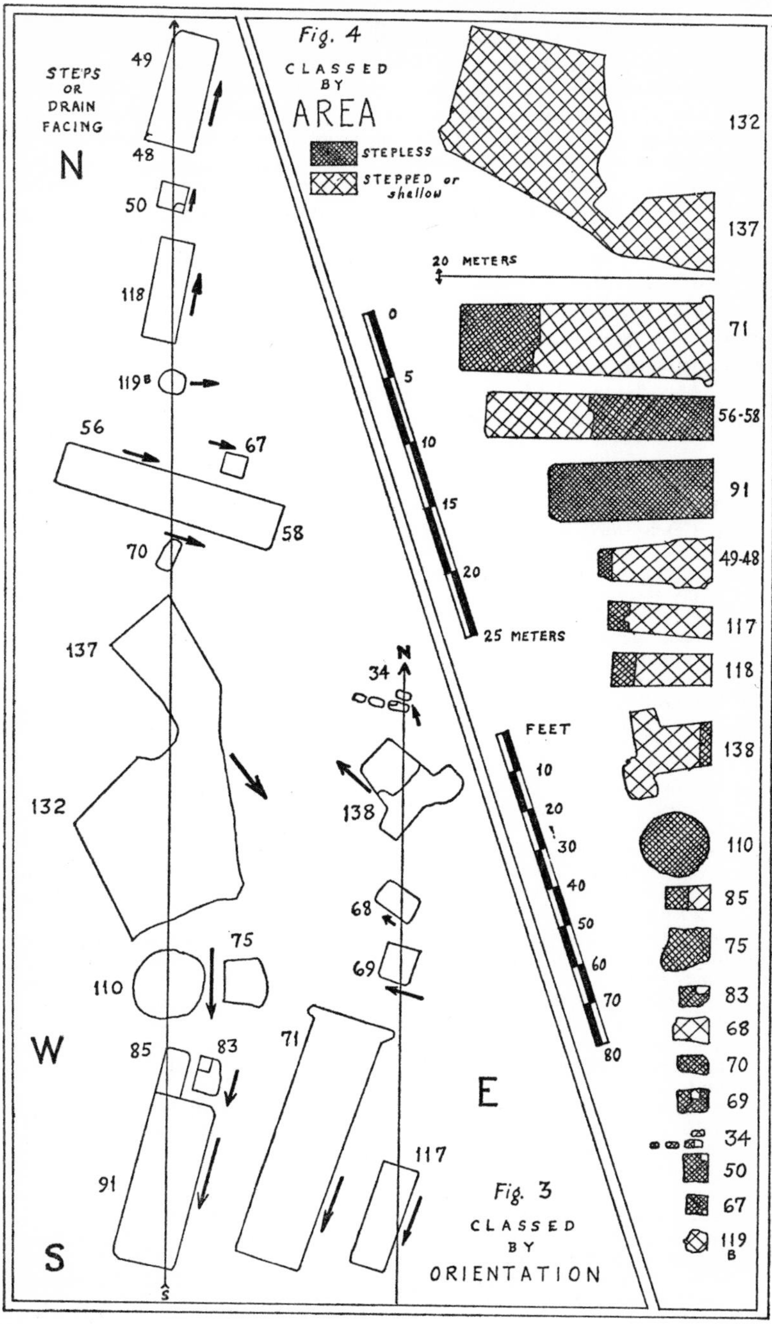

Fig. 4 CLASSED BY AREA

Fig. 3 CLASSED BY ORIENTATION

Scrutiny of biblical data for the period utilizing that type of pottery reveals no relevant fact except that 'Uzzîyâ (Ozias, Uzziah, 783-742 B.C.) according to 2 Chr 26,10 "built towers in the desert and dug many cisterns".[27] Meanwhile the only Qumran-area town attested in the Bible is "Salt City", *ir ha-melaḥ* of Jos 15,62 between "Nibšan" and En-Gedi. Martin Noth's proposal that this was the early name of Qumran itself and of 'Ozia's fort there has been accepted by de Vaux and commonly.[28] One must perhaps wonder whether it is methodically sound to expect in every random notice of the Bible a point-for-point correspondence to the fortuitous discoveries of the terrain. Still, pending positive evidence to the contrary, the rapprochement must stand as both plausible and instructive.

(b) The first members of the community of eventual Scrolls-users arrived at Qumran around 110 B.C., and "utilized the round cistern by means of a canal traced under locus 116 and 115, collecting merely the water running off the esplanade north of the ruins, built at the same time. Also during [this period] Ia were dug the cisterns 117 and 118, and they were fed by the *bassin*."[29]

---

27. This and other details of the monarch's far-flung building activities are not mentioned in the laconic notice of 4 Kgs 14, 21-22, which calls him Azaria. Azaria in 2 Ch 26,20 is the name of the priest by whom 'Ozia's usurping of priestly functions was struck with a "leprosy" which effectively terminated his regime. One is tempted to wonder whether Azaria simply took over as regent for the 25-year-old Joatham (2 Chr 26, 21; 27, 1) and signed the official acts for a long enough time to cause him to be regarded as king in 4 Kgs 14, 21, diverging from 4 Kgs 15, 32.
28. Martin Noth, "Der alttestamentliche Name der Siedlung auf chirbet kumrān", *Zeitschrift des Deutschen Palästina-Vereins* 71(1955) 111-123. It is difficult to understand how this sensible investigator (as also Farmer in footnote 52 below) finds Qumran specially suitable for a settlement from the point of view of water because Fashkha is only 2 km distant. At most one would have to say that this *disadvantage* is relatively slight, but outweighed by *other* advantages of which none can really be indicated, except the "airy [but very low] plateau" as more apt to provide cool freshness than the much higher and easily-scalable Fashkha slope.—It is perhaps not without interest to note here that the Bedouin Ta'āmira tribe destined to become the discoverers of the Dead Sea Scrolls emigrated from North Hejaz to their present haunts in search of water! Originally a group of the Bene-Harit tribe, they mingled in 1602 A.D., with the six autochthonous families of the little tribe called Bayt-'Āmir four miles south of Bethlehem. So Henri V. Vallois, "Les bédouins Taamré du désert de Judée: étude anthropologique", *L'Anthropologie* 63 (1959) 62-92, especially p. 64. *'Āmir* means "ruling"; the *t* of Ta'āmira may thus be a component borrowed from liaison with *Harit* or *Bayt;* or more plausibly perhaps a preformative of the type we have in *ta-LMûD.*
29. Roland de Vaux, "Les fouilles de Khirbet Qumrân: rapport préliminaire", *Revue Biblique* 63/4 (Oct. 1956) 537. [The details from pp. 535-548 which relate to water-installations are reproduced almost unchanged in de Vaux's 1959 Schweich Lectures, *L'archéologie et les manuscrits de la mer Morte* (London: Oxford, 1961) 1-36]. His expression is "bassin de décantation aménagé à l'arrivée du canal dans la citerne 110". He adds that a small canal from the wall closing 101 and 106, to 117, gathered runoff from the south; and a safety-drain went from 110 to the southwest.—Two small kilns of this period stand beneath what later became the cistern-stair 49.

(c) "Ib [c90-31 B.C.]. The extension of the building and the increase in number of its occupants entailed a more stable and abundant water-supply. At this moment was constructed the aqueduct bringing the winter rain-water of Wadi Qumran. It came out at the northwest corner of the ruin at a sluice, where masonry-piles broke the current, locus 137. The water gathered in a large shallow *bassin,* locus 137 and 132. A corner of this *bassin* was occupied by a bath, locus 138 (Planche Va) [our Plate IIa] . . . The outflowing water left the *bassin* by a canal opening from its southeast corner, and cutting the Ia wall of locus 116 and then the Israelite-Ia wall of locus 106. This canal in its course fed the round cistern 110 [our Plate IIbc], and cisterns 117-118. Since this new canal was at a higher level than Ia canal, the round cistern was built up higher and new branch-canals were directed to it and to 117-118 from a *bassin* in 119 *bis,* covered ordinarily by a floor to permit circulation. Overflow of the three cisterns was evacuated by a drain traced under 125, 127, 133, 134, 141, 140, and out. In locus 106, the canal turned southeast and emptied into a small *bassin* 83. This poured westward into the large rectangular cistern 91, [our plate IVa], eastward into the prolongation of the canal. This canal filled the cistern 56/58 [our Plate IVc], turned north to fill 67 then back south. At this point a branch to the north fed cisterns 49 [our Plate Ib] and 50. The canal cut the Israelite-Ia wall of locus 73, filled the little bath 68, and after a final *bassin* 69 came out at the large cistern 71 [our Plate Vb].

"The overflow of the whole system emptied from the large cisterns 91 and 71 by two trickles vanishing in the south esplanade. This water-installation, very carefully worked out, is the most striking characteristic of the Qumran ruin."[30]

A chief feature of this period was a complex little pottery-shop [our Plate VIII b] involving at least four of our smaller reservoirs. "The potter washed his mud in the shallow plastered *bassin* 75; the water came from the principal canal by a conduit emptying into a little cistern [70] adjoining the *bassin.* The bottom of the *bassin* was found covered with a layer of clean mud." The final kneading took place in a vat [68? or 69] adjoining the trench 70. The wheel was in Locus 65, a round stone-lined cavity. The kiln 64 was nearby. In Locus 84 was another kiln for smaller jars.[31]

Loci 115 and 116, which adjoin the main canal and have plastered floors, served for some use for which water was necessary; this is not a euphemism for "water-closet", a name applied plainly to Locus 51. "A conduit, branching off from the principal canal in Locus 54, emptied into Room 77 near its northeast door; this conduit, and the slope of the floor,

30. R. de Vaux, *Revue Biblique* 63, 538-9. He continues "It fits the daily needs of a relatively numerous group who had chosen to live in the desert. It also fits the special needs of a religious community which as their writings attest laid great insistence on purity. Except for the round cistern, which is Israelite, and the large cistern 91, which is for storage, all the cisterns (not counting the annexed *bassins*) have a broad stair occupying at least half their length."
31. R. de Vaux, *Revue Biblique* 63 (1956)543.

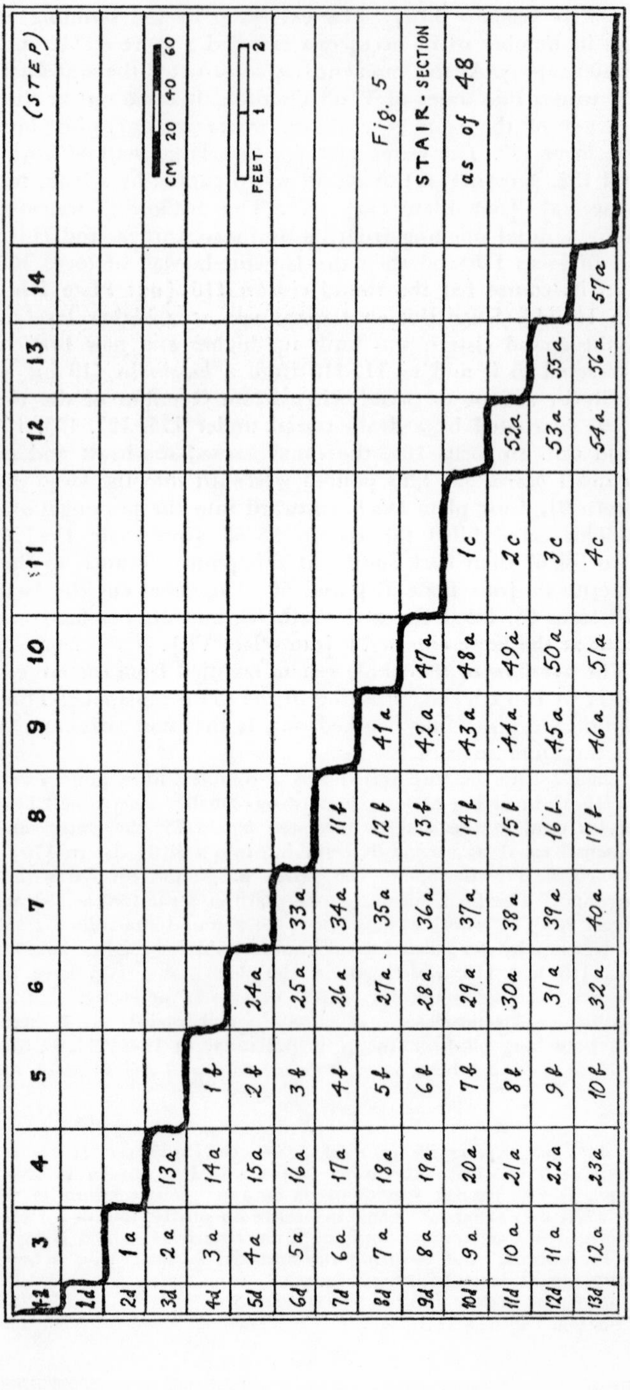
(STEP)
CM 20 40 60
FEET 1 2
Fig. 5
STAIR-SECTION
as of 48

QUMRAN RESERVOIRS

Plate I

Ia, above: Steps 48 of Reservoir 49, showing earthquake dislocation. From N and from below.—Ib, right: Reservoir 49, showing partition-trace on steps, and prolongation above floor-level rear and left. From NW.—Author's photos.

Plate II

IIa, below: Conduit, near Reservoir 110. From S.—IIb, right, above: Round Cistern 110, first constructed 750 B.C. The figure to the right is standing on the stair near the conduit-entry. From S.—IIc, right, below: Close-up of cistern 110. From S.—Author's photos.

Plate III

IIIa, above: Reservoir 138, northwest portion, showing ledges beside steps. From SE.—IIIb, below: Tiny reservoir 83, showing corner steps and entry of conduit. From SE.—Author's photos.

Plate IV

IVa, below, left: Reservoir 91, without steps, showing conduit-entry. From S.—IVb, below, center: Reservoir 85 or steps for 91. Trace of partition visible, also conduit rear and left. In upper right corner are two doorways south of "Tower", leading into Monastery and to Scriptorium. Upper left masonry includes reservoirs 110, 117, 118, 138. From S.—IVc, below, right: Reservoir 58 (foreground) cut off from Steps 56 by subsequent partition. From SE.—Author's photos.

Plate V

Va, right: Reservoir 117, showing partition trace on steps. From S.—Vb, below: Largest reservoir 71, showing north and west of it the whole masonry of the Qumran ruin. Note wall-structure where plaster has fallen away. From S.—Author's photos.

NON-QUMRANIC PARALLELS

Plate VI

VIa, above: Jib (Gibeon). Great cistern with circular stair as excavated by J. B. Pritchard since 1956. Author's photo.—VIb, below: Sabastiya, cistern with steps. From Crowfoot-Kenyon-Sukenik, *Samaria Buildings,* by permission of Palestine Exploration Fund.

NON-QUMRANIC PARALLELS

Plate VII

VIIa, above: Gezer, cis-ern. From R. Macalister, *Excavations of Gezer,* by permission of Palestine Exploration Fund.—VIIb, below: Jerusalem, Tombs of the Kings, underground vaulted cistern with steps. From M. Kon, *Qibrê ha-Melākîm,* by permission of the Dvir Press, Tel Aviv.

Plate VIII

VIIIa, above: Wadi Qumr
from east. The cliff shows trac
of deposit left by waterfall. Ne
it is a tunnel, and from the
an aqueduct leads foregrou
right to the plateau where t
"Monastery" remains stand
right of Cave 4.—VIIIb, le
Pottery workshop area 65-8
showing portion of kiln in for
ground. From NE. — Autho
photos.

permitted easy rinsing . . . : hence, a refectory." The conduit here was closed off in the next occupation-period.[32]

By far the most interesting of the cisterns is 48 [Plate Ia]-49, whose clearly partitioned steps have been equally clearly dislocated by an earthquake.[33] Comparing the earthquakes dated in historical records, with the dating-spread of coins found on the premises, warrants the conclusion that this earthquake was in 31 B.C., and that the survivors immediately abandoned the site. This abandon is in part proved by the neglect and sedimentation of the water-system. The earthquake also pushed the west wall of *bassin* 132 down the ravine.[34]

(d) Period II. The *same* community which had abandoned the site after 31 B.C. is claimed to have returned to reoccupy it anew from 4 B.C. to 68 A.D. The preliminary excavation-report states that the "pools" 49 and 50 are "interior", yet it would seem that no *roofing* has been mentioned other than that of the tower 10a, and the reed-roof over Locus 51 betrayed by abundant ash. It is remarked expressly that such plinths or other hints of roof-support as appeared in Periods

---

32. R. de Vaux, *Revue Biblique* 63 (1956) 541; 546.
33. It is noted by J. van der Ploeg, *The Excavations at Qumran* (London: Longmans, 1958) 64 that *this* reservoir was "cut out of the rock", but this would appear to mean merely that a hole had to be dug under the floor, in the sandy-rock soil, for this as for all the other reservoirs. The actual steps, if not indeed the floor, of the reservoir would seem to be *built up out of masonry* (as the *walls* are evidently in our photo), and the point will be of importance below.
34. R. de Vaux, *Revue Biblique* 63(1956) 544-5.

Observations to the Diagram of page 114 opposite

The proportion of steps to total volume in Reservoir 49-48 may be considered typical, and this is the reservoir of greatest importance and interest, although it has several steps projecting back above floor level, and a sort of annex to the east, both of which may be seen in the photo of Plate I b. The above diagram tries to take account of these irregularities without too far diverging from the normal.

Of the fourteen steps, nine are called "a" and are held to have approximately the forward extension of a normal foot, about 36 cm. Two are called "b", 46 cm., one is "c", 66 cm., and two others are represented by only 6 cm. each ("d") because they are really outside the framework of the reservoir.

To show graphically the volume used up by each step, the vertical space underneath it is divided into boxes of equal height, 20 cm., the height of the risers. Each such box is given the letter of its step, but a separate number.

The vertical area of a is	36 x 20 cm. or	720 cm^2;	57 a = 41040
b =	46 x 20 cm. or	920 cm^2;	17 b = 15640
c =	66 x 20 cm. or	1320 cm^2;	4 c = 5280
d =	12 x 20 cm. or	240 cm^2;	13 d = 3120
			6.5080 m^2

Total area of the vertical section is 2.8 × 6 m = 16.8 m^2

The available space (section of the available volume) is 10.2920 m^2.

Thus 38.74% of the space is taken up with steps, or roughly 40% and 61.26% is available for storage, or roughly 60%.

II and III were always in a re-used condition.[35] This fact, not evident in the report, is of great importance for evaluating the efficiency of the reservoirs for storing water against evaporation.

"South of the building, cistern 56 was divided in two [as appears in our Plate IVc], isolating a new cistern, 58, without stair, fed by a derivation from the canal, running along its north side . . . Toward the north, *bassin* 132 was not repaired. It became a courtyard. But a little *bassin* was kept near the aqueduct, and drained off by a new stretch of canal along the court. . . A [laundry or oven-using] industry was set up in locus 125; water was circulated here by the drain of Ib."[36]

(e) Period III. After the Scrolls-users had completely abandoned the site, it was briefly occupied by a Roman garrison about 90 A.D. They neglected the water-system, but built an awkward canal from locus 100 to 71.[37]

BETHANY; GEZER, 'AZEQA, SAMARIA

The excavator of Qumran's reservoirs declares that contemporary parallels preclude "hastily" postulating for them a cultic or even balneary scope.[38] His primary evidence is drawn from the explanation of a Bethany cistern by his colleague Père Benoit, and from the further parallels there indicated. These include Gezer and Zakariyya. Samaria and the Jerusalem "Tombs of the Kings" pool receive special notice from de Vaux.[39] The verdict of Père de Vaux has been reported as

---

35. R. de Vaux, "Fouilles au Khirbet Qumrân: rapport préliminaire sur la deuxième campagne", *Revue Biblique* 61/2 (Apr. 1954) 209-211. A further statement of p. 211 is corrected in 63 (1956) 454; "After the abandonment of cisterns 49 and 50, the canal which fed them was stopped up; but from the period I*b* on, the canal had continued all the way to the large southeast cistern. This is no innovation of Period II."
36. R. de Vaux, *Revue Biblique* 63 (1956) 546.
37. R. de Vaux, *Revue Biblique* 63 (1956) 547: "Debris-heaps formed in the northwest corner and along the face of cistern 58, covered the bottom of cistern 56, filled the *bassin* 83, and obstructed the stair (85) of cistern 91. Still, the new inhabitants needed water, and anyway they had to keep the site from being inundated by what the aqueduct kept pouring down. A bad leaky canal was built off the old one in Locus 100, [striking illustrations now as Plate XXIVb of de Vaux's 1961 Schweich volume]; it crossed the silted-up cistern 91, cut Locus 86 . . . and fell into the old canal at the southwest corner of Locus 77, thus feeding cistern 71 still in use."
38. R. de Vaux, *Revue Biblique* 63 (1956) 539. It has perhaps not been sufficiently noted that his reserves on cultic-usage were directed primarily not toward the cisterns as such but toward their partitioned staircases. "[This water-installation as described for Period I*b* above] fits the daily needs of a relatively numerous group who had chosen to live in the desert. It also fits the special needs of a religious community which as their writings attest laid great insistence on purity"!
39. R. de Vaux, *L'archéologie et les manuscrits de la mer Morte* (Schweich Lectures, London: 1961) 99: "Similar cisterns with wide descending staircases and [italics mine] ***sometimes partitions on the steps,*** are

definitive in expert surveys.[40] Hence we feel it may be useful to furnish here a detailed analysis with pictures.

Bethany. The description concerns a *cultic grotto*. Its rough natural-stone walls had two layers of plastering (*enduits*) "and as in the case of some Palestine cisterns both could have been put in at the time of the original installation". The parallels to Gezer and Jerusalem here given affect rather the mode of plastering, since up till here no cistern-usage is claimed by Benoit for Bethany and in fact its cultic scope is explicit. However, on the next page in summary it is

---

found *during the same period* . . . to which no ritual usage can be attributed [mild dissent noted regarding "Tombs of Kings" only]. It is even doubtful that they were intended for everyday [the French is *profane*] bathing" except the two small ones 138 and 68 [*RB* 1956, 539 adds "and perhaps 50"] which "were certainly baths, but archeology is impotent to say whether the baths there taken had a ritual character". Père de Vaux is quite right in contending that the *little* baths scarcely even raise the question of cultic scope. This is suggested chiefly by the *biggest* step-cisterns, and that possibility is not here envisioned by him.

40. Tacitly following de Vaux and opposing Dupont-Sommer, Frank Cross in *The Ancient Library of Qumran* [London: 1958; [2]New York: Anchor, 1961] [1]50, [2]67, says that the step cisterns have "produced much fanciful speculation. To those acquainted with Essene habits of baptism, but unacquainted with cistern-types in Roman Palestine, the pools seem admirably designed for bathing rites. Unfortunately the pools are typical examples of water reservoirs well known from other sites [here beside de Vaux is cited Parrot *RHPR* 35, 61-7, in which the only discernible relevance is the mention of Gihon spring on p. 66: see footnote 57 below] . . . On the other hand, two or three small pools are probably baths, including the shallow pool at the entrance way to the settlement. One suspects, however, that the demands of the community for water to be used for drinking and other mundane purposes, as well as water for the ordinary rites of maintaining ritual purity . . . is [*sic*] sufficient explanation for the size of the water system. Probably the ritual baptisms called for the living waters of the Jordan not far distant; possibly the waters of 'En Feškha nearby would have sufficed. In any case, we do not believe they immersed themselves in their drinking water." This insistence that the large reservoirs were not baths is not recalled on p. 177, "The central 'sacraments' of the Essene community appear to be its baptism(s) and its communal meal . . . The Essenes seem to have practised daily priestly lustrations as well as baptism"; and p. 10, "The sectarians are 'baptist' both in their general ideas of purity and in the actual practice of the rites of baptism and lustration." More nuanced, but clearly reflecting de Vaux's data, is the judgment of Joseph A. Fitzmyer, "The Qumrân Scrolls, the Ebionites and their Literature", *Theological Studies* 16 (1955: footnote 7 above) 365: "Partially roofed-over reservoirs, fitted with steps by which one could descend to reach the water-level, are not unknown in Roman Palestine [Gezer, Zakariyya]. We are not trying to exclude the possibility of [Dupont-Sommer's claim of] these installations as bathing-places; it is merely a question of reserving judgment until more convincing evidence is had." Edmund F. Sutcliffe, *The Monks of Qumran* (Westminster: Newman, 1960) 26 "Such steps are found in other contemporary cisterns in Palestine where there is nothing to suggest purificatory rites": de Vaux is *certainly* correct that the cisterns were *probably* used for water-storage; how could the water-supply be kept clean if the cisterns (except perhaps *one* large one, p. 28) were used for bathing?

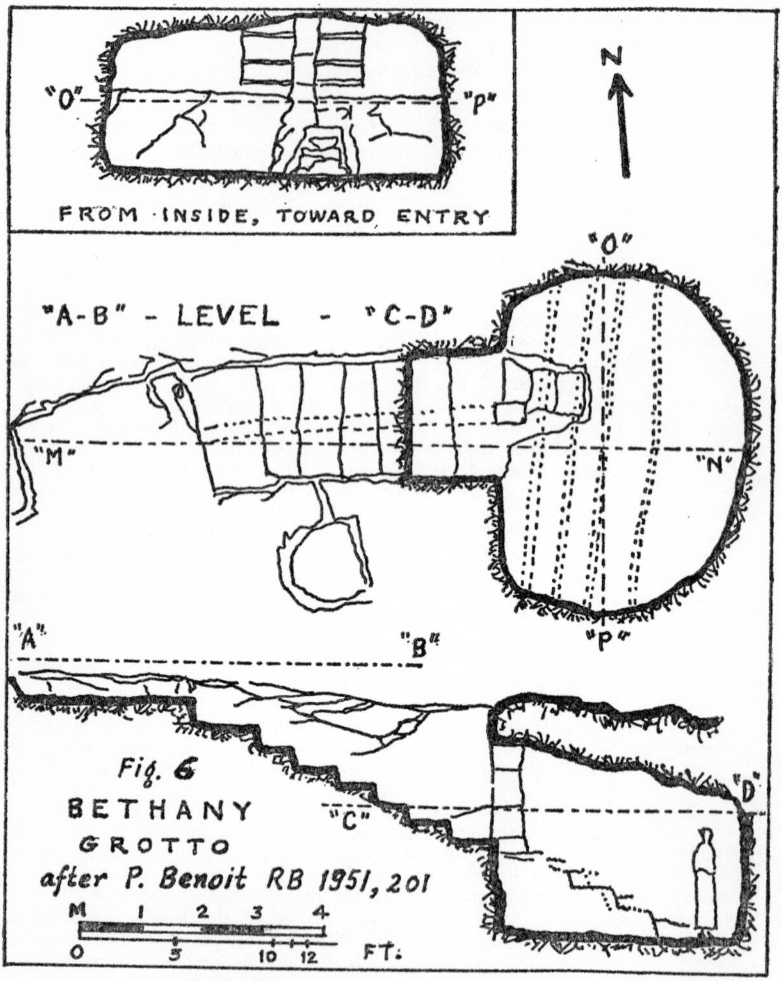

maintained that the Bethany cultic grotto had been at the beginning a cistern, similar to those studied below and to Ayn Karim.[41]

Our subjoined copy of Benoit's plan (Fig. 6) will make clear how little *structural* resemblance there is between this rock-cut vaulted-over cave staircase and any Qumran reservoir; but the mode of plastering

---

41. Pierre Benoit, "Un ancien sanctuaire chrétien à Béthanie", *Revue Biblique* 58/2 (Apr. 1951) 203-4. The Ayn Karim evidence is furnished by Sylvester Saller, *Discoveries at St. John's, Ein Karim,* 1941-2 (Jerusalem: Studium Biblicum Franciscanum, 1946) p. 65. It is a rock-cut chamber like that of Bethany, whose purpose is hazarded to be possibly burial or winepress.

is relevant, and in the further parallels will prove suggestive. As for the Roman dating of the Bethany installation, it would seem to be wholly dependent ultimately upon the dating advanced in the exploration of 'Azeqa below.

Gezer. Our photograph (Plate VIIa) reproduced from Macalister's excavation report, exhibits at once a striking similarity to the Qumran type. Its steps stretch across the whole *length* of the pool, and are thus even less practical for water-storage than Qumran, and more suitable for cultic processions, of which no question is raised.[42] It is firmly stated, however, that several of the reservoirs of this type (perhaps Fig. 7 being a sample) have their steps along the *end* or "short side" of the rectangle, and are thus even more like the Qumran examples.

Macalister adds that the steps are paved with a cement similar to that which lined the walls (as at Qumran). The photo shows two tiny steps continuing the lowest full step further downward, near the center of the pool's length. This is an interesting trait paralleled at Qumran. "The platform was a vaulted vestibule" (?!). In two such cisterns, the top step has a "pier". Possibly one who had seen such a "pier" either directly or in photograph could take it for a kind of "partition" but scarcely one in any sense parallel to the Qumran examples.

These pools are declared to be "confined to the Hellenistic stratum". Dating-criteria are not more narrowly specified; but even if they were, it would have to be remembered that Macalister's excellent pioneering was vitiated by some dating-lacunas, and much of the architecture which he confidently asserted to be Roman has now been assigned to Solomon. Finally, Macalister without verifiable basis asserts the cistern here reproduced to be similar to that of Zakariyya.

'Azeqa. We use this popularly-current biblical name for Tell Zakariyya without withdrawing our reserves regarding the absurd philology on which it is based.[43] The report of Bliss describes an underground *cave* with rock-cut entry steps as at Bethany. "The vaulted portion was probably underground at the time it was used", and we have here "probably an ancient cistern vaulted over during the Roman occupation": a dating considerably less reasoned than current Qumran methodology would allow. Bliss concludes: "Similar stepped cisterns were excavated by me at Jerusalem".[44] He does not mention which of the examples in his published volume he has in mind.

---

42. R. A. Stewart Macalister, *The Excavation of Gezer* (London: Murray, 1912) 1, 275. In the photo-volume 3, Plate 54 exhibits a cistern of considerably less obvious relevance [our Fig. 7]. It is vaulted. No partitions are discernible.
43. R. North, "Ap(h)eq(a) and 'Azeqa," *Biblica* 41/1 (Jan. 1960) 60.
44. Frederick J. Bliss [solely responsible except for the association of Macalister with Part II on The Pottery], *Excavations in Palestine* 1898-1900 (London: Palestine Exploration Fund, 1902) 21. Macalister deals further with "The Rock-Cuttings at Tell Zakarîya" in *Palestine Exploration Quarterly* 31 (1899) 25-36.

Jerusalem. In an area vaguely suggestive of the Cenacle-hill west slope (Protestant Cemetery), Bliss claims that stepped cisterns, of which a sample plan (Fig. 8 here) does indeed recall Qumran, are "a common type, all open, having rock-hewn sides, covered generally with two coats of plaster . . . approached by steps (also plastered)"[45] No dating is hazarded, and there is no suggestion of partitions along the steps.

To the imposing pool in the so-called "Tombs of the Kings" a cultic scope is assigned by an early explorer. He suggests it would have been suitable for the purification required by Levitical law after contact with a corpse. But as Père de Vaux notes, he admits simultaneously non-cultic purposes, chiefly that of draining off the inflow of surface-water which would otherwise jeopardize the monument.[46]

This "Kings" pool (Plate VIIb) does noticeably resemble those of Qumran, except for its vaulted roof, supported (now at least) by a pillar.[47] This raises the whole question of whether or how the Qumran pools are conceived to have been covered over. Certainly the impression gained from inspecting them is that no one of the reservoirs had its independent (much less *vaulted!*) roof, but that each one was either out in the open, or under the same roof as the adjacent rooms.

Samaria-Sabasṭiya. A pool pictured in the Samaria Buildings volume (our Plate VIb) shows steps quite similar to those of Qumran. They are plastered. No mention is made of partitions. The top step shows a break or irregularity in its masonry, which might have been taken to bear a rather remote resemblance to a Qumran partition. The pool is dated to the fourth century A.D. or "Fourth Roman Period".[48]

* * *

Conclusions from Parallels: 1. No example of *partition* emerges from the examples referred by Père de Vaux, though he says explicitly

---

45. Frederick J. Bliss, *Excavations at Jerusalem* 1894-1897 (London: Palestine Exploration Fund, 1898) p. 49 and Plate VI [our Fig. 8]. In Plate XXII is shown the un-Qumranoid plan of a cistern on Ophel hill with steps, but the description on p. 233 declares that access could have been only by a ladder. The Bliss figure, and the photos of Samaria and Gezer, are reproduced here by kind permission of the Palestine Exploration Fund.

46. E. Pfennigsdorff, "Die Aussenanlagen der sogenannten Königsgräber bei Jerusalem", *Zeitschrift des Deutschen Palästina-Vereins* 27(1904) 173-187. The references are from pp. 184 and 179. Père Benoit notes also C. Schick, *Palestine Exploration Quarterly* 29 (1897) 184.

47. The photo of our Plate VIIB is reproduced with permission of the publishers from Maximilian Kon, *Tombs of the Kings* (in Hebrew; Tel Aviv: Dvir, 1947) Plate III (cf. IV, large pool "B"); description p. 37.

48. J. W. Crowfoot, K. M. Kenyon, E. L. Sukenik, *The Buildings at Samaria* (London: PEF, 1942) Plate LXXII, 2 [our Plate VIB]. The pool of the "Third Roman Period" (Pl. LXXIII, 1), described on the p. 134 to which Père Benoit refers, has no perceptible resemblance to those of Qumran.

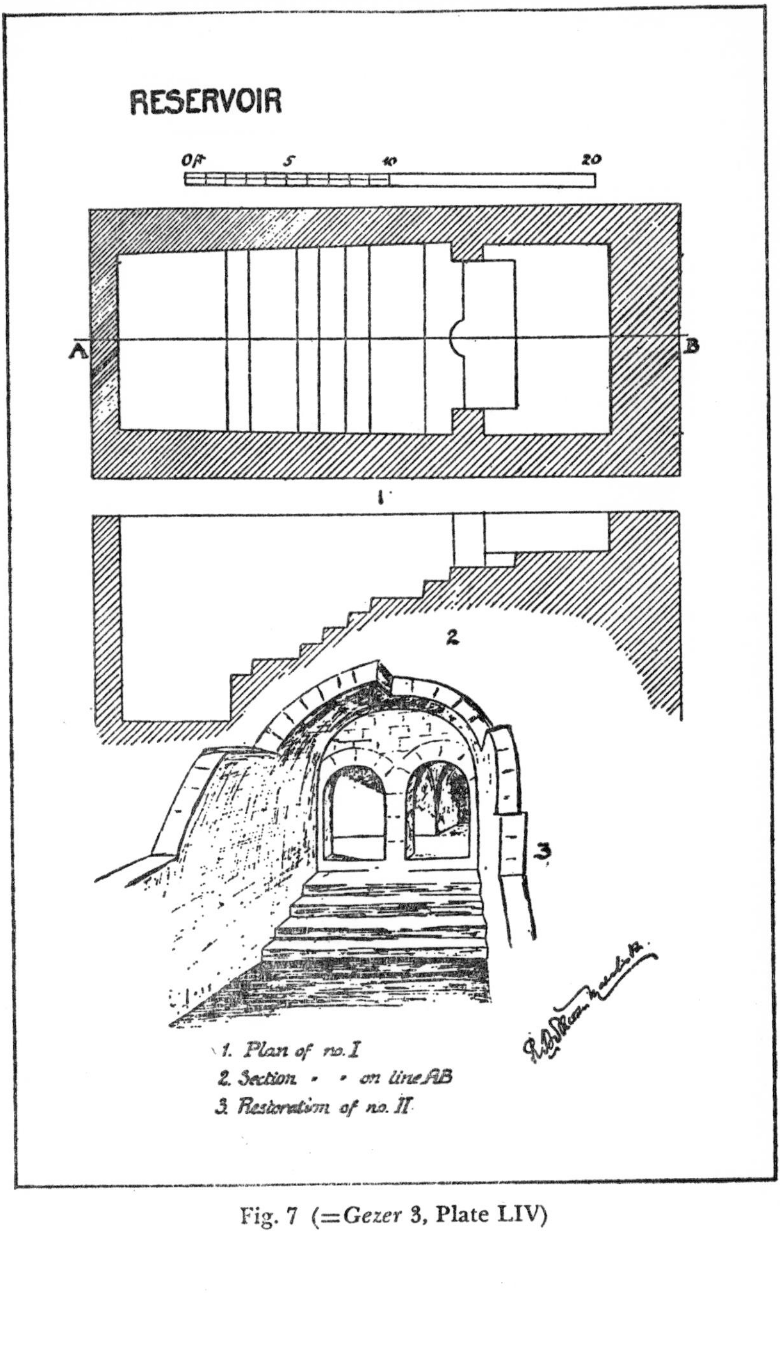

Fig. 7 (=*Gezer* 3, Plate LIV)

"with wide descending staircases *and sometimes partitions on the steps*".

2. No one of the examples contains a reliable dating except that of Samaria, which is notably post-Qumranic. Some other cases allege Roman re-use of a notably earlier structure.

3. Most of the examples have a vaulted roof, consisting in part of the natural rock under which the storage-chamber was burrowed. This cannot but be regarded as a divergence from the Qumran pattern, more significant than any of the convergences.

4. The (? cement) *plastering* of the steps and reservoir wall exhibits noticeable kinship, vitiated to an indeterminate extent by the fact that the Qumran steps are not in the same sense "rock-hewn" but are really *built up* out of masonry.

5. Cultic use is not really *excluded* by any of the examples, and is even suggested in Benoit's own and one other.

6. In no one of the alleged parallels do we have that *dense multiplicity* of *shallow broad-surfaced* chambers *in an arid zone* which constitutes precisely the unique problem of Qumran.

Conjectural Hypotheses

We have not yet reached a solution, but we have now run out of facts. In place of these, it is a poor substitute to have recourse to fantasies. Still, every science has room for legitimate constructive imaginings; so it may be pardonable or even expected to summarize briefly here those which have appeared in print as "hypotheses". These fall into three categories: (a) alternative purposes for the reservoirs; (b) theoretical likelihood of storage rather than ritual bath; (c) link with historically-attested movements.

(a) Alternatives to water-storage and ritual include: (i) filtering, (ii) tannery, (iii) industry, (iv) pisciculture, (v) dry storage.

(i) "The cisterns of Qumran seem to be constructed flat and wide to favor the *sedimentation* of foreign materials. Most of the water available must have come not from the rains but from Wadi Qumran, and wadi water would naturally have all kinds of deposits, some of which were still showing in the white streaks on the wadi cliff."[49]

(ii) At the Brooklyn *CBA* meeting of January 2, 1959, several listeners proposed that the reservoirs may have been used in part for the preparation of skins to be used as scrolls. This "tannery" hypothesis had in fact been broached by Père de Vaux.[50] But after his excavation of nearby Fashkha, he tends strongly to locate there the whole of Qumran-related retting activities, despite acknowledged misgivings of specialists regarding his evidence.[51]

---

49. Reaction of Rev. Ernest Lussier, S.S.S. after hearing my preliminary exposition of this problem at the Catholic Biblical Association regional meeting at Dover, Mass, Feb. 1, 1959.
50. So now John Allegro, *The People of the Dead Sea Scrolls* (London: Routledge, 1959) 42.
51. After further tests, and his own researches into a tannery of Hebron

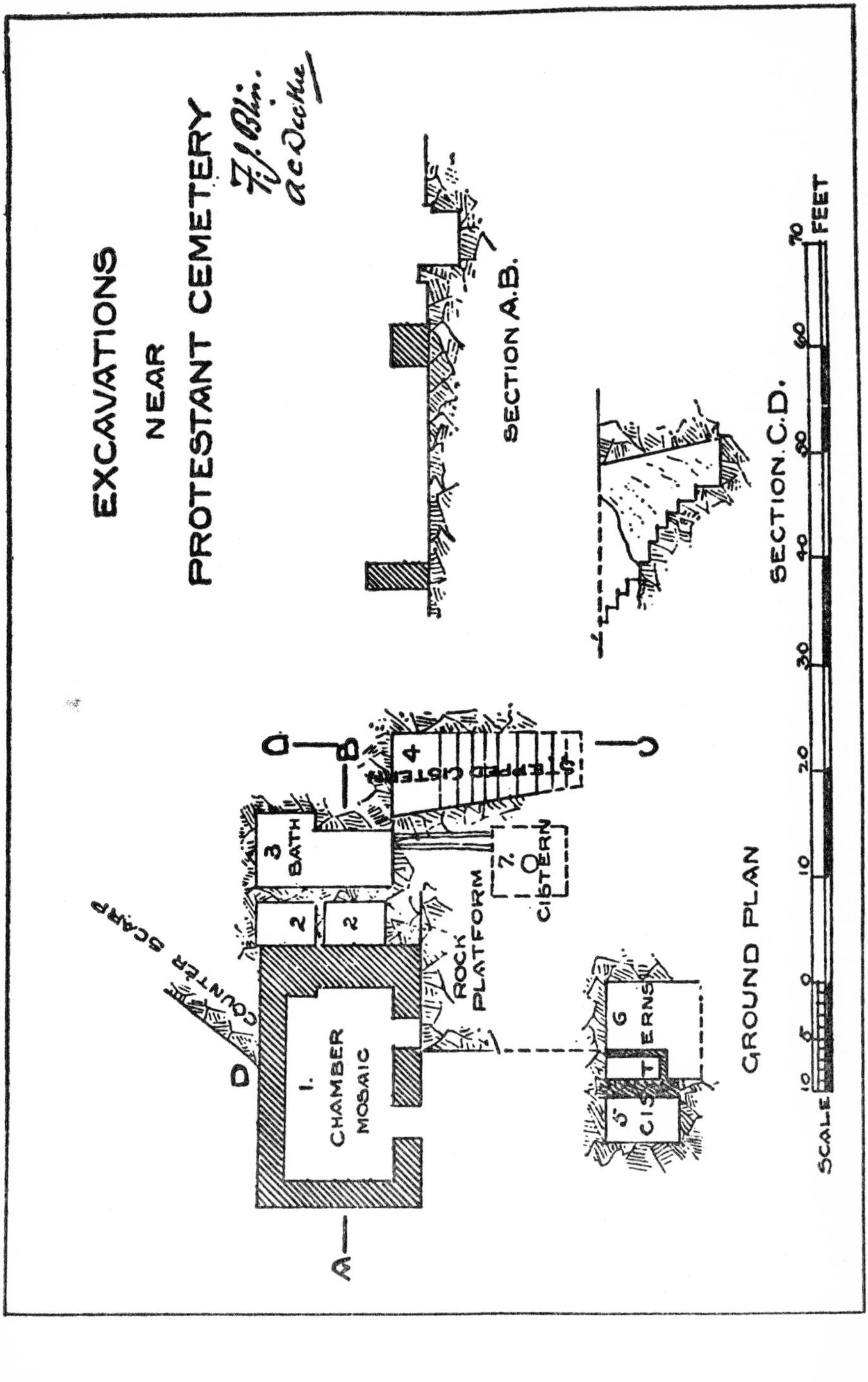

Fig. 8 (= *Excavations at Jerusalem*, Plate VI)

(iii) Interestingly noting that the name of his own community comes from Citeaux (= "cisterns"), and that its domestic usages bear considerable resemblance to those of Qumran, a subprior writes, "It is possible that they had the same experience as most American Cistercian communities. Farming is not an adequate means of support. Perhaps the Qumran community began an industry—a tannery, for example—with the intention of keeping it on a small scale. As the community grew, and their needs became greater, perhaps they gradually expanded, adding cisterns from time to time."[52]

(iv) Half a century ago it was suggested that the Qumran area harbored fish-ponds to furnish daily fare.[53] Father Sutcliffe, despite his avowed adherence to de Vaux's "certainly probable" theory of water-storage only, also shows favor for these fish-ponds.[54] We must not enhance the plausibility by imagining that fish had then as today suitable "penitential" implications; on the contrary, Jewish families often choose fish for the most festive meal of the week. The pisciculture hypothesis is favored by Zeuner for the Fashkha pools he deems unsuited for tanning.[55]

(v) All the reservoirs are connected by the elaborate conduit-system, and therefore seem to have been intended for water-storage. Still we cannot exclude the possibility that the water was at times

---

[RB 66 (1959) 235], Père de Vaux on p. 65 of his 1961 Schweich volume holds more firmly to his view that the Fashkha pools were for preparing *parchment*, as distinguished from *leather* precisely by the fact that its treatment does not utilize tannic acid, of which chemical analysis revealed no trace. He does not state whether the Qumran pools contained any of the calcium carbonate whose presence in Fashkha Pool 24 supports his hypothesis.

52. Letter of Rev. M. Edward McCorkell O.C.S.O. of St. Joseph's Abbey, Spencer, Massachusetts; February 7, 1959.—The problem of self-support at Qumran has been searchingly examined by William R. Farmer, "The Economic Basis of the Qumran Community," *Theologische Zeitschrift* 11/4 (July 1955) 295-308; 12/1 (Jan. 1956) 56-8. On p. 299 of the earlier article he claims that after immersing themselves in the Dead Sea for the extraction of bitumen, "if they didn't want to bathe at Feshkha" there would be a limited amount of "fresh" [!] water for this purpose in the Qumran cisterns. Though this will seem rather impractical to anyone who recalls the gallons of hot soapy water and rinse he needed to desalinize himself after bathing in the Dead Sea, still Farmer's suggestion may be treasured as rendering the use of Qumran reservoir-water for merely ritual immersion plausible by comparison.
53. This statement seems to be ascribed by Sutcliffe to E.W.G. Masterman, "Summary of the Observations on the Rise and Fall of the Level of the Dead Sea," *Palestine Exploration Quarterly* 45 (1913) 196; but I could detect nothing on pisciculture either here or on p. 44, nor in *any* article of Masterman up to 1924 except his "Fisheries of Galilee," *PEQ* 40 (1908) 40.
54. E. Sutcliffe, *The Monks of Qumran,* p. 36.
55. F. E. Zeuner, "Notes on Qumrân", *Palestine Exploration Quarterly* 92/1 (Jan. 1960) 27-36.

closed off from one or several reservoirs in order to use them for the storage of dry commodities or for other purposes. Apart from the permanent occlusive masonry above noted for Reservoir 58, no "plug" for a more transitory arrangement has been found, but it could have been easily improvised.

(b) Theorizing as between storage and ritual bath revolves about (i) hygiene and good taste; (ii) aridity of the area; (iii) proximity of Fashkha and Jordan; (iv) "ritual (?) repast".

(i) Like Dr. Cross, we too find it far more palatable that the votaries should not immerse themselves in their drinking water. But let us take incidental note of some Palestine usages of our hygienic twentieth century. All Jerusalem pilgrims know the tunnel of Ezechia and its Gihon and Siloam extremities, with their boys sporting and women laundering, not to speak of archeologists prowling. The water there is *flowing,* it is true; but those who come to draw it for domestic use show no great concern for how recently the boys have been dispersed.

Again, most larger Jerusalem establishments contain built-in cisterns, in which the inhabitants on occasion immerse themselves for repairs or scrutiny; and which I know to have contained a sediment of pure filth inches thick in cases where local health-department analysis pronounced the water superior to the chlorined hydrant-supply.

Ultimately, though, the relevance of Dr. Cross's observation is that not *all* the cisterns were used *always* for ritual processions. Reservoirs 91 and 58 obviously were not; indeed 58 may well have been cut off from 56 precisely for storage-functions. Granted that the step-cisterns served for the storage of uncontaminated water as long as there was that much to store! Ritual baths would just have to be interrupted for a while, even as in the best-regulated families the bathtub may be filled with water for domestic use when the municipality warns that the pipes will be turned off for repairs during a certain period. As the Qumran hot season dragged on and the water-supply gradually diminished, it would seem that one or several of the step-cisterns could be reserved for bathing. They could even be replenished by the runoff of water used for washing, eventually filtered by settling.

(ii) As to the plausibility of using *all* this storage-space for water alone, two diametrically opposite considerations suggest themselves. On the one hand it seems unlikely that the arid desert *could* have provided enough water to keep *this type* of reservoir filled and protected from evaporation during any notable part of the year.

The only single one of the twenty reservoirs which was genuinely suited to such storage was the round one, 110. But the Qumranites never built this at all; they merely found it lying there and utilized it. A round deep cistern would seem to afford better protection against evaporation and pollution, or is at any rate the most efficient use of the space and materials available.[56] We can readily understand that the arriving votaries, otherworldly and literary in their tastes, would have only vague notions of efficiency and economy in cistern-production, and still less engineering-capacity. They seem to have positively rejected this local cylindric pattern, and chosen instead to multiply on a large scale the shallow-rectangular pattern of their Jerusalem contemporaries, but without the subterranean or vaulted-roof protection needful here more than there against evaporation.

On the other hand, there are undoubtedly brief seasons of heavy rain and even melting snow rushing down in torrents from the Judean hills. The shorter these periods are, the more practical it would be to have a large number of "simple" reservoirs available to fill up all at once.[57]

(iii) We have already noted in several connections the proximity of Qumran to three other abundant sources of water. The allegation has been variously made that these rather than the reservoirs supplied facilities for the ritual baths.

Dead Sea bathing is refreshing and sanitary. Though it leaves a most unpleasant film on the body, which prolonged washing with hot soapy water scarcely removes, still this would not seem to militate against use for *symbolic* purification, and would even notably enhance the penitential austerity. The Dead Sea is less than a mile east of Qumran. Still, no one has seriously invoked this possibility.

Fashkha spring is only another mile or so farther south. We have already expressed our surprise at the view of Noth and Farmer that this fact constituted a motive for locating at Qumran *rather than* at Fashkha itself. Water could have been procured from Fashkha for daily use; the distance is no greater than the maidens of Jericho traverse daily with heavy water-jars on their heads. But it would not be feasible to fill even the smallest of the Qumran reservoirs with water carried in this way from Fashkha. That water is slightly brackish and discounseled for human drinking, but pure and refreshing for bathing and for flocks.

The *Jordan River* is some five miles northeast of Qumran. It is well known to have been favored for the ritual lustrations of various sects contemporary and akin to Qumran.[58] Despite its dirty-brown color

---

56. My mathematician confrère L. J. Heider assures me that a given area will have minimum perimeter if in circular form, and that this will result in greater economy and strength of construction; but there is no difference as regards surface exposed to evaporation, and the circular form is *less* practical when the particular structure has to be incorporated alongside others.
57. H. de Contenson, discussion following A. Parrot's report in "Congrès d'archéologie et d'orientalisme bibliques", *Revue d'Histoire et de Philosophie Religieuses* 35 (1955) 66.
58. Various baptizing sects were swarming all along the Jordan banks, according to M.-J. Lagrange, "La gnose mandéenne et la tradition

and mud-bed which many pilgrim bathers find repellent, the Jordan is "living water", fresh and flowing in accord with the highest Jewish ritual requirements.[59] John the Baptist carried on his ministry on the shores of the Jordan just about as close to Qumran as could be.[60] We may well imagine the Qumran recluses trekking as far as Jordan for baths of refreshment or ritual, but not for getting water to fill their cisterns with.

Against all three of these possibilities stands the unshaken fact that the Qumran ritual envisions its own local background. The *Serek* and *Zadokite* documents nowhere prescribe immersion; proof of this is claimed rather in the pools of Qumran; but the *Serek* speaks of *sprinkling* and this would have been more practical where water was so scarce.[61] The Essene portrayals speak more unmistakably of *bathing*, and in facilities immediately adjacent to the setting of the highly-stressed *ritual repast.* It is surprising that this point would be underrated by those who claim that the obvious resemblances between Qumran and Essenes warrant simple identification of the two groups.

(iv) Not all researchers are agreed that the "community repast" has that ritual significance which seems apparent in the documents. Notably Father van der Ploeg has claimed that the ritual elements are no more than that "grace at meals" which accompanies ordinary

---

évangélique", *Revue Biblique* 36/4 (Oct. 1927) 494-515. Pre-Qumran data were gathered by Lucien Cerfaux in "Le baptême des Esséniens", *Recherches de Science Religieuse* 19 (1929) 248-65. An early study of Wilhelm Brandt, *Die jüdischen Baptismen* (*BZAW* 18, Giessen: Töpelmann, 1910) treats the sect of Bannûs on p. 69 and the Elchasites and Sampsacans pp. 99, 114; these and other names are detailed for us by Epiphanius in his *Heresies* 19 and especially *Panarion* (ed. K. Holl, GCS, Berlin Corpus, Leipzig 1915-33; vols 25, 31, 37). The most recent and exhaustive appraisal of these materials is in Joseph Thomas, *Le mouvement baptiste en Palestine et Syrie* (Gembloux: Duculot, 1935). For the Mandeans, see footnote 69 below.

59. Jean Daniélou, "Le symbolisme de l'eau vive", *Revue des Sciences Religieuses* 32/4 (Oct. 1958) 337, notes that at Qumran "living water" is linked either with the Holy Spirit (*Serek* 4,20= Ez 36,25) or with the Torah (*Hodayot* 8; as Talmud, Strack-Billerbeck 2,433); Christ's reference to his own living water as contrasted with the well of Jacob, Jn 4,10, is paralleled in Zad 6,4; so F.-M. Braun, *RB* 62 (1955) 24; in Ez 47,8 the living water coming from Jerusalem heals the Dead Sea (Daniélou p. 341). Braun's study of Mandeism cited in footnote 68 below remarks on p. 211 concerning the Dead Sea Community, "Doubtless running water would have suited them better. On the arid plateau of Qumran, one could not hope for that, so there is not question of it anywhere except in the figurative sense."

60. Rengstorf's article "Iordánēs" (after potamós) in G. Kittel's *Theologisches Wörterbuch zum Neuen Testament* (Stuttgart: Kohlhammer, 1959) 6, 608-623 does not mention Qumran but deals with the Mandeans on p. 622.

61. Duncan Howlett, *The Essenes and Christianity* (New York: Harper, 1957) 141.

dining in any monastery or Christian home.[62] Others would find the rite more "sacramentally Eucharistic" in the basic sense of those two words: "signifying grace" and "giving thanks".[63] The "ritual bath" is further claimed to bear an essential relation to that assumed liturgical character.[64]

It must be noted that the bath before dinner could be a stringent ritual obligation even if the meal had no ritual significance at all, and more so if it involved at least a "blessing before meat". This relevance of the purification-ritual is taken for granted even by those who doubt that the Qumran meal was really a worship-service, an ersatz-sacrifice.[65]

* * *

We would conclude with Dupont-Sommer that *Serek* 3,4-9 makes sense only if the Qumran sect was essentially baptist;[66] and with Bruce, "Quite plainly the water was not required solely for the ordinary purposes of washing or drinking; the presence of several swimming-pools or baptisteries suggested that it was required for ritual purification and indicated that the community was one of a number of baptist sects which we know to have flourished in the Jordan valley."[67]

(c) May we go further and attach the water-ritual of Qumran to any other historically-attested movements? Those especially favored are

---

62. J. van der Ploeg, *The Excavations of Qumran,* translated by Kevin Smyth (London: Longmans, 1958) 213; "The Meals of the Essenes", *Journal of Semitic Studies* 2/2 (April 1957) 163-175; so Edmund F. Sutcliffe, "Sacred Meals at Qumran?" *Heythrop Journal* 1/1 (Jan. 1960) 48-65. The ritual character of the meal is maintained chiefly by Karl Georg Kuhn, "The Lord's Supper and the Communal Meal at Qumran", in K. Stendahl, *Scrolls and the New Testament* (New York: Harpers, 1957) 65-93, revised from "Über den ursprünglichen Sinn des Abendmahles und sein Verhältnis zu den Gemeinschaftsmahlen der Sektenschrift", *Evangelische Theologie* 10 (1951) 508-527; further "Repas cultuel essénien et cène chrétienne", *Les Manuscrits: colloque de Strasbourg* 1955 (Paris: Presses Universitaires, 1957) 75-92.
63. J. Gnilka, "Das Gemeinschaftsmahl der Essener", *Biblische Zeitschrift* 5/1 (Jan. 1961) 39-55; the prescribed "purity" is reduced to *Serek* 5,13 cited above.
64. Otto Betz, "Die Proselytentaufe der Qumransekte und die Taufe im Neuen Testament", *Revue de Qumran* 1/2 (Oct. 1958) 213-234, especially p. 214.
65. Joseph M. Baumgarten, "Sacrifice and Worship Among the Jewish Sectarians of the Dead Sea (Qumrân) Scrolls", *Harvard Theological Review* 46/4 (Oct. 1953) 156.
66. André Dupont-Sommer, *The Essene Writings from Qumran* (Oxford: Blackwell, 1961) 49.
67. F. F. Bruce, *Second Thoughts on the Dead Sea Scrolls* (Grand Rapids, Mich.: Eerdmans, 1956) 48. He maintains the earthquake-cistern 48 to have been one of these baptisteries; and after its destruction, 71 was constructed to replace it in this ritual function.

(i) the Mandeans; (ii) John the Baptist; (iii) the Ebyonites; and (iv) Christianity.

(i) *The Mandeans.* The claim is made categorically by Braun that Mandeism is an offshoot of Qumran Essenism.[68] Apart from the baptisms, another possible connection is Mandean emphasis on the "lustrous crown" or *k*ᵉ*lîl* noted by Gaster on *Serek* 4,7 comparing 1 Pt 5,4. Numerous recent researches into Mandeism have appeared.[69] They are synthesized in the massive study of Rudolph.[70] The Mandeans are found only in Mesopotamia, using the word "jordan" as a common noun for "water"; but we are not altogether sure whether this means they emigrated there from near the Jordan or merely adopted this term as a flight of devotion or fancy. Nor can we yet assay adequately the mutual relations of the Mandeans with Zoroastrianism on the one hand or Gnosticism on the other.

(ii) *John the Baptist.* Daniélou is the chief defender of very close links between John's disciples and Qumran.[71] He has not gone as far as some others in claiming that the Baptist himself personally in his youth was a resident member of the Dead Sea community.[72] Opposition has been expressed on the ground that the alleged similarities are

68. F. -M. Braun, "Le Mandéisme et la secte essénienne de Qumran", *L'Ancien Testament et l'Orient* (Louvain: 1957) 193-230; p. 229. Parallels are enumerated p. 211.

69. E. S. Drower, *The Mandaeans of Iraq and Iran* (Oxford: 1937); "A Mandaean Bibliography" *Journal of the Royal Asiatic Society* (1953) 34-39; and nine other titles in the bibliography of Eric Segelberg, *Masbutā: Studies in the Ritual of the Mandaean Baptism* (Uppsala: Almqvist 1958) 186; on kelîla, pp. 27-30, 111-115.—H. Lietzmann, *Ein Beitrag zur Mandäerfrage* (Berlin Academy, 1930) 597, denied any authentic connection of the Mandeans with John the Baptist.

70. K. Rudolph, *Das Mandäerproblem* (Göttingen: Vandenhoeck, 1960).

71. Jean Daniélou, *The Dead Sea Scrolls and Primitive Christianity* (Baltimore: Helicon, 1958) 16-18, citing his "La communauté de Qumran et l'organisation de l'Église ancienne", *Revue d'Histoire et de Philosophie Religieuses* 35 (1955) 105-71; William Brownlee, "John the Baptist in the Light of the Ancient Scrolls", *Interpretation* 9 (1955) 78-86; J. Schmitt, "Les écrits du Nouveau Testament et les textes de Qumran", *Revue des Sciences Religieuses* 29 (1955) 394-401; 30 (1956) 54-74.—Further J. A. T. Robinson, "The Baptism of John and the Qumran Community", *Harvard Theological Review* 50/3 (July 1957) 175-191; Karl Hermann Schelkle, *Die Gemeinde von Qumran und die Kirche des Neuen Testaments* (Düsseldorf: Patmos, 1960) 31: "We practically *must* assume personal and cultural relationships existing between John and the Qumran votaries".—Franz Zehrer, "Die Funde von Qumran und ihr Verhältnis zu den drei älteren Evangelien," *Theologisch-Praktische Quartalschrift* 109/3 (Feb. 1961) 183-6 holds it very probable that John *dwelt* for a time at Qumran.

72. M. Brändle, "Johannes der Täufer ein Schüler der Essener?" *Orientierung* 20 (1956) 257-262.—An influence in the *reverse* direction, of John the Baptist on the Essenes and Mandeans, is sustained by Jean Steinmann, *Saint John the Baptist and the Desert Tradition* (New York: Harper, 1958) 121-8, though p. 58 concludes it is probable that John himself was for a time an Essene.

either superficial or natural.[73] The question of whether John's "Baptism of penance" is a radically different thing from what is meant by those terms at Qumran must perhaps be decided by norms similar to those invoked below for Christian baptism itself.[74] But if we compare the claims sometimes made of a direct link between *Jesus* and the Qumran community, it becomes at once apparent how much more plausible such a link is in the case of John. First of all the geographical proximity is striking and indeed inescapable. The Jordan ford where tradition locates John's baptizing ministry is a scant two-hours' walk from Qumran, whereas Jesus visited this Jericho area only rarely and in transit, except admittedly for his forty-day fast.[75] Secondly, the emphasis of John upon penitence and austerity is expressed in terms and living-conditions far more similar to those of Qumran than is the humane message of the Gospels, even though they too contain the substance of a severe austerity.

For our part we admit frankly that it is impossible to conceive the Baptist preaching steadily a message so similar to that of Qumran in a desert-area so adjacent, without being fully conscious of the kinship his message bore to theirs; nay more, without actively *dissociating* himself from them unless he was willing that this kinship should be acknowledged.

(iii) *The Ebyonites.* Cullmann has found that the Judeo-Christian baptizing sect known as "The Poor" exhibits also enough other similarities to the Qumranites and/or Essenes to warrant extending the life-tenure of the old hypothesis that those Ebyonites are (Qumran) Essenes come over into Christianity.[76] Naturally his proofs will not

---

73. See footnote 29 above and now José Maria Caballero Cuesta, "¿ Fué el Bautista un esenio?" *Burgense* 3 (1962) 15-30; John is more austere and his baptism is more his own.
74. John A. T. Robinson, "The Baptism of John and the Qumran Community", *Harvard Theological Review* 50/3 (July 1957) 175-191. At Qumran, baptism is assumed to have been for sin, replacing sacrifice; whereas Jewish proselyte-baptism dealt only with ritual impurity (p. 180). "Nevertheless we look in vain in [Qumran] writings for the equivalent of a single baptism of repentance for the remission of sins . . . John was calling the people to something for which Qumran offered no parallel" (p. 181); he modified the practice of Qumran to give new emphasis on one element, not radical change. Note now the study of John H. P. Reumann, "J. A. T. Robinson's Portrait of John the Baptist", *Journal of Biblical Literature* 81 (1962) 109 (advance notice).
75. M.-J. Lagrange, *Le Judaïsme avant Jésus-Christ* (Paris: Gabalda, 1931), and footnote 58 above.
76. Oscar Cullmann, "The Significance of the Qumran Texts for Research into the Beginnings of Christianity", *Journal of Biblical Literature* 74/4 (Dec. 1955) 213-226; reprinted in K. Stendahl; *Scrolls and the New Testament* (New York: Harpers, 1957) 18-32; further "Die neuentdeckten Qumran-Texte und das Judenchristentum der Pseudoklementinen", R. Bultmann Festschrift *Neutestamentliche Studien* edited by W. Eltester (BZNW 21; Berlin: Töpelmann, 1954 ²1957) 35-51; "Secte de Qumran, Hellénistes des Actes et Quatrième Évangile", *Les Manuscrits: Colloque de Strasbourg* 1955 (Paris: Presses Universitaires, 1957) 66.

rally the votes of all experts, as Fitzmyer's dissent attests.[77] Here again, our own judgment would be that in comparison with other alleged parallels, the "Qumran-Ebyonite" links retain a genuine plausibility and title to further consideration.

(iv) *Origins of Christian Baptism.* This theme is only remotely relevant to our basic inquiry. It is thinkable, and is in fact alleged, that baptism came into Christianity not directly *from* Qumran but in groups and movements under the same influences.[78] Such a hypothesis assumes that the significance of baptism is similar in Christianity; since in *Serek* 3,4 the washing is not effective magically but depends on interior dispositions, Betz concludes that the Essene and Christian baptisms are distinguished only by the virtue of Christ's death and resurrection.[79] It would seem that at Qumran the spiritual significance of circumcision is expressed by the sprinkling and immersion.[80]

Naturally not all will admit the deeper kinship of Christian baptism with Jewish rites. "The baptismal doctrines and rites of the scrolls offer a striking contrast to Christian and even Johannite baptism in their New Testament forms. Though the Qumran Essenes practised a form of baptism by total immersion, it was a purely-ritual act. At the most these rules may have been popularly construed [but not really intended, against Kuhn] as removing sins. . . . Christian baptism was a single and unrepeatable act and, in the New Testament, has [? no] purificatory significance."[81] The question is related

---

77. J. Fitzmyer, footnote 40 above. See further J. Oesterreicher, "The Community of Qumran", *The Bridge* (New York: Pantheon, 1956) 2,91-134; Sherman E. Johnson, "The Dead Sea Manual of Discipline and the Jerusalem Church of Acts", *Zeitschrift für die alttestamentliche Wissenschaft* 66 (1954) 106-120, reprinted in K. Stendahl, *Scrolls and the New Testament* 129-142. Guido-M. Brisebois, "De momento regulae communitatis seu unionis Qumrân ad vitae religiosae originem", *Antonianum* 34 (1959) 3-31.
78. Arvid S. Kapelrud, "Dødehavstekstene og urkristendommen", *Norsk Teologisk Tidsskrift* 62/3 (1961) 113-127.
79. Otto Betz, "Die Proselytentaufe der Qumransekte und die Taufe im Neuen Testament", *Revue de Qumran* 1/2 (Oct. 1958) 217,234. See further R. Mayer, J. Reuss, *Die Qumranfunde und die Bibel* (Regensburg: Pustet, 1959) and H. H. Rowley, "The Qumran Sect and Christian Origins", *Bulletin Rylands* 44/1 (Sept. 1961) 139-143; and in T. Manson *New Testament Essays* edited by A. Higgins (Manchester: University, 1959) 218-229.
80. Thomas F. Torrance, "The Origins of Baptism", *Scottish Journal of Theology* 11/2 (June 1958) 169: "The sprinkling of sin-offering water for atonement Messianically interpreted, and the application of priestly ablution from the Temple to all initiated members of the Covenant community." His view is further elaborated in "Aspects of Baptism in the New Testament", *Theologische Zeitschrift* 14/3 (1958) 241-260.
81. Matthew Black, *The Scrolls and Christian Origins* (London: Nelson, 1961) 98. The 'no' which I query and bracket is really in the text, but does not seem to fit the author's own line of argument. On p. 95 is a further contention: "The probability is that the neophytes were admitted to the 'purer waters of baptism' in the sight of the assembled people.

to the more general one of Jewish proselyte baptism, and it seems unlikely that we will ever attain apodictic certainty as to what pre-existing significance may have been freely taken over by the founder of Christianity.[82]

* * *

We trust the reader will share our conclusion that these various conjectural hypotheses, though instructive in their way, are not of sufficient convincingness to alter the situation already created by the basic facts of the case, which we may resume as follows:

1. Qumran writings inculcate repeated and important ritual bathing (pages 100-104 above).

2. The Essenes, recognized to be at least closely linked in spirit to the Qumran movement, are portrayed as requiring a ritual bath twice daily in proximity to their dining-hall (pages 104-106).

3. These requirements seem obviously reflected in the noticeable multiplicity and structure of the Qumran reservoirs (pages 106-116).

4. Step-cisterns of similar structure, even taken singly, yield only ambiguous evidence of being either contemporary or non-cultic; and they in no way parallel the precise anomaly of multiplicity within a building-complex (pages 116-123).

5. No non-cultic explanation of the reservoirs, including that of storage or private-bath exclusively (pp. 122-8), gives full satisfaction.

The size and formation of the baptistries [*sic*] at Qumran, exposed to full view in an area which forms a natural amphitheatre, the divided partitions on entering, point to their use in some public ceremony." The claim of amphitheatre escapes me completely; surely it is not implied that observers clinging to the cliff a mile away enjoy a view of the proceedings. It is interesting to note, though, how completely this observer assumes that there was no roof or covering whatever over the reservoirs (see text accompanying footnote 35 above).

82. T. M. Taylor, "The Beginnings of Jewish Proselyte Baptism", *New Testament Studies* 2 (1956) 198, holds that Christianity had worked out its theology of baptism *before* the Jews developed true "proselyte baptism", which may have existed before 90 A.D. but not as a practice clearly distinct from ordinary baths of purification. See further N. A. Dahl, "The Origin of Baptism", *Norsk Teologisk Tidsskrift* 56/1 (Interpretationes: S. Mowinckel, 1955) 36-52; p. 44, John the Baptist and the Covenanters are "in some respects parallel, in main lines independent", because of the similar background and history of two "disruptions" of priests from the regular temple worship.

THE BAR COCHBA PERIOD

JOSEPH A. FITZMYER, S.J.

The number of historical documents pertaining to the second century A. D. in Palestine has always been small. It is consequently of interest to learn of new discoveries of original texts which come from that century and shed light on an otherwise obscure movement in the history of that part of the world. Though this movement has little direct bearing on Christianity, it is an important episode in the history of the Jewish people, for it is in effect the aftermath of the fateful destruction of Jerusalem by the Romans in A. D. 70 and the beginning of their long separation from the Holy City. That movement is the Second Jewish Revolt, which began under Bar Cochba in A. D. 132 and lasted until about 135, when the last remnants of the rebels were wiped out and the emperor Hadrian forbade the Jews to set foot in Jerusalem or even approach it within a certain radius.

In Josephus' writings we have a fairly lengthy and reasonably reliable account of the First Jewish Revolt, which began in A. D. 66 and ended with the destruction of the city of Jerusalem and of the Temple of Yahweh in 70.[1] But the details of the Second Revolt under Bar Cochba, which apparently rivalled the first in scope and duration, have been only very briefly recorded by contemporary or nearly contemporary writers. Hence any new information, no matter how meagre, helps to fill out the picture.

The New Finds

The new material has so far been published only in part and for some of it we must rely on preliminary reports. It comes from caves in at least three different wâdies which empty into the west side of the Dead Sea. The first place which yielded written documents pertaining to the period of the Second Revolt was a pair of caves in the Wâdi Murabba'ât, discovered sometime during 1951. Murabba'ât is part of the long wâdi which begins to the east of Bethlehem under the name Wâdi Ta'âmireh and ends at the Dead Sea under the name Wâdi Darajeh. The site of the caves in this Jordanian torrent-bed is about a two-hour walk westward in from the Dead Sea, being situated some fifteen miles, as the crow flies, to the southeast of Jerusalem and

1. See *Jewish War* 2. 271ff. through Book 7; *Life* 17-410.

some eleven miles south of Qumrân Cave I. The caves open southward and are found about halfway up the north side of the gorge, which is some 600 ft. deep.

News of the discovery of written material in the Murabba'ât caves arrived in Jerusalem in October 1951, and an archaeological expedition was mounted to explore and excavate four caves in that wâdi from January 21 to March, 1952. Two of them were of little importance and yielded no written material;but the other two gave definite evidence of a prolonged occupation in the Roman period, in addition to artifacts of the Chalcolithic, Iron II and Arab periods.[2] From the Iron II period of occupation of one of the caves came the earliest Palestinian papyrus (*Mur* 17)[3] to be found to date, a palimpsest dating from the eighth century, which is bound to arouse palaeographic interest.[4] From the Roman period came documents written in Hebrew, Aramaic, and Greek, which gave evidence of a trilingualism in Palestine, which was already known in the time of Herod and is now confirmed anew.[5] Some of the documents of this Roman period belong to the first century B. C.; a few are dated in the first century A. D. (to the time just prior to the First Revolt—one even in the second year of Nero [*Mur* 18]).[6] But the most important ones are derived

---

2. Details are derived from the full report and publication of the documents of the Murabba'ât caves, which are now available in P. Benoit, J. T. Milik and R. de Vaux, *Les Grottes de Murabba'ât* (Discoveries in the Judaean Desert 2; two parts, Texte, Planches; Oxford: Clarendon, 1961). Hereafter the siglum, *DJD*, will refer to this series.—See further R. de Vaux, "Les grottes de Murabba'ât et leurs documents," *RB* 60 (1953) 245-67; G. Lankester Harding, "Khirbet Qumran and Wady Murabba'ât: Fresh Light on the Dead Sea Scrolls and New Manuscript Discoveries in Jordan," *PEQ* 84 (1952) 104-9 (+ five plates); H. Seyrig and J. T. Milik, "Trésor monétaire de Murabba'ât," *Revue numismatique*, sér. VI, vol. 1 (1958) 11-26.
3. In accord with the system of abbreviation explained in *Qumrân Cave 1* (DJD 1: Oxford: Clarendon, 1955), pp. 46-8, the siglum *Mur* (=Murabba'ât) is used to indicate the texts of *DJD* 2. The system is also explained in *The Catholic Encyclopedia*, Supplement II, section 9, s. v. "Dead Sea Scrolls," #VII (where M should be changed to Mur); and in *Evangelisches Kirchenlexikon* 3 (1958) 421.
4. See F. M. Cross, Jr., *The Ancient Library of Qumran and Modern Biblical Studies* (Garden City, N. Y.: Doubleday, 1958), p. 14, n. 22.
5. Cf. *DJD* 2, p. 69; M. Smith, "Aramaic Studies and the Study of the New Testament," *JBR* 26 (1958) 304-13. It is not certain that Bar Cochba himself wrote in all three languages, but they were at least being used by those under him. See Y. Yadin, "Expedition D.," *Yᵉdîʻôt ha-ḥebrāh la-ḥaqîrat 'ereṣ yiśrā'ēl we-'attîqôtêhā* (=*Bulletin of the Israel Exploration Society* [Hereafter *BIES*]) 25 (1961) 63; *IsrEJ* 11 (1961) 50. Among the Wâdi Ḥabra texts are three letters addressed to his officers, Yehonatan and Masabbalah, one in each language (Papyrus 3,4,12). Yadin thinks that the Aramaic of these texts is to be identified with the Aramaic of the Targum Onqelos; this identification, however, must await further study.
6. The name is spelled *nrwn qsr*, just as it has often been suggested apropos of Apoc 13,18 (=666!)—if it is really pertinent.

from the time of the Second Revolt or the decades immediately preceding it (in the latter case, though the documents were written earlier, they were probably carried to the caves by the refugees who fled there toward the end of the revolt). Later on, in 1955, six Bedouin shepherds found in a hole not far from the Murabba'ât caves an important fragmentary scroll of the OT Minor Prophets in Hebrew, which had been buried with a refugee who had fled to the wâdi during the revolt and died there.[7]

About the same time as the discovery and excavation of the Murabba'ât caves (1951-2) the Bedouins found further materials related to the Second Revolt in other caves whose location was for a long time kept secret. The reluctance of the finders to reveal the name of the area was suspected by the archaeologists and scholars in Jordan to have been related to the fact that the site was across the border in Israel. The texts found in this "unknown site" were offered for sale in Jerusalem during July and August 1952.[8] They included Hebrew biblical fragments (Gn, Nm, Dt, Ps 7,14-31,22), a complete phylactery, a fragmentary text of the OT Minor Prophets in Greek,[9] a letter written to Bar Cochba in Hebrew, two Aramaic contracts dated in the "third year of the liberation of Israel, in the name of Simon ben Kosibah," two Greek and two Aramaic documents dated according to the system used in the Roman Province of Arabia (erected on the ruins of the Nabataean kingdom of Petra in A. D. 106), and finally some Nabataean papyri.[10] "The group is to be dated toward the end

---

7. See *DJD* 2, pp. 8, 50, 181.
8. J. T. Milik, *Ten Years of Discovery in the Wilderness of Judaea* (Studies in Biblical Theology 26; Naperville, Ill.: A. R. Allenson, 1959), p. 16.
9. Partially published by D. Barthélemy, "Redécouverte d'un chaînon manquant de l'histoire de la Septante," *RB* 60 (1953) 18-29. The parts preserved belong to Micah, Jonah, Nahum, Habakkuk, Zephaniah, Zechariah; they date from the end of the first century A.D. and are important evidence for the study of the Greek translation of the OT. See further, E. Vogt, "Fragmenta prophetarum minorum deserti Iuda," *Bib* 34 (1953) 423-6; P. Kahle, "Die im August 1952 entdeckte Lederrolle mit dem griechischen Text der kleinen Propheten und das Problem der Septuaginta," *TLZ* 79 (1954) 81-94.
10. One of the Nabataean papyri has been published by J. Starcky, "Un contrat nabatéen sur papyrus," *RB* 61 (1954) 161-81; see further J. J. Rabinowitz, "A Clue to the Nabatean Contract from the Dead Sea Region," *BASOR* 139 (1955) 11-14. J. T. Milik has also published a few of the documents from this site: "Un contrat juif de l'an 134 après J.-C.," *RB* 61 (1954) 182-90; "Deux documents inédits du Désert de Juda," *Bib* 38 (1957) 245-68 (II. Acte de vente d'un terrain, pp. 255-64; III. Acte de vente d'une maison, daté de 134 ap. J.-C., pp. 264-8 [a restudy of the text published in *RB* 61 (1954) 182-90]). See further J. T. Milik, "Note additionnelle sur le contrat juif de l'an 134 après J.-C.," *RB* 62 (1955) 253-4; J. J. Rabinowitz, "Some Notes on an Aramaic Contract from the Dead Sea Region," *BASOR* 136 (1954) 15-16; S. Abramson and H. L. Ginsberg, "On the Aramaic Deed of Sale of the Third Year of the Second Jewish Revolt," *BASOR* 136 (1954) 17-19.

of the first and the beginning of the second century A. D.; the *terminus ad quem* is the Second Jewish Revolt, for it was then that these documents were hidden in their caves."[11] It is now known that the site of the discovery was a cave (or caves) in the Wâdi Seiyâl (or Naḥal Ṣe'ᵉlîm), which is in Israel between Masadah and 'En-gedi. The site was explored between 24 January and 2 February 1960 by Israeli archaeologists, who found evidence of fairly recent Bedouin clandestine digging on the spot.[12] The archaeologists also found further material in the Wâdi Seiyâl caves: "traces of Chalcolithic occupation at some sites and in many caves, two Iron Age and four Roman fortresses in the region, and a group of caves inhabited during the Bar-Kokhba revolt. The most important finds were an arsenal of arrows, including the iron arrow-heads as well as the shafts of wood and cane, coins from the time of Trajan until Severus Alexander, and some fragments of scrolls, including two parchments of a phylactery containing parts of Exod. xiii, 1-16, and fragments of Hebrew, Aramaic and Greek papyri."[13]

Further material pertaining to the Bar Cochba period has come from a third spot. In 1953 and again in April 1955 Y. Aharoni, an Israeli archaeologist, conducted some explorations in the Wâdi Ḥabra (or Naḥal Ḥeber in Israel), some six kilometers, as the crow flies, slightly SW of 'En-gedi. Lacking proper equipment, he was not able to do a thorough job at that time, but he discovered that at least one cave was related to the Bar Cochba revolt. In its vicinity were found traces of two Roman camps, strategically built on the two sides of the steep cliffs forming the wâdi and so placed as to keep watch on the cave-mouth visible below them.[14] During a two-week campaign, from

---

11. J. T. Milik, *Ten Years*, p. 16. For further details about the contents of this find see J. T. Milik, "Le travail d'édition des manuscrits du Désert de Juda," *Supplements to VT* 4 (1957) [Volume du Congrès; Strasbourg: 1956]) 17-26. See further *Bib* 34 (1953) 419.
12. Y. Yadin, ["New Discoveries in the Judean Desert," *BA* 24 (1961) 34] has recently confirmed the location which was rumored several years ago in Jerusalem: ". . . according to a reliable report that reached us several months ago, [the documents were] found by Beduin in a cave of Nahal Tse'elim, north of Massada, i.e.—in Israel territory. . . . the team did indeed find traces of Beduin search parties in some of the caves." Likewise, "Les repaires de Bar Kokhéba," *Bible et Terre Sainte* 33 (1960) 6.
13. J. Aviram, "Judean Desert," *IsrEJ* 10 (1960) 125. See also M. Cassuto Salzmann, "Ricerche in Israele," *Bibbia e Oriente* 3 (1961) 24; Y. Aharoni, "Les nouvelles découvertes de la Mer Morte," *Bible et Terre Sainte* 29 (1960) 12-13; "Expedition B.," *BIES* 25 (1961) 19-33; *IsrEJ* 11 (1961) 11-24.—For the text of the phylactery see P. Wernberg-Møller, "The Exodus Fragment from Massada," *VT* 10 (1960) 229-30; F. Vattioni, "Ritrovati altri manoscritti sulla riva israeliana del Mar Morto," *RivBiblItal* 8 (1960) 71-72; "Il frammento dell' Esodo scoperto a Massada," *ibid.*, p. 180.
14. Y. Aharoni, "Hever Valley (Wadi Habra)," *IsrEJ* 4 (1954) 126-7; 5 (1955) 272-3; also M. Cassuto Salzmann, *Bibbia e Oriente* 3 (1961) 23-25.

23 March to 5 April, 1960, a team of scholars of the Israel Exploration Society (J. Aviram, N. Avigad, Y. Aharoni, P. Bar-Adon and Y. Yadin) explored the desert area about 'En-gedi.[15] In the three-chambered Naḥal Ḥeber cave they uncovered in the inmost chamber a burial niche containing a collection of baskets overflowing with skulls and also several layers of large mats covering human bones. A second spot in the cave yielded a basket of 19 metal objects: 12 bronze jugs of varying sizes, three incense shovels, two large platters, a *patera* and a key. Most of the objects were clearly identified as Roman and cultic. At a third spot there was discovered a 4 x 5 cm. fragment of animal hide on which a few words of Ps 15 and the beginning of Ps 16 were written (dated by Y. Yadin to the second half of the first century A. D.). But the most important find in this cave came from still another spot; it was a goat-skin water-bottle stuffed with bundles of colored raw wool, skeins of wool, beads, and a package which contained a batch of papyri bound together with four pieces of a wooden slat. "After having been opened, the papyri were read by Yadin and found to contain fifteen letters from the leader of the Revolt, Bar-Kochba, written in Hebrew, Aramaic and Greek."[16] According to another report four of the letters were written in Hebrew, two in Greek and the rest in Aramaic; they were letters written by Bar Cochba to officers stationed at the oasis of 'En-gedi.[17]

Finally, during the spring of 1961, when the Israeli archaeologists returned to the wâdi, a sensational discovery was made "in the same cave where the 'archives' of the second century Jewish leader Simon Bar-Kochba were found in April, 1960."[18] The number of papyrus documents discovered there in "a long, reed-like sheath" was first announced as seventy.[19] But subsequent reports have reduced the number to five documents found in a leather pouch and thirty-six in a water-skin; they too are letters of Bar-Cochba, deeds and contracts of the

---

15. See J. Aviram, "The Judean Desert Expeditions," *BIES* 25 (1961) 5-12; N. Avigad, "Expedition A.," *ibid.*, 13-18; Y. Aharoni, "Expedition B.," *ibid.*, 19-33; P. Bar-Adon, "Expedition C.," *ibid.*, 34-48; Y. Yadin, "Expedition D.," *ibid.*, 49-64; B. Lifshitz, "The Greek Documents from Nahal Seelim and Nahal Mishmar," *ibid.*, 65-73. (All are in Modern Hebrew.) See *IsrEJ* 11 (1961) 3-62.
16. J. Aviram, *IsrEJ* 10 (1960) 125-6; see further R. North, "Report from Palestine," *CBQ* 22 (1960) 317.
17. *Bibbia e Oriente* 3 (1961) 25. Y. Yadin (*BA* 24 [1961] 48; *Bible et Terre Sainte* 34 [1961] 14) now specifies that one of the Greek letters "is apparently not from Bar Kochba." In fact, in his fuller report (*BIES* 25 [1961] 49-64) he lists eight papyrus letters as Aramaic (Pap. 1,2,4,8,10,11,14,15), two as Greek (Pap. 3,6), three as certainly Hebrew (Pap. 5,7,12) and two as probably Hebrew (Pap. 9,13).
18. Reuters dispatch from Tel Aviv, dated 18 March; *Washington Post*, 19 March 1961, p. A3.
19. *Ibid.*

same period.[20] But all of this material is as yet unpublished and we are dependent so far only on preliminary reports.

So much for the new finds which have provided the material which sheds new light on the Bar Cochba period. We turn now to an attempt to relate the new material, in so far as it is known, to what was previously known.

Bar Cochba's Name

One of the most interesting features of the new data supplied by the texts found in the caves of the Wâdies Murabba'ât and Ḥabra is the spelling of the name of the leader of the Second Revolt. In English the most commonly used form is Bar Cochba (less frequently spelled Kochba, Kokhba or Cocheba). This name has clung to him in history mainly due to its use by ancient Christian authors who wrote it in Greek or Latin as *Chochebas or Chôchebas.*[21] Bar Cochba means "the son of the star." In the light of the new data this form is almost certainly to be regarded as a nickname, or at least as a name derived from a word-play on his real name. His full name is given as Simon ben/bar Kosibah in the new texts: *šm'wn bn kwsbh* (*Mur* 43,1), *šm'wn br kwsbh* (*Ḥbr* 1,3,11) sometimes spelled *kwsb'* (*Mur* 24 B 3, C 3. 30, E 2, G 3; *Ḥbr* 2,12), *kwśbh* (*Ḥbr* 14) or *kśbh* (*Ḥbr* 8). The Greek form of the name occurs in *Ḥbr* 6 as *Simôn Chôsiba,* giving us precious evidence of the pronunciation of the name.[22] His real name was, then, Simon the son of Kosibah—the latter is apparently the name of his father, and not of the locality from which he comes.[23]

---

20. Y. Yadin, "The Secret in the Cliffs: the Discovery of the Bar Kochba Letters," *Atlantic Monthly* 208/5 (Nov. 1961) 129-35. However, in a recent public lecture Yadin reported the number as 47 papyrus letters, contracts, deeds and 1 biblical fragment on skin.
21. Justin Martyr wrote *Chochebas* (*Apol.* 1.31; *MG* 6.376); likewise Orosius (7.31; *CSEL* 5.468), Jerome's translation of Eusebius' *Chronicon* (283F; *GCS* 47, 201). But Eusebius (*Eccl. Hist.* 4.6,2; 4.8,4; *GCS* 9, 306 and 316) has *Chôchebas.* This form of the name is also found in a few Rabbinical texts: *Seder 'Olam Rabbah* 30 (ed. B. Ratner, p. 146; one ms. has *br kkb'*); *Šilšelet haqqabbala* of R. Gedalya ben Yahya 40 (*br kwkb'*). See S. Yeivin, *Milḥemet bar Kôkbâ* (2nd ed.; Jerusalem: Mosad Bialik, 1953), pp. 145, 233-4.
22. See Y. Yadin, *BIES* 25 (1961) 54ff.; *BA* 24 (1961) 48. The siglum *Ḥbr* will hereafter refer to the texts of the Wâdi Ḥabra as they are cited in the *BIES* article of Yadin. An English translation of this article has appeared too: "Expedition D," *IsrEJ* 11 (1961) 36-52.
23. It has been suggested that *bn* or *br kwzyb'* in the Rabbinical writings may mean "the man of Kozeba," a town or locality mentioned in 1 Chr 4, 22 (*kôzēbā'*). But this suggestion can now be disregarded since the name is given in the new documents with a *samekh* or *śin* instead of a *zayin.* J. T. Milik [*RB* 60 (1953) 279-89] discussed the problem of the *bn X* names, whether they are always patronymics or could be designations of quality. However, in *DJD* 2, p. 126 he recognizes *bn kwsbh* as a patronymic, even though the etymology of *kwsbh* is quite obscure. This seems to be the better solution, until more evidence is forthcoming. Y. Yadin (*BIES* 25 [1961] 64) apparently also inclines

However, in Rabbinical writings his name is often given as *bn* or *br kwzyb'* (or *kwzb'*), "the son of the lie,"[24] a word-play involving the shift of the radicals *ksb* to *kzb,* the root meaning "to lie." Though the interpretation is questioned at times,[25] it still seems best to regard the Rabbinical *kôzîbâ* form of his name as due either to the Rabbis who did not approve of his anti-Roman uprising or to those who later reflected ironically on its ill-fated outcome. To them he was the "son of the lie." The other form of the name, *Kôkᵉbâ,* is likewise due to a word-play attributed to his contemporary, the great Rabbi Aqiba, who did approve of his movement. In fact, he regarded him as a messiah, and applied to him the oracle of Balaam, "A star shall advance from Jacob" (Nm 24, 17).[26] The patronymic *bar Kosibah* was changed to the Ara-

---

toward the view that *bar Kôkebâ* and *bar Kôzibâ* are nicknames. Cf. F. Nötscher, "Bar Kochba, Ben Kosba: der Sternsohn, der Prächtige," *VT* 11 (1961) 449-51.

24. Bab. Talmud, *Sanhedrin* XI.1,2; fol. 93b (ed. Goldschmidt, 7, 400); Jer. Talmud, *Ta'anith* 4. 68; *Echa Rabbah* 80. 2,5 (ed. S. Buber, p. 158): "Do not read *kôkāb,* 'star,' but *kôzēb,* 'liar.'"—J. T. Milik [*RB* 60 (1953) 277-8: *DJD* 2, p. 126] suggests that of the two forms of the name attested in the Rabbinical writings, *kwzb'* and *kwzyb',* the defective form was the more original, since the dissyllabic form **Kosba* becomes **Kozba* ("*s* s'assimilant à la sonore suivante"). The form with *z* would be a phonetic shift introduced into the writing, especially by those who only heard the name and related it to an otherwise known root. However, the trisyllabic form of the name is preserved in Greek, *Chôsiba.* When this is considered together with the Rabbinical *plena scriptio, kwzyb',* it appears that the more original form was *Kôsibah.* Hence, it is better to retain the suggestion that both *kwkb'* and *kwzb'* are the result of a play on the original name.

25. E. Schürer [*Geschichte des jüdischen Volkes im Zeitalter Jesu Christi* (5th ed.; Leipzig: J. C. Hinrichs, 1920) 1, 683; (Engl. tr. of 2nd ed. by J. MacPherson; Edinburgh: T. and T. Clark, 1905: 1/2, 298] maintains that it was "not until a comparatively late period, and only by a few individual writers, in view of his miserable collapse, [that] it was taken to mean liar or deceiver." Footnote 100 (Engl. 84): "Since Barcosiba or Bencosiba is the prevailing form, even in the mouths of such as esteemed him highly, like Akiba, it cannot have had a disrespectful meaning." It should be recalled, however, that Schürer's transliteration of the name with an *s* does not represent the real spelling of the name now known to us from the new finds, but is the frequently used German equivalent of Semitic *z* in the Rabbinical form of the name *kwzyb'.* What Schürer says might be accepted as correct, if we could be sure that R. Aqiba had not in fact used the correct form *kwsbh* (with a *samekh*), which was later normalized in the Rabbinical tradition to agree with the other form *kwzyb',* precisely because of the ill-fated outcome of the revolt.

26. Jer. Talmud, *Ta'anith* 4.68d: "R. Simon ben Yohai said, 'R. Aqiba, my teacher, expounded the passage: "There shall go forth a star (*kwkb*) out of Jacob" (Nm 24,17), as follows: "There goes *kwzb'* out from Jacob." When R. Aqiba saw Barcoziba, he said, "This is the king Messiah." Then R. Yoḥanan ben Torta said to him, "Aqiba, the grass will grow out of your jaw-bone, and the Son of David will not yet have come." ' " Similarly the Midrash *Echa Rabbah* (2.2,4 ed. S. Buber, p. 101;

maic *bar kôkebâ*, "the son of the star," whence comes our English form Bar Cochba, the name which has persisted for him in our history books.

Coins minted during the first year of the Second Revolt bear the name with a title, "Simon, Prince of Israel" (*šm'wn nśy' yśr'l*),[27] and the fuller form of the name and title is now attested in the new documents as "Simon ben Kosibah, Prince of Israel" (*šm'wn bn kwsb' nsy' yśr'l* [*Mur* 24 B 2-3] or "Simon bar Kosibah, the prince over Israel" (*šm'wn br kwsbh hnsy' 'l yśr'l* [*Ḥbr* 1]). The title, "Prince of Israel," designates the supreme rank which Bar Cochba held during the period of his leadership of the revolt. There was, however, apparently also a priestly co-leader, for other coins of the same period mention "Eleazar, the Priest" (*'l'zr hkwhn*).[28]

It is not unlikely that both the title, Prince of Israel, and the appellation, "the son of the star," are due to the messianic character of the uprising. Thanks to the discovery of the Qumrân texts, where we find a developed but complex messianic expectation formulated, it is easy for us to understand how Bar Cochba's movement could have been hailed as the event which was to free Jerusalem and redeem Israel. In the messianic expectations of the Qumrân sect the Oracle of Balaam played an important role. It is used in the third paragraph of the *Testimonia* text from Cave 4, in 1QM 11,5-7, in *CD* 7, 19-20. In the *Testimonia* text it refers to the Davidic Messiah, whereas its use in the *Testament of Levi* (18,3) is applied rather to the Aaronitic Messiah (but cf. the *Testament of Judah* 24, 1, where it is used of the

---

tr. by J. Rabbinowitz, in *Midrash Rabbah* [London: Soncino, 1951], p. 157).—Eusebius (*Eccl. Hist.* 4.6,2; *GCS* 9. 306) is also aware that *Barchôchebas* is related to *kwkb*, "star," when he says that he was "a man who was murderous and a bandit, but relied on his name, as if dealing with slaves, and claimed to be a luminary who had come down to them from heaven and was magically enlightening those who were in misery." This pejorative view of the leader of the Second Revolt agrees with that of other early Christian writers; see footnote 112.

27. It is now universally admitted that these Simon coins date from the Bar Cochba period; see A. Reifenberg, *Ancient Jewish Coins* (2nd ed.; Jerusalem: Rubin Mass, 1947), pp. 33-34, 64 (##190, 192, 193, 199); likewise *DJD* 2, p. 46. Some of the coins with the name *šm'wn* bear a star, which may refer to Aqiba's appellation of the leader as a messiah (see A. Reifenberg, *op. cit.*, p. 60 [##164, 167]). Cf. C. Roth, "Star and Anchor; Coin Symbolism and the End of Days," *'Ereṣ Yiśrā'ēl* 6 (1960) 13*-15*.

28. Perhaps this is R. Eleazar ben Azariah, the president of the Beth-Din in the place of Gamaliel II; see A. Reifenberg, *Ancient Jewish Coins*[2], 34 and 61 (##169, 170), p. 63 (##189, 189a), p. 64 (#196), p. 65 (#203); *DJD* 2, p. 47.—Y. Yadin (*BIES* 25 [1961] 59; *IsrEJ* 11[1961] 46) mentions that Ḥbr 11, a letter written by Simon bar Kosibah to two of his officers at 'En-gedi, contains a reference to a certain Baṭniyah bar Misah, who is called "our master" (*rbnw*). It is not yet determined who he is, nor what relationship he had to the rebel leader. See further "Les lettres de Bar Kokhéba," *Bible et Terre Sainte* 34 (1961) 15.

Kingly Messiah).[29] Even granting that such messianic expectations might have been rather "sectarian," and not necessarily characteristic of all contemporary Judaism, nevertheless they provide a background against which it is easy to understand how the uprising of the Jews in the second century after the horrible destruction of their "holy city" and the Temple of Yahweh in A. D. 70 could take on the colors and hues of a messianic movement. Simon ben Kosibah, as the leader of that Second Revolt, was the "Messiah," the "son of *the star.*" His revolt was dedicated to the "Liberation of Jerusalem," and the "Redemption of Israel," as the coins of his time attest.[30] We know nothing about his antecedents, and cannot even conjecture how he came to be the leader of the revolt. But at any rate he became for the Jews the "Prince of Israel," the *nāśī'*, the name reminiscent of the OT eschatological leader of the people spoken of by the prophet Ezekiel, who was to be descended from David (see Ez 34, 24; 37,25; 44,3).

The Causes of the Second Revolt

The causes of the Second Jewish Revolt have always been a subject of great debate among the historians of second century Palestine. How grateful we would be, then, if the new documents were to shed some light on this subject. However, the reports about the new discoveries and texts shed no new light on this area of our study and we are in no better position than previously. We present here a brief résumé only of what seems to be the state of the question regarding the sources today.

Ancient authorities assign various causes to the Second Revolt, most of which are not contradictory, but the problem is how to assess them. Modern historians do not always agree. E. Schürer has, however, effectively disposed of one claim that has often been put forth that the revolt was due to the permission given by Hadrian to the Jews to rebuild the Temple of Yahweh, but which was subsequently revoked by him.[31] There is really no foundation for the claim. The two reasons, however, which are seriously considered today, as having played a major rôle in causing the Jews to revolt, are those which come to us from Dio Cassius in his *Roman History* and from Spartian in his *Life of Hadrian.*

The first reason which we shall discuss is that given by Dio Cassius, *viz.* that the Emperor Hadrian, who was visiting the Near East,

---

29. See J. M. Allegro, "Further Messianic References in Qumran Literature," *JBL* 75 (1956) 182-87, Document IV. Cf. "'4Q Testimonia' and the New Testament," *TS* 18 (1957) 513-37; "The Use of Explicit Old Testament Quotations in Qumran Literature and in the New Testament," *NTS* 7 (1960-1) 297-333, esp. pp. 312 and 323. Likewise L. E. Toombs, "Barcosiba and Qumran," *NTS* 4 (1957) 65-71.
30. See A. Reifenberg, *Ancient Jewish Coins*², 60-66.
31. *GJV* 1.671.3 (Engl. tr. 289-91); similarly H. Strathmann, "Der Kampf um Beth-Ter," *PJB* 23 (1927) 103-5.

attempted to rebuild the city of Jerusalem as an important center of his empire and to erect on the site of the Temple of Yahweh a shrine to the Roman god Jupiter Capitolinus. Dio Cassius' text follows:

> At Jerusalem he [Hadrian] founded a city in place of the one which had been razed to the ground, naming it Aelia Capitolina, and on the site of the temple of the god he raised a new temple to Jupiter. This brought on a war of no slight importance nor of brief duration, for the Jews deemed it intolerable that foreign races should be settled in their city and foreign religious rites planted there. So long, indeed, as Hadrian was close by in Egypt and again in Syria, they remained quiet, save in so far as they purposely made of poor quality such weapons as they were called upon to furnish, in order that the Romans might reject them and they themselves might thus have the use of them; but when he went farther away, they openly revolted.[32]

This reason, as given by Dio Cassius, seems to fill out with details what Spartian, the biographer of Hadrian, very succinctly said of him in the following words: *sacra Romana diligentissime curavit, peregrina contempsit; pontificis maximi officium peregit.*[33] In other words, it was completely in character with Hadrian to attempt to rebuild Jerusalem after the fashion of Hellenistic cities and try to establish there the culture of the Greeks which he admired so much.

One of the problems connected with this cause for the Second Revolt is precisely the time when Hadrian began to build Aelia Capitolina. Dio Cassius' report seems to indicate that it was actually begun before the Revolt. Since this point enters into our later discussion of the dates of the revolt, it is important that we review here the reasons for thinking that Dio Cassius is correct.

The reign of Hadrian was marked by long journeys to the various parts of his empire. In the year A.D. 128 he undertook his second protracted visit to the Near East. While the data about his movements, his visits to various colonies, cities and countries, and his inspections of Roman legions and garrisons are relatively abundant, they are not, however, sufficient to establish with certainty their detailed chronological order. But it seems that he was at Antioch in Syria in autumn A.D. 129, and from there made his way to Beirut in Phoenicia, via Palmyra and Damascus. From Beirut he went to the province of Arabia, the former kingdom of the Nabataeans, and from Petra he came back to Jerash, where he apparently spent the winter of A.D. 129-

---

32. *Roman History* 69.12,1-2 (tr. by E. Cary, *Loeb Classical Library,* vol. 8, p. 449).

33. Aelius Spartianus, *Vita Hadriani,* 22.10; in the *Scriptores historiae augustae* (tr. by D. Magie, Loeb Classical Library, vol. 1, pp. 68-69). In connection with these testimonies it is customary for historians to discuss the *Epistle of Barnabas* (16,4), but the value of this text, which is corrupt in a crucial spot, is quite debatable. See E. Schürer, *GJV* 1.672 (Engl. tr. 290); H. Strathmann, *PJB* 23 (1927) 104; H. Bietenhard, "Die Freiheitskriege der Juden unter den Kaisern Trajan und Hadrian und der messianische Tempelbau," *Judaica* 4 (1948) 95-100.

30.[34] From Jerash he must have made his way to Judaea, for coins have been found commemorating his *parousia* or arrival there: *adventui Aug(usti) Iudaeae.*[35] He seems to have visited Eleutheropolis, Tiberias, Caesarea Maritima and Gaza.[36] In many of these places he was hailed as *restitutor, oikistês, ktistês, euergetês,* which titles are generally attributed to his policy of setting the Roman garrisons to work in building Hellenic-style cities in these areas.[36a] While there is no direct evidence of Hadrian's visit to Jerusalem, it is quite likely that he visited the town, given its importance in the history of Palestine, its fairly recent destruction by Roman troops, and the fact that a garrison of the *Legio X Fretensis* was still stationed there. En route to Gaza and subsequently Egypt, where he spent the winter of A.D. 130, he must have passed Jerusalem. It is likely that he ordered the rebuilding of the city as the *colonia Aelia Capitolina* at this time. At any rate, Hadrian was in Egypt by November A.D. 130, for he saluted the colossal statute of Memnon at Thebes on the 21st of that month.[37] Apparently he returned to Syria in the spring of A.D. 131 and then proceeded to visit the regions of Pontus and the Black sea.[38] He passed the winter of 131-32 at Athens. The withdrawal to these more distant places is probably what Dio Cassius has in mind, when he refers to the outbreak of the Second Revolt.

A different reason, however, is given by Spartian for the revolt, one which has nothing to do with the attempt to rebuild Jerusalem as a Hellenic city. The biographer of Hadrian records it thus: *moverunt*

---

34. The inscription on the triumphal arch at Jerash, which was erected on the occasion of Hadrian's visit there, is dated to the fourteenth *tribunicia potestas* and the 192nd year of the era of Jerash (=the Pompeian era), *i.e.* 1 October 129-30. See W. F. Stinespring, "The Inscription of the Triumphal Arch at Jerash," *BASOR* 56 (1934) 15-16; C. H. Kraeling (ed.), *Gerasa: City of the Decapolis* (New Haven: American Schools of Oriental Research, 1938), pp. 401-2; C. C. McCown, "New Historical Items from Jerash Inscriptions," *JPOS* 16 (1936) 69-78, esp. pp. 75-76; M. I. Rostovtzeff, *CRAIBL* 1934, p. 267.—On the journeys of Hadrian in general see J. Dürr, *Die Reisen des Kaisars Hadrian* (Vienna: G. Gerold, 1881); B. W. Henderson, *The Life and Principate of the Emperor Hadrian* A.D. 76-138 (London: Methuen, 1923), pp. 128ff.; B. d'Orgeval, *L'empereur Hadrien: oeuvre législative et administrative* (Paris: Ed. Domat Montchrestien, 1950), pp. 25ff.; W. F. Stinespring, "Hadrian in Palestine, 129/130 A.D.," *JAOS* 59 (1939) 360-5.
35. See H. Mattingly and E. A. Sydenham, *The Imperial Roman Coinage; Vol. II Vespasian to Hadrian* (London: Spink, 1926), p. 454 (##890-94); M. Bernhart, *Handbuch zur Münzkunde der römischen Kaiserzeit* (Halle a. d. S.: A. Riechmann, 1926), Textband, p. 103, n. 1; H. St. J. Hart, "Judaea and Rome: the Official Commentary," *JTS* n. s. 3 (1952) 172-98 (esp. pl. V, ##1-4).
36. See F.-M. Abel, *Histoire de la Palestine depuis la conquête d'Alexandre jusqu'à l'invasion arabe* (Études bibliques; Paris: Gabalda), vol. 2 (1952) pp. 74, 79ff.
36a. See R. MacMullen, "Roman Imperial Building in the Provinces," *Harvard Studies in Classical Philology* 64 (1959) 207-35.
37. Cf. *CIG* 4737.
38. See Arrian, *Periplus ponti Euxini,* 1.1 (ed. R. Hercher, 1885, p. 86).

ea tempestate et Iudaei bellum, quod vetabantur mutilare genitalia.[39] The emperor Domitian had earlier forbidden castration. Dio Cassius records, "He forbade that any person in the Roman Empire should thereafter be castrated."[40] This prohibition was repeated by the Emperor Nerva.[41] But when Hadrian came along, he interpreted the prohibition in such wise that it included circumcision.[42] The rescript which he issued apropos of it probably does not date from the beginning of his reign; it belongs more likely to the period just before the Second Revolt, and for that reason is given by Spartian as a cause of the revolt.[43] Hadrian made both castration and circumcision a crime punishable by death, by subsuming it under the existing *lex Cornelia de sicariis et veneficis.* Such a law naturally touched a major tenet of the religion of the Jews and it is not improbable that it contributed to their rebellion against Roman domination.

The widening of the prohibition of castration to include circumcision, however, was not specifically directed against the Jews. There is no evidence that Hadrian so intended it. On the contrary, when under Antoninus Pius permission was given to the Jews to circumcise their children again, the prohibition still stood good against the non-Jewish peoples.[44] Consequently, it appears that the prohibition of circumcision was a general one, but affected an important Jewish religious rite—a rite for which the Jews were as prompt to rebel as for the building of a shrine of Jupiter on the site of Yahweh's Temple in Jerusalem.

The prevailing opinion among modern historians of the period is to accept both the cause given by Dio Cassius and that supplied by Spartian, since they are not conflicting reasons and both may have been the prime factors in the uprising. Whether there were other sub-

---

39. *Vita Hadriani,* 14.2.
40. *Rom. Hist.* 67.2,3. See also Suetonius, *Domitian,* 7.1: "Castrari mares vetuit"; Eusebius, *Chronicon* 272F (*GCS* 47.190) : "Domitianus eunuchos fieri prohibuit." H. Hitzig, "Castratio," *Pauly-Wissowa Real-Encyclopädie* 3/2 (1889) 1772-3; B. d'Orgeval, *L'empereur Hadrien,* p. 324.
41. Dio Cassius, *Rom. Hist.* 68.2,4.
42. See Ulpian, Digesta, 48.8,4: "Divus Hadrianus rescripsit: constitutum quidem est, ne spadones fierent, eos autem, qui hoc crimine arguerentur, Corneliae legis poena teneri. . . ." The *lex Cornelia de sicariis et veneficis* punished murder with death. This was applied to the physician who performed the castration; the eunuch was punished with exile and loss of property.
43. This is accepted as a cause of the revolt by E. Schürer, *GJV*; M. Noth, *The History of Israel* (2nd English ed.; New York: Harper, 1960), pp. 451-2; H. Hitzig, "Circumcisio," *Pauly-Wissowa Real-Encyclopädie* 3/2 (1899) 2570-1. But it is questioned by H. Bietenhard, *Judaica* 4 (1948) 92-94.
44. See Modestinus, *Digesta* 48.8,11: "Circumcidere Iudaeis filios suos tantum rescripto divi Pii permittitur; in non eiusdem religionis qui hoc fecerit, castrantis poena irrogatur." See E. Schürer, *GJV* 1.677; E. M. Smallwood, "The Legislation of Hadrian and Antoninus Pius against Circumcision," *Latomus* 18 (1959) 334-47.

ordinate reasons we do not know for certain.[45]

It should be noted, however, that Pausanias and Chrysostom were content to ascribe the Second Revolt merely to the general disobedience and the revolutionary tendency of the Jews, who were hankering after the restoration of their ancient political state.[46] But this is a description rather of the general background of the period under Roman domination, especially since the destruction of Jerusalem in A.D. 70. After Titus left the town in ruins and a garrison of the *Legio X Fretensis* was stationed there to maintain Roman military control, the lot of the Jews in the empire was not easy. Under Vespasian the procuratorial province of Judaea was administered as an imperial province with the official name *Iudaea.* It was not a part of the *provincia Syriae,* but depended directly on the emperor and thus had the appearance of independence, at least of the neighboring Roman administration in Syria. *Iudaea* was governed by a *legatus* who resided at Caesarea Maritima. Roman colonists were settled in Flavia Neapolis (modern Nablus) and 800 veterans were given property in Emmaus. In Jerusalem itself some of the old inhabitants, both Jews and the Christians, who had returned from Pella, lived side by side with the Romans. In fact, in recent times it has become clear that more Jews actually lived in Jerusalem between the two revolts than we normally imagine, as ossuaries and other burials of the period attest. Vespasian had claimed the whole of the land of Judaea as his private property and tenant-farmers worked the land for him. The Jewish community, accustomed to pay a didrachm or half-shekel as a tax for the Temple of Yahweh, now had to contribute the same to the *fiscus iudaicus* which eventually benefited the Roman Temple of Jupiter Capitolinus. The Temple cult was no more and with it passed away the influence of the Jerusalem Sanhedrin headed by the high priest. Religious emphasis among the Jews shifted to certain forms of synagogue worship and to the study of the Torah to insure its careful

---

45. S. Perowne (*Hadrian* [London: Hodder and Stoughton, 1960], pp. 149-50) summarizes thus the grievances which the Jews could have had against Hadrian by the year 130: "First, he had declared himself the successor of Antiochus Epiphanes. He had finished Antiochus' own temple in Athens. Secondly, like Antiochus, he had adopted, or allowed others to adopt in addressing him, the style of god, of Zeus Olympios. Thirdly, he had permitted this style to appear on coins which circulated among Jewish communities. Fourthly, he had prohibited circumcision, which for the Jews was the very seal of their being and faith. Fifthly, he was on his way to patronize and caress the Greeks of Alexandria, who had shewn themselves the most ardent enemies of the Jews. Sixthly, he had gone out of his way to honour the very man who had captured Jerusalem, almost two centuries before, and had violated the Holy of Holies [*i.e., Pompey*]. Seventhly, and finally, he had given orders for the obliteration of Jerusalem, for the construction on the site of a Roman colony, called by his own name, and containing, on the very site of the ancient Temple, a shrine where he himself should be venerated."

46. Pausanias, *Periegesis* 1.5,5; Chrysostom, *Adv. Judaeos* 5, 11; *MG* 48.900.

observance (especially according to the traditions of the Pharisees and the Rabbis). The council of 72 Elders (or Rabbis) in Jamnia (Yabneh), under the leadership of R. Joḥanan ben Zakkai and later under R. Gamaliel II, took over the rule of the Jewish community in Palestine. It enjoyed a certain autonomy even though the land was still dominated by the Romans, who normally did not interfere with the workings of the council. It fixed the calendar and the canon of the Scriptures and functioned as a court of law. But both in Palestine and in the diaspora there was always the yearning for the "restoration of Israel," a yearning fed by the recollection of what had taken place after the destruction of Jerusalem in 586 B.C. When Trajan (A.D. 98-117) was occupied with the threat of the Parthians, revolts of the Jews occurred in Cyrene, Egypt, Cyprus and in Mesopotamia (toward the end of his reign, *ca.* 115-6).[47] These revolts were in part fired by the messianic expectations current among the Jews of the time. The general who finally put down the Mesopotamian revolt was the Romanized Moor, Lusius Quietus, who was subsequently rewarded with the governorship of Palestine.[48] We know little about the conditions of Palestine between the two revolts, but the fact that Lusius Quietus was sent there as governor would indicate that elements of unrest were present there too. It is to this general background of unrest among the Jews, both in the diaspora and in the motherland, that the statements of Pausanias and Chrysostom are best related. Given such hopes of a liberating messiah to come and such hankering after the freedom of old, the two causes of the Second Revolt as stated by Dio Cassius and Spartian become readily intelligible.

The Dates of the Revolt

The dates normally given for the Second Revolt are A.D. 132-5. The beginning of the revolt is usually reckoned according to the notice in Dio Cassius, that the Jews "openly revolted," when Hadrian withdrew from their vicinity to more distant regions, as we have seen. These dates have been preferred by modern historians to those supplied by Epiphanius and the *Chronicon Paschale*. The former gives the forty-seventh year after the destruction of Jerusalem as the date of Hadrian's visit to Jerusalem and the building of Aelia Capitolina, which oc-

---

47. See Dio Cassius, *Rom. Hist.* 68.32,1-3 (which ascribes much bloodshed and gruesome atrocities to the Jews in Cyrene, Egypt and Cyprus). Similarly Eusebius, *Eccl. Hist.* 4.2,1-5 (who mentions the revolts in Alexandria, the rest of Egypt, Cyrene and Mesopotamia in the 18th regnal year of Trajan). Cf. V. A. Tcherikover and A. Fuks, *Corpus papyrorum iudaicarum* (Cambridge, Mass.: Harvard Univ. Press), vol. 1 (1957), pp. 85-93; H. Bietenhard, *Judaica* 4 (1948) 66-67.

48. Dio Cassius, *Rom. Hist.* 68.32.5; Eusebius, *Chronicon* in Armenian translation by J. Karst, *GCS* 20.219.—The *Seder 'Olam Rabbah* 30 (ed. B. Ratner, p. 146) speaks of a "war of Quietus," but historians are reluctant to take this expression in a strict sense; moreover, the text may not be sound. See H. Bietenhard, *Judaica* 4 (1948) 70-77.

casioned the revolt.[49] This, however, cannot be correct, for it would equal A.D. 117, the very year of Hadrian's accession to the imperial throne. The *Chronicon Paschale* also gives a misleading date, in associating the building of Aelia Capitolina with the third year of the 224th Olympiad, in the consulship of Aelius Hadrianus Augustus and Rusticius.[50] This would be the year A.D. 119. Although we cannot date precisely the year in which Hadrian began the rebuilding of Jerusalem, it seems to have been before the Second Revolt, and most probably in the year A.D. 130. Dio Cassius' report implies that some time passed before the Jews openly rebelled. Hence the year is usually given as A.D. 132.

New light has been shed on the question by the dates given in one of the documents from a Murabba'ât cave. *Mur* 24 is an abstract of title-deeds written on a papyrus by a deputy of Bar Cochba, in whose name various farm-lands were rented out in return for crops to be paid into the "treasury" of the Prince of Israel. It belongs to a *genre* called in Greek *diastrôma* and already known from the papyri found at Oxyrhynchus in Egypt.[51] In each case a record is made of the date, the competent authority, the names of the lessees, the fact of the rental, the duration of it, and the terms (stating the exact amount of wheat which is to be paid yearly to the "treasury"); finally the signatures are appended. In *Mur* 24 there are eleven fragmentary texts of this sort, the wording of which offers at times slight variants. The item of interest to our discussion here is found in texts B and E of this document; it is the synchronism of dates which is given. We supply the text of one of the deeds in order to comment on it and explain the synchronism.[52]

Mur 24 E (*DJD* 2.131)

[*b'śryn lš*] *bṭ šnt št* [*ym*] *lg'lt*[53]	[The 20th of She] bat, the 2 [nd] year of the Redemption of
[*y*] *śr'l 'l yd šm'wn bn k* [*ws*] *b' nsy'*	[I] srael by Simon ben K [osi]-bah, the Prince of

---

49. Epiphanius, *De mensuris et ponderibus* 14; *MG* 43.259-61.
50. *MG* 92.613; ed. Dindorf, I. 474. For a modern, but isolated, attempt to defend these dates see W. D. Gray, "The Founding of Aelia Capitolina and the Chronology of the Jewish War under Hadrian," *AJSL* 39 (1922-3) 248-56. See also M. Auerbach, *Zur politischen Geschichte der Juden unter Kaiser Hadrian* (Berlin: 1924), p. 325.
51. Oxy P 274 (dated A.D. 89-97); see B. P. Grenfell and A. S. Hunt, *The Oxyrhynchus Papyri, Edited with Translations and Notes* (London: Egypt Exploration Fund, 1899), 2.259-62.
52. The lacunae in the text are restored with certainty due to the very similar wording of these parts in the other fragmentary texts, which fortunately do not have the lacunae always in the identical spot.
53. *lg'lt yśr'l*: Milik rightly understands this expression as a synonym for *lḥrwt yrwšlm*, adducing as evidence the interchange of these expressions in different dates or years on coins (see A. Reifenberg, *Ancient Jewish Coins*², 60 [#163, *lg'lt yśr'l*, ##170-2, 189-95]) and in the new documents (*Mur* 23 and 24). There is no reason to regard *lg'lt*

[*yś*] *r'l bmḥnh šywšb bhrwdys*[54]	[Is] rael, in the camp which is situated at Herodium.
[*y*] *hwdh bn rb' lhll bn grys*[55]	[Ye] hudah ben Rabba' declared to Hillel ben Garis:
'ny mrṣwny [*ḥ*] *krt*[56] *hmk*[57] *hywm 't*	"I, of my own free will, have [ren] ted from you today
h'pr[58] *šhw' š ly bḥ‹k›rty b'yr*	the farm-land, which is mine by my tenancy in 'Ir-
nḥš šḥkrt mšm'wn nsy' yśr'l	Naḥaš (and) which I have rented from Simon, the Prince of Israel.
t[59] *'pr hlz ḥkrty hmk mn hywm*	This land I have rented from you from today
'd swp 'rb hšmṭh šhm šnym	until the end of the eve of Remission, which is (in) complete years,

---

yśr'l as the more messianic title given to the revolt and *lḥrwt yrwšlm* as the more political one, as suggested by B. Kanael, "The Historical Background of the Coins 'Year Four . . . of the Redemption of Zion,'" *BASOR* 129 (1953) 20. For two hybrid coins in A. Reifenberg, *Ancient Jewish Coins*², #171-2, bear on the obverse *šnt 'ḥt lg'lt yśr* and on the reverse *š b lḥr yśr'l.*

54. *bmḥnh šywšb bhrwdys*: Milik's translation links these words with the preceding *nsy' yśr'l,* "Prince d'Israël en campagne, qui réside à Hérodium." He interprets the expression to mean that Bar Cochba had his headquarters at Herodium. However, Y. Yadin ["Were the Headquarters of Bar Cochba at Herodium?" *Hā-'Āreṣ* 10 March 1961, p. 10; see also *IsrEJ* 11 (1961) 51] has shown that the Hebrew need not mean that; the sense is rather that the contract was made in the camp at Herodium. This interpretation is confirmed by other documents found in the Wâdi Ḥabra cave in 1960, which make it unlikely that the headquarters of Bar Cochba were on Herodium. See further discussion *infra.* Cf. *Mur* 18,2, where the place in which the text is written seems to be named; likewise *Mur* 19.1,12; 115.2.
55. *hll bn grys*: The same individual is mentioned in the other deeds (*Mur* 24 B 6, C 5, [F 4-5], [H 3], J 3), and is probably the administrator in charge of the lands in the village of 'Ir-Naḥaš, near Eleutheropolis, the modern Deir Naḫḫas, about a mile and a half *ENE* of Beit Jibrin.
56. *ḥkrt*: The verb *ḥkr* means to "contract, farm," especially to "give or take in rent on a fixed rental payable in kind" (Jastrow, p. 463). The details of the text bear out this meaning.
57. *hmk*: Defective spelling of the Mishnaic Hebrew *hymk* (*hêmekā*), an alternate form of *mmk,* "from you." See M. H. Segal, *A Grammar of Mishnaic Hebrew* (Oxford: Clarendon, 1958), p. 144.
58. *h'pr*: Normally this word means "loose earth" (whence a number of figurative meanings are derived); but here it equals "a piece of farmland."
59. *t*: This form, which is found often in these documents (*Mur* 22 i 2; 24 A 8, B 18, C 16, D 11, E 8,10,13; 36 i-ii 3; 43 3,5; 44 6,7,8,9; 46 3,5), is related by Milik to the Punic *t,* a form of the *signum accusativi* (See Z. Harris, *A Grammar of the Phoenician Language* [American Oriental Series 8; New Haven: American Oriental Society, 1936], p. 76; J. Friedrich, *Phönizisch-Punische Grammatik* [Analecta Orientalia 32; Rome: Pontifical Biblical Institute, 1951] #255).

šlmwt šny [*m*] *ksh*[60] *ḥmš t ḥkyr*	[fi] scal years, five. (This is) the rent
[*š'h*]*' mwdd*[61] *lk b* [*hr*] *wdys ḥnṭyn*	[which I sha] ll pay to you at [He] rodium: wheat
[*ypwt wnqywt*] *šlw* [*št kwr*] *yn wltk*	[of good quality and pure], thr [ee ko] rs and a letek,
[*m'srt m'srt*] *t 'lh*	[tithed . . . having tithed] these
[*šth' šwql 'l gg h'wṣr*[62]] *w* [*q*] *ym*	[which you will pay into the treasury]. (This document is) valid,
[*'ly l'mt kkh*[63]]	[therefore, against me]."
[*yhwdh bn rb' 'l npšh*]	[Yehudah ben Rabba', for himself]
[*šm'wn bn kwsb' mn m'mrh*[64]]	[Simon ben Kosibah, at his command].

There are several important items in this text which shed new light on the affairs of second century Palestine. For the moment we are only interested in those which help to fix the date of the Second Revolt more precisely. These are, first of all, the date of the document itself, "the 20th of Shebat, the 2nd year of the Redemption of Israel"; secondly, the reference to the "end of the eve of Remission," and lastly the indication that the contract would last up to that time, a period of "five complete years." The "remission" (*šemiṭṭâ*) referred to is the observance of the regulation of Ex 23,10-11, according to which the land is to lie fallow every seventh year.[65] The contract is thus made to be valid up to the end of the sixth year of the current seven-year or sabbatical cycle. Until that time there are five complete years, *i.e.* years when the rental on the harvest derived from the land must be paid. This means, therefore, that the 20th of Shebat of the second

---

60. *šny mksh*: Lit. "years of the toll or tax," from the root *mks*, "to pay a toll on" (Jastrow, p. 783).
61. *šh' mwdd*: The relative pronoun *š* precedes the 1 sg. impf. Qal of *hyh* in an apocopated form; see M. H. Segal, *op. cit.*, p. 95. The 2 sg. is restored in 1. 14. The root *mdd*, "to measure," is often used for measuring off a tithe; compare *šql* in 1. 14.
62. *'l gg h'wṣr*: Lit. "on the roof of the treasury." Milik explains the expression by the shape of public granaries in the ancient East, especially in Egypt, which were great round silos with an opening on top through which the grain was poured. See J. B. Pritchard, *Ancient Near East in Pictures Relating to the Old Testament* (Princeton: University Press, 1954) #90.
63. *l'mt kkh*: Lit. "in accordance with thus"; = *'l kk* of the OT.
64. *mn m'mrh*: "At his command," the form of the suffix being an Aramaism, as in *npšh* (1. 16). This expression indicates that Hillel ben Garis was acting as a deputy for Bar Cochba.
65. It may also refer to Dt 15,1ff., which ordains that every seventh year a creditor's claims are to be remitted; *šmṭh*, the noun, is found explicitly in this connection. Cf. *Mur* 18.7.

year of the Redemption of Israel falls in the second year of the sabbatical cycle. Since Shebat corresponds roughly to January-February, the 20th of this month would equal the early part of February in our calendar.

Now Rabbinical tradition has recorded that the Temple was destroyed by Titus during *môṣā'ê šᵉbî'ît*,[66] which means the year after the Sabbath-year. Hence, the year itself was A.D. 68-69, beginning with the month of Tišri.[67] The subsequent Sabbath-years fell on 75-76, 82-83, 89-90, 96-97, 103-104, 110-111, 117-118, 124-125, 131-132.[68] The year 132-133 was, then, the first year of the new cycle and 133-134 its second year. Therefore, the document was written at the beginning of February of the year 134. This date is indicated as corresponding with the second year of the "Redemption of Israel." We have unfortunately no certitude as to what month was used as the beginning of the year in this reckoning. Milik has suggested Tišri.[69] In that case, there would be a perfect agreement of the beginning of the sabbatical cycle with that of the new era of the Redemption of Israel. In such a case, the revolt began on, or at least was officially reckoned from, 1 Tišri A.D. 132. This reckoning, however, does not agree with that proposed by Milik, *viz.* 1 Tišri A.D. 131, for he maintains that we must correct the normally accepted date. We have, however, used the same

---

66. *Seder 'Olam Rabbah* 30 (ed. B. Ratner, p. 147); cf. Bab. Talmud, *'Arakhin* 11b (ed. Soncino Press, 33.65); *Ta'anith* 29a (ed. Goldschmidt, 3.520). Milik (*DJD* 2. 125) says that Josephus mentions this year as a Sabbath year, but gives no references.
67. Mishnah, *Roš haššanah* 1,1; "There are four 'New Year' days: on the 1st of Nisan is the New Year for kings and feasts; on the 1st of Elul is the New Year for the Tithe of Cattle . . .; on the 1st of Tishri is the New Year for [the reckoning of] the years [of foreign kings], of the Years of Release and Jubilee years, for the planting [of trees] and for vegetables; and the 1st of Shebat is the New Year for [fruit-] trees . . ." (tr. H. Danby, *The Mishnah* [London: Oxford, 1954], p. 188). Josephus (*Ant.* 1. #81) also mentions an autumn New Year for "selling, buying and other ordinary affairs" (i.e. the making and dating of contracts). Cf. J. Jeremias, *ZNW* 27 (1928) 98.
68. Milik (*DJD* 2. 125) says: "L'année sabbatique la plus proche de la fin de la Révolte, 135 ap. J.-C. (date assurée par les sources romaines), est donc 130/1 et la deuxième année du cycle suivant correspond à 132/3."—The same miscalculation has been noted by S. Zeitlin, "The Fiction of the Bar Kokba Letters," *JQR* 51 (1960-1) 265-74, esp. p. 267. Cf. also L. Kadman, *The Coins of Aelia Capitolina* (Corpus Nummorum Palaestinensium 1; Jerusalem: Universitas, 1956), p. 17, who shows that a Bar Cochba coin overstruck on a coin from Gaza with the double date of the third year of the visit of Hadrian and the 192nd year of the Era of Gaza (= A.D. 131-2) gives this year as the *terminus post quem* for the outbreak of the revolt.
69. Milik is, however, aware of a complication here, when he writes, "On se rappellera cependant que le Nouvel An d'automne ne valait que pour la datation des contrats. Il reste à étudier si cette ère telle qu'elle est attestée par les monnaies ne doit pas plutôt commencer au 1er Nisan, et s'il s'agit du 1er Nisan de 131 ou de 132" (*DJD* 2.67); cf. *Bible et Terre Sainte* 33 (1960) 16. The year is certainly A.D. 132, but no evidence so far has settled the month, Nisan or Tišri.

presuppositions as he has in our reckoning, and it seems to us that his calculation is off by one year. Reckoning the Sabbath-years from 68-69 one does not arrive at 130-131.

Rabbinical tradition has preserved the notice that Bar Cochba's revolt lasted for three and a half years (*mlkwt bn kwzyb' šlš šnym wmḥṣh*).[70] This has often been suspected, because the same tradition ascribes three and a half years to Vespasian's and Titus' siege of Jerusalem, and also because it is reminiscent of the apocalyptic passages in Dn 7,25 and 9,27, which are thought to have been operative in the creation of this tradition. However, one of the new texts from Murabba'ât is dated in the "third year of the freedom of Jerusalem" (*Mur* 25 i 1) and two Aramaic contracts from the cave in the Wâdi Seiyâl are reported to be dated in the "third year of the liberation of Israel" (see above). Finally, and best of all, there is *Mur* 30.8, which contains the date the "21st of Tišri of the fourth year of the Redemption of Israel." This puts an end to a puzzling problem about the duration of the revolt as posed by the coins of the period. Coins had been found dated *šnt 'ḥt lg'lt yśr'l* ("the first year of the Redemption of Israel") or *š b lḥr yśr'l* ("the second year of the Freedom of Israel").[71] But none were dated after that year. Reifenberg's solution was to maintain that those which simply bore *lḥrwt yrwšlm* without a date were minted in the third year of the revolt, but after Jerusalem had again fallen into the hands of the Romans. It is now certain that the revolt lasted into the beginning of the fourth year at least, and so the Rabbinical tradition about three and a half years is not far off.

However, according to our calculation the 21st of Tišri of the fourth year of the Redemption of Israel would equal October A.D. 135 (according to Milik it is the year 134). Eusebius (*Eccl. Hist.* 4.6,3) mentions that the war "reached its height in the eighteenth year of the reign of Hadrian in Beththera, which was a strong citadel not very far from Jerusalem; the siege lasted a long time before the rebels were driven to final destruction by famine and thirst." The eighteenth regnal year of Hadrian is normally reckoned as 11 August 134-135.[72] If our reckoning of the beginning of the era of the "Redemption of Israel" is correct, and *Mur* 30 is to be dated to the 21st of Tišri A.D. 135, then Eusebius' statement just quoted must be taken more seriously and exactly than it normally is. For it is usual to regard it as meaning that the revolt came to an end in Hadrian's eighteenth year.[73] However, what Eusebius actually says is that the war came to a head or a climax in Hadrian's eighteenth year (*akmasantos de tou polemou*

---

70. *Seder 'Olam Rabbah* 30 (ed. B. Ratner, p. 146); cf. Jerome, *Comm. in Danielem* 9; *ML* 25, 577-8. The Midrash, *Echa Rabbah* 2.2,4 (ed. S. Buber, p. 101), attributes three and a half years to the siege of Beth-Ter alone; this is impossible.
71. A. Reifenberg, *Ancient Jewish Coins*^{2}, ##189, 197; see also p. 35.
72. See Spartian, *Vita Hadriani*, 4.7, where it is recorded that Hadrian's regnal year is to be reckoned from the 11th of August.
73. So E. Schürer, *GJV* 1.695 (Engl. tr. 310) and many others.

etous oktôkaidekatou tês 'êgemonias kata Bêththêra . . . tês te exôthen poliorkias chroniou genomenês), and that the siege lasted a long time. The Armenian text of Eusebius' *Chronicon,* moreover, lists that the Jewish war came to an end in Hadrian's *nineteenth* year.[74]

Further corroboration of this is derived from another source. As a result of the final defeat of the Jewish rebels and the conclusion of the "Jewish war" Hadrian was acclaimed *imperator* for the second time. For a long time the title *Imp. II* was not found with certainty in any inscription before A.D. 136. But it is now known that the second acclamation occurred toward the end of Hadrian's nineteenth *tribunicia potestas.*[75] The twentieth began on 10 December A.D. 135, and the earliest occurrence of *Imp. II* is thus dated before that. If the revolt had already begun its fourth year by the 21st of Tišri (= October) 135, it is hardly likely that Hadrian's troops had as yet put an end to it. So his second acclamation as *imperator* must have occurred between October and 10 December A.D. 135. This still leaves open the question whether the year is to be reckoned from 1 Nisan or 1 Tišri. But it confirms the data advanced above for the termination of the revolt in the year A.D. 135.

Rabbinical tradition has, however, recorded that Beth-Ter fell on the 9th of Ab (July). But this date probably represents a conflation of the celebrations of three fast-days rather than the recollection

---

74. Karst's German translation for the 19th year (*GCS* 20.221): "Der jüdische Krieg, der im Palästinerlande war, endigte, indem übel hergenommen die Juden kaum der Vernichtung entgingen." Cf. H. Strathmann, *PJB* 23 (1927) 100, 111 n. 2.
75. The evidence is complicated. Several inscriptions are known from the year A.D. 134-5 without any mention of Hadrian's second acclamation. The latest of these are *CIL* 3, #XXXV (dated 15 Sept. 134; cf. *CIL* 16, #79); *CIL* 16, #82 (dated 14 Apr. 135). Earlier ones of the same year are: *CIL* 3. #XXXIV; 6. #973; 9. #4359; 10. #7855. On the other hand, it is clearly found in several inscriptions dated to the *trib. pot.* XX (i.e. after 10 December 135): CIL 6.#976, 975; *Papyri Osloenses* (edd. S. Eitrem and L. Amundsen), 3. #78 (dated before 31 May 136); R. Cagnat, *Inscriptiones graecae ad res romanas pertinentes,* 3. #896; and probably also in *CIL* 14. #4235 (where [*trib. pot. X*]*X* is restored and the date is 14, 19, 24, or 29 Dec. 135). This would give a date between April and 10 December 135. However, the second acclamation occurs in an inscription which is dated in the *trib. pot. XVIIII,* hence before 10 December 135. See *CIG* 12 *Suppl.* (1939), #239; W. Peek, *Archaiologikê Ephêmeris* 1931, p. 113, #9; C. Seltman, "Appendix," *Hesperia* 17 (1958) 85; F. M. Heichelheim, "New Light on the End of Bar Kokba's War," *JQR* 34 (1943-4) 61-3. It may also occur in an undated fragmentary inscription whose restoration is not certain (*CIL* 2, #478); see also *CIL* 6. #974. Since the date of the "21st of Tišri of the fourth year of the Redemption of Israel" is found in *Mur* 30.8, the interval in which the second acclamation took place thus becomes October to 10 December 135. However, it should be noted that there are a few inscriptions of the year 136 which do not mention *Imp. II* (*CIL* 14, #2088; 3. #749), and that S. Perowne *Hadrian,* 165) reckons the fall of Beth-Ter in A.D. 136. Cf. B. W. Henderson, *Life and Principate,* 218, n. 4.

of an actual historical date: one fast-day commemorated the three great Jewish defeats. As the Mishnah puts it, "Five things befell our fathers on the 17th of Tammuz and five on the 9th of Ab. . . . On the 9th of Ab it was decreed against our fathers that they should not enter into the Land [of Israel; Nm 14,29ff.], and the Temple was destroyed the first and the second time, and Beth-Tor [=Beth-Ter] was captured and the City was ploughed up."[76]

The Period of the Revolt Itself

The information about the course of the revolt is meagre indeed. From what there is it seems that Jerusalem was wrested once again from the control of the Romans. This is certainly implied in the coins which were minted with the inscription *lḥrwt yrwšlm*, "Of the Liberation of Jerusalem." It is not improbable that the cult of Yahweh on the site of the old Temple was resumed, and that this was commemorated by the coins struck with the title *'l'zr hkwhn*, "Eleazar, the Priest." That an attempt was made by the Jews to rebuild the Temple itself at this time would not surprise us, although there is no definite information regarding this point.[77]

Did Bar Cochba attempt to reinforce Jerusalem at this time? The archaeologists, who have studied the problem of the "Third Wall" of Jerusalem, of which Josephus speaks (*JW* 5. #147), are not of one mind regarding it. The line of an ancient wall which has been traced roughly from the old Russian colony (now in Israeli Jerusalem), past the front of the present American Consulate in Jordanian Jerusalem, to the American School of Oriental Research, has been regarded by E. Robinson and more recently by E. L. Sukenik and L. A. Mayer as the third north wall of the city of which Josephus speaks.[78] However,

---

76. *Ta'anith* 4.6 (tr. H. Danby, p. 200). Josephus (*JW* 6. #250) also knows of the tradition which assigns the double destruction of Jerusalem to the same day of the month: "But now in the revolution of the years had arrived the fated day, the tenth of the month Lous, the day on which of old it had been burnt by the king of Babylon." H. St. J. Thackeray's comment: "This is in accordance with Jer. lii. 12f., where the burning of the temple by Nebuzaradan, captain of Nebuchadrezzar's guard, is stated to have occurred on the 10th day of the 5th month (Heb. Ab = Lous in the Syrian calendar). In 2 Kings xxv. 8, on the other hand, the day is given as the 7th Ab; while, in Jewish tradition, the anniversary of the double burning has always been kept on the 9th Ab. A fictitious symmetry between corresponding events in the two sieges has probably been at work" (*Loeb Classical Library*, 3.448-9).

77. See S. Yeivin, *Milḥemet Bar Kôkbâ* 78f. Possibly the obscure reference in the *Epistle of Barnabas* (16, 1-7) should be considered in this connection; see note 33 above and H. Bietenhard, *Judaica* 4 (1948) 95ff.

78. *The Third Wall of Jerusalem: An Account of Excavations* (Jerusalem: Hebrew University Pres, 1930). W. F. Albright, *The Archaeology of Palestine* (Pelican A199; 5th ed.; Harmondsworth: Penguin, 1960), p. 158, favors this view. Cf. W. Ross, "The Four North Walls of Jerusalem," *PEQ* 1942, 69-81.

H. Vincent has maintained still more recently that this wall coincided roughly with the line of the present-day north wall of the Old City. For him the ancient wall which lies considerably to the north of it is nothing more than remnants of the rampart set up as an outer defence of the city under Bar Cochba. It is the "wall of Bar Cochba."[79] But W. F. Albright is inclined to follow the view of Sukenik and Mayer. This is a knotty problem in which the experts do not agree themselves; it must await further excavation and investigation for a solution. But it deserves mention here for the possible connection it may have with the Second Revolt.

If this is all true, it is difficult to understand how Dio Cassius (*Rom. Hist.* 69.13,1) could write, "At first the Romans took no account of them [the Jewish insurgents]. Soon, however, all Judaea had been stirred up, and the Jews everywhere were showing signs of disturbance, were gathering together, and giving evidence of great hostility to the Romans, partly by secret and partly by overt acts." This statement, however, is a brief summary of the whole revolt, and perhaps the liberation of Jerusalem itself was at first regarded as a minor, local skirmish by the Romans. Yet it was a local skirmish which apparently spread rapidly to all parts of Judaea.

Once Jerusalem had been liberated and Israel redeemed, the Prince of Israel had to organize the land for the continuation of the revolt. The administrative machinery and the division of the land into toparchies which had been set up by the Romans were apparently retained by Bar Cochba. He controlled the land of Judaea, especially the fertile Shephelah, and from the new documents we learn additional names of villages and districts under his control. In addition to Jerusalem, which name is probably to be read in *Mur* 29.9,11; 30.8 (see *DJD* 2. p. 205), the following places came under his administration directly or indirectly: Herodium (*Mur* 24 B4,C4,E3,I4), Teqoa' (*Mur* 47.6; *Ḥbr* 1 and 14), 'En-gedi (*Mur* 46.4; *Ḥbr* 12), Qiryat 'Arabayah (15), 'Ir-Naḥaš (*Mur* 24 B 8, C 7-8, E 6-7), Beth Mašiko (*Mur* 42.1,4), *Meṣad Ḥasîdîn* (identified by Milik with Khirbet Qumrân, *Mur* 45.6) and Kepar Biš, Kepar Šaḥalîm, Kepar Dikrîn (the three villages mentioned in Rabbinical writings as destroyed by the Romans [*Echa Rabbah* 53b; *Ta'anith* 4.69a; *Gittin* 4.6,3]). Y. Yadin conjectures that Bar Cochba also controlled Masadah at this time.[80] To this list must be added the place of his last stand, Beth-Ter (Eusebius, *Eccl. Hist.* 4.6,3).

Herodium is mentioned as the center of a toparchy in *Mur* 115.2, 21, a Greek document of remarriage dated A.D. 124. In the time of Bar Cochba it probably continued to be the center of the toparchy, for we learn that a camp was situated there (*Mur* 24 E3). Indeed,

---

79. H. Vincent and M.-A. Stève, *Jérusalem de l'Ancien Testament: Recherches d'archéologie et d'histoire* (Paris: Gabalda, 1954), vol. 1, pp. 146-74.

80. *BIES* 25 (1961) 63.

Milik has suggested on the basis of the phrase, *šm'wn bn kwsb' nsy' yśr'l bmḥnh šywšb bhrwdys,* that Bar Cochba as the warlike Messiah had made his headquarters at Herodium, and that it was from there that he withdrew to Beth-Ter as the Romans closed in about him. As we indicated in note 54, the Hebrew need not be so interpreted. Moreover, new information from the Wâdi Ḥabra texts suggests that it is quite unlikely that his headquarters were there. In Pap 12, as Y. Yadin has pointed out,[81] Bar Cochba writes to two of his officers at 'En-gedi:

mšm'wn br kwsb' l'nšy 'yngdy	From Simon bar Kosiba' to the men of 'En-gedi,
lmsbl' [*w*]*lyḥw* [*n*]*tn b*[*r*] *b'yn šlwm bṭwb*	to Masabbala' [and] to Yehonatan ba[r] Ba'yan, greetings! In ease
'tn ywšbyn 'klyn wš[*w*]*tyn mn nksy byt*	you are living, eating and dr[i]-nking off the goods of the house
yśr'l wl' d'gyn l'ḥykn lkwl dbr	of Israel, and you care not a whit for your brothers. . . .

This rebuke is addressed to Masabbalah and Yehonatan at 'En-gedi. This fact must be coupled with a bit of information found in another papyrus, *Ḥbr* 15, which reads as follows:

šm'wn lyhwdh br mnšh lqryt 'rbyh šlḥt lk try ḥmryn dy tšlḥ
'mhn (*tr!*) *gbryn lwt yhwntn br b'yn wlwt msblh dy y'mrn*
wyšlḥn lmḥnyh lwtk llbyn w'trgyn w't šlḥ 'ḥrnyn mlwtk
wymṭwn lk hdsyn w'rbyn wtqn ythn wšlḥ ythn lmḥnyh
. . . . . *hw' šlm*

Simon to Yehudah bar Menasseh at Qiryat 'Arabayah. I have sent to you two asses, with which you will send [2] (two?) men to Yehonatan bar Ba'yan and to Masabbalah that they gather and [3]send to the camp, toward you, palm-branches and citrons. And you send other men from your own quarters [4]and let them bring to you myrtle and willow twigs. Prepare them and send them to the camp.[5] . . . . . Farewell.

From this letter it is obvious that Bar Cochba is sending the two asses to 'En-gedi via Qiryat 'Arabayah. There is no spot between Herodium and 'En-gedi which can be identified with this name. Yadin, following Mazar, has identified Qiryat 'Arabayah with *Birat 'Areva' deBêt-leḥem,* mentioned in the Midrashim in connection with the birthplace of the Messiah, the modern village of 'Arṭas, near the pools of Solomon. If this identification is correct, the route which the asses are to take to go to 'En-gedi leads in the opposite direction. In another text (*Ḥbr* 1) Bar Cochba orders the same Masabbalah and Yehonatan bar Ba'yah (*sic*) to punish the men of Teqoa' (*kwl gbr tqw'y*), who were spending time repairing their houses. Teqoa' apparently pertained to the jurisdiction of the officers stationed at 'En-gedi. Consequently, it would be strange, if Bar Cochba's own headquarters were at Herodium,

---

81. *Hā'Āreṣ* (10 March 1961), p. 10; see also *BIES* 25 (1961) passim.

that he would give such orders to the officers of 'En-gedi, given the relative proximity of Teqoa' to Herodium itself. It is better, then, to regard Herodium merely as one of the camps under Bar Cochba's control, the administrative center of a toparchy as in the days of Roman domination. His headquarters are better sought either in Jerusalem or in Beth-Ter. Sending the letter to Yehudah bar Menaššeh from one of these spots with the instruction that he should send men on to 'En-gedi is certainly more logical. The note was probably delivered to Yehonatan and Masabbalah, who kept it in their archives and carried it with the other missives of their chief to the cave in the Wâdi Ḥabra, when they fled there before the advancing Roman soldiers.

'En-gedi thus emerges as a source of supplies for the rebel chief. The oasis there was cut off from the rest of Judaea by the desert and was rich in produce. There was also a small port there for commercial traffic by boat on the Dead Sea. From the rebuke addressed by Bar Cochba to Yehonatan and Masabbalah it would appear that it was something of a sinecure for them, when their lot was compared to that of their "brothers."

Besides the military, priestly and intellectual leaders of the period of the Second Revolt, Simon ben Kosibah, Eleazar (ben Azariah?), and the Rabbi Aqiba, we now know of many other Jews who were engaged in the uprising, thanks to the new documents. Their names are preserved on the skin and papyrus documents which they carried with them to the caves of refuge. There is no need to retail them all here, but the more important ones are the names of the officers under Bar Cochba. In addition to Yehonatan bar Ba'yah (or Ba'yan) and Masabbalah bar Šim'ôn[82] there were Yešua' ben Galgulah, who is addressed as *rwš hmḥnyh* (*Mur* 42.2), and, if Y. Yadin's conjecture is correct,[83] Šim'ôn bar Matatyah, who is stationed at Masadah. Just where Yešua' ben Galgulah had his camp is not certain. The administrators (*hprnsyn*) of the village of Beth-Mašiko address him as *rwš hmḥnyh,* when they write explaining the sale of a cow by an inhabitant of their village to a certain Joseph ben Aristion (*Mur* 42), but no indication is given there where that camp is situated. However, two other letters are addressed to him by Bar Cochba himself.

MUR 43

mšm'wn bn kwsbh lyš'	From Simon ben Kosibah to Yešua'
bn glglh wl'nšy hkrk[84]	ben Galgulah and to the men of the fort,

82. In a Greek letter (*Ḥbr* 3) they are addressed as *Iônathê kai Masabala.* Y. Yadin [*BIES* 25 (1961) 57] suggests the vocalization *Masabbalah* on the basis of Josephus (*JW* 5. #532), which has *masbalos* and *masambalos.*

83. *BIES* 25 [1961] 63, apropos of a Wâdi Seiyâl text not yet published; see *Supplements to VT* 4 (1957) 21.

84. The reading of this word is doubtful. Milik at first read *wl'nšy ḥbrk,*

šlwm m‘yd ’ny ‘ly t šmym	greetings! I call the heavens to witness against me that
yps[*d*] *mn hgll’ym šhṣlkm*	(if) any of the Galileans who are with you is mistreated,
kl ’dm š’ny ntn t kblym	I shall put irons
brglkm kmh š‘st[*y*]	on your feet, as I have done
lbn ‘plwl	to ben ‘Aphlul.
[*š*]*m‘wn b*[*n kwsbh*] *‘l* [*npšh*][85]	Simon b[en Kosibah], for [himself].

The second letter (*Mur* 44) reads as follows:[86]

mšm‘wn lyšw‘ bn glgwlh [	From Simon to Yešua‘ ben Galgulah [the head of the camp],
šlwm štšlḥ tbw ḥmšt]	greetings! You should send and bring five [
kwryn ḥ[*ṭy*]*n* [ ]*.š lbyty* [	kors of wheat [ ]. . . to my house [

"aux hommes de ta compagnie" [*RB* 60 (1953) 277], a reading which was accepted by F. M. Cross, Jr. [*RB* 63 (1956) 47: "La première lettre du mot est sûrement ḥeth"]. This reading was judged "graphically impossible" by H. L. Ginsberg [*BASOR* 131 (1953) 25], who read instead *wl’nšy hkrk*, "and to the men of the fort." Milik now reads (*DJD* 2, p. 160) the first letter as a *he* and the second as a *beth*, and understands the word as a name of a village mentioned by Jerome as *Caphar Barucha* and by Epiphanius as *Kapar Baricha*, situated about 3 mi. east of Hebron. According to this latest suggestion of Milik, *Yešua‘* would be the commander of a camp at *Kᵉpar ha-Baruk*. But since the construction is peculiar (with an article and without *kᵉpar*), and the reading is not at all certain, it seems preferable not to introduce a proper name here. So we retain Ginsberg's suggestion, *hkrk*, "the fort."

85. This restoration, if correct, would mean that Bar Cochba himself has written the letter, and it would be a precious autograph. The phrase *‘l npšh* is certainly found elsewhere in the new texts (normally in contracts, *Mur* 18,9; 19,26; 21,21.23; 24 C 19, D 20; 27,6; 28,11.12; 29 verso 3 [where it is parallel to the Greek *cheiri ‘eautou*]; 36,6; but also in a letter, *Mur* 42,10). However, Y. Yadin [*BIES* 25 (1961) 58; *IsrEJ* 11 (1961) 45; *Bible et Terre Sainte* 34 (1961) 16] suggests that since at least one Bar Cochba letter (*Ḥbr* 8) was signed *šm‘wn br yhwdh* (a secretary?), it might also be the case here. Possibly we should read then *‘l* [*m’mrh*], as in *Mur* 24 C 20 (where Milik has written [*mn*] but admits in the note that *‘l* is also possible).

86. Our translation is different from that of Milik, who believes that the text of this letter is intact. However, the grammatical difficulties which his translation encounters (e.g., the continual shift in person and number) make it unlikely that his interpretation is correct. There is not one line which joins necessarily with the beginning of the next, and the photo suggests that possibly we do not have the full width of the original papyrus letter. Hence we have tried to translate the lines only in the most obvious way and leave the rest blank except for line 1, where the restored title is derived from *Mur* 42,2. Milik's translation of *tšbt* (line 6) as "pendant le sabbat" is almost certainly wrong; the sign of the accusative *t* suggests that some verb is missing in the preceding line.

’ṣlk bd‘t wttqn lhn [	near you with knowledge (?); and you should prepare for them [
mqwm pnwy yhw bw ’ṣlk [	a free (?) place. Let them be in it near you [observe]
tšbt ḥzw ’m yḥpṣw lbw [	the Sabbath. See (to it) that they be pleased at heart [
whtḥzq wḥzq t mqwm [	Take courage and fortify [that] place [
hw’ šlwm wpqdty t my [	Farewell! And I have ordered the . . . [
šytn lk tḥṭyn šlh ’ḥr [	who will give you his wheat, other [
hšbt yṭlwn.	the Sabbath they will take up.

In general, the new texts from the caves of Murabba‘ât, Ḥabra, and Seiyâl reveal Bar Cochba as an administrator, giving orders to subordinates and settling problems which have arisen in the land under his control. Like the Roman Emperor before him, he is the proprietor of the land. Farms are rented out in his name and a yearly rent had to be paid in kind into his granaries. This appears from the *diastrômata* in *Mur* 24, where the land is rented from Simon the Prince of Israel (*mšm‘wn nsy’ yśr’l,* E 7). The deputy, Hillel ben Garis, acts as an administrator of the lands of *‘Ir-Naḥaš* on his command ([*mn*/‘*l*] *m’mrh,* C 20). The Wâdi Ḥabra texts are reported to contain similar details about the leasing of government-owned lands to a four-man syndicate which, in turn, subleased the plots among themselves. Amid the details which concern him Bar Cochba shows himself respecting the traditional Jewish feasts. In *Mur* 44 he is apparently ordering Yešua‘ ben Galgulah to provide hospitality for a caravan transporting grain over the Sabbath. He orders that Eleazar bar Ḥittah be sent to him "immediately before the Sabbath" (*Ḥbr* 8). He provides that the palm-branches and citrons be brought for the celebration of the feast of Succoth in one of the camps, and orders Yehudah bar Menaššeh to make similar provision where he is (*Ḥbr* 15). In other letters he orders the arrest of a certain Yešua‘ bar Tadmorayah (whose sword must be taken from him), confiscates wheat, seizes property, and even gives instructions about the harvesting of ripe and unripe grain. It is an abundance of such details which come to light in the new documents, which also reveal that the simple people in Palestine were leading fairly normal lives despite the revolt. They still exchanged property, married, and made their contracts of various sorts.

The list of the few names of villages which were controlled by Bar Cochba given above scarcely exhausts the places which were under his authority. Dio Cassius (*Rom. Hist.* 69.14,1) mentions that the Romans finally captured "fifty of their most important outposts and nine hundred and eighty-five of their most famous villages were razed to the ground". Where Dio Cassius got such figures, we do not know, but they do give some indication of the extent of the control over the land which Bar Cochba must have had.

All of these details confirm the data given in Dio Cassius about the mode of warfare which was practised by the rebels. "They did not dare try conclusions with the Romans in the open field, but they occupied the advantageous positions in the country and strengthened them with mines and walls, in order that they might have places of refuge whenever they should be hard pressed, and might meet together unobserved under ground."[87] It was probably a guerrilla-type warfare, well organized on a village and toparchy basis, and resembling that of the Maccabees, especially in the early days of their struggle.

At first sight it might seem that the caves in the Wâdies Murabba'ât, Seiyâl and Ḥabra were actually the outposts (*phrouria*), of which Dio Cassius speaks (*Rom. Hist.* 69.14,1). The evidence found in them, however, indicates rather that they were used as places of refuge, like the *anaphygai* also mentioned by him (69.12,3). For it appears that Yešua' ben Galgulah fled from his camp to the cave in the Wâdi Murabba'ât, taking with him various household objects, family archives, the letters from his chief, Bar Cochba, and perhaps also his family.[88] Similarly, Yehonatan and Masabbalah fled from their camp at 'En-gedi to the cave in the Wâdi Ḥabra with a whole collection of letters from their chief.

Among the documents taken by the refugees to the caves were biblical scrolls and texts. From the Murabba'ât caves have come fragments of Gn, Ex, Nm (*Mur* 1), Dt (*Mur* 2), Is (*Mur* 3) and the large fragmentary scroll of the Minor Prophets (*Mur* 88). The latter was found in a hole near the caves, in which a refugee had been buried. Milik mentions that this is the oldest concrete example of a tomb-genizah, of which the Rabbinical writers speak.[89] The text of this scroll is fragmentary in many places, but a substantial portion of ten of the twelve books is preserved (Jl 2,20.26-4,16; Am 1,5-2,1; 7,3-8,7; 8,11-9, 15; Abd 1-21; Jon 1,1-4,11; Mi 1,1-7,20; Na 1,1-3,19; Hb 1,1-2,11; 2, 18-3,19; So 1,1; 1,11-3,6; 3,8-20; Ag 1,1-2,10; 2,12-23; Za 1,1-4). Further, there is a phylactery (*Mur* 4), and possibly a Mezuzah (*Mur* 5). We have mentioned the biblical texts from the other areas earlier in our discussion. In all these biblical documents the remarkable aspect is the close agreement of their text with the *Textus Receptus* of later centuries. Milik lists for the text of the Minor Prophets (*Mur* 88) only 59 variants, the majority of which are simply cases of *scriptio plena* for *defectiva* or vice versa (about 30) and additions written above the line possibly by the copyist himself (about 8). Many of the others are quite insignificant (prepositional exchanges like *beth* for *kaph*, *'el* for *'al*, etc.).[90] When these texts are compared with the bibli-

---

87. *Rom. Hist.* 69.12,3.
88. For the artifacts found in the Murabba'ât caves, see *DJD* 2, pp. 29-48.
89. *DJD* 2, p. 181; see Bab. Talmud, *Megillah*, fol. 26b.
90. See *DJD* 2, pp. 183-4, 205. Milik had previously pointed out that the only significant variant in the whole scroll was Hab 3,10: *zrmw mym*

cal texts from the Qumrân caves, where a number of texts manifest different recensions, it looks very much as though we have in the Murabba'ât scrolls the stabilization of the text effected by the council at Jamnia. Indeed, they apparently determined not only what books belonged to the Palestinian canon of the OT, but also what recension was to be copied in the future, with what spelling and in what script. The script of the Murabba'ât biblical texts bears a very strong resemblance to the script employed by the scribes in the medieval manuscripts. For this reason the biblical texts from the Bar Cochba period are important for the data which they supply for the study of the transmission of the OT.

In the new material which has been published so far there are strikingly few references to the enemy Romans. The letter of the administrators of Bet-Mašiko to Yešua' ben Galgulah explains that they do not come up with Joseph ben Aristion, who has bought the cow, to give evidence of the purchase, because "the Gentiles are drawing near to us" (*hgyym qrbym 'lnw*), *Mur* 42.5. Milik has reported that a short letter from the Wâdi Seiyâl addressed to Bar Cochba by Šim'ôn ben Matatyah mentions *hg'ym* who have moved their camp (*qṣryhm*).[91] But the only explicit reference to the Romans found so far is in *Ḥbr* 11, an Aramaic letter which mentions *rhwmyh* (*i.e., Rhômāyēh*).[92] Perhaps the texts found this year will supply further information about the Romans, who were systematically advancing through the country and wiping out the pockets of resistance, thus driving the refugees to the caves.

THE END OF THE REVOLT AND THE LAST STAND AT BETH-TER

Just where the emperor Hadrian was all during the Second Revolt is not clear. After leaving Palestine and Syria in A.D. 131, he went to Pontus and the Black Sea area and from there to Athens for the winter. On the 5th of May A.D. 134 he was once again in Rome.[93] By this time the revolt was well under way. He must have returned to Judaea afterwards, to judge by a remark of Dio Cassius about the outcome of the war, which we shall quote later.

The initial lack of concern on the part of the Romans about the Jewish uprising stemmed from the attitude of the Roman governor of Judaea, a certain Tineius Rufus (Eusebius, *Eccl. Hist.* 4.6,1). He undoubtedly underestimated the movement and soon it grew to proportions which were beyond his control. Dio Cassius (*Rom. Hist.* 69. 13,1) mentions that "all Judaea had been stirred up." This is to be

---

'bwt (as in Ps 77,18) instead of the MT *zrm mym 'br* (*Supplements to VT* 4 [1957] 20).

91. *Ibid.* p. 21.

92. *BIES* 25 (1961) 60; *IsrEJ* 11 (1961) 45. On p. 56 Yadin mentions that *hgw'yn* also occurs in one of his Hebrew documents.

93. *CIG* 3.5906, which is dated *pro g' Nônôn Maïôn apo Rômês*; the year is given as *dêmarchikês exousias to iê', 'ypatos to g'*. See F.-M. Abel, *Histoire* 2, 93.

understood not in the restricted sense of Judaea (as opposed to Samaria and Galilee), but in the sense of the Roman province, which included those areas as well. We have already seen the solicitude of Bar Cochba for the Galileans, who apparently had joined his ranks. Dio Cassius (*ibid.*) further adds that "many outside nations, too, were joining them through eagerness for gain." The result was that the rebels were getting the better of the Roman garrisons and aid had to be given to the governor. Leaving his own province in the charge of Caius Severus, the legate of the *Legio IV Scythica*, Publicius Marcellus, the governor of Syria, came to the aid of Tineius Rufus, as a Greek inscription attests,[94] probably with the *Legio III Gallica*. Eusebius (*Eccl. Hist.* 4.6,1) records that military aid was sent by the Emperor. E. Schürer[95] has made a catalogue of the Roman legions which took part in the Judaean war, using the various direct and indirect references to it found in inscriptions. The following groups of Roman soldiers were engaged at some time or other in putting down the rebellion: *Legio X Fretensis* and *Legio VI Ferrata* (both resident in Judaea), *Legio III Cyrenaica* (brought in from the province of Arabia), *Legio III Gallica* (probably brought by the Governor of Syria), *Legio XXII Deiotariana* (brought in from Egypt), *cohors IV Lingonum, cohors I Damascenorum, cohors I Thracum*; besides, several detachments of *Legio I Italica, Legio V Macedonica, Legio X Gemina* and *Legio XI Claudia*.[96] Apparently the *classis syriaca* was also somehow involved in the war.

But this was not enough. Finally "Hadrian sent against them his best generals. First of these was Julius Severus, who was dispatched from Britain, where he was governor,[97] against the Jews" (Dio Cassius, *Rom. Hist.* 69.13,2). Although Eusebius gives the impression that Rufus Tineius was always in charge of the operations against the Jewish rebels (*Eccl. Hist.* 4.6,1), it was actually Sextus Julius Severus who had the supreme command in the last period and who finally

---

94. *CIG* 3.4033-34: *'ênika Poublikios Markellos dia tên kinêsin tên Ioudaikên metebebêkei apo Syrias.*
95. *GJV* 1.687-9, n. 116 (Engl. tr. 303, n. 96). See further F.-M. Abel, *Histoire* 2, 92.
96. An epitaph of a Roman soldier, found at Beisân (ancient Scythopolis), shows clearly that the *Legio XI Claudia* was in Palestine at this time and engaged in operations in the north as well as at Beth-Ter. See M. Avi-Yonah, "Greek and Latin Inscriptions from Jerusalem and Beisan," *Quarterly of the Department of Antiquities in Palestine* 8 (1939) 57-9. This inscription shows that in fact the *Legio XI Claudia* was present during the Roman counter-offensive, and that the inscription at the spring in the village of Bittîr also dates from this period: CENTVR . VEXILL . LEG . V . MAC . ET . XI . CL [*CIL* 3/14.155; cf. *ZDPV* 29 (1906) 55, n. 1].
97. This is confirmed by his *cursus honorum* given in a Latin inscription (*CIL* 3.2830): *leg(ato) pr(o) pr(aetore) imp(eratoris) Traiani Hadriani Aug(usti) provinciae Daciae, co(n)s(uli) leg(ato) pr(o) pr(aetore) Moesiae inferioris, leg(ato) pr(o) pr(aetore) provinciae Britanniae, leg(ato) pr(o) pr(aetore) provinciae Iudeae, leg(ato) pr(o) pr(aetore) provinciae Suriae.*

succeeded in putting an end to the rebellion.

> Severus did not venture to attack his opponents in the open at any one point, in view of their numbers and their desperation; but by intercepting small groups, thanks to the number of his soldiers and his under-officers, and by depriving them of food and shutting them up, he was able, rather slowly, to be sure, but with comparatively little danger, to crush, exhaust and exterminate them. Very few of them in fact survived. Fifty of their most important outposts and nine hundred and eighty-five of their most famous villages were razed to the ground. Five hundred and eighty thousand men were slain in the various raids and battles, and the number of those that perished by famine, disease and fire was past finding out. Thus nearly the whole of Judaea was made desolate, a result of which the people had had forewarning before the war. For the tomb of Solomon, which the Jews regard as an object of veneration, fell to pieces of itself and collapsed, and many wolves and hyenas rushed howling into their cities" (Dio Cassius, *Rom. Hist.* 69.13,3-14,2; tr. E. Cary).

Not only the Roman sources mention the great number of Jews who perished in this war, but also the Rabbinical and Christian writings. The former abound in many legendary and imaginative details, but there can be little doubt about the correctness of the substantial account.[98] Eusebius reports (*Eccl. Hist.* 4.6,1): "He [Rufus] destroyed in heaps thousands of men, women and children, and, under the law of war, enslaved their land." The slow process of searching out the rebels, of starving them and of killing them off, recorded by Dio Cassius, is now confirmed by the discoveries in the caves of Murabba'ât, Seiyâl and Ḥabra, to which the Jews fled. The burial niche in the Wâdi Ḥabra cave, with its "collection of baskets overflowing with skulls" and "layer upon layer of large mats covering human bones,"[99] gives eloquent testimony to the Roman mop-up operations. Whole families must have taken refuge in the caves at the advance of the Roman troops; there they died of hunger and thirst.[100] In the case of the Wâdi Ḥabra cave two Roman camps were built in a strategic position atop the cliffs of the gorge so as to keep watch on the opening of the cave, lest the refugees try to escape.[101]

To judge from the Rabbinical writings the greatest opposition to the Romans occurred in Judaea in the region called *har hammelek,*

---

98. Cf. E. Schürer, *GJV* 1.694; Engl. tr. 311.
99. *BA* 24 (1961) 39-40; Cf. *IsrEJ* 4 (1954) 126-7; 5 (1955) 272-3.
100. This is the conclusion too of the archaeologists who explored the various caves; see Y. Aharoni, *IsrEJ* 4 (1954) 127; 5 (1955) 272-3; Y. Yadin, *BIES* 25 (1961) 51; R. de Vaux, *DJD* 2, p. 48.
101. "These camps resemble those found around Masada. They are built with a wall of rough stones *ca.* 1 m. thick, except on the side which touches the cliff. The gates are protected by *claviculi* which, unlike those found in the camps around Masada, turn outwards. Inside the camps were traces of various square and round constructions. These camps seem to have had no other strategic or military purpose than to keep watch on the cave-mouths visible directly below them in the cliff side, at present very difficult of access" [*IsrEJ* 4 (1954) 126-7].

"The Royal Mountain."[102] The same sources relate that during the revolt R. Aqiba had preached that salvation would come to the Jews from Judah and Benjamin, while the other tribes would be the objects of divine rejection.[103] The great Rabbi's preaching fired them to an almost fanatical enthusiasm for wiping out the Romans. It will be remembered that Dio Cassius recorded the caution of the Roman general, Sextus Julius Severus, who was aware of the "desperation" of the Jews (*Rom. Hist.* 69.13,3). With such militant fury they managed to annihilate the *Legio XXII Deiotariana*.[104] But in the end the *har hammelek* was devastated, Jerusalem fell to the Romans and the last stand was made at Beth-Ter.

Most of the sources are silent about the recapture of Jerusalem by the Romans, and consequently we do not know exactly when it occurred. Possibly it happened during the second year of the revolt or a little after it, and that is why no coins were issued in the third year or the fourth year of the Liberation of Jerusalem. Neither Dio Cassius nor Eusebius mentions the Roman recapture of the town. However, a vague reference to it may be found in the contemporary writer, Appian, who lived both at Alexandria and at Rome in the time of Hadrian, and who wrote: "Jerusalem, the greatest city, which Ptolemy I, king of Egypt, had destroyed [?], and when it was repopulated again Vespasian razed, and Hadrian again in my own day (did the same). . . ."[105] Was it at the fall of Jerusalem that Hadrian returned to the Near East? Both Appian and the Mishnah (*Ta'anith* 4.6: the fall of Beth-Ter and the ploughing up of the City on the 9th of Ab) refer to a destruction of the city under Hadrian. This must refer to what had been built anew since the days of Titus and perhaps under Bar Cochba himself; but it was a destruction in view of the building of Aelia Capitolina.

According to Eusebius (*Eccl. Hist.* 4.6,3); the war reached its height at Beth-Ter, a strong citadel not very far from Jerusalem.[106]

---

102. See J. T. Milik (*DJD* 2, p. 126) for an attempt to identify the town and the region connected with this name in the Rabbinical literature. It is apparently the area about Eleutheropolis (Beth Gubrin).

103. See L. Ginzberg, *The Legends of the Jews* (Philadelphia: Jewish Publication Society of America, 1928), 6.408.

104. Julius Africanus ascribes it to the Pharisees who served the Romans poisoned wine. See A. Harnack, "Medicinisches aus der ältesten Kirchengeschichte," *Texte und Untersuchungen* 8/4 (Leipzig: J. C. Hinrichs, 1892), p. 44.—Y. Yadin [*BA* 24 (1961) 42] suggests that the 19 metal vessels which were found in a basket in the Wâdi Ḥabra cave and which are clearly Roman objects were actually booty taken by Bar Cochba's fighters from the Romans and carried off with them to the refuge-cave. Cf. *BIES* 25 (1961) 52-3.

105. *De bello syr.* 50 (=*Roman History* 11.8,50; ed. H. White, *Loeb Classical Library*, 2.199).

106. The spelling of the name of this place varies in the sources. The Greek mss. of Eusebius have *Bêththêra, Biththêra*; Latin texts have *Bether* (Jerome, *In Zach.* 8.9; *ML* 25.1574), *Bethera*; Rabbinical sources also vary: *byttr, bytr, btr.* We have followed E. Schürer in regarding

There the siege lasted a long time before the rebels were driven to final destruction by famine and thirst and "the instigator of their madness paid the penalty he deserved." Beth-Ter is identified today with *Khirbet el-Yehûd* ("the ruin of the Jews") a site on a hill-top about 400 m. WNW of the modern village of *Bittîr*. It overlooks from the south the Wâdi el-Gharbi, through which the railroad makes its way from Jerusalem to Jaffa. The modern village of Bittîr has preserved the ancient name of the place where Bar Cochba made his last stand; it is situated some six and a half miles WSW of Jerusalem.

According to F.-M. Abel, the space within the roughly ellipse-shaped fortified enclosure, which crowns the summit of the hill and of which there are still some traces here and there, scarcely measures 300 x 150 metres.[107] Hadrian had apparently had a road built from Jerusalem to Eleutheropolis in A.D. 130, which made its way through the valley at the foot of the hill itself. The eighth milestone is found in the valley below the ruins, and is dated to the year 130. In order to take the citadel, the Roman general had to lay siege to the area. Traces of the Roman *circumvallatio* are still visible today to the north and the west of the ruins. They permit one to reconstruct a wall of about 3800 metres, doubled in some places, and fitted with a watch-tower. The size of the *circumvallatio* and its position suggest a rather lengthy siege, thus confirming the suggestion made by Eusebius. Detachments of the *Legio V Macedonica* and the *Legio XI Claudia* left their names on the road to the spring; they seem to have been at least part of the Roman troops which were engaged in this final stage of the war.[108]

There is little information about the siege itself and the conquest of Beth-Ter in the sources. Of all the Rabbinical legends related to this struggle few are regarded as trustworthy by modern historians. E. Schürer and F.-M. Abel retain only one as having some credibility: that before Beth-Ter fell, Bar Cochba killed his uncle, the Rabbi Eleazar of Modin, a pious old man who apparently wanted to come to terms with the Romans.[109] There is no reason to doubt the sub-

---

byttr as the most probably correct form. It is probably the same place as *Baithêr*, a town in Judah in the vicinity of Bethlehem, mentioned in Codex Alexandrinus at Jos 15,59. The word occurs in a phrase not found in the MT, and the Codex Vaticanus of the LXX reads *Thethêr*. —W. D. Carroll ["Bittîr and its Archaeological Remains," *AASOR* 5 (1923-4) 78] tries unconvincingly to derive the form from *bêt-har* (*bêttar*), "in view of the mountainous location of the place," and with reference to Ct 2,17.

107. Abel, *Histoire*, 2,94.

108. On Beth-Ter see A. Alt, "Die Ausflüge," *PJB* 23 (1927) 9-29 (pp. 12-15: "Reste der römischen Zirkumvallation um Beth-Ter"); A. Schulten, "Anhang: Beth-Ter," *ZDPV* 56 (1933) 180-4; W. D. Carroll, *AASOR* 5 (1924) 77-103; A. Dowling, "Interesting Coins of Pella and Bittîr," *PEFQS* 38 (1907) 295-7; H. Strathmann, *PJB* 23 (1927) 114-8; E. Zickermann, "Chirbet el-jehud (bettir)," *ZDPV* 29 (1906) 51-72.

109. Jer. Talmud, *Ta'anith*, 4.68d-69a; Midrash, *Echa Rabbah* 2.2,4. Cf. *GJV* 1.695 (Engl. tr. 311); Abel, *Histoire* 2, 95.

stantial historicity of the accounts about the massacre of the Jews when the citadel was finally taken.

Dio Cassius (*Rom. Hist.* 69.14,3) records at the end of his account: "Many Romans, moreover, perished in this war. Therefore Hadrian in writing to the senate did not employ the opening phrase commonly affected by the emperors, 'If you and your children are in health, it is well; I and the legions are in health.' " The losses on both sides were apparently heavy, and for that reason the Emperor despite the successful outcome of the war for Rome did not feel that he could send back the usual report to the senate in Rome. This notice found in Dio Cassius suggests, therefore, that in the final stages of the war Hadrian was once again in Judaea. At any rate, as a result of the victory over the Jews Hadrian was soon acclaimed *imperator* for the second time, and soon thereafter the title appears on his inscriptions. Within a short time he contracted an illness which was to prove fatal.

Sextus Julius Severus was rewarded by the Senate for his victory over the Jews,[110] and subsequently became the governor of the province of Syria. Apparently Tineius Rufus resumed the control of Judaea, for he is remembered in Jewish tradition as the tyrant and to him is attributed the death of the great Rabbi Aqiba.[111] Once Beth-Ter had fallen, many Jewish captives were sold into slavery by the Romans in markets set up at Mamre ("in tabernaculo Abrahae," Jerome, *In Zach.* 11,4; *ML* 25. 1573; "in mercato Terebinthi," Jerome, *In Jer.* 6.18,6; *CSEL* 59:390) and at Gaza (later called "Hadrian's Market"); others were carried off to Egypt.

Aelia Capitolina

The fate of the Jews was sealed. Not only were they defeated and massacred or enslaved, but an imperial edict added the crowning ignominy: they were forbidden access to their "Holy City"—an edict which still has its consequences today. Eusebius in his *Ecclesiastical History* has recorded:

> Hadrian then commanded that by a legal decree and ordinances the whole nation should be absolutely prevented from entering from thenceforth even the district around Jerusalem, so that not even from a distance could it see its ancestral home. Ariston of Pella tells the story. Thus when the city came to be bereft of the nation of the Jews, and its ancient inhabitants had completely perished, it was colonized by foreigners, and the Roman city which afterwards arose changed its name, and in honour of the reigning emperor Aelius Hadrian was called Aelia. The church, too, in it was composed of Gentiles, and after the Jewish bishops the first who was

---

110. *CIL* 3. 2830: "Huic [senatus, a]uctore [imp(eratore) Tra]iano Hadriano Aug(usto) ornamenta triumphalia decrevit ob res in [Ju]dea prospere gestas. [d(ecurionum)] d(ecreto)."
111. Cf. P. Benoit, "Rabbi Aqiba ben Joseph Sage et héros du Judaïsme," *RB* 54 (1947) 54-89, esp. pp. 87-89.

appointed to minister to those there was Marcus" (4.6,3-4).[112]

The Bordeaux Pilgrim at the beginning of the fourth century knows of the custom of the Jews who were then permitted to come once a year (probably on the 9th of Ab) to the area of the old Temple, not far from Hadrian's statue, to anoint the stones, to rend their garments and to weep in mourning over the fate of Jerusalem.[113] But it was no longer the same old city.

Hadrian built *colonia Aelia capitolina* on the site of the former Jerusalem. The *cardo maximus* of the new city led from north to south, roughly along the route of the present-day *Sûq* in the Old City, beginning at the Damascus Gate (or Bâb el-'Amûd, "the gate of the Pillar," the name which is derived from the column erected at the north end of the *cardo maximus*, as can be seen on the Madaba Map[114]) and ending at the south wall. The *decumanus* coincided roughly with the *tarîq bâb Sitti Maryam* and led to the triple arch in the east wall of the city, which is called today the *Ecce Homo* Arch.[115] Thus it was that the old Temple Area was completely excluded from the new Roman colony.

The *Chronicon Paschale* for the year A.D. 119 (miscalculated; see above) records the following details in Hadrian's new city:

> He destroyed the Temple of the Jews in Jerusalem and built there two public baths (*ta dyo dêmosia*), the theater, the *capitolium* (*to trikamaron*), the four-porticoed nymphaeum (*tetranymphon*), and the circus (or amphitheater, *dôdekapylon*), which was previously called the "Steps" (*Anabathmoi*), and the Square (*tên Kodran*). He divided the city into seven districts (*amphoda*), and set his own deputies up as district-rulers; to each of them he assigned a district. To this day each district goes by the name of its district-ruler. He

---

112. Cf. Justin Martyr, *Apol.* 1.47,6.—During all this period we hear very little about the Christians in Palestine and any part which they may have had in the revolt. Justin Martyr (*Apol.* 1.31,6) records: "In the recent Jewish war, Bar Kocheba, the leader of the Jewish uprising, ordered that only the Christians should be subjected to dreadful torments, unless they renounced and blasphemed Jesus Christ" (tr. *Fathers of the Church* 6,67; he is also quoted by Eusebius, *Eccl. Hist.* 4.8,4). P. Orosius (*Hist. adv. paganos* 7,13; *CSEL* 5,468): " . . . ultusque est [Hadrianus] Christianos, quos illi [Iudaei] Cocheba duce, cur sibi aduersum Romanos non adsentarentur, excruciabant; praecepitque, ne cui Iudaeo introeundi Hierosolymam esset licentia, Christianis tantum ciuitate permissa; quam ipse in optimum statum murorum exstructione reparauit et Aeliam uocari de praenomine suo praecepit." Eusebius' *Chronicon* (in Jerome's translation, 283F; *GCS* 47,201): "Chochebas, dux Iudaicae factionis, nolentes sibi XPianos aduersum Romanum militem ferre subsidium omnimodis cruciatibus necat."
113. *Itinerarium Burdigalense* 591; *CSEL* 39.22.
114. M. Avi-Yonah, *The Madaba Mosaic Map with Introduction and Commentary* (Jerusalem: Israel Exploration Society, 1954), p. 52.
115. See H. Vincent and F.-M. Abel, *Jérusalem: Recherches de topographie, d'archéologie et d'histoire. Tome second: Jérusalem nouvelle* (Paris: Gabalda, 1914), p. 29: The *Ecce Homo* Arch is judged by Vincent to be "un débris de la porte orientale d'Aelia Capitolina."

gave his own name to the city, calling it Aelia.[116]

Not far from the intersection of the *cardo maximus* and the *decumanus maximus,* which was situated roughly at the Seventh Station of the *Via dolorosa,* the agora of Aelia was constructed. The remains of the gate of Ephraim were incorporated into its approach, and some remnants of its colonnade can still be seen today in the Russian hospice. At the edge of this forum the temple of Jupiter Capitolinus was erected, the *capitolium* or *Trikamaron* (so named because of its triple-vaulted cella).

On the old Temple Area was constructed the Square, the *Kodra,* a sanctuary sacred to Zeus and the area where the cult of Hadrian himself was carried out.

The Romans were once again in control of the city and the land The garrison of the *Legio X Fretensis* took up its quarters anew on the upper hill of the city in the vicinity of the towers which remained from the old palace of Herod (near the Jaffa Gate). Over the gate leading to Bethlehem a dedication to the founder of the colony was inscribed together with the emblem of the Roman Legion, a wild boar. Beginning with Eusebius, this figure has often been interpreted as a mockery intended to prevent the Jewish nation from attempting to enter the city which once belonged to it: "in fronte eius portae, qua Bethleem egredimur, sus scalptus in marmore significans Romanae potestati subiacere Iudaeos."[117]

But Roman contingents were scattered throughout the land as well. The new discoveries in the caves of the Wâdi Murabba'ât show that the Romans settled down there as well, perhaps to prevent survivors of the revolt, who had not been sold into slavery, from taking further refuge there. In the Murabba'ât caves were found two coins with the counter-minting of the *Legio X Fretensis,* a contract dated as late as A.D. 171 (?), and a Greek fragment mentioning the Emperor Commodus (180-192). It seems as though Roman soldiers stayed on in this area until the end of the second century.[118]

The defeat of the Jews in the Second Revolt sealed the fate which was to exclude them ever since from the city and the Temple area which for so many years had been the rallying point of the nation. After the destruction of Jerusalem in A.D. 70 the hope lived on that it would be rebuilt and restored to the nation. This hope began to see realization in the appearance of the messianic figure of Bar Cochba—but only to be disappointed. He was the last political leader whom the Jews had, until the foundation of the State of Israel in 1948.

That hope of a return to Jerusalem and of a restoration of the Temple is still echoed in the fourteenth and seventeenth blessings of

---

116. *MG* 92.613. Our interpretation of the expressions follows that of H. Vincent, *Jérusalem nouvelle,* pp. 6-18.
117. *Chronicon* 283F (in Jerome's translation; *GCS* 47,201).
118. See *DJD* 2, p. 48.

the *Šemônēh ʿEśrēh*:

And to Jerusalem, Thy city, return in mercy, and dwell therein, as thou hast spoken; rebuild it soon in our days as an everlasting building, and speedily set up therein the throne of David.

Accept, O Lord our God, Thy People Israel, and receive in love and favor both the fire-offerings of Israel and their prayer; and may the service of Thy people Israel be ever acceptable unto thee. And let our eyes behold Thy return in mercy to Zion.

NEW UNDERSTANDING OF THE GOSPELS

DAVID MICHAEL STANLEY, S.J.

Nowadays, there is considerable interest among Catholics in a relatively recent phenomenon, frequently described as "the new understanding of the Gospels," or "the new approach to the Gospels." If I were asked to select the salient features of this movement in Catholic Scriptural scholarship, I should say that it consists in (1) a more discerning appreciation of the Gospels *as literature*, and (2) a deeper insight into *the historical process* which produced them. When I speak of "the Gospels as literature," I refer to the various literary forms they display and to their doctrinal content, their biblical theology. When I speak of "the historical process which produced the Gospels," I understand the phrase in a twofold sense. It signifies, in the first place, the various moments in the creation of the four Gospels. In the second place, it connotes also the events of the Christian salvation-history which they record.[1]

In his justly celebrated prologue to the third Gospel, St. Luke describes the authoritative source of the evangelical traditions, the members of the apostolic college, as "the original eye-witnesses, who became ministers of the Word" (Lk 1,2). This characterization of the first disciples of Jesus, it will be noted, is a double one, and merits our attention here inasmuch as it is concerned with the two essential elements that must function in any understanding of the nature and purpose of our Gospels: event and the Word.[2] It comprehends the sacred history of man's redemption through Jesus Christ as well as the "good news" (for that is what "gospel" literally means), the authoritative interpretation or expression of that history's meaning in the apostolic preaching.

The Gospel narrative, as the record of the historical process through which Christian salvation became a reality, reposes upon the testimony of competent, reliable eye-witnesses. Indeed, the very character of the records themselves provides evidence of the manner in

1. For the description of Salvation-History, cf. "The Conception of our Gospels as Salvation-History," *Theological Studies* 20 (1959) 561-589.
2. In Hebrew, the same term denotes both event and word: *dabar*. For an informative discussion of the implications of this, cf. John L. McKenzie, "The Word of God in the Old Testament," *Theological Studies* 21 (1960) 183-206.

which, under the supervision of the primitive Christian community, they attained their definitive form, and so provides additional motives for the credibility of what they narrate.

However, Peter, John, and the other "original eye-witnesses" had a more formative function than that of simply attesting to the brute facts upon which their kerygma, or message, reposed. They "became ministers of the Word." As the hierarchical heads of a new religion, they testified above all to something which transcended mere ocular testimony: God's definitive entrance into human history, the significance, for man's redemption, of the life, death, and resurrection of Jesus of Nazareth, the *propter nos et propter nostram salutem* of the Creed.[3] Thus in addition to, or rather upon the basis of, their attestation of a certain historical reality, they proclaimed their own Christian faith in the divine meaning of that reality.[4] Without this element, their words would not be "the Word," "the Word of God" (Acts 13,5; cf. 10,36), "the Word of the Lord" (Acts 15,36), "the Word of this salvation" (Acts 13,26).[5]

In the books we call the Gospels, this "witness of faith" is to be found in the inspired interpretation of the events set forth by the sacred authors. And the principal means of grasping the evangelists' message, as Pius XII has pointed out, is by discerning "the distinctive genius of the sacred writer," especially by a careful study of "the literary forms which he used."[6]

Accordingly, we wish, in the space at our disposal, to discuss two facets of this "new understanding of the Gospels": their literary character, and the structural development by which they evolved. Such a review of the progress made in Gospel studies should bring us a more discriminating sense of their historical value as well as a more profound reverence for their Christology.

To situate our discussion, however, we must begin by inquiring into the factors which led Catholic scholars to take this "new look" at the Gospels. The three most influential factors are, in the order of their appearance: the development, after the first World War, of an Historico-literary method of investigation known as Form criticism (Formgeschichte),[7] the publication of the encyclical *Divino afflante Spiritu* in 1943, and the portentous discovery, in 1947, of certain

---

3. In Acts 10, 34-43, Peter's discourse exemplifies in a striking way the consciousness of the apostolic preachers of their twofold role as witnesses.
4. When we turn to the evangelists or other inspired writers, this "incarnational" nature of their testimony is not to be forgotten. It is because the words and deeds of Jesus come to us "incarnated" in the sacred writer's faith that he is author, *in a true sense,* of what he records.
5. L. Cerfaux, "Témoins du Christ d'après le Livre des Actes," *Angelicum* 20 (1943) 166-183.
6. *Acta Apostolicae Sedis* 35 (1943) 314.
7. The significant works for a study of the beginnings of *Formgeschichte* are: M. Dibelius, *Die Formgeschichte des Evangeliums* (Tübingen: 1919); K. L. Schmidt, *Der Rahmen der Geschichte Jesu* (Berlin: 1919); R. Bultmann, *Die Geschichte der synoptischen Tradition* (Göttingen: 1921).

Jewish sectarian documents at Qumran, popularly known as the Dead Sea Scrolls.[8]

The Positive Values in Form Criticism

Form criticism was first applied to the Gospels by certain German scholars in an attempt to renew Gospel studies, which had reached an impasse thanks to the sterility of "the Higher Criticism," the investigation of the documentary sources underlying the sacred books. While certain postulates of the Form critics are demonstrably false,[9] and others require a certain refinement,[10] we may say at once that, as an heuristic method which seeks to trace the steps which led to the formation of the Gospels, Form criticism is not necessarily unacceptable. Indeed, it has produced fruitful and lasting results.

One fundamental postulate is that the Gospels are compilations of small units, narratives or sayings. One may judge the truth contained in this assertion by recalling the impression of completeness given by the self-contained passages from the Gospels which appear in our Mass formulae, as contrasted with many of the excerpts from the epistles, so frequently obscure or unintelligible when read out of context.[11] Starting from the conviction that our Gospels are actually a mosaic of independent units, the Form critic turned his attention to the study and classification of the various literary forms which these units exhibit. One important consequence has been an increased awareness of the variety of historical narrative, ranging from family memoirs or popular stories to reports by eye-witnesses, which our Gospels contain.

The Form critic is also keenly interested in what he calls the *Sitz im Leben,* the original situation or historical context of a given narrative or saying. Attention has thus been drawn, for instance, to the liturgical character of the risen Christ's command, at the conclusion of St. Matthew's Gospel, to practice Christian baptism (Mt

---

8. From the already vast literature on this subject, we suggest two helpful studies by Catholics: Roland E. Murphy, O. Carm., *The Dead Sea Scrolls and the Bible* (Westminster, Md.: 1956); Kurt Schubert, *The Dead Sea Community: its Origin and Teachings* (New York: 1959).
9. For example: the sociological postulate that the community as such is creative (it is rather conservative); the assumption that the primitive Church was the anonymous, unrestrained crowd in which, *ex hypothesi,* myths and legends take their origin. An additional false assumption, made by some Form critics, is that all that can be attained by a study of the Gospels is "the Christ of faith," not the "Jesus of history."
10. Cf. the helpful critique of *Formgeschichte* by Pierre Benoit, "Réflexions sur la 'formgeschichtliche Methode'," *Revue Biblique* 53 (1946) 481-512. Also, R. W. Catterall, "Form Criticism," *Clergy Review* 41 (1956) 157-162.
11. Some Form Critics have pushed this principle too far, denying the historical value of the general framework of the public life: cf. the balanced criticism of this tendency by C. H. Dodd, "The Framework of the Gospel Narrative," *Expository Times* 43 (1931-32) 396-400, in which he shows that the Markan summaries, when read continuously, give a fairly clear picture of Jesus' movements in Galilee.

28,19). In this way, we have come to learn a great deal from the Gospels about the day-to-day life of the primitive Church: her methods of winning and instructing converts, the shaping of her doctrines and policies by drawing out the implications of Jesus' words and actions, the development of her social life, her ascetical life, her liturgical life.

Because the Form critic has been primarily concerned with the historical evolution of the various literary forms found in the Gospels, an evolution caused, he is convinced, by the way in which these data were preserved, his interest has been re-awakened in the apostolic tradition which preserved them. This new respect for the formative role played by tradition in the production of the New Testament Scriptures has been one of the most beneficial results of Form criticism. Oscar Cullmann, the eminent Swiss Lutheran theologian, has remarked, "Since the Reformation, we have had a false notion of the origin of the Gospels . . . . Whilst Catholicism has never forgotten that Tradition preceded the Scripture, the Reform theologians paid no attention to the fact that between Jesus' lifetime and the composition of the Gospels lies a period of at least thirty years."[12]

I might restate this by saying that Form criticism has reminded us all that the Gospels were from the beginning the Church's books, written by her members under her direction, providing us with the church's picture of Jesus Christ, and presenting, in addition, an intimate, heart-warming glimpse of the Church's faith and life.

"Divino afflante Spiritu . . . "

The encyclical letter of Pius XII "on the most opportune way to promote biblical studies" may be justly regarded as a *magna charta* for the Catholic Scriptural scholar by reason of its liberating attitude towards biblical science and the urgency of its appeal for the advancement of Scripture studies within the Church. The Holy Father insisted that full liberty be given the Catholic exegete to solve "the many important questions" concerning the Bible which are as yet unanswered. He drew attention to the very small number of Scriptural texts whose meaning has been authoritatively settled.[13]

The Pope urged the Scripture scholar to "go back in spirit to those remote centuries of the East."[14] To do this, he must make use

---

12. Oscar Cullmann, "Les récentes études sur la formation de la tradition évangélique," *Revue d'Histoire et de Philosophie Religieuses* 5 (1925) 472.
13. *Acta Apostolicae Sedis* 35 (1943) 319. In the opinion of John L. McKenzie, this is "perhaps the most important statement of the encyclical": cf. "Problems of Hermeneutics in Roman Catholic Exegesis," *Journal of Biblical Literature* 77 (1958) 197-204.
14. *Acta Apostolicae Sedis* 35 (1943) 314. The differences between the biblical, Semitic mentality and that of modern, western culture (which is Greek in origin) are clearly brought out by Gregory Dix, *Jew and Greek: a study in the Primitive Church* (London: 1953) 1-18; and by Célestin Charlier, "Méthode historique et lecture spirituelle des écritures," *Bible et Vie Chrétienne* 18 (1957) 7-26.

of all the findings of modern science. Above all, he must study the various literary forms; and for this, the method of Form criticism is recommended, since "the sacred books need not exclude any of the ancient Near Eastern forms of expression in human language, provided they are compatible with the divine sanctity and veracity."[15] While of course the Holy Father did not neglect the divine nature of the Bible, his preoccupation with the human aspect of the sacred books and his repeated insistence that they must be studied as literature have given a new orientation and a powerful impetus to the study of the Gospels.

The Discoveries at Qumran

The third formative influence on the new understanding of the Gospels was the fortuitous discovery, in the early spring of 1947, of a number of documents belonging to a Jewish sect which flourished during the period contemporary with our Lord and with the apostolic Church of the first century. Since the reader is doubtless familiar with the story of this astonishing find, we shall confine our attention to their value as background material for the Gospels.[16]

In the first place, these writings develop certain theological themes, familiar to us from the Gospels. The doctrine of "the two ways," is one of these. Mankind is considered as consisting of two opposing groups, those who act with rectitude and those whose conduct is evil. Jesus taught a similar doctrine: "the gate leading to destruction is wide; the road there is easy to travel . . . how narrow is the gate leading to life; the road there is difficult . . . ." (Mt 7,13-14). In the theology of Qumran, men are led by one of these "two ways" under the direction of "the spirit of truth," or "the prince of light"; or of "Belial," "the spirit of perversity," "the angel of darkness." According as men are good or evil, they are "the sons of light" or "the sons of darkness." The reminiscences of the vocabulary of the Fourth Gospel in such terminology are clear.

The theme of the desert as a place where God is to be found and his presence enjoyed is another Qumran motif which finds echoes in the New Testament. By their retreat into the desert, the Qumranian sectaries believed they were preparing for the coming of the messianic age. An Isaian text from which they drew inspiration (it is cited twice in the rule of the community) is one that recurs in John the Baptist's preaching. "In the desert, make ready the way of the Lord . . ." (Is 40,3). Echoes of this "desert spirituality" followed at Qumran are found in the epistle to the Hebrews and in the Apocalypse.[17]

---

15. *Acta Apostolicae Sedis* 35 (1943) 315-316.
16. Cf. John M. Oesterreicher, "The Community of Qumran," *The Bridge*, volume 2 (New York: 1956) 91-134.
17. Cf. the balanced study by Joseph Schmitt, "Les écrits du Nouveau Testament et les textes de Qumran," *Revue des Sciences Religieuses* 29 (1955) 381-401; 30 (1956) 55-74.

Three moral attitudes are basic both in Christianity and in the morality of Qumran: a hatred of impurity, a great mistrust or contempt of wealth, the practice of brotherly love.

A feature of the Qumran community which is of paramount interest to Catholics, since it has helped us appreciate the dominant role of the Church in the formation of our Gospels, is the structural parallelism it offers to the primitive Christian Church. This Jewish group is marked by a strong sense of unity in doctrine, religious practice, fraternal love. The repeated use of the term *yaḥad* to describe themselves (the word means "community") is proof of this sense of oneness, which, as in the Christian community of Jerusalem, was symbolized by the practice of communal living.[18]

The carefully hierarchized organization of the Qumran community which recalls several features of the earliest Christian Church is a reminder, if one be needed, that Christianity in its origins was not a "democratic" institution, consisting (as the first Form critics gratuitously assumed) of an unorganized, anonymous collectivity, capable of producing without any restraint a crop of mythical tales about Jesus of Nazareth. At Qumran, the *mebaqqer* or superintendent presided with jurisdiction over the *rabbim*, "the many" as the community was called, acting towards them like a father and a shepherd. In addition, there was a council of the elders, who with the superintendent jealously guarded the purity of doctrine and practices of Judaism as they understood it.

The use of the corresponding Greek terms in New Testament descriptions of the early Church indicates a similarity of organization.[19] It was the apostolic college with Peter at its head which ruled the Church, and it is not without significance that the discourses in Acts, which are regarded by modern scholars as samples of the earliest apostolic preaching, are credited to St. Peter. Thus the oral tradition out of which our Gospels were created was not the product of a nameless, irresponsible crowd, but emanated from the apostolic hierarchy under the direction of him who had replaced Christ upon earth.[20]

These then are the three principal factors, I would suggest, that

---

18. This sense of community is emphasized in Acts 2, 44-45; 4,32-35; 5, 1-11. The phenomenon is of paramount importance for any proper evaluation of the historical character of the evangelical traditions recorded in the Gospels. It is inconceivable that any group possessing such a lively consciousness of its unity and distinctive nature should permit the introduction of novelty, not to say myth, into its traditional picture of the risen Lord Jesus.
19. In the New Testament, the term *episkopos* corresponds to *mebaqqer*, *hoi polloi* to *rabbim*, *epi to auto* to *yaḥad*, *hoi neōteroi* (*neaniskoi*) to the "novices" or "postulants," *hoi presbyteroi*, to the elders in the community.
20. That Peter was regarded as holding Jesus' place in the primitive Christian community is clear from a comparison of Acts 5,15-16 with Mk 6,56. —The intense resistance which the Qumran covenanters offered to the change of calendar (from solar, the traditional, priestly reckoning of time, to lunar, adopted in late Judaism by the official caste in Jeru-

have provided us with a new approach to the Gospels. We must now review the ways in which the study of the Gospels as literature has increased our understanding of them.

The Literary Character of the Gospels

Perhaps today more successfully than hitherto has an attempt been made to "go back in spirit" to the culture and the thought-patterns of the period which produced the Gospels. Recent studies[21] of the psychology and modes of expression which constitute the ancient Semitic or biblical mentality have given an insight into the world in which Jesus Christ lived. We have come to realize the existential quality of Palestinian modes of thinking, its concreteness, its love of imagery and symbolism. We have come to appreciate the (to us) strange kind of logic which governs the thought of the biblical writer, articulated as it is by keywords and parallelism rather than syllogistic argumentation.

We have only to recall the importance attached to the name of anything or anyone, in the view of the sacred writers, to become conscious of how widely their thought diverges from that of the Greeks, which we have inherited. To us, the names assigned to things are purely conventional or equivocal: "a rose by any other name would smell as sweet." In the eyes of the Semite, the name comprehends and expresses the full reality of a thing, the total significance of a person or his function. When God changes Abram's name to Abraham, he is, from the biblical point of view, simply a different person. "Your name will be Abraham: for I have made you the father of many nations" (Gn 17,5). Jesus' naming Simon "Rock," Peter, constitutes him head of the Church (Mt 16,18).

Our modern consciousness of the importance of symbolism, the result of twentieth century developments in psychology, has also aided our interpretation of the Gospels. To trace the metamorphosis of biblical symbols under the creative impact of the sacred history is a most informative, as well as fascinating task. The richness and dynamic vitality of the symbol, in contrast with the abstracted poverty of the scientific term has been well defined by Austin Farrer. "Symbol endeavours, as it were, to *be* that of which it speaks, and imitates reality by the multiplicity of its significance."[22] Perhaps no New Testament writer has exploited the potentialities of the symbol so successfully as the evangelist St. John, for whom Jesus' miracles are "signs," or symbols that induct us into the mystery of his mission and his person. To describe the creative dynamism of the power to forgive sins, which the

---

salem) provides a striking instance of how this well-organized community resented any derogation from what they regarded as religious custom.

21. Cf. Thorlief Boman, *Das Hebräische Denken im Vergleich mit dem Griechischen* (Göttingen: 1954); Claude Tresmontant, *Études de métaphysique biblique* (Paris: 1955).
22. Austin Farrer, *A Rebirth of Images: the Making of St. John's Apocalypse* (London: 1949) 19.

risen Christ confers upon his disciples on Easter evening, St. John represents the glorified Jesus as "breathing into" them, as "the Lord God breathed into the nostrils" of the little clay doll he had molded, "so that man became a living being" (Gn 2,7:cf. Jn 20,22).

The second area of Gospel studies in which progress has been made is in the investigation of what Pius XII called "the distinctive genius" of each evangelist, that is, his personal conception of New Testament salvation-history. For each of the four evangelists, as we now know, has his own distinctive way of answering the question, "What manner of man is this?" Where Mark depicts Jesus Christ as the Son of God who reveals, by his actions, his divinity no less than his complete humanity, Luke portrays him as the second Adam, the Saviour of mankind, who fulfills, by what he is and what he teaches, the religious aspirations of that Hellenistic civilization that Luke knew and loved. For John, Jesus is the incarnate Word become man in order to become our interpreter of "the God no man has ever seen" (Jn 1,18).

If we are to penetrate the secret of "the distinctive genius" of the authors of the Gospels, we must study each of their books as a literary unity and so endeavor to grasp its individual message. St. Matthew's Gospel may serve as an illustration of what I mean.

In many ways, of course, the First Gospel resembles that of Mark or Luke. Not only does Matthew tell the same story, with the help of much the same sources. His theological outlook is also, in many respects, similar to theirs. He regards, as do they, the destruction of sin as the aim of Jesus' earthly career. He is no less conscious than they of the redemptive character of Jesus' death and resurrection. Moreover, the tragedy of Jesus' rejection as their Messias by God's chosen people is no less operative in the structuring of Matthew's Gospel than in that of Mark or Luke.

Matthew is however rightly renowned for his love of order and symmetry, his habit of omitting the irrelevant, his discipline and sense of proportion. His carefully constructed account of Jesus' life exemplifies such qualities admirably.

To illustrate the principal theme of his story, Matthew has employed certain family reminiscences of Jesus' infancy. A genealogy shows Jesus deeply rooted in his people's past. The story of Jesus' virginal conception and birth reveals how, in him, sacred history has made an utterly new beginning. The fidelity of the Magi, set in sharp contrast with the faithlessness and perversity of Herod, presages the choice of the Gentiles in place of the Jews in God's Kingdom, represented here below by the Church. The divine frustration of Herod's attempt upon the life of the infant Jesus foreshadows the final triumph of God's redemptive plan for mankind through the death and resurrection of Christ.

The Matthean account of Jesus' public ministry progresses in an orderly, yet dramatic manner. The first stage in Jesus' mission, after his messianic investiture at his baptism by John, shows him winning the ear and heart of the Galilean crowds by his proclamation of the imminent establishment of God's sovereignty in this world and by his merciful, liberating work of healing those held under Satan's domination by diseases of various kinds. As his reputation grows and the work expands, we see him call the Twelve and entrust them with a share in his mission of preaching and curing men's ills. Soon, opposition from the vested interests of Judaism, represented by the scribes and Pharisees, begins to appear. Matters come to a head with their demand of "a sign" in proof of the validity of Jesus' claims. He excoriates his adversaries' bad will (they insinuate he is a tool of the devil), and promises only the "sign" of his own death and resurrection.

From now on, we see a decline in Jesus' popularity with the crowds, who by their apathy and obtuseness offer a kind of passive resistance to his teaching. Thus, in this second stage of Jesus' public life, we see him concentrating more and more upon the instruction of his faithful adherents. He does not entirely abandon the fickle populace however, but teaches them through the parable: a brief, somewhat paradoxical story, calculated to arouse their curiosity and lead them to further inquiry.

St. Matthew shows, by contrast with the decline of Jesus' appeal to the generality of Galileans, the heart-warming growth of the disciples' faith, which develops to a climax in Peter's profession of loyalty at Caesarea Philippi. Matthew takes advantage of Peter's dramatic avowal, in which he has perceived the virtualities of faith in Jesus' divinity, in order to record Christ's appointment of Peter as head of his future church.

Thereafter, in Matthew's story, Jesus avoids publicity, avoids debate with his adversaries, whose opposition is continually on the increase, until he reaches Jerusalem for the *dénouement* of his earthly career. A series of skirmishes with the Judean religious authorities reveals to us the gradual mounting of Jesus' anger until it bursts forth in a tragic and terrible denunciation of the bankruptcy of contemporary Judaism.

With this episode, Jesus' public ministry comes to an end. Events now move swiftly: Jesus is betrayed, arrested, unjustly condemned, maltreated, crucified. Matthew brings his book to a triumphant conclusion with a glimpse of the joyful reunion between the disciples and the risen Christ upon a certain mountain in Galilee.

When we attempt to analyze Matthew's literary procedure, we find that he has constructed the main body of his book, containing the account of Jesus' public ministry, by alternating narrative with discourse. He divides his material into five booklets (possibly to recall the five books of the Old Law), each devoted to some facet of "the Kingdom of Heaven." As we read the carefully selected episodes and the skillfully composed sermons of Matthew, we gradually become conscious that, behind the immediate reality of Jesus' Galilean ministry, our author is giving us an insight into the nature and mission of the future Christian Church. She stands revealed, in the Sermon on the

Mount, as the perfect flowering of the Old Testament religious spirit. Subsequent discourses of Jesus disclose her orientation to the Gentile mission, her mysterious supernatural character, the brotherly love that must animate her members, her ultimate liberation, by means of the destruction of the Temple, from the Judaism out of which she took her rise.

It is this ecclesiastical character of the Matthean Gospel which has made it the Church's favourite for use in her liturgy. It is also this quality which enables us to grasp the peculiarly Matthean features of the picture of Jesus Christ and his work, which this inspired book presents. He is, before all else, Emmanuel, "with us is God," as is stated in the prologue (Mt 1,23); and the author returns to this conception in the last words of the risen Christ which he records, "Remember, I *am with you* all the time until the end of history" (Mt 28, 20). It is his desire to remain with us in his Church which has most appealed to St. Matthew about Jesus, "the Son of the living God" (Mt 16,16). It is this purpose of his mission which best characterizes the "Good News" as set forth by the first evangelist.

Some Discoverable Literary Genres

We must now attempt to evaluate the progress towards a fuller understanding of our Gospels made in recent years, thanks to the study of the many literary forms which they exhibit. Here two *caveats* must be borne in mind.

The first is contained in the observation of Pius XII, already cited, that "the sacred books need not exclude any of the ancient Near Eastern forms of expression . . . compatible with the divine sanctity and veracity." This should caution us against excluding *a priori* certain literary genres, current in Semitic culture, but alien to our western modes of expression. True reverence, surely, does not approach the sacred books with the conviction that there are certain ways God should (or should not) have transmitted his revelation. To put ourselves to school to the evangelists in order *to learn from them* the literary vehicles or forms God did choose is obviously the only truly scientific method. It happens also to be the attitude proper to Christian humility.

The second principle is that, in itself, the literary analysis of any narrative does not give us warrant to assert or deny its historical value.[23] It may indeed set limits to our assertion of the historicity of certain features of a narrative, in the sense that it provides a clearer insight into *the kind of history* thus presented. The parables in the

23. Cf. J. Cambier, "Historicité des évangiles synoptiques et Formgeschichte," in *La Formation des Évangiles* (Bruges: 1957) 211. This collection of essays gives a fairly comprehensive view of the advances made by Catholic scholarship in the understanding of the Synoptic Gospels. For a similar collection concerning the Fourth Gospel, cf. *L'Évangile de Jean: études et problèmes* (Bruges: 1958).—A useful study of New Testament literary forms is that of A. Robert, article "Littéraires (Genres)" *Dictionnaire de la Bible Supplément,* V, cols. 405-421.

Gospels, which often provide a kind of symbolic history of the fortunes and destiny of the Church, are obviously a different genre from the accounts of the passion of Jesus. Again, the Markan account of the institution of the Eucharist (Mk 14,22-25), with its schematic and highly liturgical features, is strikingly different from the Markan narrative of the storm at sea (Mk 4,35-41). Indeed, the Lukan version of the Last Supper (Lk 22,14-20) exemplifies another genre, in which a theological motif (the fulfillment of the passover sacrifice in the Eucharist) has dictated the somewhat artificial, stylized presentation of the events.[24]

What literary genres has modern scholarship discovered in our Gospels? In the first place, each of these books as a whole is now seen to possess a distinctive genre, which we may call the Gospel-form. Since, in some respects, it represents the written account of the apostolic kerygma or preaching, it has as its principal theme the "Good News" of salvation in Jesus Christ. But while the Gospel preached by the apostles was aimed at the non-Christian world to produce *metanoia,* conversion, the written Gospel is directed to the Christian convert (like Luke's Theophilus), to provide a deeper comprehension of the meaning of the faith already accepted. "These things were written," John informs his reader, "in order that you may grow in your belief that Jesus is the Messias, the Son of God. . . ." (Jn 20,31).[25] From this it becomes evident that, for a valid interpretation of our Gospels, it is necessary to attend constantly to the dialogue between the author and his (Christian) reader. For the witness of the evangelist is, before all else, the witness of faith, and it is with this in mind that he has carefully recorded the testimony of "the original eye-witnesses."

Subordinated to this general Gospel-form are many other genres: the parable, the liturgical formula, the summary, the *midrash,* the popular story, the eye-witness account, the constructed scene, the sermon, the ode, the canticle, etc. All of these forms, whether fictional (like the parable), poetic (like the *Magnificat*), or historical or didactic, express a certain kind of truth, indeed *inspired* truth, which is, consequently, the object of Christian faith. The discerning of the literary form simply tells us better *how* it is to be believed: it does not eliminate any part of Scripture from the body of revelation. Nothing is more disconcerting for the teacher of Scripture, who has pointed out the fictional nature of a biblical book or passage, than the remark, "So we don't have to believe that any more."

It may be helpful to illustrate some of these literary forms by examples from the Gospels. As a brief instance of the eye-witness

---

24. A more complete discussion of this point will be found in "Liturgical Influences on the Formation of the Four Gospels," *Catholic Biblical Quarterly* 21 (1959) 33-35: the view exposed is that of Pierre Benoit, "Le récit de la Cène dans Lc XII, 15-20: étude de critique textuelle et littéraire," *Revue Biblique* 48 (1939) 357-393.
25. This is a more accurate translation of the Greek *present* subjunctive than the usual rendering, "that you may believe . . ."

account (the Passion narratives are too lengthy to be cited here), we may take Mark's description of the call of the first disciples.

> "Now as he was walking past them by the lake of Galilee, he watched Simon and Andrew, Simon's brother, casting their net into the lake,—they were fishermen. Jesus said to them, 'Come and follow me: I will make you go fishing for men.' And immediately, dropping their nets, they followed him. Walking along a little farther, he saw James, Zebedee's son, and his brother, John. They were in their boat, repairing their nets. At once, he called them; and abandoning their father Zebedee, who was in the boat with the hired men, they set off after him" (Mk 1,16-20).

Despite the schematic nature of the account, the results of continued re-telling in oral tradition, the description retains certain details which must go back to an eye-witness. The picture of Jesus walking by the lake is described from the viewpoint of one of the disciples. The mending of the nets, the sketch of Zebedee with his hired men, are further details given by someone who actually saw the episode.

In contrast with this type of narrative, there is the form we have designated as the constructed scene. There are, of course, many clear instances in the Gospels of sermons attributed to Jesus, which have been given their actual form by Matthew or John. To admit that such discourses, as they stand, are the work of the sacred writers, is by no means to deny that Jesus was the author of the various sayings from which they were composed.

This same principle must function in the evaluation of the literary form which is a construction by the sacred writer from *incidents* which occurred on different occasions. To admit, where the evidence demands it, that a certain incident related by an evangelist is a complex of several happenings is not to assert that it did not happen at all. St. Luke gives a striking example of this technique in his description of Jesus' visit to Nazareth during his public life. By the use of certain traditions, some of which were unknown (it would seem) to Mark or Matthew, the third evangelist builds up this episode to form the opening of Jesus' public ministry. In its author's eyes, Jesus' rejection by the Nazarenes is symbolic of the failure of Israel to understand him and his mission.

It is not merely that St. Luke is better informed about Jesus' Nazareth experiences than the other Synoptic writers, although only he tells us about the Scriptural passage Jesus read in the synagogue, and of the admiration of the townsfolk at his eloquence, of his references to Elias and Eliseus, of the Nazarenes' attempt to kill him. A careful analysis of the Lukan narrative results in the impression that two, or even three, quite distinct events have been fused into one. There was a day when Jesus read the Scripture lesson, and the people were lost in admiration of him, taking a certain local pride in a hometown boy who had achieved prominence. This may be the same occasion to which Matthew refers in passing (Mt 4,13), a visit early in Jesus' public ministry. There was another incident, perhaps that described by Matthew and Mark (Mt 13,54-58; Mk 6,1-8), when Jesus' fellow-citizens reacted quite differently: they became disillusioned in him, and he, in turn, refused to work miracles merely to prove his powers. To this, St. Luke adds some fragments of a sermon (it would appear) on the call of the pagans to the Gospel, which so angered the villagers that they made an attempt on Jesus' life.

These brief illustrations of literary forms found in our Gospels may serve to exemplify the twofold purpose of the evangelists, which we alluded to earlier. These sacred writers do witness faithfully to real events, to actual words of Jesus. Peter's frank avowal before the Sanhedrin applies also to these sacred writers: "We cannot but declare what we have seen and heard" (Acts 4,20). At the same time, they show themselves "ministers of the Word": they press into the service of the Gospel the various traditions about Jesus they have received. Their main purpose is not simply "biographical" in the modern sense of the term: it is "evangelical," to witness to God's definitive entry into human history, in the person of his Son, Jesus Christ. They are interested undoubtedly in the "historical," not for its own sake, but because of "the Good News" it contains.

The formation of our Gospels

The second area in which we have achieved a "new understanding of the Gospels," as I remarked at the beginning of this study, is that of the historical process which produced them. While a great deal is still unknown about the manner in which the Gospels were composed, a certain degree of reasonably solid progress has been made, as a result of the critical examination of the books themselves and of a clearer perception of the nature and history of the primitive Church.

Attention has been directed to the various centres of interest around which certain traditions crystallized: a liturgical interest, which produced written accounts of Jesus' passion probably quite early in the apostolic period, for use in the "breaking of the bread";[26] a catechetical interest, which employed certain sayings and stories for the instruction of converts; an apologetic interest, which used certain incidents for the defense of orthodox doctrine and practice; a didactic interest, which evoked Jesus' authority to settle questions arising within the community itself; an ecclesiastical interest, which grew with the Church's consciousness of her own distinctive spirit and destiny; and, finally, an historical interest, which exercised a preponderant role, because of the unique character of Christianity as an historical religion.[27]

The revival of interest in the Synoptic problem, i.e., the study of

---

26. That instruction is combined with sacrifice in the Christian liturgy is one of its distinctive traits: cf. Augustine Bea, "The Pastoral Value of the Word of God in the Sacred Liturgy," *The Assisi Papers* (Collegeville: 1957) 76.
27. Gregory Dix, *Jew and Greek* (London: 1953) 5: "Christianity is the revelation of Divine Truth from beyond all history and all time, but it is so, only because it is the only fully historical religion. It is the only religion which actually *depends entirely upon history*."

the mutual dependence of Matthew, Mark, and Luke, has led to the plausible hypothesis that several Greek translations of Aramaic documents relative to the Gospel materials constituted the sources upon which the evangelists drew.[28] The findings of the Form critics have revealed the existence of certain complexes, now incorporated in our Gospels, antedating their composition. Indeed, St. Luke had long ago asserted that before he wrote "many had tried their hand at drawing up an account of the events" (Lk 1,1) which form the subject-matter of our written Gospels. It appears fairly certain that the series of episodes narrated by the Synoptics, which begins with Peter's profession of faith and extends to Jesus' transfiguration (cf. Mt 16,13-17,20) and the cure of the lunatic boy, pre-existed, in literary form, our inspired Gospels. This sequence is unique because of the specific chronological connection between the various episodes it recounts—a fairly solid indication that it formed a written source taken over by the evangelists.

The existence of an authoritative Gospel framework, composed in the very early days of the Church and handed on as normative for missionary preaching appears today to be accepted widely. Paul himself testifies that he handed on just such an authoritative version of the "Good News," received from his predecessors, the apostles (cf. 1 Cor 15,3.11). In fact, Paul's letters provide evidence, at least in one instance (his account of the institution of the Eucharist: 1 Cor 11,23-25), of the great care, as regards form and expression, with which these evangelical traditions were handed on. That this was probably the customary practice in the early Church with respect to the oral transmission of the materials later enshrined in our Gospels seems clear from what is known of the way in which contemporary Jewish teachers insisted upon the accurate memorizing, by their disciples, of certain doctrines.[29]

It is moreover Peter himself who is indicated as the principal author of this apostolic preaching.[30] In the opinion of the great majority of modern New Testament critics, the speeches in Acts are genuine summaries of this primitive preaching; and analysis reveals that the speeches attributed to Paul in Acts are basically the same in outline and in content as those ascribed to Peter. Granted that Luke, as Paul's travelling-companion, was well acquainted with Paul's sermon schemes, it seems evident that he followed, as indeed we saw him assert in his letters, the traditional evangelical form which Peter had originally composed.

Recent attempts at a study of the distinctive biblical theologies, represented by various stages of the development, particularly, of

---

28. For a helpful survey of recent developments concerning this question, cf. Francis J. McCool, "Revival of Synoptic Source-Criticism," *Theological Studies* 17 (1956) 459-493.
29. Harald Riesenfeld, *The Gospel Tradition and its Beginnings: a study in the Limits of "Formgeschichte"* (London: 1957) 16ff.
30. C. H. Dodd, *The Apostolic Preaching and its Developments* (London: 1936).

Christology, in the apostolic age, have succeeded in tracing the steps in the evolution of Christian dogmas. We are thus able to evaluate the contributions, in the expression of the Christian revelation, made by men like Peter, Stephen, Paul, Matthew, and John.[31] Above all, it has become more evident perhaps than formerly that Jesus Christ himself was not only the one Person to whom all these apostolic preachers and thinkers bear witness, but that he was the primary source of the Christian religion, as the one who fulfilled in an utterly new, thoroughly creative manner, all the prophetic hope and aspirations of Old Testament history.[32] The twofold testimony of the evangelists, to the historical reality of the events and of the Person they present (i.e., their eye-witness testimony), and to the supernatural significance of these events and of this Person, the Son of God (i.e., their witness of Christian faith), points infallibly to Jesus Christ, postulates his historical existence as well as his divine character. As John L. McKenzie has recently remarked, "If the apostolic preaching was the creative agent of this synthesis, then the disciples were greater than their master."[33]

I should like, in closing, to point out one very important result of this "new understanding of the Gospels," for the simple reason that it may not, in the minds of many, appear to be a gain at all. We have come to realize the impossibility of writing a life of Christ in the modern biographical sense. Modern biblical scholarship has demonstrated the futility of trying to fix, in a chronological pattern, the majority of the events that made up the public ministry of Jesus. It would seem to be the part of scientific candor, no less than of Christian humility, to admit that all such attempts are foredoomed to failure, for the very good reason that this was not the way God willed to have us learn Christ. Our astonishing ignorance of the exact dates of Jesus' birth and of his death are a striking proof of this: these facts, however important in our eyes, simply do not form part of the New Testament revelation. But to appreciate the impossibility of composing a life of Christ, to suit modern standards, possesses certain advantages. And not the least of these is a clearer perception of the profound truth there is in the statement of Père Lagrange: "The Gospels are the sole life of Jesus Christ that could be written. Our task is to understand them as best we can."[34]

---

31. One splendid instance of this type of study has been provided by Krister Stendahl, *The School of St. Matthew* (Uppsala: 1954).
32. Bruce Vawter, "Messianic Prophecies in Apologetics," *Proceedings of the Catholic Theological Society of America* 12 (New York: 1960) 97-119.
33. John L. McKenzie, "Messianism and the College Teacher of Sacred Doctrine," *Proceedings of the Society of Catholic College Teachers of Sacred Doctrine* 12 (Notre Dame: 1960) 48.
34. M.-J. Lagrange, *L'Évangile de Jésus-Christ* (Paris: 1936) vi.

THE GOSPEL MIRACLES

RAYMOND E. BROWN, S.S.

This article is an attempt to probe the pre-literary relationships between the Synoptic tradition and the Johannine tradition. On first look the two traditions are startlingly different on the whole question of miracle. In the Synoptic tradition miracles are narrated one after the other in almost embarrassing profusion. Some 200 of the 425 verses of Mk 1-10 deal directly or indirectly with miracle, a statistic which means that almost one half of the Marcan narrative of the public ministry concerns the miraculous.[1] In Jn, on the other hand, we have seven miracles narrated during the public ministry.[2] The pressing of the crowds with their sick, the constant pleading for help, the wonder-struck awe, the excited reports of what has been done, in short the whole color of the Synoptic miracle narrative had faded in Jn.[3] Rather, the miracles of Jn seem to serve primarily for long interpretative discourses. But not only the number and the circumstances of miracles differ in the two traditions. For Jn the might and wonder of the miracle seems to have been submerged in the concept of miracle as sign, a change which touches on the very nature and function of the miracle. Nevertheless, despite these obvious differences, we hope to show that, once we have made allowance for the peculiar genius of each tradition, their concept of miracle is not as diverse as might first seem.

From the time that Quadratus made apologetic use of the gospel miracles in his *Apology to Hadrian* (c. 125 A.D.) the interpretation of miracle seems to have been inextricably bound up with the defense of the Christian faith. While the apologetic usefulness of the miracle has had the advantage of leading the best theological minds in the Church to study and comment on it, nevertheless, this constant apologetic coloring of the exegesis of the gospel miracles has been a mixed blessing. The history of the apologetic of miracles is too well known to

1. The figures are given by Alan Richardson, *The Miracle Stories of the Gospels* (London: SCM paper back ed., 1959) 36.
2. Changing of water to wine at Cana (2,1-11); healing of the official's son (4,46-54); healing at Bethesda (5,1-15); multiplication of the loaves (6,1-13); walking on the water (6,16-21); healing the blind man (9); raising Lazarus (11).
3. In Jn 7 and 8 we do get a picture of the excitement of the crowds, but this is not immediately connected to a miracle.

present.[4] As exegetes we need but express our gratitude that the overemphasis on the transcendent value of the miracle (as an exception to "the laws of nature") has now given place among Catholic scholars to an emphasis on the religious context of the miracle and on its role as a sign.

With particular reference to the purpose and interest of our article, we might note that while the miracle is useful to apologetics as a guarantee of the credibility of revelation, this perfectly valid use of the gospel[4a] must not lead us to the assumption that such an apologetic purpose dominated Jesus' own use of miracles. The question that concerns us in a purely scriptural study of the miracle is not how we can use the gospel miracles in defending the faith but what role miracles played in the gospel tradition. Once and for all, miracles are important external signs of revelation. But, beyond this, Jesus' miracles had a more primary, internal role *in his ministry* as acts through which he gave revelation; side by side, the word and the miraculous deed gave expression to God's entrance into time.[5] This is not novel once we realize that in the OT Yahweh is pictured not only as a God who speaks (e.g., through the prophets) but also, nay chiefly, as a God who acts. His actions[6] in salvation history were effective signs of his protection of his people; they accomplished what they signified. It is not surprising, then, that when God's Son came to establish God's dominion

4. For an excellent summary see John A. Hardon, S. J., "The Concept of Miracle from St. Augustine to Modern Apologetics," *TS* 15 (1954) 229-257. Also Louis Monden, S. J., *Le miracle, signe de salut* (Desclée de Brouwer; 1960) 45-55 (he has an excellent bibliography on "miracle"). Modern opinions are clearly summarized in Robert Gleason, S.J., "Miracles and Contemporary Theology," *Thought* 37 (1962) 12-34.

4a. The Vatican Council (DB 1813) has defined that miracles can be known with certainty and that they can be used to establish the divine origins of the Christian religion.

5. The Hebrew term used for what we would call a miracle is *môpheth,* translated in the LXX by *teras.* (The Deuteronomist often adds a synonym to *môpheth* namely *'ôth*—LXX, *sēmeion.*) As a translation, *teras* actually overplays the prodigy element in *môpheth* for the Hebrew term refers to any symbolic act, e.g., of a prophet, and need not refer to anything extraordinary. When something extraordinary is described, *niphla'* can be added. It is interesting that the NT never uses *teras* alone to refer to the miraculous acts of Jesus and the Apostles, but always combines it with *sēmeion;* perhaps this is an attempt to avoid overemphasizing the prodigy element. *Teras* is used in secular literature, however, for the miracle worked by the Hellenistic wonder worker (more frequently than *dynamis* or *sēmeion*). The word "miracle," from the Latin *miraculum* (never used in the NT), has not preserved the NT nuance of avoiding the prodigious element. See A. Lefèvre, "Miracle," *VDBS* 5, col. 1300.

6. It is interesting that there are very few miracles worked by and for individuals in the OT; rather God's miracles are centered on the whole people. Really, the only important instances of private miracles are those of Elias and Eliseus in 3 Kgs 17 to 4 Kgs 13; these men heal, multiply food, and bring the dead back to life. This is why Jesus seemed like a second Elias; see our article "Three Quotations from John the Baptist in the Gospel of John," *CBQ* 22 (1960) 297-298.

over men, he was also a God who acts as well as a God who speaks.[7]

1. The Synoptic *dynameis*

The ordinary term in the Synoptic Gospels for miracle is *dynamis,* an act of power. With Jesus God's power erupts among men (Acts 10,38), and the entrance of God is centralized in one individual. The powerful divine deeds which were worked on a national scale in the OT are now channeled through Jesus.

The Synoptic Gospels describe Jesus' ministry as one of announcing the coming of God's kingdom. The material which the Synoptists give us pertaining to the public ministry can be divided between preaching (mostly in parables[8]) and working miracles. This is in harmony with Peter's kerygmatic summary of the ministry in Acts 10,36-38 which mentions precisely preaching and healing (Acts 2,22 is more general: "mighty works and wonders and signs"). Therefore, it is clear that in the Synoptic Gospels Jesus' miracles are to be connected to the coming of the kingdom.[9]

Now there is no question that Jesus' miracles caused people to wonder and admire, and led many to faith. Nevertheless, it is evident that, at least in Jesus' mind, the element of proof or credential was not primary in the miracle for he consistently refused to work a miracle simply as a proof.[10] Whether the request came from the devil, Herod, the Pharisees or the people, Jesus would not perform miracles just to show that he was sent by God.[11] Since his miracles inevitably attracted attention, he sought to avoid this by performing his miracles privately, away from the crowd.[12] He minimized the purely prodigious element of the miracle which could not lead to understanding or faith. As he said, "If someone should rise from the dead, they will not be convinced" (Lk 16,31). He admitted that false prophets could

---

7. As Augustine puts it, "Gesta Verbi sunt verba."
8. Mt, more than Mk or Lk, correctly characterizes many parables as parables *of the kingdom.*
9. A. George, "Les miracles de Jésus dans les évangiles synoptiques," *Lumière et Vie* 33 (1957) 7-24. Edwyn Hoskyns and Noel Davey, *The Riddle of the New Testament* (London: Faber paperback ed., 1958) 117-126.
10. The overemphasis on the apologetic aspect of the gospel miracles has actually played into the hands of those who oppose the credibility of miracles. Bultmann's view is that the miracle stories have been added to the Gospels to gain understanding for Jesus as a wonder worker: Jesus needed the same credentials as Apollonius of Tyana and the rabbinical wonder workers. For a detailed critique of Bultmann's assumptions about the lack of historicity in the gospel accounts of the miracles, see V. Taylor, *The Formation of the Gospel Tradition* (London: Macmillan, 1953) 119-136. (See n.22 below)
11. Mt 4,5; Lk 23,6-12; Mk 8,11-13; Mt 12,38-42; Mk 15,31-32; Mk 6,1-6.
12. Mk 7,33; 8,23; 9,25. As Ian Hislop, O.P., "Miracles and the Gospels," *Blackfriars* 39 (1958) 57-60, points out, enthusiastic reaction to Jesus as a wonder worker is on the same surface plane as reaction to him as one possessed or mad. Both reactions are superficial; the astonishment has simply taken different directions.

work prodigies that would come close to deceiving even holy men (Mk 13,22-23).

The connection of the miracle with the coming of the kingdom lies in another direction. The miracle was not primarily an external guarantee of the coming of the kingdom; it was one of the means by which the kingdom came. In particular, Jesus' miracles were the weapons he used to overcome Satan.[13] The temptation story was set at the beginning of the public ministry in Mt and Lk to tell us that the coming of the kingdom involved a tremendous struggle with Satan. From the time of man's sin until the coming of Jesus, Satan had a certain dominion over nature and over man. He would not yield this dominion to God without a fight, a fight that culminated in Gethsemani and Calvary, the hour of the power of darkness (Lk 22,53).[14] So much of Jesus' energy and time was taken up in this struggle that he could virtually identify his ministry with the casting out of demons. As his ministry drew to a close, he said, "Behold *I cast out demons* and perform cures today and tomorrow, and the third day I finish my course" (Lk 13,32). The expelling of demons was the infallible sign of the coming of the kingdom: "If it is by God's spirit that I expel demons, then it follows that the dominion of God has at last overtaken you" (Mt 12,28). The reason for this is that in the NT demoniacal possession is not so much the result of a league with Satan as an expression of bondage under Satan's dominion.

In a wider field of application beyond that of demoniacal possession, sickness itself is part of the realm of Satan. We all know that in the OT sickness and suffering were explained as the result of sin, and that this explanation was inadequate. However, this inadequacy does not vitiate the concept. Jesus himself refused to draw any one-to-one equivalence between sickness or misfortune and actual sin: the fact that a man was sick or suffering did not prove that he (or his parents) had committed an actual sin (Jn 9,3; Lk 13,1-5). Nevertheless, it is good theology that human suffering is one of the consequences of original sin, that some sufferings are the penalties of actual sin. And Jesus' whole attitude toward sickness implies that it belongs to the

---

13. Although Satan entered OT theology as a relatively late comer, he assumed great importance in the last pre-Christian centuries. The NT picture is best summed up in I Jn 5,19: "The whole world is in the power of the Evil One." For the development of the concept of Satan's dominion see James Kallas, *The Significance of the Synoptic Miracles* (London: SPCK, 1961) 38-76. This can be supplemented from the Dead Sea Scrolls with their dualistic picture of a world divided into the dominions of light and darkness.

14. In Jesus' ministry the two kingdoms are pitted against one another. This is the logic of Mk 3,22-27: Jesus' expulsion of demons is not a case of Satan's kingdom divided against itself, but of God's kingdom vs. Satan's. The stronger one (see Mk 1,7) has come to bind the strong man and take over his dominion. Satan recognized this: Mk 1,24 tells us the demons cried out, "What have you to do with us, Jesus of Nazareth? Have you come to destroy us?"

disorder characteristic of the realm of evil and is intimately connected with sin. This is the real logic (often overlooked) in healing the paralytic as a sign that his sins are forgiven (Mk 2,1-12) : if Jesus had power over one, he had power over the other.[15] It is this connection between sickness and evil that explains the frequency of possession in the gospel narrative. Diseases that might be analyzed medically as epilepsy (Mk 9,14-29), or as arthritis (Lk 13,10-17), are directly connected with Satan and his kingdom. Indeed, the very vocabulary used to describe illness and healing seems to reflect a concept of sickness as almost personalized evil. In Lk 4,39 we hear that Jesus "rebuked" a fever, much as he would rebuke a demon.[16] Also, sickness is referred to as *mastix* (a castigation or whipping; Mk 3,10; 5,10; 5,29. 34), almost as if it were directly inflicted by Satan.[17] We may see this, too, in the use of "save" in reference to healing, a concept which we have overspiritualized. The term "save" includes not only spiritual regeneration, but also, and primarily, deliverance from the evil grasp of sickness, from the dominion of Satan—there is no dichotomy of soul and body in Hebrew thought; the whole man is saved.[18]

This concept of the gospel miracle as an invasion of the kingdom of Satan and a means of establishing God's dominion affects other aspects of the Synoptic miracle narratives. Kallas[19] makes the plausible suggestion that the frequency of miracles worked on the sabbath day is not just accidental. Jesus' purpose in choosing the sabbath for his miracles was not just to raise a test case for the Law; rather, it was primarily to emphasize his miraculous work as a renewed creativity. God had rested from the work of the first creation on the sabbath; now he had resumed his creative work as he established his dominion, saved man from Satan, and re-created him in His own image.[20]

The ultimate expression of the miracle as the triumph of God's kingdom over Satan is found in Jesus' restoration of life to the dead.[21]

---

15. The same connection lies behind Jas 5,15: the man's sickness is removed and his sins are forgiven.
16. *Epitimaō*: for rebuking demons in Mk 1,25; 3,12; 9,25. Notice Mk 8,33: he *rebuked* Peter saying, "Get behind me, *Satan*!"
17. Kallas, *Significance* 79.
18. See the use of "save" in Mk 5,23; 5,34; 6,56; 10,52. We should note, however, that the term "save" seems to have been used for deliverance from sickness in secular literature as well. See Arndt and Gingrich, *Lexicon*, p. 496. For a treatment of the question, see Richardson, *Miracle Stories of the Gospels*, 62.
19. *Significance of the Synoptic Miracles*, 64.
20. Mk 3,4 and esp. Lk 13,16: "Ought not this woman, a daughter of Abraham whom Satan bound for eighteen years, be loosed from this bond on the sabbath day?" It is quite obvious that in resuming the creative work on the sabbath, Jesus is tacitly affirming his own divine prerogatives. (Mt 12,5-8)
21. Notice the climactic position of death in the order of miracles in Mt 11,2-4: miracles dealing with the blind, lame, lepers, deaf, and the *dead*. These are the signs that Jesus is the stronger one who is to come (Mt 11,3 and 3,11). Jn, in situating the Lazarus miracle as the final and

Death, as a by-product of man's sin (Gn 3,19; 1 Cor 15,56), was a particularly strong element in Satan's dominion (1 Jn 3,14). As Paul puts it, "The last enemy to be destroyed is death" (1 Cor 15,26). Thus, in raising from the dead (Mt 9,18; Lk 7,12), Jesus manifests an especially strong intervention of *dynamis* and reveals that "God has visited his people" (Lk 7,16). The revelation of God's kingdom is even more obvious in the central miracle of the Gospel, the resurrection of Jesus from the dead. It was this miracle, understood as the glorification of Jesus, that revealed that he was the Lord, Messiah, Savior and King (Acts 2,32-33.36; 5,31)

The explanation of some of the nature miracles also consists in seeing them as a revelation of God's dominion which is replacing that of Satan.[22] It is a commonplace that the Hebrew did not properly evaluate secondary causality, and that disasters caused by natural forces were often attributed directly to God or, later, to Satan. However, beyond this undeniable fact there is the valid theological observation that the sin of man did introduce certain elements of disorder into nature. Satan had established a certain dominion over all that creation which had been subordinated to man. Thus, as Paul tells us, all creation has been groaning in travail until the time of deliverance (Rom 8,22; 2 Pt 3,12-13). The great struggle of the last times will shake not only men's souls but also the very heavenly bodies as Satan is forced to give up his dominion over them (Mk 13,25; also Eph 2,2 where Satan is called "the prince of the power of the air"). In Jesus' announcement of the coming of God's kingdom, then, we would expect some sign that the powers of nature were being made subject through Jesus. In the words of Ps 8,7, "You have given him rule over the works of your hands, putting *all things* under his feet."

A good example of the nature miracle as a victory over Satan is found in the stilling of the storm (Mk 4,37-41). When the raging of nature threatens to destroy the group in the boat, Jesus stands and rebukes (*epitimaō*) the wind, just as he rebukes sickness and demons. To the sea he says, "Be silent" (*phimoō*, literally "to muzzle"), the same type of personal command that he gives to the demon in Mk 1,25.[23] And after his command the sea is tranquilized, much as a

---

climactic miracle of the gospel narrative, is a faithful interpreter of the NT appreciation of the importance of the raising of the dead.

22. The nature miracles offer commentators a great deal of difficulty. Taylor's treatment of the miracle stories (*supra,* n. 10) is marred by his failure (pp. 136-141) to see the place of the nature miracles in the ministry of Jesus. However, Ph.-H. Menoud, "La signification du miracle selon le Nouveau Testament," *RHPR* 28-29 (1948-1949) 179, is correct when he states that the modern distinction between nature miracles and miracles worked on men is too rigorous. There is no real distinction in the gospel treatment of the two types of miracles. See Wm. Neil, "The Nature Miracles," *ExpT* 67 (1956) 369-372.

23. Perhaps there is a hint of the ancient mythological concept of the sea as the spawning-place and special preserve of the evil monster. Certainly the idea was still alive in NT times (Ap 13,1).

demoniac after the expulsion of the demon: nature has been restored to order. Perhaps a similar explanation is applicable to the walking on the water (Mk 6,45-52); in the Matthean account, at least, the miracle causes the disciples to recognize Jesus as God's Son (Mt 14,33).

Thus, many of the gospel miracles (healing the sick, raising the dead, some nature miracles) reveal the triumph of God's kingdom by destroying Satan's hold on men and nature.[24] One part of this revealing function of the miracles lies in the fact that they fulfill OT prophecies. Throughout the prophets we hear of a period of supreme divine intervention into the life of God's people, a period of overflowing divine mercy for those who have remained faithful. This will be the day when the Lord will comfort Sion and make her deserts into gardens (Is 51,3); imprisonment and suffering will come to an end (Is 61,1-3). Jesus presented his miracles as a fulfillment of the prophesied deliverance. When the disciples of the Baptist came to ask Jesus if he was the one to come, he answered them in terms of the OT prophecies. His healing of the blind, the lame, the lepers, and his raising the dead, and his preaching to the poor fulfill Is 61,1-3 (good news to the poor; sight to the blind; consoling the afflicted), Is 35,5-6 (the blind see; the deaf hear; the lame jump about), Is 26,19 (the dead rise). Of course, Isaias probably meant these things as a figurative description of the messianic blessings, but Jesus is fulfilling them literally.

At times this fulfillment of OT prophecy seems to become the prime purpose of the miracle. For instance, the multiplication of the loaves, sparked by Jesus' compassion for the crowds (Mk 6,34), seems designed to show God's care for his people and the abundance of his blessings as foretold by the prophets. The people were like sheep without a shepherd (Mk 6,34); and, as Ez 34,11 had foretold, God himself was pasturing them. The multiplication of food echoed back to the divine miracles of the exodus and foreshadowed the messianic banquet.[25]

* * *

Here we come to an important step in our consideration of the Synoptic miracle. Hitherto we have been insisting that the miracles themselves were part of the coming of the kingdom, especially in as much as they were acts of divine power, opposing that of Satan. They were part of the picture of divine intervention foretold by the prophets. Yet, once we admit that certain miracles may have been worked primarily to fulfill this OT prophetic picture, we are approaching another concept of miracle as symbolic action. And we must admit that sometimes in the Synoptic gospels the main purpose of a miracle does seem

---

24. This is the only real significance of miracles which Kallas, *Significance . . .* allows. Thus, he would tell us (p. 92) that the multiplication of the loaves is a conquest of the disorder of nature which leaves men hungry. Again the miraculous catch of fish in Lk is seen as a reparation of nature's evil unproductivity. There is not the slightest indication of this in the gospel text. Kallas is carrying a good theory too far.
25. Neil, *ExpT* 67 (1956) 372. Also, Menoud, *RHPR* 28 (1948-9) 181 sees a reference to the liberation from need as described in Ap 7,16-17.

to be symbolic. In the miraculous draught of fishes (Lk 5,1-11) there may be an element of divine compassion[26] toward the poor fishermen; but, as Lk 5,10 points out, the chief purpose of the miracle is the symbolism of the great numbers of men to be caught by the disciples as fishers of men.[27] Thus, the miracle is a symbolic action prophetic of the nature of the kingdom.[28] The miraculous withering of the fig tree (Mk 11,12-14. 20-25) also seems to be a symbolic action prophetic of the rejection of Judaism. If, as a prophet, Jesus performed the healings, multiplications, and raisings of an Elias, he also performed the symbolic actions by which prophets like Isaias, Jeremias, and Ezechiel illustrated their ministry.[29]

If there are a few miracles in the Synoptic tradition whose main purpose is symbolism, there are many more where symbolism plays a secondary role.[30] For example, in the opening of the eyes of the blind, besides the above-mentioned deliverance from sickness and evil, we may see a symbolism of the spiritual opening of the eyes through faith in Jesus. At times this secondary symbolism is quite pronounced. Between two sections which describe how the disciples are slowly growing in faith (Mk 8,11-21 and 27-30), we find the narrative of the blind man who was healed by stages and only with difficulty (8,22-26). As Richardson[31] suggests, the miracle seems to symbolize the slowness of opening the ears to the meaning of the Gospel message. Certainly Jesus

---

26. Richardson, *Miracle Stories of the Gospels*, 29-30, stresses that we should not put too much emphasis on compassion as a motive for the gospel miracles. However, there is a place for messianic compassion (as distinguished from mere humanitarian compassion) in the miracles.
27. One may ask if there is not an element of the prodigious here: a miracle to impress the disciples and cause them to follow Jesus. However in Mk-Mt, which do not narrate the miracle, the disciples follow Jesus without having seen any prodigy at all. Some scholars hold the theory that Lk's miracle is the same as the one described in Jn 21, and that the post-resurrectional setting in Jn is the more original position of the narrative. If this is true, there would be no need of impressing the disciples with Jesus' power after the resurrection.
28. Richardson, *Miracle Stories of the Gospels*, brings out very well the symbolic aspect of the miracles. At times, however, he exaggerates, and he seems to divorce the symbolism from the reality of the miracles. It is in reaction to Richardson that Kallas goes to the other extreme (*supra*, n. 24) of denying symbolism and writing it off as a Church creation.
29. Perhaps symbolic action is the explanation of that very difficult miracle of the coin in the fish's mouth (Mt 17,24-27). At first this miracle seems to resemble very closely the action of a Hellenistic wonder worker; but, as one of the three Petrine sections of Mt, it is probably connected to the theme of Peter's primacy.
30. Of course, the distinction between primary and secondary purposes in a gospel miracle is from our viewpoint. It is doubtful that either the evangelist or Jesus himself would have so distinguished; for them the symbolism would have been an essential part of the miracle.
31. *Miracle Stories of the Gospels*, 84-85. We should note that this miracle is of indisputable antiquity. The use of spittle and the seeming difficulty encountered by Jesus seem to have embarrassed the authors of Mt and Lk who omit the miracle.

often hurled the challenge to hear, as if he were speaking to the spiritually deaf.

Was this secondary symbolism intended by Jesus, or was it a later insight of the evangelists? We have no doubt that by a grouping such as that mentioned in Mk 8, the evangelist has heightened the symbolism of the healing of the blind. Yet, it would be hypercriticism to deny Jesus a symbolic use of his miracles. For instance, in the healing of the centurion's servant (Mt 8,5-13) and of the daughter of the Syrophoenician woman (Mt 15,21-28), the intention to make the miracle an occasion for teaching on the conversion of the Gentiles seems to come from Jesus himself. And, as we have pointed out, there are some miracles whose primary purpose seems to be symbolic,[32] and whose symbolism would therefore stem from Jesus himself. Undoubtedly, in the kerygmatic use of Jesus' miracles in the early Church there was a deepening and an extension of symbolism, but the road had been opened by the Master.

In summation, then, the Synoptic Gospels present the miracle as an instrument in the revelation of God's kingdom. Most of the miracles were actions[33] whereby the dominion of God was actually established over man and nature.[34] A few of the miracles were more symbolic in purpose, teaching men about the kingdom rather than directly bringing this kingdom about.[35] This symbolic aspect may be found on a secondary level in many other miracles which, besides establishing God's kingdom, helped to teach men about the demands and constitution of that kingdom (e.g., its relation to the OT; its difficult demand for faith and cooperation; its demonstration of God's merciful love; its future extent and success). Thus the miracle stories were part of the *kerygma* and *didache* of the Synoptic tradition.

The acceptance of either or both of these aspects of the Synoptic miracle involved faith on the part of those who were the subjects or the witnesses of the miracle. For instance, the salvation from the power of Satan involved in the healings is the result *both* of Jesus' action and of the corresponding faith that it arouses. In fact, several times Jesus attributes the salvation directly to the faith of the person healed: "Your

---

32. It might be asked if the primary purpose of the Transfiguration were not pedagogic. Certainly it was an eruption of the divine *doxa* into the public ministry. Yet, the heavy Sinai symbolism seems to be an attempt to draw the attention of the disciples to the appearance of God to Moses. The relation to Gethsemani, drawn out by Lk (9,32.34b; 22,45), may stem from the evangelist himself.

33. Perhaps we may take a term from modern apologetics and call them sign-acts. Although the Synoptists do not call the miracles signs, the *dynameis*, in order to be effective, had to lead people to see the power behind the actions; they had to be signs.

34. Since the miracle had such a vital role in the establishment and proclamation of the kingdom, small wonder that in sending out the Twelve (Lk 9,1) and the seventy(-two Lk 10,17) Jesus specified the power to heal and exorcise as the essential part of their commission to preach the kingdom.

35. These miracles might be called sign-symbols.

faith has saved you" (Lk 8,48; 17,19; 18,42). Faith calls forth the *dynamis* of Jesus (Mk 9,24; Mt 15,28; Lk 5,20; 7,9) because it represents a readiness to accept God's dominion.[35a] Indeed, faith can put God's *dynamis* at the service of men so that they in turn can work miracles: "All things are possible to him who believes" (Mk 9,23; 11,22-23). As Fitzer[35b] puts it, faith is a sphere in which God's power comes to fruition, and this power is seriously hindered by unbelief (Mk 6,5-6; Mt 17,19-20). In its variety this faith may vary from initial trust in Jesus' power to a complete belief in what he is.[35c] Faith thrives and deepens and increases in the presence of that exercise of divine power which is the miracle.

2. The Johannine *erga* and *sēmeia*

In our study of Jn we may proceed by first discounting those differences from the Synoptic tradition which are really only surface differences. The reduction of the number of miracles in Jn is guided in part by the stated purpose of the Fourth Gospel. Jn 20,30-31 tells us that the signs narrated were chosen from among many because they were especially suited to encourage the faith of the reader. Nevertheless, in reducing the number of miracles (a tendency contrary to that of Mt and Lk which increase the number of miracles found in Mk), Jn further weakens any temptation to regard Jesus as a type of Hellenistic wonder worker. The same effect is accomplished by the omission of most of the expressions of wonder and awe that usually accompany miracles in the Synoptic tradition.

In comparing Jn and the Synoptic Gospels on the type of miracle narrated, we do not find much difference.[36] The multiplication of the loaves, followed by the walking on the water, is found in both traditions; and the Cana miracle which is peculiar to Jn is a nature miracle of the same type as the multiplication.[37] The healing of the royal official's son (Jn 4,46-54) is probably the same miracle narrated in the Synoptics as the healing of the centurion's boy (Mt 8,5-13; Lk 7,1-10). The healing of the cripple at Bethesda (Jn 5,1-15), and of the blind

---

35a. Here, again the biblical approach to the miracle differs from the apologetic: most often a gospel miracle does not so much lead to faith as presuppose it (at least initial faith). See H. Holstein, S.J., "Le miracle, signe de présence," *BiViChr* 38 (1961) 49-58.

35b. G. Fitzer, "Sakrament und Wunder im Neuen Testament," *In Memoriam Ernst Lohmeyer* (Stuttgart: 1951) 180.

35c. The suggestion that the only type of faith involved in accepting miracles is that of trust in a wonder worker is an oversimplification—Taylor, *Formation of the Gospel Tradition*, 132.

36. L. Cerfaux, "Les miracles, signes messianiques de Jésus et oeuvres de Dieu, selon l'Évangile de saint Jean," *Recueil Lucien Cerfaux* 2 (Louvain: 1954) 41-42.

37. Besides the theme of messianic abundance, the theme of replacement of Jewish institutions also appears. Menoud, *RHPR* 28 (1948) 182, points out that while, at first glance, the Cana miracle resembles that of pagan metamorphosis, it really fits into the theme of Jesus' ministry as a new creation. It is an act of revelation, not simply a prodigy.

man (9), and the raising of Lazarus (11) are individual examples of types known from the Synoptics.

It is on the meaning of the Johannine miracle that we must center our attention, and perhaps we may find a key to this in Jn's vocabulary. Although others (including the editor of the Gospel) refer to Jesus' miracles as "signs," Jesus himself consistently refers to them as "works."[38] What is the origin of the Johannine term "works"? The term occurs but twice in the Synoptics for Jesus' miracles (Mt 11,2; Lk 24,19); so, if the term is an authentic one on the lips of Jesus, it is a case of Jn's preserving vocabulary lost in the Synoptic tradition. An OT background for the term may be found in the work or works of God accomplished on behalf of his people, beginning with creation and continuing with salvation history.[39] The use of *ergon* for creation is quite prominent in the LXX beginning with Gn 2,2. In salvation history a prominent example of the *works* of God may be found in the exodus (Ex 34,10; Ps 65[66],5; Ps 76[77],12; Dt 3,24 and 11,3—in the latter two passages a variant reading with *terata*). It is interesting, in this connection, that in Acts 7,22 Stephen calls Moses "a man mighty in words and *works*." By the use of the term "works" for his miracles Jesus was associating his ministry with creation and the salvific works of his Father in the past: "My Father works up to now, and so do I work as well" (5,17).[40] So close is the union of Jesus and the Father in the works of the ministry that the Father himself may be said to perform Jesus' works (14,10).

The concept of "work" in Jn is wider than that of miracles; in 17,4 Jesus can sum up his whole ministry as a "work": "I glorified you on this earth by completing the work you have given me to do." Not only are Jesus' miracles works; his words are works too: "The *words* that I say to you people are not spoken on my own; it is the Father, abiding in me, who performs the *works*."[41] Nevertheless, miracles are prominent among the works given Jesus by the Father to complete (5,36), "These very works that I perform give testimony for me that the Father has sent me."

38. *Ergon* or *erga* is used of Jesus' doing his Father's work or the work he was sent to do some eighteen times. Only once do others speak of his "works" (7,3); the other seventeen times Jesus is using the term himself.
39. Cerfaux, *Recueil*, 2, 47.
40. It is to be noted that the last passage is in the context of a sabbath miracle. Thus, Jn is in perfect harmony with the idea we suggested above (n. 20) for the Synoptic Gospels, viz., working miracles on the sabbath is a creative action.
41. Jn 14,10. "Words" and "works" are companions in Jn; this can be seen in Jn's custom of having a work followed by an interpretive speech. We might note, with Gleason, *Thought* 37 (1962) 14, that the great works of God in the OT are often followed by an interpretation, e.g., the song of Ex 15 after the crossing of the sea. Menoud, *RHPR* 28 (1948) 185, points out the correlativity of "word" and "work." Word reminds us that the value of the miracle is not in its form but in its content; the miraculous work reminds us that the word is not empty, but an active, energetic word designed to change the world.

Thus, while Jn does not present the ministry of Jesus precisely in the Synoptic terms of announcing the coming of God's kingdom, Jn does agree with the Synoptics in presenting the miracles of Jesus as an integral part of the ministry (or "work") and as a manifestation of God's power.[42] The Synoptic emphasis is on God's power overcoming that of Satan. Jn is quite aware of the opposition of Satan (14,30; 16,33) and is even more dualistic than the Synoptics. Yet, the connection between the miracles and the destruction of Satan's power is not emphasized in Jn. The complete absence of exorcisms represents a remarkable difference from the Synoptic picture. In one place, however, Jn does seem to highlight death as almost a personal force to be overcome. In the Lazarus story, in the presence of death Jesus trembles angrily because of the emotions that flare up within him (11,33.38: *embrimaomai, tarassō*). It is interesting that we encounter similar expressions when Jesus is troubled (*tarassō*) at the presence of Satan in Judas (13,21), and at the cleansing of a leper (*embrimaomai*) in Mk 1,43.[43] If this vocabulary evidence has any force, we might have one example of a miracle in Jn that is a direct attack on Satan.

* * *

The term in Jn used by others and by the editor himself to refer to Jesus' miraculous deeds is "sign." Once again we have a term not used by the Synoptics in the same way as in Jn. In the Synoptics we might distinguish two usages of "sign": (a) in an eschatological sense: the signs of the last times and of the parousia;[44] (b) of miracles demanded of Jesus as an apologetic proof by non-believers.[45] The latter use of signs has a pejorative connotation, for Jesus refuses to give such signs since they are requested by an evil and faithless generation. In

---

42. Although Jn does not use the Synoptic term *dynamis* to describe Jesus' works, Jn 5,19 comes close to the idea: "The Son has no power (*dynatai*) to do anything on his own—only what he sees the Father doing." Throughout Jn it is quite clear that the Son acts with the same power as the Father.
43. The sternness of Jesus with the leper can scarcely be explained except in terms of leprosy considered as the work of Satan. Kallas, *Significance of the Synoptic Miracles,* 31, points out that leprosy was a religious contamination, and a healed leper was obliged to offer sacrifice signifying God's reacceptance of him into the community. Thus in healing leprosy Jesus was removing a curse which separated man from God's service.
44. Mt 24,3.24.30. In 24,24 the familiar combination "signs and wonders" refers to the prodigies of the false prophets (see also 2 Thes 2,9; Ap 19,20). The eschatological use of "signs" stems from the prophetic books and the apocalyptic seers of the OT (see Dn 3,99; 6,28), and is frequent in Ap. It is interesting that in Acts 2,19 Peter adds "signs" to the citation of the eschatological passage from Joel. Josephus, *War,* 6:288-309, refers to the miraculous events connected with the fall of Jerusalem as "signs and wonders."
45. Mt 12,38-39; 16,1-4; Lk 23,8 (see 1 Cor 1,22). This usage probably stems from the occasional OT use of "sign" as a divine mark of credence, e.g., Tob 5,2 (LXX): "What sign can I give him [that he may believe that you sent me as your representative]?" In a similar way the Pharisees are demanding Jesus' credentials. See D. Mollat, "Le semeion johannique," *Sacra Pagina* 2 (Paris: 1959) 213-215.

Acts we encounter a third use of "sign": (c) "signs and wonders" have become a simple description of miracles.[46] In Acts 2,22 (under the influence of the Joel citation) Jesus is called a man attested by "mighty works and wonders and signs" (note that the standard Synoptic term for miracle, *dynamis*, is equated with *teras* and *sēmeion*).[47] "Signs and wonders" are also used to refer to the miracles of the Apostles,[48] as is "signs" alone.[49]

The comparison of these different NT usages of "sign" with that of Jn offers difficulties. While Jesus does not speak of his own works as signs, the use of that term by others is scarcely the same as its use by non-believers in the Synoptics [(b) above]. Only in Jn 2,18 and 6,30 where disbelievers demand a sign are we close to the Synoptic usage. More typically Johannine and less Synoptic is the case where people come to believe in Jesus because of the signs.[50] Nevertheless, we should note that this is not a satisfactory form of belief, for Jesus speaks harshly of it (2,23-25; 4,48; 6,26). Evidently Jesus is not satisfied with having his miracles looked on as mere credential cards; he wants an understanding of what they reveal.[51] The most characteristic Johannine use of a "sign" is as a favorable designation of miracle, and this is very different from the Synoptic use. The evangelist refers to Cana as the first of Jesus' signs (2,11), and to the healing of the official's son as the second of the signs (4,54). He says that the Baptist worked no sign (10,41) while Jesus performed many (20,30). In 12,37 the evangelist complains that the Jews had not believed even though Jesus had performed so many signs. Clearly, then, in many passages of Jn "sign" is the equivalent of miracle (with a certain deemphasis on the prodigious aspect).[52] This usage is in part the same as that of Acts [(c) above],

---

46. For a history of this combined term see S. V. McCasland, "Signs and Wonders," *JBL* 76 (1957) 149-152. This use in Acts may be the influence of septuagintal language on Luke; however, the use is Pauline too (Rom 15,19; 2 Cor 12,12).
47. Also in 2 Cor 12,12; 2 Thes 2,9.
48. Acts 2,43; 4,30; 5,12; 6,8, etc. (Rom 15,19; Heb 2,4).
49. Acts 4,16.22; 8,6; (8,13 with *dynamis*); Marcan appendix 16,17.20.
50. Jn 2,23; 3,2; 6,2.14; 7,31; 9,16; 12,18.
51. Nevertheless, those who believe because they have seen signs have taken one step on the road to salvation; they are quite different from those who refuse to see, the wilfully blind (3,19-21; 12,37-41). Those who demand signs in the Synoptic tradition (Mt 16,1-4) are close to the Johannine wilfully blind.
52. *Sēmeion* is a somewhat narrower term than *ergon*; it is not used of the whole ministry of Jesus. However, even words may be signs, e.g., in 12,33 (18,32) and 21,19 there is a statement which serves as a sign (*sēmainō*) of how Jesus or Peter is to die. This symbolic use is, C. H. Dodd claims, close to that of Philo who uses *sēmainō* of the symbolic significance of OT passages [*The Interpretation of the Fourth Gospel* (Cambridge: 1954) 141-142]. Yet, as he recognizes, the real parallelism is to prophecy.

    Are there non-miraculous signs in Jn? When the term *sēmeion* appears, *de facto* it refers to miraculous deeds. But Dodd suggests that the evangelist considered actions such as the cleansing of the Temple

although the Johannine tradition, with its distrust of the marvelous, disapproves of the combination "signs and wonders": "Unless you people can see signs and wonders, you will not believe" (Jn 4,48—only use).

The relation of the Johannine signs to the eschatological signs spoken of in the Synoptics [(a) above] is interesting. Dodd's theory of realized eschatology in Jn is well known.[53] In Johannine thought the signs that are to mark the end of time are perhaps already found in Jesus' miraculous signs.[54] This is not too far from Jesus' statement in Mt (12,39.41) that no sign will be given except the sign of his own preaching, and that the signs of the times are already present to be interpreted by the Pharisees (Mt 16,3).

Thus, there are some distant parallels in the NT for the Johannine use of "sign"; the main background for this use, however, seems to be in the OT. In particular we should recall the signs wrought by God in the exodus story.[55] Exodus motifs are frequent in Jn;[56] and if the evangelist saw that Jesus had replaced so many of the institutions of the exodus, it was no great step to see his miracles as signs corresponding to the signs by which God delivered Israel. We are told that God multiplied signs through Moses (Ex 10,1; Nm 14,22; Dt 7,19); yet the people refused to believe. In Nm 14,11 God asks, "How long will they not believe in me despite all the signs which I have performed among them?" This is very much like Jn 12,37, "Even though he had performed so many of his signs right in front of them, they refused to believe." Jn answers the problem with a reference to the arm of the Lord (Is 53,1) which had been at work in these signs. Dt 7,19 speaks of "signs, wonders, the mighty hand, the outstretched arm." Jn 20,30 ends the Gospel on the note of the signs Jesus had performed before his disciples, just as Dt 34,11 ends on the note of the signs and won-

---

as signs. Probably he did; the Jews did not, however (2,18). The fact that the cleansing of the Temple is followed by 2,23 which mentions that Jesus did many *signs* in Jerusalem is not probative, for 2,23-25 is simply an editorial transition to c.3. 4,54 points to no sign between the two Cana miracles. Another candidate for a non-miraculous sign might be 3,14-15 where the raising up of the Son of Man is compared to the serpent of the exodus narrative; the comparison is drawn from Nm 21,9, where (LXX) it is said that Moses set the serpent on a *sēmeion.*

53. One cannot subscribe to the view that there is no final eschatology in Jn or that the passages referring to final eschatology (5,26-30) are intrusive interpolations made by an ecclesiastical redactor. Nevertheless, it is true that the burden of Jn's eschatology is realized. For examples see our pamphlet commentary, *New Testament Reading Guide* #13 (Collegeville: 1960) p. 13.
54. Mollat, *Sacra Pagina,* 2, 216-217. In a similar vein I Jn 2,18 seems to have fitted the notion of antichrist into realized eschatology: the antichrists are lapsed Christians.
55. Mollat, *Sacra Pagina,* 2, 213-215; Cerfaux, *Recueil,* 2, 43.
56. Theme of the new tabernacle (1,14); the paschal lamb (1,29; 19,14.29. 36); bronze serpent (3,14); comparison of Christ with Moses (1,17; 5,45-47); the manna (6); the water from the rock (7,38-39); the feast of Tabernacles (7-8).

ders which Moses performed before Israel. Nm 14,22 connects God's glory to his signs, two terms very characteristic of Jn. Just as God's signs showed his glory, so Jesus' signs showed his glory (2,11; 12,37,41).

* * *

Both the Johannine terms for miracles, "works" and "signs," share as a background the OT description of God who acts on behalf of man.[57] "Work" emphasizes more the divine perspective of what is accomplished, and so is a fitting description for Jesus himself to apply to his miracles. "Sign" expresses the human psychological viewpoint, and is a fitting description for others to apply to Jesus' miracles.

In this concave-convex description of miracle as "work" and "sign," we find that, as the background in the exodus story might lead us to expect, the Johannine tradition presents the miracle as a work of revelation which is intimately connected with salvation. Yet, while in the OT the physical deliverance accomplished by God's work on behalf of his people is in primary focus (a deliverance with deep spiritual overtones, of course), in Jn the reference to spiritual deliverance is primary and the symbolic element is stronger. Here, again, Jn differs from the Synoptic tradition. As we have seen, most of the mighty deeds in the Synoptic Gospels are a direct part of the deliverance of the world from Satan; there is a symbolic element, but most of the time this is secondary.[58] In Jn, however, the symbolic element has become primary. We do not mean that the material action, like healing, can be dispensed with, but that there is little emphasis on the material results, and great emphasis on the spiritual symbolism. If Jesus heals the royal official's son and grants him life (*zaō* in 4,50.51.53), the commentary that follows this miracle and that of Bethesda[59] makes it clear that the life that Jesus communicates is spiritual life (5,21.24). If Jesus restores the blind man's sight, the interchange that follows (9,35-41) shows that Jesus has given him spiritual sight and reduced the Pharisees to spiritual blindness. If Jesus gives life to Lazarus, the

57. Both the terms *ergon* and *sēmeion* occur in the accounts of the exodus; the Synoptic term *dynamis* is rare. [*Dynamis* is frequently used for "army, host"; but it occurs for God's powerful deeds only in Ex 9,16 (v.l.) and Dt 3,24 (LXX).]

58. We made the allowance that some miracles in the Synoptic tradition have primarily a symbolic significance, e.g., loaves were multiplied to reremind people symbolically of messianic abundance. In the case of such a miracle it seems that in Jn this primary symbolism becomes stronger, e.g., the people connect the multiplication with the expected messianic miracle of the manna (6,30-31) and see in Jesus the Mosaic prophet-to-come (6,14). Also the secondary symbolism is stronger. There is a hint in the Synoptics that the food was to be understood on a spiritual level (Mk 8,11-21) and even a hint of eucharistic symbolism (comparing Mk 6,41 with Mk 14,22). Both of these themes are developed at length in Jn 6. To take another case, if we compare Jn's account of the walking on water with that of the Synoptics, we find that all the elements of amazement are lost in Jn, and that the divine title of Jesus (6,20) is highlighted.

59. A. Feuillet, S.S., "La signification théologique du second miracle de Cana," *RechSR* 48 (1960) 62-75.

remarks of Jesus (11,24-26) show that the restoration of physical life is important only as a sign of the gift of eternal life. This Johannine attitude wherein the spiritual import of the miracle clearly dominates over the material effect is a natural consequence of Jn's incarnational theology. The Word has become flesh, and now flesh of itself avails nothing. The world of spirit has been brought into the world of time, and this penetration results in a transformation.

Perhaps the best OT parallel for this dominant symbolism in the Johannine sign is the prophetic symbolic action.[60] The sign performed by the prophet (e.g., Is 20,3) was important only in what it graphically portrayed, e.g., God's coming judgment, or God's intervention. In Jn, with its partially realized eschatology, Jesus' symbolic actions not only prophesy God's intervention, but contain it. The physical health, sight, and life are accompanied by the gift of spiritual life and faith. Thus, Dodd[61] is correct in referring to the Johannine miracles as *signa efficacia* (whereas we may classify the prophets' symbolic actions as *signa prophetica*). But to modify this terminology we may call Jesus' miracles also *signa prophetica*. The prophetic aspect consists in this: the spiritual life and sight which have been attached to physical miracles during the ministry of Jesus will be poured forth without such intervention once Jesus is glorified and the Spirit is given. Thus, the miracle is a sign, not only qualitatively (material standing for spiritual), but also temporally (what happens before *the hour* prophesying what will happen after the hour has come). That is why the signs of Jesus are concentrated in the first half of Jn; for once the hour has come (13,1), there is no more mention of Jesus' performing signs. It is in the period of the hour that his "work" is accomplished (17,4; 19,30); the hour is the watershed between the miraculous prophetic sign and the reality prophesied.[62]

By way of parenthetical remark, we might add that the prophetic element in the miraculous sign is what allows the Johannine narrative of the miracle to bear so often a secondary sacramental significance.[63] The sacraments are the great means of pouring out spiritual life once Jesus has been raised up. From his side come blood and water, the Eucharist and Baptism (19,34); from the very heart of Jesus flows the water of the Spirit (7,38-39). The sacraments are the efficacious signs of the post-ascensional period, as the miracles are the efficacious and

60. While we say that the account of the exodus is the ultimate source for the Johannine concept of sign, we must also recognize the strong influence of the prophetic symbolic action. Mollat, *Sacra Pagina*, 2, 213; C. H. Dodd, "Le kerygma apostolique dans le quatrième évangile," *RPHR* 31 (1951) 272.

61. *Ibid.*

62. The hour refers to the passion-death-resurrection- (theological) ascension of Jesus. It is the hour of his return to the Father, begun on Holy Thursday and completed on Easter Sunday.

63. See our article, "The Johannine Sacramentary Reconsidered," *TS* 23 (June 1962).

prophetic signs of the period before the hour has come.[64]

Returning to the primary symbolism of the Johannine signs, we can now understand the type of belief that is demanded in Jn of those who observe the signs. As we have mentioned,[65] there are two preliminary unsatisfactory stages in reaction to the signs:

(a) That of those who refuse to see the signs with any faith, e.g., Caiphas (11,47). Such people refuse to come to the light (3,19-20); it would have been better for them if their eyes were physically incapable of sight (9,41; 15,22). Their wilful blindness can only be explained as a fulfillment of the lack of faith predicted in the OT (12,37-41).

(b) That of those who see the signs as wonders and believe in Jesus as a wonder worker sent by God. Jesus regularly refuses to trust himself to this type of faith (2,23-25; 3,2-3; 7,3-7) which is not real belief in what Jesus truly is.

But there is also a satisfactory reaction to signs:

(c) That of those who see what is signified by the signs, and learn who Jesus is and what he has come to do, and so believe in him (4,53; 6,69; 9,38; 11,40).[66] It is this comprehension of the sign that leads one to see the true glory of Jesus (2,11). And it is thus that the works that Jesus performs give testimony for him (5,36), and Jesus can challenge men to put faith in his works (10,38).[67] At the Lazarus miracle Jesus thanks the Father (11,41-42) for the sign that will lead people to believe in him as the resurrection and the life.

Of course, there is a still higher type of faith which can arrive at the identity of Jesus without the use of signs, that of those who have believed without seeing (20,29). They believe on the word of the

---

64. P. H. Menoud, "Miracle et sacrement dans le Nouveau Testament," *Verbum Caro* 6 (#24, 1952) 139-154, insists that sacraments did not take the place of miracles because miracles are reported side by side with sacraments in the Acts. For Menoud sacraments refer back to the historical act of salvation and re-present it, while miracles (in the Church) announce eschatological fulfillment. All of this is true but does not concern the Johannine picture. As Menoud admits, "Thus the Johannine notion of sign establishes a relation between miracles and sacrament" (146). See Fitzer, *Lohmeyer Memorial,* 171-172: "The miracle is to be understood as the sign of the presence of God in Christ. The sacrament is to be understood as the sign of the presence of Christ in the Church."

65. *Supra,* n. 51. O. Cullmann, "*Eiden kai episteusen,*" *Aux sources de la tradition chrétienne* (Mélanges Goguel; Paris: 1950) 52-61.

66. There are stages in this belief: the disciples who believed at Cana are still growing in faith in 6,60-71. Full faith comes only after the Resurrection (20,28).

67. "Even though you will put no faith in me personally, put your faith in these works so that you may come to know and understand that the Father is in me and I am in the Father." The most complete meaning of this is in sense (c), that the gospel miracles can lead men to believe, not only that Jesus was sent by God, but just who he is. He is asking for belief in his works, not solely as the credentials of a wonder worker, but as the revealing acts of one who is teaching. This is clear if the whole verse is quoted and the proper emphasis is given to the purpose clause which concludes the verse.

Apostles (17,20), and Jesus blesses them and prays that they may see his glory (17,24).

In this emphasis on faith as a necessary accompaniment of the miracle Jn is in perfect harmony with the Synoptics. We saw that in the Synoptic tradition faith is an active partner with the miracle (i.e., the faith of the healed person is said to save); so in Jn faith is part of the *ergon* (6,29): "This is God's work: to have faith in him whom He sent."[68] In exalting a faith that has no dependence on miraculous signs, Jn has moved out of the sphere of the ministry of Jesus into that of the Church, and into the ultimate development of the sign, the sacrament.

* * *

Perhaps we might conclude our article by drawing together the conclusions of our comparisons:

1) The circumstances of the miracle are somewhat different in the two traditions. Jn gives very little emphasis to circumstances that would highlight the miracle as a prodigy; and in so doing, Jn brings us more easily to the theological purpose of the miracles in Jesus' ministry.

2) The vocabulary for the miracle is different. Jn's *ergon* and *sēmeion* have OT roots, and help to show the continuity between the Father's actions and those of Jesus. Once again the Johannine vocabulary avoids any stress on the prodigious.

3) In neither tradition are the miracles merely appendages to the ministry of Jesus, convenient credentials; rather they are an essential part of proclaiming and introducing the kingdom of God (Synoptics) and of the work of Jesus given him by the Father (Jn).

4) The predominant element in most of the Synoptic miracles is that of an action of divine power delivering man from Satan's evil grasp. The miracles are God's intervention on behalf of his people as foretold in the OT. The didactic or symbolic element in the miracle (what it tells about the kingdom) is secondary in most miracles. In Jn the symbolic element (what the miracle teaches about Jesus[69]) is predominant. The Johannine miracle is conceptually close to the prophetic symbolic action.

5) Faith is emphasized in both traditions, but in Jn this faith is more clearly distinguished from trust in the wonder worker.

When we look over these comparisons, we realize that there are differences between the two traditions. The differences, however, are really differences of emphasis. The developments in the Johannine picture of the miracle are perfectly consonant with the stated purpose of the Gospel, i.e., to use the event of Jesus' life to give meaning to the faith of the later Christians.

---

68. See G. Bertram, "*Ergon*," *TWNT* 2, p. 639.
69. In Jn Jesus is the personification of God's kingdom. What the Synoptics say about the kingdom, Jn often applies to Jesus, e.g., the Johannine "I am" similes take the place of the synoptic parables of the kingdom.

CHANGING STYLES IN JOHANNINE STUDIES

THOMAS AQUINAS COLLINS, O.P.

It is immediately evident to those interested in the matter that a remarkable change has taken place in Johannine studies over the past half century. The change regards both the conclusions reached on difficult questions and the very pre-occupation of present day Johannine scholars. Today in Johannine studies the center of gravity has, indeed, shifted from the man to the book. As Dr. A. Hunter has observed, fifty years ago discussion of the fourth Gospel began with questions of authorship, date and provenance. When these questions had received an answer, the other questions were taken up. Nowadays, the discussion generally starts with the other questions.

New studies on the very text of the fourth Gospel show significant changes from earlier positions. At the turn of the century, and for some decades afterwards, the critics were intent on the studies of vivisection, partition and rearrangement of the original order of the fourth Gospel. The authenticity and proper position of the sixth chapter claimed special attention. Nowadays many experts agree with Dr. Dodd that it is "the duty of an interpreter at least to see what can be done with the document as it has come down to us before attempting to improve upon it."

The whole story of the changing styles in Johannine studies is a fascinating one but only its highlights can be underscored here. We hope that it proves interesting and useful especially to those beginning their study of the Gospel according to St. John. Like all Gaul, this paper is divided into three parts: I. From Sanday to Bultmann; II. From Bultmann to Barrett; III. The Catholic Contribution. With respect to this third section, may I say here that I do not particularly favor the consideration of Catholic biblical scholarship as something apart from the main stream of modern biblical studies. The reasons for so doing in this instance will be offered at the beginning of the third section. Finally, I feel compelled to call attention to the debt I owe to many in fashioning a conspectus of this sort. I willingly acknowledge that debt.

I. From Sanday to Bultmann[1]

We begin this conspectus with Professor William Sanday, Lady

1. The chief sources for the main lines of this conspectus are: William

Margaret Professor and Canon of Christ Church, Oxford. In the first of his eight Morse Foundation Lectures at Union Seminary, New York, October 1904, Sanday began with a penetrating survey and criticism of the Johannine literature of his day. He laments the radical trend these studies have taken and contrasts it with the not too distant past (1870-1900) when "opinion had seemed to gravitate more and more towards a sort of middle position in which the two sides in the debate could almost reach hands to each other."[2]

The chief works opposed by Professor Sanday are those of Jülicher,[3] Schmiedel,[4] Réville,[5] and Loisy.[6] From the conclusions of these he profoundly dissents. His own view of the origin of the Fourth Gospel, his chief concern as it was the chief concern of all writers at the turn of the century, may be found in these words of Lecture VIII:[7]

> I do not hesitate to say that this theory of the late origin of the Gospel is not one that will work, or bear to be consistently carried out. On the other hand, if we assume the traditional view, all the evidence falls into line; we have an adequate cause for the authority which from the first attached to the Gospel; and, allowing for the scantiness and critical drawbacks of the materials from which our evidence is drawn, we have a picture quite as satisfactory as we can expect of its gradually expanding circulation.

Dr. Archibald M. Hunter,[8] professor of New Testament at the University of Aberdeen, Scotland, rightly portrays Sanday as the conservative leader of British scholars at the turn of the century:

> At the beginning of the century most British scholars, led by William Sanday, still clung to the apostolic authorship, and were ready to use the Gospel almost equally with the Synoptists as a source for the life and teaching of Jesus.

If, in November 1903, Sanday could sadly lament the radical trend Johannine studies had taken, he soon had cause to rejoice. Two British

---

Sanday, *The Criticism of the Fourth Gospel* (Oxford: 1905). V. H. Stanton, *The Gospels as Historical Documents,* III, (Cambridge: 1920). P. H. Menoud, *L'Évangile de Jean d'après les recherches récentes,* Cahiers theol. 3 (Neuchâtel-Paris: 1947). E. B. Allo, "Jean" in *VDBS,* 4 (1949) 815-843. A. M. Hunter, *Interpreting the New Testament;* 1900-1950 (Philadelphia: Westminster Press, 1951). W. F. Howard, C. K. Barrett, *The Fourth Gospel in Recent Criticism and Interpretation* (London: 1955), New Edition. W. Grossouw, "Three Books on the Fourth Gospel" in *NT* 1 (1956), 36-46. *L'Évangile de Jean* (Desclée De Brouwer: 1958), a symposium; cf. especially P. H. Menoud, "De Bultmann à Barrett," pp. 11-40. This entire volume on modern Johannine studies is a mine of information.

2. *Criticism of the Fourth Gospel,* 6.
3. A. Jülicher, *Einleitung in das N.T.* 4th ed. (Tübingen: 1901).
4. P. W. Schmiedel, "John, Son of Zebedee" in *Encyclopedia Biblica,* vol. 2, p. 2503 ff. (New York: The Macmillan Company, 1901).
5. Jean Réville, *Le quatrième évangile, son origine et sa valeur historique* (Paris: 1901).
6. Alfred Loisy, *Le quatrième évangile* (Paris: 1903).
7. William Sanday, *Criticism of the Fourth Gospel,* 247.
8. A. M. Hunter, *Interpreting the NT,* 78.

authors, James Drummond,[9] Principal of Manchester College, and Professor V. H. Stanton[10] of Cambridge, published works which "did better than I hoped to do the very thing that I desired."[11] Drummond, like most at the turn of the century, was concerned with the origin of the Fourth Gospel: he devoted only 60 pages to the *Character* of the Gospel and spent the remaining 500 pages on the *Authorship*. He had entitled his work: *The Character and Authorship of the Fourth Gospel.* Drummond's book was the ablest of its kind in the conservative tradition. He found the external evidence all on the same side of the fence and judged that most of the internal evidence squared with the external.[12]

At the time of Sanday's Morse Lectures (1904), only the first part of Dr. Stanton's studies had been published. However, what had appeared was enough to convince Dr. Sanday that Stanton, too, was on the right track. Prof. Schmiedel, in the above-cited article in *Encyclopedia Biblica,* rejected all notion of "genuineness" and linked the question of Johannine authorship to the question of the historicity of the Fourth Gospel. Schmiedel held that in the final analysis the questtion of the historicity of the Gospel is the more important one.[13]

Back in England, the "advanced" scholars had a champion in E. F. Scott[14] whose brilliant work on the Fourth Gospel was a distinct challenge to the labors of Drummond for the conservative side. Dr. Scott spent comparatively little time on the problem of apostolic authorship; he simply assumed with Continental scholars that the work was non-apostolic and dated from the beginning of the second century.[15] Scott's chief concern was with the purpose and theology of the Fourth Gospel. His studies had convinced him that the Evangelist, whoever he was, intended to make Jesus and his doctrine intelligible to the Hellenistic world.

Turning back to Germany and to F. Spitta,[16] we find a new trend. Spitta was looking for a genuine Johannine source behind the present Fourth Gospel. He settled on a document which he claimed originally contained both the sayings and the deeds of Jesus, written with a purely historical interest in view. An elaborator transformed this earlier source, more trustworthy than the Synoptics, into a theological treatise. This elaborator also added chapter 21, he incorporated some

9. James Drummond, *An Inquiry into the Character and Authorship of the Fourth Gospel* (London: 1903).
10. V. H. Stanton, *The Gospels as Historical Documents,* Part I (Cambridge: 1903). Part III, The *Fourth Gospel,* was not printed until 1920.
11. William Sanday, *Criticism of the Fourth Gospel,* 2.
12. A. M. Hunter, *Interpreting the NT,* 78.
13. P. W. Schmiedel, *Enc. Bib.,* 2, col. 2518.
14. E. F. Scott, *The Fourth Gospel* (Edinburgh: T. & T. Clark, 1906).
15. A. M. Hunter, *Interpreting the NT,* 79.
16. F. Spitta, *Zur Geschichte und Literatur des Urchristentums,* vol. I (1893), pp. 156-204; *Das Johannes-evangelium als Quelle der Geschichte Jesu* (Göttingen: 1910).

material from other sources, not always in the proper chronological order, and he added many explanatory glosses.

With the studies of Wendt,[17] Soltau,[18] and Wellhausen,[19] the whole question of the composite character of the Fourth Gospel became acute.[20] All were sincere in their research into Johannine sources. All produced brilliant works in their attempts to support the thesis that the present Gospel of St. John is composed of various literary strata. The following significant remark from the pen of Julius Wellhausen should often be recalled when discussing this period of Johannine study.[21]

> Literary criticism is of far more limited significance for the historical relations of the Fourth Gospel than for exegesis. In spite of its different strata it can historically be regarded as essentially a unity. It should be assumed that the amplifications for the most part originate from the same circle within which the basic document arose and found its first readers.

A strong reaction set in against this concentrated attack upon the integrity of the Fourth Gospel. The veteran scholars, Zahn[22] and B. Weiss,[23] as well as the textual critic, C. R. Gregory,[24] hastened to defend the Gospel's integrity. To this group should be added the name of Heinrich Appel,[25] a pastor who wrote a lucid critique on the genuineness of the Fourth Gospel, with special reference to the latest critical studies.[26]

Dr. Scott's brilliant work, cited above, was followed by F. C. Burkitt's book on the transmission of Gospel history.[27] Dr. Burkitt maintained that the Fourth Gospel was written "to prove the reality of Jesus Christ."[28] He insisted upon the fact that the Evangelist was not an historian; for the Evangelist, the true realities were not events but ideas, said Burkitt. We ought not, therefore, attempt to learn the

---

17. H. H. Wendt, *Die Lehre Jesu,* ed. 1, (Göttingen: 1866). Cf. also: *Das Johannes-Evangelium* (Göttingen: 1900) and *Die Schichten im vierten Evangelium* (Göttingen: 1907).
18. W. Soltau, *Unsere Evangelien, ihre Quellen und ihr Quellenwert* (Leipzig: 1901).
19. J. Wellhausen, *Das Evangelium Johannis* (Berlin: 1908).
20. Cf. V. H. Stanton, *Gospels,* vol. III, p. 32 ff. and W. F. Howard, *Fourth Gospel,* 60-69, for further material on the composite character of the Fourth Gospel.
21. J. Wellhausen, *Evangelium Johannis,* 119. Cited by Stanton, *Gospels,* 40.
22. Th. Zahn, *Das Evangelium des Johannes unter den Händen seiner neuesten Kritiker* (Leipzig: 1911).
23. B. Weiss, *Das Johannesevangelium als einheitliches Werk* (Göttingen: 1912).
24. C. R. Gregory, *Wellhausen und Johannes,* ed. 2, (Leipzig: 1910).
25. H. Appel, *Die Echtheit des Johannesevangeliums* (Leipzig: 1915).
26. Howard, *Fourth Gospel,* 66.
27. F. C. Burkitt, *The Gospel History and its Transmission* (Edinburgh: 1906).
28. Burkitt, *Gospel History,* 256.

course of events from the Evangelist; we shall only be disappointed.

The first volume of Hastings' Dictionary of Christ and the Gospels[29] appeared in 1906. The articles on the Fourth Gospel by J. S. Riggs,[30] R. H. Strachan,[31] and W. R. Inge[32] betray the perceptible change that is taking place in critical orthodoxy at this period. True, Riggs holds the traditional line. Strachan, however, while still considering the Fourth Gospel to be from the pen of the Apostle John writing from Ephesus, concludes that the Fourth Gospel is really the testimony of a group of eye-witnesses: "With John's as the guiding mind, they conjointly made themselves responsible for the statements contained in the book."[33] In this article, Dr. Inge contends strongly for the symbolic or allegorical approach over the historical.

America, at this period, was not lacking in experts on the Fourth Gospel. Most noteworthy was Yale's Professor B. W. Bacon[34] whom Howard[35] calls "the most ingenious, brilliant, and persistent writer on the Johannine problem." Bacon's views varied considerably over his long career.

Before the outbreak of World War I, four more writers in English published significant works on Johannine studies. F. W. Lewis[36] was the first in England to try his hand at reconstructing the Fourth Gospel according to the alleged original order. Working through internal evidence, Lewis attempted to prove that a number of Johannine passages could not have originally held the place they now occupy in the Gospel. Following Spitta, Lewis called attention to the fact that each of the transposed passages is about the same length. With this purely material aspect of the text as a beginning, Lewis claimed that a disturbance of the leaves of the original manuscript would account for the present arrangement.

In 1911, Dr. James Moffatt[37] published an exhaustive survey of all the tangled mass of critical theory that surrounded the Johannine writings. Howard[38] wrote of this work: "No book or brochure or article of any importance, written in English, German, French or Dutch, can have escaped Professor Moffatt's searching eye."

Germany produced three outstanding pre-World War I writers on

---

29. James Hastings, *Dictionary of Christ and the Gospels,* vol. I (Edinburgh: 1906).
30. J. S. Riggs, "John the Apostle" in *D.C.G.* pp. 866-869.
31. R. H. Strachan, *D.C.G.,* vol. I, pp. 869-885.
32. W. R. Inge, *D.C.G.,* vol. I., pp. 885-895.
33. Cf. Howard, *Fourth Gospel,* 27.
34. B. W. Bacon, *Introduction to the New Testament* (New Haven: 1900); *The Fourth Gospel in Research and Debate* (New Haven: 1910); *The Gospel of the Hellenists* (New York: 1933), edited by C. H. Kraeling.
35. Howard, *Fourth Gospel,* 29.
36. F. W. Lewis, *Disarrangements in the Fourth Gospel* (London: 1910).
37. James Moffatt, *Introduction to the Literature of the New Testament* (Edinburgh: 1911).
38. *Fourth Gospel,* 32.

the Fourth Gospel: J. Weiss,[39] W. Bousset,[40] and W. Heitmüller.[41] These three writers agree on the following points: (1) John the Apostle died early in the first century, A.D. (2) John of Asia (whose name became attached to the Apocalypse) is identical with John the Presbyter. The study of the close relationship between the Fourth Gospel and the Apocalypse was particularly attractive to Weiss and Bousset.

As we have already noted in this conspectus of modern Johannine studies, J. Réville and A. Loisy attracted a great deal of attention by their studies at the turn of the century. Réville represented what we might call left-wing Protestant scholarship, while Alfred Loisy had not yet, at this time, abandoned the Catholic Church. Both these writers agreed that the author of the Fourth Gospel was more of a theologian than an historian. Réville rejects the notion that the Fourth Gospel came from the hand of the last of the twelve Apostles for the following reason: how explain the fact that a long period elapsed before the Gospel was accepted as having full apostolic authority? Réville held that the Fourth Gospel must be interpreted in the light of the Prologue.

The work of A. Loisy on the Gospel according to St. John appeared in two editions, twenty years apart.[42] In his first edition (1903), Loisy did not differ materially from the critical attitude of Réville. Loisy thought that the author of the Fourth Gospel (which he held to be a literary unity, in his first edition) was an Alexandrian Jew who had studied St. Paul and had composed the Fourth Gospel around 100 A.D. This author, consequently, was neither John the Apostle, nor John the Presbyter, nor even one from among the intimate companions of Jesus. Eighteen years later (1921), Loisy published a second edition of this work which contained certain significant changes in his opinions. In this second edition, he abandoned his support of the literary unity of the Fourth Gospel in favor of an extensive redactional theory.

Conditions throughout the world during the period of 1914-1918 were hardly conducive to scholarly research. Yet as a result of studies during this period, some important Johannine works did appear. In England, such writers as Gardner,[43] Strachan,[44] and Jackson[45] made valuable contributions to the study of the Fourth Gospel.

---

39. J. Weiss, *Die Offenbarung des Johannes* (Berlin: 1904); "Literaturgeschichte des N.T." in *R.G.G.*, ed. I:3, 2199-2201 (1912); *Das Urchristentum* (1917), ed. by R. Knopf, pp. 611-624.
40. W. Bousset, *Die Offenbarung Johannis,* in Meyer's series of commentaries, ed. 1 (1896), ed. 2 (1906). "Ist das vierte Evangelium eine literarische Einheit?" in *Th. R.*, xii, 1-12; 39-64 (1909). "Johannesvangelium" in *R.G.G.*, ed. 1:3, 608-633 (1912).
41. W. Heitmüller, *Das Johannes-Evangelium* in *Die Schriften des Neuen Testaments,* ed. 1, ii (1906); ed. 3, iv (1918).
42. A. Loisy, *Le quatrième évangile,* ed. 1 (1903); ed. 2 (1921).
43. P. Gardner, *The Ephesian Gospel* (London: 1915).
44. R. H. Strachan, *The Fourth Gospel, its Significance and Environment* (London: 1917); ed. 3 revised and rewritten (1941).
45. Latimer Jackson, *The Problem of the Fourth Gospel* (Cambridge: 1918).

In 1920, two outstanding scholars gave us permanent contributions to Johannine studies: R. H. Charles[46] and Dr. V. H. Stanton.[47] Dr. Charles held for separate authors for the Fourth Gospel and the Apocalypse, a position which he supported with a wealth of philological arguments.

Of interest to students of the sixth chapter of St. John is the suggestion of Dr. Stanton that the present position of the Bread of Life discourse just after the miracle of the feeding may be accounted for by the Evangelist's customary use of that miracle in presenting Jesus as the living bread:[48]

> We may then reasonably conjecture that he was led to place the whole of this discourse-matter where he does, just after the miracle of the feeding, from his having been accustomed to use that miracle in this instruction of Christian assemblies as a text for setting forth Jesus as the living bread.

In post-World War I Germany, the publication of E. Meyer's study of the origin of Christianity[49] aroused considerable interest. Meyer follows Schwartz and Wellhausen in holding for an early death of John the Apostle. An unknown author, says Meyer, wrote both the Gospel and the Johannine Epistles.[50] This unknown author intended to offer his work as the production of the Beloved Disciple who is John the Son of Zebedee: "How this can be denied is one of the many things which remain incomprehensible to me in the assertions of modern criticism."[51]

The first systematic study of the Fourth Gospel according to the method of form-criticism was made by H. H. Windisch.[52] Like Meyer, Windisch was especially attracted to the study of the dramatic structure of the Fourth Gospel. As a result of his studies, Windisch concluded to the literary unity of the Gospel which was skillfully composed of the following elements: (1) Detailed stories, dramatically presented (i.e., the story of the man born blind in chapter 9, and the trial before Pilate in chapter 18). (2) A blend of stories and polemical speeches (i.e., the healing of the lame man in chapter 5 and the feeding of the multitude combined with the walking upon the water in chapter 6). (3) A series of related single scenes [i.e., in chapter 1, 19-34 and 35-51, which Windisch sub-divides into two acts: (a) The witness of John the Baptist, divided into two series of dialogues and a

---

46. R. H. Charles, *A Critical and Exegetical Commentary on the Revelation of St. John,* ICC Series (Edinburgh: 1920).
47. V. H. Stanton, *Gospels,* Vol. III (1920).
48. Stanton, *Gospels,* Vol. III, p. 239 ff.
49. E. Meyer, *Ursprung and Anfänge des Christentums* (Berlin: 1923).
50. In Vol. I (1921), p. 20, Meyer suggests that Jn 5, 43 dates the Gospel as later than Bar Cocheba's revolt. This "precarious position" (*ita* Howard p. 71) was abandoned in an additional note at the end of Vol. III (1923), p. 650.
51. Cited in Howard, *Fourth Gospel,* p. 70.
52. H. Windisch, "Der Johanneische Erzählungstil" in ***Eucharisterion,*** ii (Göttingen: 1923), pp. 174-213.

witness testimony; (b) the winning of the first disciples, consisting of short dialogues organically connected].

During the last twenty years no name has been more closely associated with the method of form criticism than that of Martin Dibelius.[53] In his study of the structure and literary character of the Fourth Gospel, Dibelius concluded that the Evangelist did not create the miracle-stories peculiar to his Gospel, but rather made use of traditions belonging essentially to the type called *Novellen.* These are popular stories, extremely vivid and concrete. In the case of the stories found in the Fourth Gospel, the Evangelist's own inner experience gave them a special illumination which is communicated to the reader by means of certain parentheses and appended dialogues. These were, of course, from the hand of the author himself, according to Dibelius.[54] For Dibelius, then, the redactor is the Evangelist himself. Except for the last chapter of the Fourth Gospel, Dibelius defended the fundamental unity of the Johannine narrative.[55] The most significant aspect of all Dibelius' studies is the emphasis he placed on the study of the Johannine world of ideas.[56] Rudolph Bultmann, especially, will probe still further in that world.

R. Bultmann (whose important commentary will be considered in the proper place later) and Walter Bauer were the first to adopt this newer religious historical approach to the background of the Fourth Gospel. What they attempted was to unify the phraseology and concepts which are common to Johannine, Ignatian, Syrian, and Egyptian mysticism by postulating a common origin in Gnostic myths and cults which arose in Persia, spread westward, and left deposits on the soil of Palestine and Syria.[57]

We close this period of German scholarship with the brief mention of three authors who contributed works bearing on the religious background of the Fourth Gospel. Dr. J. Grill,[58] G. Bert,[59] and Dr. G. Kittel[60] were all interested in the possible relationship between the fourth Gospel and Philonic, mythological and Jewish theological parallels. Dr. Grill suggests that in the sixth chapter of St. John we have the introduction of the mystical meal from the cult of Dionysus.[61]

In England a number of important works were published in the decade of 1920-1930. We have already discussed the contribution of Dr. Stanton. Dr. Garvie,[62] in 1922, offered this solution to the problem

53. M. Dibelius, "The Structure and Literary Character of the Gospels" in *HThR* 20 (July, 1927), 151-170.
54. Howard, *Fourth Gospel,* 75.
55. *Ibid.,* p. 76.
56. *Ibid.*
57. *Ibid.,* p. 79.
58. J. Grill, *Untersuchungen über die Entstehung des vierten Evangeliums,* I (Tübingen: 1902); II (Tübingen: 1923).
59. G. Bert, *Das Evangelium des Johannes* (Gütersloh: 1922).
60. G. Kittel, *Die Probleme des palästinischen Spätjudentums und das Urchristentum* (Stuttgart: 1926).
61. Cf. Howard, *Fourth Gospel,* 83.
62. A. E. Garvie, *The Beloved Disciple* (London: 1922).

of the composition of the Fourth Gospel: (1) In the background is the Witness, the disciple whom Jesus loved; he is not, according to Dr. Garvie, the Son of Zebedee. Rather he was a wealthy Jerusalemite with close connections with the family of the High Priest. (2) In the foreground stands the Evangelist, a disciple of the Witness, who may be John the Presbyter. This Evangelist wrote the Prologue and edited the teachings of the Witness, while at the same time joining to the publication some of his own comments. (3) Finally, there is the Redactor, who plays a rather minor role in the theory of Dr. Garvie. Yet to him are attributed chapters 6 and 21, as well as other short passages. Dr. Garvie holds strongly for the historical value of the Fourth Gospel.[63]

We may close our consideration of this decade with mention of two major works from the hands of English scholars: G. H. C. Macgregor's commentary on John in the Moffatt series,[64] which appeared in 1928, and J. H. Bernard's great ICC commentary,[65] which appeared in the same year. Both these authors agree that the Son of Zebedee did not write the Fourth Gospel, that there is the authority of an eye-witness behind the Gospel, and that certain textual dislocations and additions must be admitted to exist in our present text.

The next decade (1930-1940) saw more emphasis placed upon the problem of the composition of the Gospel and upon the origin and interpretation of Johannine thought, rather than upon the problems of authorship and date. Actually this has become the prevailing trend of the last twenty years. C. H. Roberts' discovery of the tiny (3½ by 2½ inches) fragment containing a few words from the Fourth Gospel (18, 31-33 and 37-38) proved beyond a reasonable doubt that a codex of the Fourth Gospel was circulating in mid-Egypt before the middle of the second century A.D.[66] For all practical purposes, the debate over the later composition of the Fourth Gospel terminated with this discovery. If not a direct proof, it was at least a strong confirmation of the traditional thesis that the Fourth Gospel dated from the end of the first century A.D.

If the newly-discovered papyrus had strongly influenced the dating of the Gospel, it had by no means solved the problem of Johannine authenticity. As Menoud remarks, there are other factors of as much importance as the date, for the determination of Johannine authorship.[67] There is, for instance, the question: Does a study of the literary characteristics and the theology of the work prove, or even strongly incline us towards, Johannine authorship? The responses given to this question by the critics in the 1930's were still hesitant. Most Catholic

---

63. A. E. Garvie, *Beloved Disciple,* 240.
64. G.H.C. Macgregor, *The Gospel of John* (London: 1928).
65. J. H. Bernard, *The Gospel according to John* (Edinburgh: 1928), 2 Vols.
66. C. H. Roberts, *An Unpublished Fragment of the Fourth Gospel in the John Rylands Library* (Manchester: 1935). Cf. also P. Benoit in *RB* 45 (1936) 269-272.
67. Menoud, *Évangile de Jean,* 9.

scholars were responding with an unqualified affirmative.[68] The more important defenders of Johannine authenticity at this period were: F. Büchsel,[69] W. Oehler,[70] W. Michaelis,[71] as well as P. Feine,[72] E. Redlich,[73] C. J. Wright,[74] and A. T. Olmstead.[75]

Towards the end of this decade, three outstanding studies on the literary composition of the Fourth Gospel rightly claimed the attention of all Johannine scholars. Their authors were: E. Hirsch,[76] whose work appeared in 1936, R. Bultmann,[77] whose commentary on St. John began to appear in 1937 and was completed in 1941, and E. Schweizer,[78] whose study of Johannine style characteristics in 1939 began a new era in the study of the literary unity of the Fourth Gospel.

Schweizer's study completely undermined the theories of Hirsch. Its application by Ruckstuhl in our decade would undermine the theories of Bultmann and Jeremias. In considering the work of Schweizer, it is useful to recall that older writers such as Spitta and Wendt (as well as Hirsch) felt certain that non-Johannine additions could be separated from genuine Johannine material. Much of the work of these scholars on the Fourth Gospel was directed to establish and defend this hypothesis. Schweizer set himself to the task of discovering whether such a distinction between non-Johannine and Johannine material would stand the test of minute literary analysis. He was convinced that any investigation must begin with the objective criterion of philological evidence. He would begin with genuine Johannine vocabulary and constructions.[79]

There are many Johannine words and expressions which never, or hardly ever, appear in the other canonical books of the New Testament. On the other hand, many words, phrases, and constructions proper to the other books of the New Testament never, or hardly ever, are found in the Fourth Gospel. Schweizer's method was first to establish the existence of true Johannine literary characteristics, and secondly to try to discover if these genuine Johannine characteristics are found to be spread throughout the Fourth Gospel. As we shall see in a moment, Schweizer devised an ingenious formula to demonstrate the results of his investigations.

---

68. *Ibid.*, 10.
69. F. Büchsel, *Das Evangelium nach Johannes* (Göttingen: 1934).
70. W. Oehler, *Das Johannesevangelium, eine Missionsschrift für die Welt* (Gütersloh: 1936).
71. W. Michaelis, *Einleitung in das Neue Testament* (Bern: 1954) ed. 2.
72. P. Feine, *Einleitung in das Neue Testament* (Leipzig: 1954) ed. 10.
73. E. B. Redlich, *An Introduction to the Fourth Gospel* (London: 1940).
74. C. J. Wright, *Jesus, the Revelation of God* (London: 1950).
75. A. T. Olmstead, *Jesus in the Light of History* (New York: 1942).
76. E. Hirsch, *Das vierte Evangelium in seiner ursprünglichen Gestalt verdeutscht und erklärt* (Tübingen: 1936); *Studien zum vierten Evangelium* (Tübingen: 1936).
77. R. Bultmann, *Das Evangelium des Johannes* (Göttingen: 1941).
78. E. Schweizer, *Ego Eimi* (Göttingen: 1939).
79. *Ibid.*, p. 15.

Schweizer studied the familiar "I am" passages[80] in the Fourth Gospel to establish the characteristics to be applied to the Johannine Epistles, the Synoptic Gospels, and the remaining books of the New Testament.[81] He devised a formula to show how often a word or a phrase appeared in (1) the Fourth Gospel, (2) the Johannine Epistles, (3) the Synoptic Gospels, and (4) in the rest of the New Testament canonical books. The following example will show clearly Schweizer's method.

ekeinos: 42+6/11+0

This formula indicates that *ekeinos* is found 42 times in the Fourth Gospel, 6 times in the Johannine Epistles, 11 times in the Synoptic Gospels, and not at all in the other books of the New Testament. The next step was to determine truly Johannine material on the score of distribution of truly Johannine literary characteristics. If truly Johannine literary characteristics are found to be spread out fairly evenly throughout the whole Gospel, then evidently a strong case can be presented for homogeneity and unity of authorship. If, on the other hand, certain undisputed Johannine literary characteristics are found to be unaccountably (the qualification is important) lacking in certain passages, then these passages may be considered non-Johannine. What did Schweizer actually discover through his investigations?

He found that (1) in those passages of the Fourth Gospel which have always been held to be rather suspect (i.e., the pericope of the Adulterous Woman, Jn 7,53-8,11), Johannine style characteristics are entirely lacking. (2) In those passages most closely parallel to traditional Synoptic material, the Johannine literary characteristics are rare and infrequent.[82] (3) The account of the Marriage Feast of Cana also lacks Johannine characteristics, but accountably so.[83] (4) Aside from these cases, Schweizer concluded: speaking generally, the whole Gospel exhibits practically the same linguistic characteristics throughout. Therefore, *no distribution of sources can be drawn on the basis of diverse linguistic characteristics*, as Spitta, Wendt and Hirsch had attempted to do. Schweizer clearly showed that Johannine literary characteristics are to be found in all of the alleged distinct sources. Consequently these cannot be said to be from another hand on the basis of style characteristics. E. Ruckstuhl, who completed and strengthened the work of Schweizer, added further proof in support of the same conclusion.[84] We may say that if John did use written sources

---

80. E.g., Jn 6, 35; 8, 12; 10, 7; 10, 11; 11, 25; 15, 1; 14, 6.
81. Cf. Menoud, *Évangile de Jean,* 15.
82. E.g., Jn 2, 13-19; 4, 46-53; 12, 1-8; 12, 12-15.
83. With respect to Schweizer's treatment of the passage containing the account of the Marriage Feast of Cana, Menoud notes that we have here the only defective moment in an otherwise carefully worked out analysis. Schweizer failed to note that in Jn 2, 4 we actually do have two typically Johannine expressions: (1) *Woman* used by Jesus to designate his mother (cf. Jn 19, 26), and (2) *hour* with the personal pronoun (cf. Jn 7, 30; 8, 20; 13, 1; 16, 21). Cf. Menoud, *op. cit., Évangile de Jean,* 15, footnote no. 2.
84. Cf. notes 104-106.

or traditional gospel material, he re-worked this material until it bore the imprint of his own style and language. Though Menoud mildly criticizes some small deficiencies in Schweizer's methods, he concludes: "Mais, en elle-même, sa méthode parait juste, utile et féconde."[85]

Joachim Jeremias[86] was pre-occupied with the study of the literary characteristics of St. John's Gospel in an effort to establish the authentic text of the Evangelist as distinct from that of the redactor. From an analysis of Jn 21,24 Jeremias tried to show that the non-Johannine characteristics there are found in other parts of the fourth Gospel. Therefore, he concluded, these passages in which the non-Johannine characteristics are found can be said to be non-Johannine passages.[87]

Jeremias later revised his opinions in the face of the compelling evidence of Ruckstuhl in favor of the general uniformity of style throughout the fourth Gospel. Jeremias offered an interesting opinion on the origin of the Bread of Life discourse: it comes from a pre-Johannine eucharistic homily.[88]

In 1940, Francis Noel Davey edited and published *The Fourth Gospel* from the notes of Sir Edwyn Hoskyns.[89] A second edition appeared in 1947. For Hoskyns, the Gospel according to St. John is a strictly theological work.[90] After giving all sides of the debate on the problem of the authorship of the Gospel, Hoskyns cannot be sure who actually wrote the Gospel. Of this he is sure, however: whoever did write the work fashioned it into one whole and was complete master of his material.[91]

Dr. Strachan, as we have already observed, published a thoroughly revised third edition of his work on the Fourth Gospel in 1941. The author reversed himself on the questions of both authorship and composition of the Gospel. In his Preface he writes:[92]

> I have found it necessary to join the ranks of those who are convinced that the Gospel is essentially a literary unity, and have withdrawn my previous attempt to isolate certain portions as editorial revisions or insertions. The theory also that in certain places the sequence of thought has been disturbed owing to dislocations caused by disarrangements of pages in an original codex, I find unconvincing.

---

85. Menoud, *Évangile de Jean,* 16.
86. Jeremias, "Johanneische Literarkritik", *ThBl* 20 (1941) 33-46.
87. Jeremias considered the Fourth Gospel to be pretty much of a literary unity. He thinks an editor made certain additions and that perhaps the leaves of the original document became displaced. Cf. Menoud, *Évangile de Jean,* 25-26, for a summary of Jeremias' conclusions.
88. J. Jeremias, *The Eucharistic Words of Jesus* (Oxford: 1955). This is a translation of the second German edition which appeared in 1949. Cf. also: J. Jeremias, "Joh 6, 51c-58—redaktionell?" in *ZNW* 44 (1952/53) pp. 256 ff.
89. Sir Edwyn Hoskyns, *The Fourth Gospel,* ed. 2 (London: 1947).
90. *Ibid.,* p. 17.
91. *Ibid.,* p. 48.
92. R. H. Strachan, *The Fourth Gospel,* ed. 3 (London: 1941) v.

After treating of the various suggestions as to transpositions of texts in the Gospel, Strachan writes:[93]

> In the two cases . . . where an improved itinerary would be provided, the argument has a certain weight, but not sufficient in my opinion to warrant transposition. This Evangelist is not interested in itineraries.

Finally, the author also abandons his previous opinion with respect to the authorship of the Fourth Gospel.[94]

> As one who has made the attempt, I would like to state frankly that after further reflection on the style and thought of the Evangelist, I have abandoned my own theory of redaction adopted in previous editions of this book. . . .

These, indeed, are forthright and decisive revisions of opinions. Coming at the beginning of a new trend in Johannine studies, they are significant.

II. From Bultmann to Barrett[95]

Since the end of World War II, Johannine studies have made great strides under the capable hands of many competent scholars.[96] These scholars have produced and are producing solid studies on the Fourth Gospel, varying from short, technical notes to full scale studies. Of the latter type, the outstanding works of the period are those of Bultmann,[97] Dodd,[98] and Barrett.[99]

Menoud[100] is certainly correct when he observes that it is Bultmann especially who is responsible for a great deal of the new vigor evident in more recent Johannine studies through his works on the Fourth Gospel and on New Testament Theology. Father D. M. Stanley[101] concludes an article on Bultmann thus:

> The work of Rudolph Bultmann is not only admirable for its testimony to the renewed vitality of German Protestant thought. It is, in many of its aspects, a valuable contribution to Catholic Scripture studies in the middle of the twentieth century.

In his book, Bultmann dates the Gospel from the end of the first century. Against Dodd, he holds that its unknown author should be sought in Eastern Christianity rather than in the traditional Roman

---

93. *Ibid.,* 81.
94. *Ibid.,* 81, footnote no. 2.
95. The chief sources consulted for this part of the conspectus of Johannine studies are: *L'Évangile de Jean*; W. Grossouw, "Three Books on the Fourth Gospel" in *NT* 1 (1956) 36-46; W. F. Howard-C. K. Barrett, *The Fourth Gospel in Recent Criticism and Interpretation* (London: 1955) ; F. M. Braun, "Où en est l'étude du quatrième évangile?" in *ETL* 32 (1956) 535-546.
96. Cf. Ph. Menoud, "De Bultmann à Barrett" in *L'Évangile de Jean* (Desclée de Brouwer: 1958) 31-40.
97. R. Bultmann, *Das Evangelium des Johannes* (Göttingen: 1941) . Cf. also: *Theologie des Neuen Testaments* (Tübingen: 1953) .
98. C. H. Dodd *The Interpretation of the Fourth Gospel* (Cambridge: 1953) .
99. C. K. Barrett, *The Gospel According to St. John* (London: 1956) .
100. Ph. Menoud, *Évangile de Jean,* 11.
101. D. M. Stanley, "Rudolph Bultmann: A Contemporary Challenge to the Catholic Theologian" *CBQ* 19 (1957) 347-355.

Province of Asia.[102] According to Bultmann, the Fourth Gospel as we have it reflects the long process which produced it. For Bultmann, the process is not finished yet. It is the duty of the textual critic to finish the task.

J. Schneider[103] claimed that Bultmann had really destroyed the true unity of chapters 6, 7, and 10. Schneider insisted that this unity is evident to anyone who understands that the Evangelist is working according to laws of literary composition proper to himself. Two other important recent studies concluded to the literary unity of the Gospel according to St. John: the monographs of E. Ruckstuhl[104] and B. Noack.[105] Ruckstuhl completed the studies of Johannine characteristics begun by Schweizer, which we considered above. He demonstrated through his studies that these Johannine characteristics, far from being proper to any single source, are fairly well distributed among the various sources isolated by Bultmann.[106] Therefore, no decisive argument can be deduced for a distinction of sources from the positions of Johannine literary characteristics, since these are found in all the sources alleged to differ one from the other.

Dr. Dodd published his work on the Fourth Gospel in 1953.[107] It was justly acclaimed throughout the scholarly world. The work is not intended as a commentary on the Fourth Gospel, but is restricted in scope to the attempt to establish some general principles and lines of direction for the interpretation of the Gospel according to St. John. For the most part, purely critical questions are left aside. Dr. Dodd accepts the Johannine authorship of the Gospel and attempts to answer the questions: "From what spiritual current does this Gospel originate?" "What is its background and also its 'foreground'?" In other words, what is the writer's aim and for whom did he primarily intend his work?[108]

Dodd's answer is to place the Gospel against the background of what he calls "the higher religion of Hellenism." This spiritual movement is derived by Dodd mainly from the spirituality of the Hermetic writings and, to a less degree, from the writings of Philo Judeus. Dodd thinks that the Fourth Evangelist intended his work for

> non-Christians who are concerned about eternal life and the way to it, and may be ready to follow the Christian way if this is presented to them in terms that are intelligibly related to their previous religious interests and experience.

---

102. Cf. Bultmann's *Theologie des Neuen Testaments,* cited above, p. 357.
103. Cf. J. Schneider, "Zur Komposition von Joh. 10" in *Con N.* 11 (1947) 220-225; "Zur Frage der Komposition von Joh. 6, 27-58 (59)" in *In Memoriam Ernst Lohmeyer* (Stuttgart: 1951) 132-142. Also: "Zur Komposition von Joh. 7", *ZNW* 45 (1954) 108-119.
104. E. Ruckstuhl, *Die literarische Einheit des Johannesevangeliums* [Freiburg (Schweiz): 1951].
105. B. Noack, *Zur johanneischen Tradition* (Copenhagen: 1954).
106. Cf. E. Ruckstuhl, *Einheit,* 20-179.
107. C. H. Dodd, *The Interpretation of the Fourth Gospel* (Cambridge: 1953).
108. *Ibid.* p. vii.

Dodd also thinks that the Evangelist wanted to appeal especially to the devout and thoughtful persons who professed this higher Hellenistic religiosity. Consequently, the author of the Fourth Gospel cast his message in a form which was *prima facie* acceptable to this spiritual outlook. Dr. Dodd tries to prove all this by means of parallels, taken from the *Corpus Hermeticum* and *Philo*.[109] Bultmann, for one, refuses to be convinced.[110]

W. Grossouw[111] has thus indicated the significance of this answer of Dodd:

> One might say that Dodd shows a certain reaction with regard to the way in which of late years the Old Testament and Jewish backgrounds of the Gospel are stressed, a reaction in favor of a stronger Hellenistic outlook, which also appears in other recent publications.

On the question of the literary unity of the Gospel of St. John, Dr. Dodd is another of the recent writers who insists on interpreting the work as it has come down to us:[112]

> . . . Meanwhile, the work lies before us in an order which (apart from insignificant details) does not vary in textual tradition, traceable to an early period. I conceive it to be the duty of an interpreter at least to see what can be done with the document as it has come down to us before attempting to improve upon it. This is what I shall try to do.

Dr. Dodd is well aware that many attempts have been made to rearrange the Fourth Gospel. He admires the patience of their authors and ingenuity of the suggestions made. He is convinced, however, that the theological movement of the Fourth Gospel is far more important for its interpretation than the improvements that may be made in chronology by rearrangements of the text.[113]

What is probably one of the greatest commentaries on the Greek text of St. John appeared in 1955, when C. K. Barrett published his *The Gospel according to St. John*.[114] The work was immediately hailed as "the standard critical commentary on the Greek text for our generation" and as a work which "marks a decisive stage in the study of the Johannine Gospel." These and other tributes of reviewers bear testimony that Dr. Barrett has, indeed, written a great commentary on the Fourth Gospel.

The dominant characteristic of his own work is caution. This is particularly evident in his investigation of the questions of authorship and date. Barrett thinks that a disciple of John the Apostle wrote chapters 1-20 of the Fourth Gospel.[115] This disciple was a bold thinker, well read in both Judaism and Hellenism. His work was too daring

109. Cf. W. Grossouw, NT 1 (1956) 38.
110. R. Bultmann, "The Interpretation of the Fourth Gospel" in *NTS* 1 (1954-55) 77-91. (This article, although entitled in *NTS* in English, is actually written in German.)
111. *NT* (1956) 38-39.
112. C. H. Dodd, *Interpretation of the Fourth Gospel*, 290
113. *Ibid.*, 340
114. C. K. Barrett, *The Gospel according to St. John* (London: 1955).
115. *Ibid.*, 113.

and original for official backing in the primitive Church and the author probably died with the work still unpublished. Only gradually did the main body of the Church come to realize that this author had really defeated the Gnostics with their own weapons and that he had vindicated the permanent validity of the primitive Gospel. Consequently, the Gospel was edited, together with chapter 21, based probably upon material which the original author himself left at his death.

This Evangelist of the Fourth Gospel, whom Barrett calls "perhaps the greatest theologian in all the history of the Church," was by this time forgotten. But because he had put into his Gospel references to the Beloved Disciple, the book was "put out on its long career as the work of John, foe of heretics and beloved of his Lord."[116]

Regarding the question of date, Dr. Barrett reaches the wide limits of 90-140 A.D. and does not feel that it is possible to narrow them further without recourse to a hypothesis regarding authorship. "John itself is a quite credible product of any date between 90 and 140. None of the attempts to shift either date is successful."[117]

Turning to the important question of the literary composition of the Fourth Gospel, Dr. Barrett again shows himself to be a cautious scholar. He does not consider any theory of textual displacement proved. He agrees with Strachan that "this Evangelist is not interested in itineraries."[118] He agrees with Dodd that the movement of the Fourth Gospel is dictated by theological rather than by chronological and topographical considerations.[119] Like Hoskyns and Dodd, Dr. Barrett attempts to interpret the Johannine text as it has come down to us.

The final full scale commentary to be considered is that of R. H. Lightfoot.[120] Like many of his predecessors in the field of Johannine studies (Westcott, Holland, and Hoskyns), Dr. Lightfoot did not live to give his book its final form. When he died, the commentary proper had been completed and was ready for publication. Except for minor changes, then, the commentary is printed as Lightfoot left it. From other material left by Lightfoot, the editor, C. F. Evans, has written an Introductory Essay with appropriate subdivisions.

Lightfoot tells us that his work is a religious and theological exposition of the text of St. John.[121] The text is that of the Revised Version. Though he does not intend to discuss in detail questions of introduction, Dr. Lightfoot does express his opinion on the questions which interest us in this conspectus. He thinks that evidence from papyrus proves the Gospel was in existence a little before or a little after 100 A.D.[122] He regards the attribution of the Fourth Gospel to the Son of Zebedee as an opinion which "still receives support and

116. *Ibid.*, 114.
117. *Ibid.*, 108-109.
118. Cf. note 93.
119. Cf. Barrett, *Gospel acc. John,* 20.
120. R. H. Lightfoot, *St. John's Gospel* (Oxford: 1956).
121. *Ibid.*, p.v.
122. *Ibid.*, 1.

has never been shown to be impossible."[123] He points out that whereas we have some reliable knowledge of John, the Son of Zebedee, we have none whatever about John the Presbyter or any other figure to whom the authorship has been assigned.[124] Lightfoot joins Hoskyns, Dodd, and Barrett on the question of the unity of composition of the Fourth Gospel. In the absence of textual evidence to support suggested re-arrangements, Dr. Lightfoot says that it is reasonable to hold that no attempt should be made to alter the order of the text as we have it.[125] The unity of this Gospel, Lightfoot thinks, is not only a unity of structure, it is also a unity of themes.[126]

III. The Catholic Contribution

To appreciate the approach of Catholic Biblical scholars to Johannine studies during the past fifty years, it is necessary to understand, at least in broad outline the conditions of Catholic biblical scholarship at the turn of the century. The best analysis known to this writer is that of Dom Charlier:[127]

> For the greater part of the nineteenth century the leaders of Catholic thought had held aloof from this movement of new ideas which was changing world opinion. They took up a defensive attitude. Never in all its long history was the Church's biblical exegesis so wilfully conservative and at times even retrogressive. Nothing at all was known of the work done in Germany except that it was extremist. Renan's Life of Christ, which wrecked the faith of a whole generation, only made this work more suspect, and it was rejected wholesale in the name of a tradition which was blinded by fixed and narrow ideas. It was for Leo XIII to broaden this narrow outlook. His encyclical *Providentissimus* (1893) encouraged many to get to grips with independent criticism.

We who are now enjoying the fruits of those early years of struggle and strife find it difficult to appreciate the confusion which existed in the minds of the faithful who watched this struggle take place. Dom Charlier writes:[128]

> Eyes accustomed to narrow and rigid limits had suddenly to focus themselves on the boundless perspectives of the new sciences, where established fact jostled with arbitrary hypothesis. It was thus that a whole brilliant generation of our young people died of a kind of intellectual indigestion.

Charlier rightly notes that the Church has always frowned upon those who, through cowardice or lack of confidence try to stifle the legitimate development of her tradition. "In this respect a diehard conservatism is as harmful as an irresponsible liberalism."

The great sin of the conservatives was to continue to impose upon the books of the Bible patterns of thought wholly foreign to the

---

123. *Ibid.*, 2.
124. *Ibid.*, 7.
125. *Ibid.*, 8.
126. *Ibid.*, 21.
127. Dom Celestin Charlier, *The Christian Approach to the Bible* (Westminster: 1958) 17.
128. *Ibid.*, 18.

mentality of the Sacred Writers and those for whom they wrote. Like the poor, these "conservatives" are always with us. Our own day is by no means entirely free from the same type of opposition to scientific exegesis which Lagrange and others like him had to face at the turn of the present century. This writer has long held the view that the real source of difficulty is to be found in the domain of philosophy and theology. Dom Charlier is in complete agreement:[129]

> The real trouble is to be found in the field of philosophy and theology. Our exegetes have followed the rules of logic, which were developed for and by the western mind. Their procedure in the sciences is conditioned by this western approach. They have not thought it necessary to transpose their thought or to strip it of its idiom. Generally they have presupposed that the minds of all people were moulded, as theirs were, in the idiom of Aristotle, Descartes and Kant. They have applied western standards of philosophy, psychology and logic to texts which were conceived in a totally different atmosphere. Not enough notice has been taken of a whole world of thought and feelings which is radically different from their own world. What is even more unpardonable, no real attempt has been made to get inside that world to appreciate its peculiarities. This is the real barrier which has kept men from that vital truth which the Bible has to give them.

Attempts to solve this problem by the addition of a few pious reflections to a sterile exegesis have failed miserably. The whole intellectual approach to the study of these oriental books needs to be re-created from the inside.[130] During the past quarter century, better trained Catholic professors of Sacred Scripture have contributed a great deal towards a better understanding of what the Sacred Writers intended to communicate to their readers. True, there is still some fear of the new exegesis, especially on the part of those teaching Apologetics. This is understandable. It is not an easy thing to discard faulty interpretations of texts long used to "prove" a thesis in theology. This fear springs from a lack of knowledge concerning the true nature and principles of modern Catholic exegesis. I suggest that when all our professors of theology are required to undertake graduate studies in Sacred Scripture, much of the tension between the two fields will disappear. Only then will the much discussed and long hoped for integration between theology and exegesis take place.

We hope that this brief consideration of some aspects of the struggle for survival of early Catholic scientific exegesis will help to explain the fact that the number of outstanding Catholic contributions to the solution of the Johannine problem has been rather small during the last half century. Though small, these contributions were significant. Their fruits are beginning to appear in the works of younger Catholic writers. In our survey of Catholic authors who have contributed to the study of St. John's Gospel during the past fifty years, we will not be concerned with those works mainly intended to nourish the spiritual

---

129. *Ibid.,* 20.
130. *Ibid.,* 21.

life of the faithful, but shall concern ourselves exclusively with critical studies.

In 1904, the first outstanding Catholic commentary on the Fourth Gospel in this century made its appearance.[131] It was quickly recognized that P. Calmes had written the best exposition of St. John's Gospel ever to appear in French, and one of the best ever written in any language up to that time. True, there were faults from a critical point of view, especially in the introduction;[132] but no one could reasonably deny that this Catholic commentary was a work of the first rank.

P. Calmes, while holding for John the Apostle as the author, claims that the Fourth Gospel underwent certain modifications just before its publication. Calmes believed that John the Apostle completed the work before his death, but that he had not perfectly organized it. Calmes felt certain that the last chapter was written after the book was finished. With respect to the sixth chapter of St. John's Gospel, Calmes admits that the beginning of the chapter is somewhat disconcerting, from a chronological point of view. However, he also points out that St. John is more concerned with the movement of his thought than with chronological sequences. Nor, he adds, is the Fourth Evangelist too concerned with a purely logical and didactic exposition of his teaching. P. Calmes suggests that in interpreting the sixth chapter of St. John, we must attempt to separate in the chapter that which is doctrinal and that which is historical.[133] P. Calmes' work quite clearly set the tone of the Catholic scholarship of the period.

In 1906 there appeared a second edition of J. Knabenbauer's commentary on St. John, which had first appeared in 1898.[134] This was the last of the old-style, ponderous commentaries, with its innumerable citations from all the great commentators of the past and with but a minimum of up to date critical scholarship. Knabenbauer holds that the Apostle John wrote the Fourth Gospel in Asia Minor. By this he means *all* the parts of the Gospel, including the pericope of the Adulterous Woman, chapter 21 and the two verses of this chapter which terminate the Gospel, verses 24-25. Knabenbauer seems to think that the work came to us in the exact state in which it left the pen of the Apostle. Even in 1906, this type of commentary was unacceptable to our best Catholic scholars.

About this time, J. E. Belser[135] published in German a commentary which was intended to meet the needs of Catholic scholarship in the spirit of the new scientific method in exegesis. Unfortunately, reviewers of the work found that the author was not so scientific, after all.[136]

---

131. Th. Calmes, *L'Évangile selon saint Jean* (Paris: 1904).
132. Cf. *RB* 13 (1904) 436ff.
133. Calmes, *Évangile selon saint Jean,* 74.
134. J. Knabenbauer, *Commentarius in Quattuor S. Evangelia* IV, *Evangelium Secundum Joannem* (Paris: 1898), ed. 2 (1906).
135. J. E. Belser, *Das Evangelium des heiligen Johannes, übersetzt und erklärt* (Freiburg: 1905).
136. Cf. *RB* 15 (1906) 493 ff.

In France, M. Lepin published two substantial works in refutation of the now widespread critical theories on Johannine authorship and authenticity. His works were especially directed against the opinions of Réville and Loisy. Like most Catholic scholars of the period, Lepin was particularly concerned with defending (1) Johannine authenticity and (2) Johannine historicity.[137]

The problem of the identity of John the Presbyter had been studied by Dom John Chapman at the turn of the century. He published his findings as a small monograph in 1911.[138] Dom Chapman's main conclusions were: (1) the presbyters were not Apostles but disciples of the Apostles, and (2) John the Presbyter is really John the Apostle. As P. Lagrange noted in his review of this work,[139] Dom Chapman's argumentation actually seems to provide fuel for the fire of his opponents.

Though lacking reliable evidence for his archeological opinions, F. Tillmann[140] published a solid commentary on St. John's Gospel, intended for the general public. The work has undergone several revisions and has been greatly expanded through the years.[141] Amongst the more important positions taken by Tillmann is that which inverts the order of chapters five and six in the Fourth Gospel. Tillmann was an industrious, progressive Catholic Johannine scholar, as the various and improved editions of his commentary reveal.

The highwater mark of Catholic Johannine scholarship was reached in 1925, when P. Lagrange published his monumental *Évangile selon saint Jean*.[142] Non-Catholic as well as Catholic scholars paid high tribute to this masterful work. These words of Sir Edwyn Hoskyns are well worth recalling:

> With the vast wealth of technical European scholarship at his back, Lagrange produced a commentary in which massive learning is controlled by mature judgment and set forth with extreme delicacy and reserve of expression.[143]

The following are some of the more important general conclusions of P. Lagrange concerning the character and purpose of the Fourth Gospel: (1) the Fourth Gospel is just what it presents itself to be, an historical book. If it is also a didactic book, this is because it is a gospel in which Jesus himself is the Teacher. (2) The Fourth Gospel is a record of concrete deeds rather than the product of the Evangelist's fertile imagination. (3) The author, however, is not a mere chronic-

---

137. M. Lepin, *L'Origine du quatrième évangile* (Paris: 1907); *La valeur historique du quatrième évangile*, 2 vols., (Paris: 1910).
138. Dom John Chapman, *John the Presbyter and the Fourth Gospel* (Oxford: 1911). This was first written in *MSS* in 1903-1904. It is referred to by Sanday, *Criticism of the Fourth Gospel*, 252, in 1905.
139. Cf. *RB* 20 (1911) 459 ff.
140. F. Tillmann, *Das Johannes-evangelium übersetzt und erklärt* (Berlin: 1914).
141. For example, the work was expanded from 292 pages, in 1914, to 364 pages in 1931.
142. M. J. Lagrange, *Évangile selon Saint Jean* (Paris: 1925).
143. Cf. Hoskyns, *Fourth Gospel* 2, 25.

ler, but a writer who has well understood the profound significance of the events he has seen and recorded. This significance, however, lies in the actual history which has been narrated symbolically by the Fourth Evangelist. (4) Like its predecessors, this Johannine Gospel must be considered primarily as a record of the events of Jesus' ministry, to which the author bears authentic witness.

Lagrange is well aware of the difficulties presented by the critics against the Johannine authorship of the Fourth Gospel. He suggests that perhaps the apostle used a secretary in the composition of his work, and to this secretary he gave a certain amount of liberty in the choice of expressions.[144] Such use of a secretary would in no way be contrary to the thesis of Johannine authorship, but it would go far towards explaining and accounting for certain literary peculiarities of the Gospel.

In his fine study of the sixth chapter of the Gospel according to St. John, P. Lagrange makes the interesting suggestion that perhaps Jn 6,51-58 was not spoken by Christ in the exact historical circumstances where we now find it. Lagrange thinks that it was more likely to have been an intimate colloquy between Jesus and his disciples which John placed in its present position in order to present an imposing ensemble of eucharistic teaching.[145] The suggestion is certainly an attractive one.

In 1927 A. Durand[146] published his commentary on St. John in the *Verbum Salutis* series. Intended for the general public, the work, on the whole, is acceptable enough. Its weakness may be summed up in the one word indecision.[147] Though a professional biblical scholar, the author very often fails to assist his readers to resolve a problem which he himself has posed. Too often he simply refuses to indicate the prudent stand to be taken on debated questions. Durand holds that the Apostle John wrote the Gospel at Ephesus. He proposes 97-100 A.D. as the extreme limits beyond which we cannot go in assigning a date for the Fourth Gospel's appearance. He favors the present order of chapters, 4, 5, 6 and 7, but notes that serious attention now has to be given to the possibility of textual dislocations.

The outstanding Catholic commentary on the Fourth Gospel to appear in the decade 1930-1940 was that of F. Braun in the *La Sainte Bible* series.[148] The work bears clear testimony that Catholic Johannine studies had come of age. Writing for readers who are well-informed but not necessarily biblical specialists, Braun produced a well-balanced and compact little commentary. Like many others, he leans heavily upon the work of P. Lagrange. Amongst his positions, Braun thinks the Gospel was written by the Apostle John at Ephesus about the year 100 A.D. Though he keeps it in its proper place in his commen-

144. Lagrange, *Évangile selon Saint Jean,* CXIX.
145. *Ibid.,* 195.
146. A. Durand, *Évangile selon Saint Jean* (Paris: 1927).
147. Cf. *RB* 37 (1928) 454.
148. F. M. Braun, *Évangile selon S. Jean* (Paris: 1935), vol. X in Pirot-Clamer's *Sainte Bible.*

tary, Braun is strongly inclined to transpose chapter 6 to a position between chapters 4 and 5.[149] He also thinks that 21, 24 is from the hand of John himself, not from one of the Ephesian presbyters. After twenty-five years, Braun's work can be still read with pleasure and profit.

After World War II, a noteworthy commentary on St. John was published in German by the competent Johannine scholar, A. Wikenhauser.[150] Though deliberately stripped of scientific dress for the benefit of the general reader, this work cannot hide from the eyes of the biblical expert the solid basis on which it is founded. A simple introduction acquaints the reader with the traditional Catholic positions on the problems of authorship, composition, and theology of the Fourth Gospel. An excellent commentary, which clearly demonstrates the author's competence, follows. Some of Wikenhauser's positions are: (1) Except for the Appendix (chapter 21), the pericope of the Adulterous Woman (7,50-8,11), and 5,3b-4, John the Apostle wrote the Fourth Gospel. (2) Ephesus is most probably the place of composition, while 90-100 A.D. seems the most likely decade for its date. However, in his introduction to the New Testament,[151] Wikenhauser adds, "but it is not impossible that some parts had already been committed to writing before 90 A.D." And finally (3) Wikenhauser favors the chapter order 4, 6, 5, and 7, as well as other transpositions of pericopes in chapters 7, 9, 10, 12.

Fresh evidence that Catholic Johannine scholarship had reached new heights came with the publication of the Johannine volume in the *Bible of Jerusalem series.*[152] The introduction to the Fourth Gospel by D. Mollat is splendid. The French text is very well presented and the accompanying notes form a veritable commentary on the Johannine text. Mollat looks upon the Fourth Evangelist not only as a trustworthy witness to Evangelical tradition but also as an inspired exegete of that tradition. The Fourth Gospel is essentially a kerygmatic work. What is special to it, in contrast to the other Gospels, is its spiritual element and its liturgical as well as sacramental emphasis. Mollat accepts the traditional opinions regarding authorship, date and place of composition, but he does not allow his conclusions to outstrip the evidence on these matters. He prefers the order of our present text and suggests that the difficulties involved in accepting that order be solved by (1) admitting the successive stages of composition during which the Apostle retouched or added to his basic composition, or (2) admitting the possibility that the present text was edited by disciples who gathered together what writings they found after the Apostle's death. In any case, the work is thoroughly Johannine. After noting the various attempts to work out a plan for the Gos-

---

149. *Ibid.*, p. 350.
150. A. Wikenhauser, *Das Evangelium nach Johannes übersetzt und erklärt* (Regensburg: 1948).
151. A. Wikenhauser, *New Testament Introduction* (Freiburg: 1958), p. 319.
152. *L'Évangile et Les Épîtres de Saint Jean* in *BJ* series by D. Mollat and F. M. Braun (Paris: 1953).

pel, Mollat suggests his own plan; this centers around the city of Jerusalem and especially the various festive occasions associated with the Holy City.

In 1959, F. M. Braun published a work[153] of high quality on the history of the fourth Gospel in the early Church. From his studies on the problems of the unity of the fourth Gospel and the Johannine writings, the fortunes of Jn in the second century, and the identity of the author of Jn, Braun suggests that (1) during the years A. D. 95-100 the five Johannine writings were put into final form in this order: Ap, 3 Jn, 2 Jn, 1 Jn and Jn; (2) one author used three different disciple-scribes for the writing of the Ap, the Epistles, and Jn; (3) the author of Jn is "the disciple whom Jesus loved", John the son of Zebedee.

As reviewers have pointed out,[154] the most important section of this major Johannine study is the author's successful refutation of the long accepted thesis that the Gnostics were the first true patrons of the fourth Gospel. After a very careful consideration of the evidence from Egypt, Rome and Syria-Asia Minor, Braun shows that in all three areas the evidence, though varying in degrees of certitude, points to an acceptance of Jn in orthodox circles in the second century. As Raymond E. Brown aptly remarks in his review, ". . . Braun's study should serve as a long overdue funeral service for the theory of the Gnostic patronage of Jn."

If, in this survey of critical Catholic works on the fourth Gospel, the number of works of high quality is relatively small, the same must not be thought of Catholic special monographs and scientific articles on specific difficult problems. As a matter of fact, the number of the latter is very large and growing still larger.[155] Throughout the world and in most modern languages Catholic scholars are continually producing excellent studies on Johannine theology, textual criticism, sources of Johannine thought, style characteristics of the fourth gospel, and similar areas of scientific research. As we move along in the second half of this century, Catholic Johannine scholarship is solidly entrenched in biblical scientific circles. The works of the École Biblique's Boismard and the American Raymond E. Brown, for instance, assure us that the future of Catholic Johannine studies is in good hands. However, the story of these and other outstanding Catholic Johannine scholars belongs to another chapter in the history of Johannine studies in the twentieth century.

SUMMARY

In reviewing the story of Johannine studies over the past half cen-

---

153. F. M. Braun, *Jean le Théologien et son évangile dans l'église ancienne* (Paris: Gabalda, 1959).
154. Cf. the review of Raymond E. Brown in *CBQ* 22 (April, 1960) 219-222.
155. Cf. the long bibliographical list in the recently published *Bibliographie Biblique* (Montreal: 1958). The Johannine studies are listed on pages 130-144.

tury, we note the following shifts of emphasis: (1) On the question of authorship, a very decided change has taken place. Very few critics now defend the direct apostolic authorship of the fourth Gospel, though it must be admitted that the conservative opinion does not seem so indefensible to the critics as it did twenty-five or thirty years ago.[156] Another change regards the value to be placed on the identification of the author of the fourth Gospel. J. A. T. Robinson writes:[157]

> The question of authorship is still important, if only because the narrative is patently presented as that of an eye-witness and if that claim is groundless it affects our total assessment of it . . . But the question of authorship is not, I believe, the decisive one for the valuation of the Gospel as history. The decisive question is the status and origin of the Johannine tradition. Did this come out of the blue round about the year A.D. 100? Or is there a real continuity, not merely in the memory of one old man, but in the life of an on-going community, with the earliest days of Christianity? What, I think, fundamentally distinguishes the "new look" on the fourth Gospel is that it answers that question in the affirmative.

(2) Vivisection, partition and rearrangement of the Johannine text is of little concern to the modern scholar. The work of Schweizer, Ruckstuhl and others has pretty well established the basic integrity of the fourth Gospel text as we know it. Most moderns (e.g., Dodd, Barrett, Lightfoot, etc.) prefer to see what they can do to interpret the text as it has come down to us. (3) With respect to date, most critics accept A.D. 100, and Ephesus still polls the majority vote as the place of origin.

The future of Johannine studies seems bright. There is much work to be done, especially with regard to the further clarification of Johannine thought, as well as possible relationships to the Qumran material. The fact of the relationship seems certain enough; the question remains as to its degree and kind. At any rate, the present Johannine styles are likely to remain for some decades to come without significant changes.

---

156. A. M. Hunter, *Interpreting the NT,* 86.
157. J. A. T. Robinson, "The New Look On The Fourth Gospel," in *The Gospels Reconsidered* (Oxford: 1960) 154-166. In the same work, cf. also W. C. Van Unnik, "The Purpose of St. John's Gospel", pp. 167-196.

LIVING WATER IN JOHN

FRANCIS J. McCOOL, S.J.

One of the tasks of exegesis, and not the least important at that, is constantly to review the interpretations of key-texts in the Scriptures which have become widely accepted, to see if the knowledge gained by recent study confirms or suggests some modifications in what is being placidly repeated in the schools. A case in point is the interpretation which is generally given to the figure of "living water" employed by Our Lord in his first interchange with the Samaritan woman. Both Catholic and non-Catholic interpreters alike have maintained for a long time that this figure denotes directly a life-giving power, either the Spirit or commonly among Catholic exegetes a modification of this idea, namely sanctifying grace. So Zahn asserts that the phrase denotes neither the Person of Jesus nor His word but the Spirit[1]; Bernard agrees[2] as does Strack-Billerbeck stating that *hydōr zōn* means "der Geist des neuen Lebens . . . der seinerseits Leben für das ewige Leben wirkt."[3] The Catholic interpreters who follow this trend give interpretations which are both more specific and better adapted to the minutiae of the text. Père Lagrange states that the gift which Jesus bestows "is evidently what the Church calls sanctifying grace which John (1 Jn 3,9) describes by another metaphor as the *sperma* of God which abides in him who is born of Him, a seed which is already the eternal life (1 Jn 5,11) ".[4] Here Lagrange appears to be influenced by St. Thomas who interprets *hydōr zōn* as *gratia Spiritus Sancti* and explains that this grace is fittingly termed *water* because it produces effects in the supernatural order which resemble those produced by that element in nature: it cleanses, refreshes, quenches, while it receives the epithet *living* "quia ita ipsa gratia Spiritus Sancti datur homini quod tamen ipse fons gratiae datur, scilicet Spiritus Sanctus."[5] Durand, Leonard and

---

1. T. Zahn, *Das Evangelium von Johannes*[4] (Leipzig: 1912) 237-238.
2. J. Bernard, *The Gospel according to St. John* (Edinburgh: 1928) 1, 139.
3. H. L. Strack & P. Billerbeck, *Kommentar zum Neuen Testament* [2] (Munich: 1956) 2, 433. The passage is John 4, 10-14.
4. M.-J. Lagrange, *Évangile selon Saint Jean*[7] (Paris, 1948) 108.
5. S. Thomae Aquinatis, *Super Evangelium S. Joannis Lectura*[5] (Turin-Rome: 1952) 110.

many other Catholic interpreters repeat this interpretation without however contributing anything notable of their own.

However, there has always been another way of reading these verses, dating very probably from a period as early as that of Ignatius of Antioch[6] and which has been again proposed in our time by interpreters as respected in their different confessions as Rudolf Bultmann and Alfred Wikenhauser. For these men the metaphor *hydōr zōn* denotes directly and immediately the *revelation* of Jesus which of course in its turn gives life. Bultmann expresses it in these terms: "In the common parlance of the East *hydōr zōn* is flowing water or spring water, as is presupposed in the reply of the woman in v. 11f. But the reader understands without more ado that something else is intended here: the revelation which Jesus imparts, as Jesus' words in v. 13f. immediately make clear."[7] Wikenhauser agrees: "The context is better served if we see behind the water no special gift but as behind the Light and the Bread which Jesus is (8,12; 6,35) the revelation which He brings, therefore the salvation that He brings to mankind in His words and His deeds."[8] Bultmann, if not Wikenhauser, considers his exegesis as opposed to the dominant interpretation. "To think of a specific gift of Jesus here, e.g. the Spirit, is inaccurate and is unsupported by the text." We should interpret Water here as elsewhere Light and Bread, viz. Jesus' revelation as a totality, or himself under the aspect of Revealer. Since these two interpretations are in Bultmann's eyes at least mutually exclusive, we may see St. John's thought in clearer focus if we compare the reasons for both readings in the light of the text itself.

The reasons which have persuaded so many exegetes to see the Spirit, or the Spirit present in sanctifying grace, behind the figure of living water are as classical as is the opinion itself. First, as Lagrange said, there are the parallel passages 1 Jn 3,9 and 1 Jn 5,11 where the other metaphor of a seed which both is and gives eternal life can hardly be interpreted except as meaning the presence of the Spirit in sancti-

---

6. R. Bultmann, *Das Evangelium des Johannes*[15] (Göttingen: 1957) 135, n.7 relates the following text of Ignatius of Antioch with our passage: *hydōr zōn kai laloun en emoi, esōthen moi legon deuro pros ton patera* (Ad Romanos 7,2). The reference to John is unmistakable, even if we do not read *hallomenon* for *kai laloun* as Lightfoot suggests (*Apostolic Fathers,* 2,224). Bultmann interprets the "living water" here as the Spirit. We are interested however more in the activity which Ignatius assigns the Spirit here. It is not that of conveying revelation, at least apparently; the Spirit here speaking within the Saint invites him to paradise. However this way of thinking of the "living water", when taken together with the prominent place which *hydōr zōn hallomenon* possessed in the Gnostic speculations of the second century suggests that the equation "living water=revelation," was not unknown in the Syria of that period.
7. Bultmann, *Evangelium des Johannes,* 132.
8. A. Wikenhauser, *Das Evangelium nach Johannes*[2] (Regensburg: 1957) 107.

fying grace. We should interpret the related figure here in the same fashion. But there is another text, Jn 7,37-39, which seems even more peremptory. Here, as in our passage, Jesus invites the onlookers to approach Him and drink and promises refreshment which will never fail—for, depending on the punctuation you prefer, streams of living water will flow from either the belly of Christ or that of the believer, satisfying in the latter case both himself and others. The important point, however, is that the Evangelist here identifies the reality behind the figure: He meant by this the Spirit which those who believed in him were to receive (7,39). While an author is free to use a symbol in different ways in the same book—as John indeed does with water in 19,34,[9] still the closeness of the thought-content here and in our passage urges us to transfer this Johannine interpretation to 4,10-14. Zahn notes in this regard that in addition to these two passages Jesus is described twice elsewhere in the early part of this gospel as the one who is to baptize with the Spirit (1,33; 3,5).

Secondary only to the argument from parallel passages is that derived from the background in the light of which our text must be interpreted. All are agreed that chapter 4 is one of eschatological fulfillment. The evangelist is eager to stress that the moment in which the woman met Jesus is that in which the Messiah proclaims himself openly as the fulfillment of the hopes of Israel offering the living water which leads to eternal life and inaugurating the eschatological cult which alone in the future will be acceptable to God. But it is a well known fact that the goods of the eschatological kingdom and in particular the Holy Spirit, the special gift of the period of fulfillment, have been symbolized both in the Old and the New Testament by the element of water.[10] In the light of these texts it is not unreasonable to connect the use of the figure here with the Holy Spirit.

Some minor considerations of a confirmatory nature have been drawn from the vocabulary employed in the texts. Bernard notes that the term *dōrea* which is applied here to living water always indicates the gift of the Holy Spirit in the Book of Acts.[11] He also calls attention to the strangeness of the term *hallomenou* here. This term is not applied elsewhere (apparently), he says, of the action of water but it and the related *ephallomai* are applied to the action of a divine Spirit. In this connection Abbott, who is Bernard's source on this point, reads the Johannine phrase as referring to the action of the Holy Spirit

---

9. No one will deny that John saw a symbolic meaning in the effusion of blood and water from the side of Christ. What this meaning actually was still remains a subject for dispute. However the patristic interpretation, viz. that the sacraments of baptism and the eucharist sprang from Christ's sacrificial death is by far the most probable.
10. For the more important texts, cf. Wikenhauser, *Evangelium nach Johannes,* 106.
11. Bernard, *Gospel acc. John,* 138.

which is vehement like that of rushing waters.[12] Psychologically this way of applying an apparently unsuitable term to a symbol can be explained by a subconscious transfer to it of an epithet which really is appropriate to the reality the writer has in mind throughout. Thirdly, the living water which becomes a fountain is related by John to eternal life, whereas in the Biblical tradition the Spirit is preeminently the Giver of Life.[13] Zahn also points out how well the details of the figure fit the dominant interpretation. In the figure Jesus distinguishes between the spring, the flow of water and the sea or river into which the water empties. What John is saying here is that the Spirit not only quenches man's thirst for God but becomes the starting point of a new vital movement which runs through the short period of earthly life until it is absorbed into eternal life.[14]

It is clear that the minutiae of John's text are certainly reconcilable with the interpretation suggested both by the parallel passages and the suggested Old Testament background.

Why then do Bultmann and Wikenhauser, to name but two, persist in preferring another interpretation? Here again we shall do well to move from the general to the particular. The fourth, if any gospel, is emphatically the gospel of revelation and in our passage Jesus proffers a gift to the woman, the gift of God, i.e. the most important gift man can receive because it is irreplaceable. Now throughout the gospel a single gift is offered to men under three distinct figures, that of Light (8,12 and *passim*), Bread (6,27.35) and Water. The figure of light is slightly different from the other two since it does not evoke an object like them but denotes the state of enlightenment produced by the activity of Jesus. This figure clearly points to the revelation which Jesus gives or is as the source of illumination which is needed and suffices for eternal life. The other two figures evoke realities which man constantly needs for life. It will be wise here to note how John opposes the bread and water given by Jesus with their counterparts in nature. He who drinks the water that I will give him will never be thirsty—and the reason for this is quickly given—for the water that I will give him will become a spring of water within him, bubbling up for eternal life. The reality referred to is clearly permanent and inexhaustible—it is a constant spring which gives eternal life. Equally so is the reality figured under bread. It is a food which lasts for eternal life [6,27] . . . I am the bread that gives life. No one who comes to me will ever be hungry, and no one who believes in me will ever be thirsty [6,35]. Now, granted the strong unity of symbolic thinking which runs through the fourth gospel, it is not unreasonable to suppose that these extremely similar symbols point to the same reality. But it

---

12. *Ibid.*, 141.
13. St. John himself restates this tradition in 6,63: "The spirit alone gives life."
14. Zahn, *Evangelium von Johannes*[4], 240.

is admitted by the majority of commentators that the reality evoked by the figure of bread over the greater part of chapter 6 is the revelation which Jesus brought to men. Therefore it may be that this is the reality intended under the figure of water.[15]

This conclusion is strongly suggested by the present position assigned to our passage in the fourth gospel. It seems quite probable that John has ordered several of his longer sections in pairs. Chapters 5 and 6, no matter what order we read them in, seem to belong together and very probably, as Bultmann suggests, the story of Cana should be read with the Cleansing in the Temple as presenting two antithetical aspects of the ministry which is to be described. At all events, it seems wise to read the Samaritan episode in tandem with the episode about Nicodemus.[16] Everything in these units seems to suggest this: 1) the literary construction employed—the centerpiece of each event is a dialogue followed by passages which further develop the subject-matter of each; 2) the typical persons who are presented—a man, a teacher, a Pharisee is opposed to a woman who is also a schismatic and a sinner; 3) the identity of action in each case for in both John presents an initial confrontation of the person with Jesus; 4) antithetical reactions: Nicodemus is for the moment at least at a loss [3,9] which permits Jesus or John to develop the idea that Jesus' coming is the judgment of the world (3,19) and to dilate on the negative side of this event. The Samaritan despite her handicaps illustrates the positive results of this event; she accepts Jesus as the Messiah (4,29) and contributes in part, if not decisively, to Jesus' acceptance by her fellow-citizens. Since the chapter on Nicodemus evokes the rejection of the light i.e. the revelation brought by Jesus (3,19f), it seems that John wished to balance this by a picture of its acceptance which would lead us to see in the living water a symbol primarily of revelation.

Moreover, there is a parallelism within the Samaritan dialogue itself which may lead us to this conclusion. Jesus as Messiah does two things in the dialogue: he offers the gift of living water and he proclaims the imminent inauguration of the eschatological worship of God: the hour is coming and is already here when the true adorers will worship the Father in Spirit and in truth (4,23). Wikenhauser is undoubtedly right in insisting on the eschatological nature of this worship. The opposition is not between external and internal cults but between the cultic systems then in vogue and the new worship which will deprive both Jerusalem and Garizim of their functions. As both we and John know the cultus which was instituted by Christ was an external reality just as much as were the cults of the Jews and the Samaritans. It is interesting to realize therefore that if we interpret the living water mentioned earlier as revelation, Jesus here in John

---

15. This parallelism is the most convincing reason adduced by both Bultmann and Wikenhauser.
16. So Bultmann, *Evangelium des Johannes,* 77.

presents the definitive revelation which gives life and announces the advent of the definitive Christian worship—the two basic elements in the new dispensation.

However, we should note in passing that the element of spirit intrudes here upon our notice. The basis of the new worship is spirit and truth and the cult corresponds to the nature both of God and the true adorers. The true adorers are those who have become sons of God—i.e. they share in his nature because born of the Spirit (4,23; 1,12; 3,3-8). The nature of God is that of spirit i.e. He is the Person who fills His worshippers with divine life. This is a point which we must remember later.

Now the general character of the Gospel, the position of this passage in the greater whole and the parallelism within the dialogue itself combine to suggest the interpretation of living water as the revelation expressed in Jesus' words and works. But are not all these indications counterbalanced by the meaning of water in the Old Testament prophecies of the glorious culmination where it signifies so often the gift of the Spirit? Bultmann is unruffled by this consideration for he reads John here as elsewhere not in the light of the Old Testament but in that of Gnostic Dualism where water is the symbol for divine revelation. He argues for this background from the peculiar nature of Johannine dualism in which all goodness and virtue are denied the goods of this world and attributed to those of the upper, unseen world, but especially from documents such as the Odes of Solomon which betray a similar Gnostic frame of mind. We mention this here only because such images as Bultmann cites from the Odes [e.g. the Word of Truth comes from the mouth of a singer like a stream of water (12); I drank and was inebriated by the spring of immortality i.e. revelation (11,6)] recall to mind an earlier tradition which we have not yet mentioned, the sapiential tradition of Israel. Here water symbolizes Divine Wisdom, the fear of the Lord which proceeds from instruction, Torâ, all of which are presented as givers of life.[17] Nor is John untouched by this tradition. As is clear from his gospel he insists on the close connection between revelation (knowledge) and life. This is evident in the Prologue. Peter insists in 6,68 that Jesus has words of eternal life and Jesus Himself proclaims in 14,6 "I am the Way, the Truth and the Life": i.e. He bestows Life precisely because he communicates the definitive revelation of God. More to our purpose perhaps is to note that the parallel passage in 7,38: "if any one is thirsty, let him come to me and drink" or "and let him who believes in me drink" reflects the influence of this sapiential tradition.[18] We can hardly therefore exclude all such influences on the use of the term water in our passage.

---

17. Wisdom: Prv 13,14; Sir 15,2-3; 24,30-33; Fear of the Lord: Prv 14,27; Torâ: Sir 24,23-29.
18. Bernard, *Gospel acc. John,* 283.

We appear to have arrived at an impasse. For reasons naturally different in content but quite weighty for all that, seem to support both positions. Perhaps the reason for this is that these two interpretations are not so mutually exclusive as Bultmann appears to believe. We have a hint of this from an authority as ancient as St. Thomas who besides interpreting *aqua viva* as *gratia Spiritus Sancti* also notes that in our passage Jesus *explicat virtutem suae doctrinae* and proceeds to show how Jesus' *doctrina* is both *optima aqua* and *aqua viva,* noting in his development the relationship of water to Divine Wisdom.[19] Perhaps St. John's conception is more inclusive than we thought. A more recent scholar, Father de la Potterie, has come to this conclusion with regard to other Johannine texts which are discussed in almost the same terms as is our own.[20] The famous text I Jn 2,27, "you shall retain in your hearts the *chrisma* with the Spirit that you received from him and you do not need to have anyone teach you," a text which, as he says, can seem to favor a certain type of illuminism led de la Potterie to attempt to determine the meaning of *chrisma* in this verse and in 2,20. It has been debated whether *chrisma* here denotes the action of the Holy Spirit teaching the Christian interiorly or the word of truth received in baptism. After a detailed study which appears convincing to this writer at least, de la Potterie concludes that *chrisma* in this section of I Jn is the *word of God,* not so much in so far as it is preached exteriorly in the community but in so far as it is received by faith in men's hearts and remains active there, *thanks to the action of the Spirit.*[21] Only this synthesis of viewpoints gives full justice to the texts. This conclusion is established not only by a minute analysis of the texts in question but also by recalling John's concept of the function of the Holy Ghost as He works in the hearts of Christians. To realize how John conceived this, we may well begin with the basic fault he attributes to the Jews: you do not allow his word to remain in you (5,38). It is not the external promulgation of revelation which conduces most to salvation but permitting it to penetrate the mind and will. Now it is precisely here that the activity of the Spirit enters and has full play. The Paraclete, the Spirit of Truth remains with the Christians always (14,13-17). But we should note how He acts. He always seems to act in relation to the revelation which Jesus has given: he teaches by recalling everything which Jesus taught i.e. he uncovers what his teachings really say and imply (14,26; 15,26; 16,13f). He is the abiding principle who constantly and permanently vivifies the revelation of Jesus by recalling it, developing its potentialities and aiding Christians to practice it.

---

19. St. Thomas, *Super Evangelium Joannis,* p. 111-112. In discussing this point Thomas appeals to the following texts from the Wisdom Literature: Sir 24,29; Wis 5,9; Ps 41,2 and Ps 35,9.
20. "L'onction du chrétien par la foi" in *Bib* 40 (1959) 12-69, especially p. 45.
21. I. de la Potterie, *Bib* 40 (1959) 44.

Let us turn now to our text in the light of these considerations and especially in view of de la Potterie's interpretation of *chrisma* and see what help, if any, they can give us. First, in connection with a gospel as carefully composed as John's it is important to attend to the minutiae of the text. Especially is this true in our section where Jesus' part in the discourse is clearly motivated by the situation in which he found Himself. When the woman wonders that He a Jew should address her, Jesus replies that if she realized the gift at his disposal and who He was, she would realize that in truth their positions were reversed—she was the needy one; he possessed the essential gift which because of the context He calls living water. Let us now examine this term in the light of the entire context. It is an element as extrinsic to Jesus as the water of Jacob's well was to the woman. In this context Jesus is not the source of the water but offers it.[22]

Next Jesus promises that if this water is drunk a transformation will take place; the water imbibed will become itself a spring in the person who receives it i.e. a source of ever increasing water which is ordered to eternal life. Holding to the relationship between the terms in the figure it seems best to interpret the element extrinsic both to Jesus and the drinker as the definitive revelation—the words of eternal life as shown by Jesus in His words and works. In the light of similar figures such as "come to" "receive" Christ and especially in the phrase: let him drink who believes in me in 7,38, the figure "drink" suggests the appropriation in faith of the divine message externally proposed. The transformation mentioned would then be the same divine message vivified by the Spirit of truth, constantly brought before the mind and its depths plumbed, a process which is both ordered to and itself participates in eternal life. Bultmann is certainly correct when he implies that the Spirit is not explicitly mentioned in the text. But when we think of John's teaching on the interior work of the Spirit, when the element of spirit is evoked in connection with the new cultus, when the Spirit is expressly connected with the passage in c.7 and perhaps in view of some of the vocabulary used here, it seems hard to maintain that the divine Spirit was completely absent from his mind as he wrote these verses.

If this suggestion be true, John's description of the process of salvation would be even more complete here than in I Jn 2,20.27. There using the figure *chrisma* he begins at the second stage—the acceptance of the revelation by faith due to the activity of the Spirit of God as well as that of the believer. Here, however, the entire process is described, beginning with the external proposition of the word of God under the symbol of living water. This would surely be appropriate at the hour when Jesus first met the Samaritan woman and revealed to her and her fellow-citizens not only His title but His essential functions.

---

22. This in contradiction to 7,38.

ABBREVIATIONS

Gn Ex Lv Nm Dt Jos Jgs Ru 1Sm 2Sm 3Kgs 4Kgs 1Chr 2Chr Ezr Neh Tb Jdt Est Jb Ps (Hebrew numeration) Prv Eces Ct Wis Sir Is Jer Lam Bar Ez (ek) Dn Os Joel Am Abd Jon Mi Na Hb So Ag Zech Mal 1Mc 2Mc—Mt Mk Lk Jn Acts Rom 1Cor 2Cor Gal Eph Phlp Col 1Thes 2Thes 1Tim 2Tim Ti Phlm Heb Jas 1Pt 2Pt 1Jn Jude Ap

AASOR	Annual of the American Schools of Oriental Research
AbTANT	Abhandlungen zur Theologie des Alten und Neuen Testaments
AJSL	American Journal of Semitic Languages
AmiCl	Ami du Clergé
ANEP	J. Pritchard, Ancient Near East in Pictures Relating to OT
ANET	J. Pritchard, Ancient Near Eastern Texts
ArOr	Archiv Orientální
ATD	Das Alte Testament Deutsch
BA	Biblical Archaeologist
BASOR	Bulletin of the American Schools of Oriental Research
BH	Biblia Hebraica, Kittel (-Eissfeldt)
Bib	Biblica
BIES	Bulletin of the Israel Exploration Society=Yediot
BiViChr	Bible et Vie Chrétienne
BJ	Bible de Jérusalem
BK	Bibel-Kommentar
BO	Bibliotheca Orientalis
BWANT	Beiträge zur Wissenschaft des Alten und Neuen Testament
BZ	Biblische Zeitschrift
BZAW BZNW	Beihefte zur Zeitchrift für die Alt/Neutestamentliche Wissenschaft
CAD	Chicago Assyrian Dictionary
CBQ	Catholic Biblical Quarterly
CCD	Confraternity of Christian Doctrine Bible Translation
CIG	Corpus Inscriptionum Graecarum
CIL	Corpus Inscriptionum Latinarum
CML	G. Driver, Canaanite Myths
Con N	Coniectanea Neotestamentica

CRAIBL	Comptes-Rendus, Académie des Inscriptions et Belles-Lettres
CSEL	Corpus Scriptorum Ecclesiasticorum Latinorum Vindobonense
DCG	J. Hastings, Dictionary of Christ and the Gospels
ETL	Ephemerides Theologicae Lovanienses
ExpT	Expository Times
FRLANT	Forschungen zur Religion und Literatur des Alten und Neuen Testaments
GCS	Die griechischen christlichen Schriftsteller (Berlin Corpus)
GJV	E. Schürer, Geschichte des jüdischen Volkes im Zeitalter Jesu Christi
GLECS	Groupe Linguistique des Études Chamito-Sémitiques
Greg	Gregorianum
HAT	Handbuch zum Alten Testament
Ḥbr	Wadi Ḥabra finds
HPR	Homiletic and Pastoral Review
HThR	Harvard Theological Review
HS	Bonner Bibel
HUCA	Hebrew Union College Annual
ICC	International Critical Commentary
IsrEJ	Israel Exploration Journal
JAOS	Journal of the American Oriental Society
JBL	Journal of Biblical Literature
JBR	Journal of Bible and Religion
JCS	Journal of Cuneiform Studies
JEA	Journal of Egyptian Archeology
JJS	Journal of Jewish Studies
JNES	Journal of Near Eastern Studies
JPOS	Journal of the Palestine Oriental Society
JQR	Jewish Quarterly Review
JRAS	Journal of the Royal Asiatic Society
JSS	Journal of Semitic Studies
JTS	Journal of Theological Studies
MG	Migne, Patrologia Graeca
ML	Migne, Patrologia Latina
MT	Masoretic Text
MVAG	Mitteilungen der vorderasiatisch-ägyptischen Gesellschaft
Mur	Wadi Murabba'ât Documents
NT	Novum Testamentum
NTS	New Testament Studies
Or	Orientalia
OTS	Oudtestamentische Studiën
PE[F]Q	Palestine Exploration Quarterly
PJB	Palästinajahrbuch
QM	Qumran, Milḥamâ
PRU	C. Virolleaud, Palais Royal d'Ugarit
RB	Revue Biblique

RechSR	Recherches de Science Religieuse
RevScPhTh	Revue des Sciences Philosophiques et Théologiques
RGG	Religion in Geschichte und Gegenwart
RHPR	Revue d'Histoire et de Philosophie Religieuses
RivBiblItal	Rivista Biblica Italiana
RSV	Revised Standard Version
Scr	Scripture
ThBl	Theologische Blätter
ThR	Theologische Revue
ThWNT	Theologisches Wörterbuch zum NT
TLZ	Theologische Literaturzeitung
TS	Theological Studies
TTZ	Trierer Theologische Zeitschrift
UM	C. Gordon, Ugaritic Manual
VD	Verbum Domini
VDBS	Vigouroux, Dictionnaire de la Bible, Supplément
VT [Sup]	Vetus Testamentum [Supplement]
WMZANT	Wissenschaftliche Monographien (Neukirchen)
ZAW	Zeitschrift für die alttestamentliche Wissenschaft
ZDPV	Zeitschrift des Deutschen Palästina-Vereins
ZNW	Zeitschrift für die neutestamentliche Wissenschaft
ZTK	Zeitschrift für Theologie und Kirche

GENERAL INDEX

SCRIPTURE INDEX